The authors include such leading sociologists and political scientists as Seymour Martin Lipset, Paul Seabury, Kenneth N. Walker, E. Wight Bakke, George Z. F. Bereday, and Myron Glazer.

This is the first volume in a new series, *Student Movements — Past and Present.*

SEYMOUR MARTIN LIPSET, Professor of Government and Social Relations, is also Research Associate at the Center for International Affairs, Harvard University. He is the author of *The First New Nation* (Basic Books, 1964), *Political Man,* and *The Social Bases of Politics* and has edited *Class, Status, and Power* and other works. He has contributed numerous articles to scholarly journals.

Student Politics

STUDENT MOVEMENTS—PAST AND PRESENT

General Editor: Seymour Martin Lipset

1. STUDENT POLITICS, edited by Seymour Martin Lipset

Student Politics

SEYMOUR MARTIN LIPSET, Editor

BASIC BOOKS, INC., PUBLISHERS
New York   London

The Authors

ORLANDO ALBÓRNOZ, Professor of Sociology at the Central University of Venezuela, was Senior Research Associate with the Comparative Student Project and a Lecturer at Harvard University. Among his books are *La sociología en Venezuela, Valores sociales en la educación venezolana,* and most recently *El maestro y la educación en la sociedad venezolana.*

PHILIP G. ALTBACH, Lecturer in Education and Research Associate in the Center for International Affairs at Harvard University, has been associated with the Comparative Student Project. He received his Ph.D. from the Comparative Education Center of the University of Chicago, and spent 1964–1965 doing research in India under a grant from the U. S.-Indian Comparative Education Exchange Project. He has written for such journals as the *Comparative Education Review, Harvard Educational Review,* and *The New Leader.*

E. WIGHT BAKKE, Professor of Economics at Yale University, has been associated with the Inter-University Committee on Labor Problems in Economic Development and has done research on student movements in Mexico, Colombia, Japan, and India. Among his many publications are *Citizens without Work, Organization and the Individual, A Positive Labor Market Policy,* and *Unions, Management, and the Public* (with Clark Kerr).

JOSEPH BEN-DAVID is Associate Professor of Sociology at the Hebrew University in Jerusalem. During the academic year 1964–1965, he was a Visiting Professor at the University of California and a Research Associate at the Institute of International Studies associated with the Comparative Student Project. He has written widely in the sociology of education, science, and the professions.

GEORGE Z. F. BEREDAY is Professor of Comparative Education at Columbia University. He is author of *Comparative Method in Education.* He is joint editor of *The World Year Book of Education,* general editor of *Columbia Comparative Education Series,* and was editor of the *Comparative Education Review.* He was Exchange Professor at the University of Moscow in 1961 and Fulbright Professor at the University of Tokyo in 1962.

RANDALL COLLINS has been a Research Assistant in the Institute of International Studies at the University of California at Berkeley and worked with Professor Ben-David on his research in connection with the Comparative Student Project.

JOSEPH DiBONA, Assistant Professor of Education at Brooklyn College, is associated with the Comparative Student Project. He received his Ph.D. in education from the University of California at Berkeley.

MYRON GLAZER, Assistant Professor of Sociology at Smith College, is associated with the Comparative Student Project. He received his Ph.D. in sociology from Princeton University and has done research in Chile.

SEYMOUR MARTIN LIPSET is Professor of Government and Social Relations at Harvard University and Director of the Comparative Student Project, established by the Institute of International Studies at the University of California at Berkeley, of which he has been Director. He has been visiting professor at the University of Warsaw and at the Free University of Berlin. Among his many publications are *The First New Nation, Political Man,* and *Agrarian Socialism.* He is co-author of *Union Democracy* and *Social Mobility in Industrial Society.*

DAVID NASATIR is Assistant Professor of Education and Sociology at the University of California at Los Angeles. He also taught at the University of Buenos Aires. He holds a Ph.D. in sociology from the University of California at Berkeley and has been associated with the Comparative Student Project.

PAUL SEABURY is Professor of Political Science at the University of California, Santa Cruz. During 1965–1966, he was at Harvard as a Research Associate of the Center for International Affairs. Among his publications are *The Wilhelmstrasse,* 1954; *Power, Freedom and Diplomacy,* 1963; *Balance of Power,* 1965; and *The Rise and Decline of the Cold War,* 1967. He received the Bancroft Prize in 1964 for his book, *Power, Freedom and Diplomacy.*

GLAUCIO A. D. SOARES is Director of the UNESCO Latin American Graduate Faculty of Sociology in Santiago, Chile. He served for two years as co-Director of Comparative Student Project while on the staff of the Institute of International Studies at Berkeley. His book, *Economic Development and Political Radicalism,* will appear soon.

METTA SPENCER is a Research Sociologist in the Center for International Affairs at Harvard University and is associated with the Comparative Student Project.

KENNETH N. WALKER is Assistant Professor of Sociology at the University of Toronto. He is a Ph.D. candidate at the University of California at Berkeley and worked as a Research Associate in the Institute of International Studies on the Comparative Student Project.

JEAN-PIERRE WORMS is Research Associate at the European Center of Sociology in Paris. He was a Harkness Fellow in Sociology at the University of California in 1964–1965. During the fall semester of 1965, he was at Harvard University. He has written widely on problems of political sociology and is co-author of *Evolution des modes de rémunération,* with J. Doufy et al.

Preface

This volume is devoted to an analysis of the role of students in politics and higher education, with particular emphasis on the emerging nations. It is designed to focus academic interest on this subject by presenting articles which attempt to provide some analytical coherence to extant research in the field, as well as report on some recent findings. It is hoped that this book will stimulate further thought and empirical research in an area which has assumed substantial importance.

Social science research has long taken an interest in education. Studies of teachers, educational administration and finances, and government-school relations are an established part of the literature. Yet, relatively little attention has been paid to the role of the student as a dynamic force in educational and political change. (Students have, of course, been studied frequently as subjects by social psychologists.) Students themselves have remedied this situation by dramatically pointing out their important role. Student political activity, particularly, has reached the headlines during the past decade and has focused the attention not only of government officials but of social scientists as well.

It is hardly necessary to document the importance of student organizations and movements in recent years. In the developing areas, a number of governments have been shaken or toppled by student agitation. Student movements in South Korea, Turkey, South Vietnam, Indonesia, Bolivia, Venezuela, and other nations have played a leading role in overturning governments. In Japan, the militant Zengakuren captured world headlines in its successful campaign to force the resignation of the Kishi government in 1960. In Burma, the Ivory Coast, Bolivia, Brazil, Poland, the Soviet Union, China, and many other countries governmental authorities have taken strong action to limit the scope of student political opposition. Student action has also had effects, both positive and negative, on the educational process. In India, the much discussed problem of "student indiscipline" has caused the interruption of university life on many campuses and has become a major headache for a beleaguered government. Students in Nigeria, Argentina, and other countries have agitated about academic issues and often have achieved their ends.

Student political activity is, of course, not limited to the newly develop-ing nations. Indeed, one of the major causes of an increase in interest in student political activity has been the growth of a "new left" in the United States and the dramatic events of the Berkeley student "revolt" of 1964. While Berkeley and its repercussions have been discussed in detail in a political context, the fact is that Berkeley acted as a catalyst not only for student activity, but also for scholarly interest in student agitation and political organizations. Indeed, it is hardly possible to pick up an American mazagine without reading some article, more often than not written by a professor, devoted to student unrest. Thus, the political awakening of the American student, even if limited to a very small minority of the total stu-dent population, has stimulated interest not only in student unrest, but in the broader problems of student movements and higher education in the United States and abroad.

It is important to note that the campus has not suddenly exploded, that there is a substantial tradition of student political concern and activity, and that students have played an important role in revolutionary move-ments through the years. One need only point to the crucial role of the Russian students in the nineteenth and early twentieth centuries in pav-ing the way for, and in creating, many of the revolutionary movements which led to the Russian Revolution of 1917. Chinese students also were a key element in the revolutionary upsurge of the early twentieth century and caused much of the intellectual ferment, as well as supplying the ca-dres, which contributed to the overthrow of the Manchu dynasty and to later political developments in China up to and including the Communist last thrust to power in 1945–1949. Less dramatic, although not less im-portant in their specific contexts, were the activities of student groups in nineteenth-century Western Europe which often provided the ground swell of revolutionary movements.

In spite of this record, scholars have tended to neglect student move-ments. Marxists, though often the beneficiaries of student protest, have felt that the predominantly bourgeois students could not have played a crucial role in creating, leading, and sustaining "proletarian" movements, and non-Marxists seem to have shared their bias. Many social scientists have been baffled by the web of related factors which must be untangled in order to investigate student activity. The facts that student "genera-tions" last for only a few years and that student organizations and move-ments are markedly unstable and often do not leave good records behind them have not made the task of analysis easier. Fortunately, this hiatus seems to have ended. The concern with the factors which affect the development processes—political, economic, and social—has resulted in a major focus on students as emerging elites. Knowledge of the values and activities of students is basic to any effort to evaluate prospects for development.

There is clearly a need for more research and analysis in this area. The active role of student organizations and movements in stimulating educational reform and in creating "modernizing" forces within their society must be given careful consideration. Studies of the forces which produce varying patterns of student behavior in both the industrialized nations and in developing societies have important implications not only for social and educational policy, but as a means of studying the larger societies of which the students are an integral part. Students may help initiate basic changes, but they also reflect the larger social systems.

Most of the research reported in this book has been sponsored by the Inter-University Study of Labor Problems in Economic Development using funds made available to it by the Ford Foundation and Carnegie Corporation. The Committee in charge of the study has made grants to Professors Bakke, Glazer, and Lipset, the first two for field research in different countries, the third to develop a series of survey studies of student attitudes and behavior in underdeveloped countries. Sections from the studies of Bakke and Glazer are included here. The other chapters (with the exception of that of Professor Bereday) are an outgrowth of researches which were originally sponsored in whole or part by the Institutes of International Studies and Industrial Relations and the Survey Research Center of the University of California at Berkeley, as part of a program of comparative survey studies, which was organized in conjunction with the Inter-University study. The various Berkeley-initiated projects drew on monies made available for the purpose by the Institute of International Studies, from funds derived from Ford and Carnegie and State and Federal grants designed to support comparative research. During the past two academic years, these projects have also been supported by the Center for International Affairs of Harvard University from a Ford Foundation grant.

With the exception of the first chapter, originally published in the review, *Minerva,* the contents of this volume formed a special issue of the *Comparative Education Review.* In some cases, however, the material has been revised.

Cambridge, Massachusetts
May 1967

Seymour Martin Lipset

Contents

Approaches to the Study of Student Political Behavior

—————————————— PART I ——————————————

University Students and Politics in Underdeveloped Countries[1]

SEYMOUR MARTIN LIPSET

—————————————— 1 ——————————————

The University in Underdeveloped Countries

The tasks of the universities in the underdeveloped countries of the world are fundamentally not very different from what they are in more highly developed societies. They must transmit in a more differentiated and more specific way the cultural heritage—the history, the scientific knowledge, the literature—of their society and of the world culture of which their society is a part; they must train persons who will become members of the elites of their societies to exercise skills in science, technology, management, and administration; they must cultivate the capacity for leadership and a sense of responsibility to their fellow countrymen, and they must train them to be constructively critical, to be able to initiate changes while appreciating what they have inherited. The universities must contribute new knowledge to the world's pool of knowledge and must stimulate in some of the students, at least, the desire to become original contributors to this pool, as well as equipping them with the knowledge and discipline which, given adequate endowment, will enable them to do so. Regardless of whether the university system seeks to educate only a very small fraction of the stratum of university age or a quite large proportion, these tasks remain the indispensable minimum. A university system which fails to perform these functions, however useful it might be in other respects, is not doing its job. It will become parasitic on the university systems of other countries and will be unable to cope with the tasks of national development.

In the underdeveloped countries, the role of the universities is especially important because the elites of the modern sector of the society are drawn

3

very largely from the reservoir of persons with university training. There is no class of indigenous business enterprisers who, without university training, have taken or are likely to be allowed to take the main responsibility for economic development—as they did in Europe and America in the nineteenth century. There is no class of highly skilled artisans from whom significant technological innovations will come forth. There is very little research in most new states, apart from the little that is done in universities —although the balance is now beginning to change in favor of non-university research establishments. Much of the intellectual journalism, e.g., analytical commentary on public policy, emanates from the universities. Thus the universities alone must not only produce much of the elite which must modernize the society, but they are also almost solely responsible for the conduct of intellectual life in general in their own countries. A substantial proportion of the political elite, too, is bound to emerge from the ranks of university graduates, even in a time of populistic politics.

The universities of the underdeveloped countries bear the burden of being, in an age of nationalism, institutions part of whose task it is to propagate a universal culture and to contribute to its growth, while simultaneously cultivating and developing the indigenous, actual or potential national culture and enhancing national life. The task of interpreting the indigenous cultural inheritance through linguistics, anthropology, sociology, historiography, literary history, and criticism must also be conducted according to standards and procedures of universal validity. Not only do the substance and procedure of university study partake of universality, but they are from the beginning of the modern age, and still at present, derived from the accomplishments of academics and amateurs of the Western, Central, and Northern European culture area, including the North American, the very areas of the world against which the twentieth-century nationalism of Asia, Africa, and Latin America is asserting itself. The situation is not made easier politically and pedagogically by the fact that in Africa, and in major areas of Asia, university teaching and scientific writing are still conducted in the languages of the former colonial powers. Even where this is not so, a university to perform its functions well must still, and will for some time to come, depend on books and periodicals written and printed in the metropolitan countries. Moreover, the universities of the underdeveloped countries must still share the performance of their tasks with the metropolitan universities, which for much of the world carry the major responsibility for advanced training in science and scholarship.[2]

Under these circumstances, the universities are bound to be subject to pressure from their politically sensitive fellow countrymen and from the opinion of their academic colleagues overseas. They will also be under pressure from their own student bodies, who at the most sensitive and reactive stage of life are being subjected to a discipline which is alien to their own indigenous social and cultural traditions and on their performance on which, assessed by "alien standards," their future will largely depend. Universities to be successful must form a community which embraces students as well as teachers and research workers. Universities must develop a culture of their own. This culture must go beyond the bodies of specific knowledge which are taught and cultivated and extend to a vague ethos of attitudes and sensibilities, of standards and canons of judgment which must be assimilated and cannot be explicitly taught.[3]

It is difficult enough to infuse such a culture into a new generation even in societies where the culture of the university is more or less integral to the indigenous culture. It is even more so in underdeveloped countries, where it is still in greater or lesser measure an alien culture, alien to the background from which the students come.

The central tasks of the university cannot be performed without the assimilation of the student body into the university community, which is a graded community, inevitably hierarchical by virtue of differences in age and competence. This task is not an easy one, but on its effective performance depends the success of the university in the performance of its essential functions.

University students are not, however, merely prospective members of the elites of their countries. Particularly in the underdeveloped countries, university students do not just prepare themselves for future roles in public life; they play a significant part in the political life of their countries even during their student period. The intensity of the university students' political activity is in some sense a measure of the failure of the university as an academic community. This is not necessarily and always so, but it does seem to be so in the underdeveloped countries where universities operate under severe handicaps of unfavorable traditions and a paucity of resources, human and financial, and where student politics are frequently associated with the rejection of the intellectual leadership of the faculty of the universities.

Quite apart from the influence of the life of the university itself on the students' disposition toward politics, the position of the student in an underdeveloped society is itself conducive to political preoccupations. For one thing, the modern educated classes of the former colonial countries of Asia and Africa were the creators of the political life of their countries. University students and, where there were no universities, secondary school students, played important roles as adjuncts to the movements for independence. Students at overseas universities became nationalists in the course of their sojourn in a foreign country, and they organized political bodies which, at least in the case of the African countries, were the first steps toward independence. Much of the political life of the colonial period allowed little freedom in terms of normal political activity, and strikes and demonstrations became major forms of political activity. Students were ideally suited, by the disposition of adolescence in situations of relatively safe rebellion against authority, for such activities. The political tradition then engendered has persisted into independence.

Their self-consciousness as a distinctive group with high status and with relative immunity from severe repression has also continued into independence. In societies where learning has been associated with religion and earthly authority, students, as aspirants to that learning, have enjoyed great respect. University students, too, are quite often the offspring of families of some eminence in their respective countries. Their status as kinsmen of the incumbent elites, and as prospective members of the elite themselves, affords them a special position among oppositional groups. They tend to be confident that the harsh suppression to which other opposition groups are subject will not fall to their lot. This, too, encourages their entry into the political sphere.

It should also be pointed out that public opinion in underdeveloped countries is not constituted by the views of a large and educated middle class of professional and business men and women. Because of the small size of the educated middle class, students in certain underdeveloped countries make up a disproportionately large section of the bearers of public opinion; their various affinities of education, class, and kinship with the actual elites give them an audience which students in more developed countries can seldom attain.

Finally, university students in underdeveloped countries are the heirs of a European tradition of student politics. In Germany and Russia, student politics gave much animation to the movement for national renewal and progress in the nineteenth century.[4] In France, too, in the nineteenth and twentieth centuries, university students have been significantly drawn toward revolutionary, agitational, and demonstrative politics. The traditions

of European liberalism, rationalism, and nationalism found their main re-
cipients in underdeveloped countries, within the ranks of the educated
classes. All these movements have left behind a precipitate which has
entered into the nationalist and oppositional politics of the underdeveloped
countries, both those which have recently been colonial and those long independent.

Endemic to all progressive societies has been a tension between the intellectuals, religious and secular, who seek to transmit and affirm traditional
views and those engaged in research and artistic creativity whose roles require them to criticize, revise, and supplant tradition. The latter value new
discoveries and innovation, not the reproduction, copying, or transmis-
sion of old discoveries and ideas. Originality, departure from what is
established and officially accepted, is a central value in the outlook
of the modern intellectual. More generally, in the tradition of the intellectual classes of Western society, there are important currents of long
duration and great intellectual value which have set the intellectuals against
established authority.[5] These include scientism, romanticism, revolutionary
apocalypticism, and populism. These traditions largely form the characteristic outlook of the intellectuals outside universities. Universities have
been institutions established by or supported by the authoritative center of
society—political and ecclesiastical—and they have been more integrated
into the tasks of training young persons for careers connected with the central functions of society and culture. But they, too, by their stress on scientific discipline and detachment from the idols of the market place,
have nurtured a critical attitude. Especially in the social sciences has there
been a tension between the affirmation of the dominant systems of practices and beliefs and a critical attitude toward those systems.[6]

It is this anti-traditional outlook of modern Western intellectual life
which has found reception among the intellectuals of the underdeveloped
countries, and it provides the point of departure of the youngest generation
of intellectuals in those countries.

A not unimportant factor which has encouraged the presence of critical,
anti-traditional opinions and groups on campuses is the tradition of corporate autonomy of the university, which became established on the European continent in the Middle Ages. The norm has become strong enough
in recent years in the United States, and for a longer time in Great Britain
and France, to protect the freedom of social scientists and others to present
views in writing and in the lecture halls, which are antithetical to the economic, political, and religious views of those who govern the university or

the society. In tsarist Russia, university autonomy operated at times to allow the adult sections of illegal revolutionary groups to hold meetings in university precincts, without interference by the police. In Venezuela, in recent years, terrorists have exploited this tradition of university autonomy by using the university precincts as a sanctuary from the police. Seemingly, the recognition that a university must have freedom if it is to carry out its function as a source of innovation has been more powerful in many countries than the threat such freedom might pose to the political and economic self-interest of the dominant elites.

The way in which such norms arise has been described in the case of Meiji Japan, whose late nineteenth-century leaders imitated Humboldt and the Prussian educational reformers in consciously recognizing the need to differentiate between the "indoctrination" function of primary education and the "creative" role of the universities in fostering research and training leaders. The initial educational ordinances drawn up by the Minister of Education, Arinori Mori, in the 1880's were explicitly concerned with such distinctions. He

believed that primary education, by being based on the doctrines of Japanese nationalism and militarism, would help teach the people to be loyal to the state while they were still in the formative period of their lives. But he also believed that if education were limited to the primary level, leaders could not be produced with sufficient grasp of science and technology to contribute to the prosperity of the nation. He was therefore convinced that, in both research and instruction, universities and professional schools should assume the task of preparing such leaders and that *sufficient and appropriate freedom should be allowed for this purpose....*[7]

It is, therefore, not surprising that university students, when they develop political concerns, should be more radical than the classes from which they come even in the underdeveloped nations. In the United States, where, until recently, university students have not played a notable part in public or political affairs, they are much more prone to favor the Democratic party and to support liberal and even socialist measures than is the middle class in general.[8] Likewise, in Britain and most European countries, the leftist parties are considerably stronger among university students than they are in the rest of the middle class.

Students and Politics in Communist Countries

The situation in the various communist countries, of course, has been quite different, particularly in Stalin's time. Public oppositional politics have rarely been possible. It is noteworthy, however, that students and intellectuals have played a major role in the movements to liberalize the totalitarian regimes. This was especially true in Poland and Hungary in 1956. In Poland the chief critical magazine was a student journal, *Po Prostu* (Plain Talk), which served as the main rallying point for the liberal elements as long as it was allowed to exist.[9] In Hungary, also, the university student body was a major force in the groups leading the uprising.[10] In the Soviet Union, intellectuals, particularly young ones, including students, have played a major role in demands for reform, insisting on more freedom and more intellectual integrity. A former student of Moscow University now living abroad reports that while

it is difficult to give exact figures, . . . my estimate of the proportion of Soviet students whose political discontent was revealed during the thaw of 1956 would be from one-fourth to one-third of the total. With the exception of the professional activists, the remaining played the familiar role of "the masses": their attitude toward the political avant-garde was sometimes sympathetic, sometimes uncomprehending, but rarely hostile.[11]

During 1956–1957, following the 20th Party Congress, there were open attacks on the leadership of the Young Communist League, with demands for more freedom and democracy:

Illegal and semilegal student journals with such characteristic titles as *Heresy* and *Fresh Voices* began to appear; they discussed art and ideology, ridiculed socialist realism, and attacked the local Komsomol leaders. Wall newspapers began to print "undesirable articles. . . ." Finally during the Hungarian uprising an account of the events, as gathered from a British Broadcasting Company [*sic*] broadcast, was posted on a bulletin board in the University of Moscow. . . .[12]

In Communist China, the year 1957 witnessed the "Hundred Flowers" campaign, in which criticism was openly encouraged by Mao Tse-tung and other party leaders. The results startled the regime, since for five weeks it was exposed to a barrage of sharp attacks by older intellectuals and students. As one Frenchman present in China during this period reported: "What really shook the party was a feeling that it faced the loss of its control over the youth. Young people brought up under communist rule had become the loudest in denouncing the party which had vested its hopes in them."[13]

Some indication of the nature of the criticism may be found in the pamphlet, *Look! What Kind of Talk Is This?* published by a party organization, the Peking Student Union, on June 14, 1957, as a collection of critical attitudes to be dealt with in reindoctrination sessions. The statements so presented "are not anti-socialist; they are anti-party, anti-Kuomintang, anti-imperialist, anti-Stalin, pro-Tito."[14]

There is, of course, no reliable way of estimating the extent of critical sentiments and behavior among university students in communist (or even other, more accessible) countries from evidence concerning protests which have become known. While such sentiments and actions are extremely important, it may be that most of the students passively support the status quo. Survey data based on samples of total student populations gathered in Warsaw in 1958 and 1961, and in Zagreb in 1961, do not, however, support this hypothesis. The Polish data clearly indicate that the bulk of the students were socialist, anti-Marxist, favorable to freedom and civil liberties, and egalitarian (as indicated by support for a narrow range in the distribution of income), and that 45 per cent had played an active role in the anti-Stalinist demonstrations of October 1956. Less than one-quarter (24 per cent) approved of the activities of the communist youth organization, and 72 per cent voiced dissatisfaction with them. Sixty-eight per cent favored some sort of socialism, but only 13 per cent identified themselves as Marxists, and 68 per cent indicated clear opposition to Marxism.[15] A survey of Yugoslav students at the University of Zagreb suggests greater support for the official ideology. Over half (53 per cent) stated that they accepted Marxism fully while another 19 per cent indicated partial acceptance. On the other hand, when asked their opinion of the leaders of the official League of Students, less than half (43 per cent) approved of them, while 53 per cent would have preferred other leaders. And 26 per cent of the respondents indicated that they sometimes thought they would be "more satisfied" if they could live abroad.[16]

The history of student politics in the countries of Eastern Europe and China still arouses old memories and calls forth corresponding responses from the present rulers of these countries. The efforts of students and intellectuals were of notable importance in undermining pre-communist regimes in these countries, and current efforts at their suppression may be consciously related to an awareness of that history.[17] In his classic study of tsarist Russia, set consciously in a Tocquevillian framework, Leroy-Beaulieu noted:

The schools ... have always been the hotbeds of radicalism and the higher the school, the more imbued with the revolutionary spirit the young people who graduate therefrom. ... Science and education, no matter how watchful the supervision they are subjected to—by the wants which they create, by the confidence in right and reason which they inspire, by the curiosity they arouse and the comparisons they suggest—invincibly predispose to criticism, to free investigation, hence to liberalism, to the spirit of innovation.[18]

The university students in particular were among the few to engage in demonstrations demanding freedom and major economic reforms from the mid-nineteenth century on. Many of these early protests began as struggles for greater rights for students within the universities and then widened their objectives as they met with repression. A report by a faculty commission of the University of Moscow, written in 1901, traced the causes and nature of every student disorder back to the 1850s. It

noted that since 1887 they had become almost annual.... This upward trend of student disorders was confirmed by statistics on expulsions from the university, which had doubled in the six years from 1894 to 1899, as compared to the preceding seven years. During the later period, a total of 1,214 students were expelled from the University of Moscow....[19]

Student strikes and demonstrations became even more prevalent after 1899, reaching a climax in 1905, when the universities were closed by the government.

In 1901, the workers were to learn the value of the street demonstrations from students. These demonstrations, first organized by the university students of St. Petersburg... spread rapidly to other universities and were promptly joined by sympathetic workers and other elements of the urban population.[20]

The freedom which was won by the students for themselves, in the form of autonomy given to the universities in 1905, helped facilitate revolutionary disturbances.

The student movement was being led by a group of extreme radicals, mostly Social Democrats and some Socialist Revolutionaries and others.... Overriding the liberal professors who sought a return to normal academic life, the students opened the doors of the universities to mass meetings of the workers. Since the police could not enter the universities except at the request of the university council, these meetings were held in complete freedom. Here, in closed quarters, revolutionary speeches were made and strikes organized; here the revolutionary parties made their plans without interference.[21]

Sixty years ago, Bernard Pares included students, with the intelligentsia, as the carriers of the revolutionary outlook in tsarist Russia. His analysis emphasized some of the determinants that have been pointed to in recent analyses of the politics of university students in underdeveloped countries:

The universities, long the fortress of criticism, had united within their walls a number of young men who were never again in all their lives to meet so many of their fellows under the inspiration of a common ideal. Here they were still young in heart and brain, and as yet unhampered by the practical concerns of life. They did not represent any ruling class; naturally, their interests were quite as much social as political; and students or ex-students, especially those who crossed the frontier, might be expected to carry on a scheme of social propagandism as wholehearted and as all-embracing as any other of the enthusiasms of the Russian nature. The universities were by their merits, as by their defects, a very focus of revolution.[22]

In China, students played a major role in the downfall of the Manchu Dynasty at the turn of the century. In large numbers, they backed Sun Yatsen and helped spread radical ideas of modernization and democracy throughout the country.[23] Later, with the overthrow of the monarchy in 1911, university students rallied around the ideas of Ch'en Tu-hsiu, a professor at Peking, who called, in effect, for a thoroughly democratic and egalitarian society. Student politics reached a climax in May 1919, when the huge student demonstration which began in Peking inaugurated the second Chinese Revolution. "The movement spread across the country. In it a new note sounded when workers in factories struck in support of the student demands for a new regime."[24] Many of the intellectuals and students who took part in these movements, including Ch'en Tu-hsiu, were to be among the founders of the Chinese Communist party in 1921. Student movements, demonstrations, and strikes played a major role in undermining Chiang Kai-shek during the 1930s as well. They tended to favor a united front between the Kuomintang and the communists.[25] In December 1931, a mass student demonstration in the capital, Nanking, demanded immediate united resistance to Japan. After this the student movement turned increasingly to the left and the Kuomintang attempted to suppress it. Again at the end of 1935 and in 1936, massive student demonstrations played an important role in pressing the government to accept the new United Front strategy of the communists and "the effect of the post-war [World War II] student riots was to hasten the downfall of Chiang's government and the communist victory."[26]

Historical patterns of student politics comparable to the Russian and Chinese cases may be described for other communist states. Although communist ideology forbids the party from acknowledging the fact that university students have provided both the initial leadership and a large part of the mass base in countries in which the party has taken power on its own, the facts bear out this assertion. That the Castro movement developed from student activities in the University of Havana is well recognized. Less well known is the fact that the Communist party of Cuba, itself, was founded after a massive student demonstration in the University of Havana. José

Antonio Mella and other expelled student leftists founded the party in 1925.[27] The first Vietnamese communist movement, the Association of Vietnamese Revolutionary Young Comrades, was founded by Ho Chi Minh in 1925 from among "large numbers of young men who had escaped from the repressions following the Hanoi Students' Movement in 1925." Among those veterans of the 1925 Student Movement who joined the communists following its suppression was Pham Van Dong, now Prime Minister of the Democratic Republic of Vietnam.[28] The Yugoslav Communist party also secured a large proportion of its leadership from the student movement. Before World War II, the communist student organization (SKOJ) was much larger than the rest of the movement, and its members played a major role in the partisan resistance.[29]

University Students in Underdeveloped Countries

In the underdeveloped or emerging countries, the critical attitude of the educated stratum resembles the reactions of intellectuals in pre-communist Russia and China. Their concern is, from a nationalist standpoint, with the modernization of their country, which would permit it to take its place with the leading countries of the modern world. The long absence of sovereignty adds only a complication to the responses to social, economic, political, and cultural backwardness vis-à-vis the then dominant centers of modern civilization. Great Britain, France, Germany—these were the models of modernity, and it was the retrograde position of their own country in comparison with one of these countries or with a vague composite image of all of them which provided the point of departure for the radical criticism of their own countries. Where their own countries were under colonial rule, it was only a simple step to link the backwardness of the country with the interests and intentions of the ruling foreign power.[30] The attraction of the foreign model was associated with a revulsion against the backwardness of indigenous institutions. At the same time, the politicized students and their older intellectual confrères were nationalists, and they could not lightly accept their own xenophilia and their own implicit denial of the vitality of their own indigenous inheritance.[31]

As Seton-Watson has noted, the disproportion between the modern education imparted by the universities in Eastern Europe during the nineteenth and early twentieth centuries and the backwardness of the rest of the nation made sensitive young people painfully aware of the cultural and economic backwardness of their own country.

They belonged to the nineteenth or twentieth centuries. But their less fortunate compatriots in the villages were living in the eighteenth or sixteenth centuries. . . . They felt themselves obliged to serve their peoples, to raise them to their level, and to fight against all those who had, or appeared to have, an interest in keeping them in their backward state.[32]

And the same reforming tendencies which emerged in the universities of Eastern Europe have been paralleled in Latin America:

From the [Latin American] university, came the liberal movements of the 19th century and the progressive movements—Christian or Marxist—of the 20th century. Naturally the ideological *avant garde* did not escape conflicts with the conservatives and the beneficiaries of older socio-political structures. And as these latter held power in the previous generation, there was an effort—unavowed but real— of the political elite to halt the spreading influence of the university.[33]

The concern with modernization and development has gone hand in hand with the international stratification system, in which the elite of each nation makes international comparisons and uses international standards to locate themselves as higher or lower with respect to various characteristics which are accorded international prestige.[34] The elites of the emerging nations see themselves and their countries as parts of the suppressed strata of the world though they themselves may be among the well-to-do not only within their own country but even by a world standard. Awareness or concern with the inferior position of the nation is most acute among those who have received or are receiving a university education, since the culture which that conveys is so obviously part of a universal culture and the university community has such close ties with the international community of scholars and universities.[35] Many of its leaders have been trained in the more advanced, higher-ranking nations, and hence are more likely to be especially prone to feelings of national inferiority.[36] Those who seek to maintain traditional institutions within the country, who favor only moderate change, are perceived as reinforcing the inferior status of the country.

Thus the conflict between the values of intellectuals and students and of traditional institutions is intensified with an increase in national concern for modernization and for the international position of the country. Although the inherent logic of modern university education is in principle at variance with traditional values even in culturally and linguistically more or less homogeneous countries, the conflict becomes more pronounced in new states where the university and modern cultures are either at present or in the recent past of patent foreign origin and where the language of intellectual communication so often is one which is alien to the indigenous culture.

The behavior of universities and intellectuals in developing countries should not be perceived solely or even primarily as merely a reaction to changes instigated by others. Rather, as John Friedman has argued, the "modern" intellectuals must be placed alongside those directly concerned with economic innovation as the principal agents of social change and economic growth. "The one is active in the realm of values and ideas, the other in the realm of technology and organisation. But the actions of both will tend to undermine the established order of things."[37]

The university trained "modern" intellectual has three essential tasks, "each of which is essential to the process of cultural transformation: he mediates new values, he formulates an effective ideology, and he creates an adequate, collective [national] self-image."[38] These place him in direct conflict with the traditionalist forces in his nation. Thus one of the central tasks of the study of the social requisites for development is the analysis of the conditions which influence the responses of the intellectuals and university students. It is interesting to note that the late C. Wright Mills, in his more direct concern with facilitating political revolution, also suggested that students and intellectuals, rather than the working class, may be an "immediate radical agency of change." As a sociologist, he urged the need "to study these new generations of intellectuals (including university students) around the world as real live agencies of historic change."[39]

The University Situation and the Conflict of Generations

The behavior of university students in underdeveloped countries, while to some degree identical with or derivative from the characteristics of adult intellectuals in those countries, is also a function of certain elements peculiar to the situation of the university student. University students live on the boundary between the last stage of adolescence, with its freedom from the burdens of adult responsibility, and the first stages of adulthood, with its complex of pressing tasks and difficult decisions. University students are generally at an age which is defined as biologically adult; many nonstudents of the same age have often already entered upon adult activities, married, earn money and spend it as they wish. Students are often at the age where they may vote and marry, and many do both. Yet few university students earn all their livelihood; many remain financially dependent on their parents, and the society at large still treats them in many ways as irresponsible adolescents, permitting and even approving of a certain amount of sowing of "wild oats." They may even violate the laws in various minor ways without being punished. In many societies the university is responsible for student conduct, and the corporate autonomy of the university is often a symbol, as well as a bulwark, of the immunity of the students from external authority on their dependent condition.[40]

Max Weber in his great lecture on "Politics as a Vocation" observed that youth has a tendency to follow "a pure ethic of absolute ends," while maturity is associated with "an ethic of responsibility." The advocate of the first fears that any compromise on matters of prinicples will endanger the "salvation of the soul"; the proponent of the second fears that an unwillingness to confront the complex "realities of life" may result in "the goals . . . [being] damaged and discredited for generations, because responsibility for *consequences* is lacking."[41] Thus, if some university students are inclined to be irresponsible with respect to the norms of adult society, they are also inclined to be idealistic. They have not established a sense of affinity with adult institutions; experience has not hardened them to imperfection. Their libidos are unanchored; their capacity for identification with categories of universal scope, with mankind or the oppressed or the poor and miserable, is greater than it was earlier or than it will be later in life. Their contact with the articulated moral and political standards of their society is abstract; they encounter them as principles promulgated by older persons, as impositions by authority, rather than as maxims incorporated into and blurred by their own practice. Increasingly in the modern world, which includes the highly educated sector of the emerging nations, equality, efficiency, justice, and economic well-being are presented as the values of the good society. Poverty, racial discrimination, caste systems, social inequality, administrative and political corruption, and cultural backwardness are all violations of such principles.[42] In all countries, of course, reality is usually at variance with principles, and young persons, especially those who have been indulged in adolescence and are alienated from the authority of their elders or of their parents, teachers, and other rulers of the institutional system, feel this strongly. Educated young people everywhere consequently tend disproportionately to support idealistic movements which take the ideologies or values of the adult world more seriously than does the adult world itself.[43] Youthful idealism, even when it leads to rejection of adult practices, is often "expected and respected. . . .

[Thus] in Latin America . . . the young are surrounded by a mystique which seems to make people believe all their views are somehow 'purer' and less corrupt than those of their elders."[44] The propensity of highly and even moderately educated youth to be radical, and of older persons to be conservative, is not peculiar to either advanced or underdeveloped countries. Within conservative as well as left-wing groups or parties, youth movements or affiliates tend to give the adult organization trouble by their tendency to demand that the party or church live up to its principles.[45]

In underdeveloped societies, the institutions such as the family, church, and school, through which young men and women have had to pass before they entered the university, are usually concerned with transmitting the culture already accepted by the elders rather than inculcating into them a culture which is only in a barely incipient state. An approximately similar situation exists even in "modern" societies, but the situation is much more acute in societies in which most of the older generation lives in a traditional indigenous culture much different from the culture the young person encounters in his contacts with the modern sector of his own society. The resulting hostility against the efforts of authority to impose on him a culture with which he has no sympathy disposes him to accept an anti-authoritarian political culture once he becomes interested in political things.[46]

The older generations are more attached to traditional norms regarding topics such as familial authority, women's rights, authority, religion, etc., than are the younger. Differences in attitudes are also linked to education; the better educated favor "modern" values.[47] University students being both younger and more highly educated are specially inclined to diverge from the prescriptions of tradition in their cultural and political beliefs.[48]

It is common for social movements and most parties in developing countries, especially when they are out of power, to have programs which correspond to many of the vague aspirations and resentments of the younger educated generations.[49]

The most dramatic recent demonstrations of university students as the most aggressive proponents of "modern" values have occurred in Korea, Bolivia, South Vietnam, and the Sudan, where students together with the army have undone governments. The Syngman Rhee regime in Korea was finally overthrown in 1960 as a result of student demonstrations, and similar activities have been directed against the military regime in 1964.[50] This latter year has witnessed the downfall of governments in the other three countries following demonstrations begun by students.

The need of a younger generation to establish its independence corresponds to the tactic of revolutionary movements to seek recruits among those who are not yet integrated into the institutional system. Revolutionary movements give young people an idealistic rationale for breaking with their families, which may be defined as part of the reactionary system. The higher the degree of parental control exercised before youth leave home for university, the more violent the need to demonstrate "autonomy" once they are "free."[51]

Resistance to the pressure of adult authorities which try to impel them toward the burdens of adulthood, of regular employment, regular family life, etc., is intensified by uncertainty as to whether the roles toward which they are being impelled will actually be available. The poor employment prospects for university-educated youth in many underdeveloped countries enlarge the reservoir of late adolescent rebellion from which revolutionary politics can draw support.

Students engaged in the courses of study which entail something like apprenticeship for a definite profession, e.g., engineering, medicine, and preparation for secondary school teaching, where employment prospects are fair, are likely to be less rebellious than students in courses of study without determinate destinations and in which the pattern of instruction does not require personal contact between teachers and students. The most insecure of all are those without specific aims or prospects and who therefore will have to compete with multitudes of other arts graduates, equally poorly qualified, for a small number of inconsequential posts.[52] In the past decade the rapid expansion of the university student population in much of Asia has increased this source of student insecurity. Unemployment or low-status employment awaits many graduates.[53]

The ecological concentration of universities within a limited area, bringing together many young men and women in a similar situation in life and isolating them for the most part from the motley routine of adult life, contributes to the perpetuation of student restlessness. This is as true of universities in underdeveloped countries as it is of those in advanced countries.

Like a vast factory, a large campus brings together great numbers of people in similar life situations, in close proximity to each other, who can acquire a sense of solidarity and wield real power. In Tokyo there are over 200,000 students on the various campuses in the city; the comparable figures for Peking and Calcutta are about 100,000; in Mexico City there are over 65,000; and in Buenos Aires, there are close to 70,000 students in the university. It is relatively easy to reach students; leaflets handed out at the campus gates will usually do the job. These facilitate quick communication, foster solidarity, and help to arouse melodramatic action. The organization of campus life at the new African universities, as well as in the colleges and universities of India and Pakistan, even where the numbers run only into a few thousand, has the same result. The politicians' awareness that students have contributed so much in the past to the independence movements and to revolutionary movements makes them appreciate the students' political potential in the politics of the immediate present.[54] They are aware of their value in increasing the size of demonstrations and of the heat which can be given to demonstrations by their youthful excitability.[55]

The Political Situation in the Country at Large

In large measure, student political behavior is anticipatory adult political behavior, particularly in developing countries, where even student demands for better universities, teachers, and research facilities are part of the struggle for national development. Consequently, student behavior will often reflect the state of adult politics, even if in a more extreme reformist fashion.

For the most part, "being dynamic" is the main element in the student political demands addressed to the authorities of their respective countries. "Being dynamic" means making dramatic exertions in the direction of modernity. This entails Draconic measures against "remnants of neo-colonialism," against chiefs, against foreign enterprisers, having a rapid rate of economic growth and scoring "anti-colonialist" points in the international arena of the United Nations. Governments which give an air of going about their business in a tough-minded and aggressive way appear dynamic. In Iran, students criticize the regime as conservative, while many identify the military government in Pakistan as dynamic. This is clearly brought out in surveys of student opinion in both countries, which asked identical questions. In Iran only 8 per cent believe that the standard of living is going up for the people, as contrasted with 52 per cent in Pakistan.[56]

Two surveys of "francophone" African students studying in French universities report that majorities of those interviewed stated that there is a conflict of views and/or interests between themselves personally, or the youth of their country generally, and their governments.[57] The proportions indicating such differences were lower among those from the two countries with avowedly radical regimes, Guinée and Mali, than from students from other mainland African states.[58] However, one investigation which also included students from the Malagasy Republic (Madagascar) found that they had the least disagreement with their regime.

The characteristics of the dominant elites, and the connections between those elites and the universities, influence the degree of identification with, or opposition to, government policy by the university community at large, or subsections within it. In his analysis of Japanese educational developments since the Meiji Restoration, Ronald Dore points out that the original opposition to government policies came from the staff and students of the less well-connected private universities which were identified with the various "outgroups" among the middle classes in the larger society. The imperial (state) universities were close to the government and supplied the large majority of the higher civil servants and political leaders of the Restoration period.

By the twenties, when industrialists began to exercise more influence on Japanese life, both staff and students began to be attracted by revolutionary ideologies which demanded drastic social changes. In the post-World War II period of rapid growth, prosperous capitalism, and bourgeois domination of parliament, Dore suggests, the private universities have become much more identified with the regime than the state universities. The latter

have preserved the "devotion-to-high-principle" strain in the Confucian scholar-ruler tradition of the oligarchy and remain the home of the politically minded intellectual—now typically "alienated" and forming the nucleus of political opposition.[59]

The extent of concern with politics among students in different countries is in part a function of the degree of tension in the larger polity. It has been argued that the

apparent greater student interest in national politics among Latin American students is probably a reflection of more general political uncertainty and instability in Latin America. . . . Thus national politics become a matter of concern to everybody.[60]

Where, in a condition of political tension, the existing adult elites and counter-elites are ill-organized and ineffectual, student organizations are likely to become more important in the political sphere.

. . . if young persons can gain sufficient influence to change on occasion the course of national political life, then . . . other power centres must be in such disarray as to elevate the relative power of any organized group.[61]

Thus, countries in which governments may be toppled by the political action of the military are often the same nations in which student activity is of major significance. Korea, Bolivia, the Sudan, and South Vietnam are the most recent cases in point.

The Student within the University

Academic standards are relevant. The greater the pressure placed on students to work hard to retain their position in university or to obtain a good appointment after graduation, the less they will participate in politics of any kind. Such an emphasis on rigorous training will be related to some extent to the professionalization of the teaching staff. Where the staff is part-time, as in most of Latin America, students will be more inclined to give their attention to non-academic concerns, including politics. Students are also more available for politics in universities which do not hold the undergraduates to a demanding syllabus. This is the case in Japan and India. Within the university, of course, similar variations hold. Fields such as the natural sciences, which generally require more concentrated study and work than the arts subjects or the social sciences, will inhibit the inclination of students toward politics. Where there is sufficient concern for standards of instruction and student numbers are accordingly restricted to a level compatible with adequate instruction, as in engineering and medical faculties in India, student indiscipline is less marked.

An analysis of the behavior of Indian students which seeks to account for differences among universities indicates that the colleges with better trained and more devoted staffs experience relatively few incidents of student indiscipline. The students most likely to be involved in such activities appear to come from the arts faculties of institutions and departments of low standing, which require low per capita investment, which do not inculcate into the student a sense of self-esteem in the pursuit of knowledge and which offer fewer employment opportunities.[62]

The weak concern for academic standards in India is reflected in the admission standards of many of the larger universities which admit students, some suggest a majority, who do not have the background to carry on university level work.

... the Vice-Chancellor of one of the greatest and oldest universities in India ... recognized the futility of his university's task but suggested that it nevertheless fulfilled a social function. "We keep tens of thousands of young people off the streets," he said, "and instead of letting them become delinquents we turn them, instead, into communists.[63]

That it is possible to restrain student political activity is suggested by a recent study of the Arab world which reports that in "... Egypt and Syria, recently, the regime has been ... successful in curbing political activities by increasing the number of examinations, stiffening the requirements to stay enrolled, trying to emphasize science and technology...."[64]

Nonetheless, efforts to raise standards in an atmosphere impregnated with traditions of student agitation may themselves arouse unrest and political activity. The student generation which is subjected to demands for greater exertion may find their chances to gain a degree reduced. In various parts of Asia there have been

spectacular student demonstrations in recent years, some of them with disturbing political overtones, ... apparently caused by well-intended government measures to up-grade the curriculum. For example, a recent outburst of student agitation in Pakistan stemmed from the government's attempt to implement the report of the country's Educational Commission pointing the way to a lengthening and improvement of a number of curricula. But stiffer and tougher courses proved burdensome not only on those without the intellectual qualifications, but also on those with but slender means; and angry demonstrations, student strikes and walkouts, even destruction of campus property, have been the result.[65]

In Venezuela, in a deliberate effort to reduce student opposition politics, the University of Caracas adopted a "no repeating rule" in 1963, which provided that a student who failed more than twice was to be dropped permanently from the rolls of the university. This rule, however, was not enforced until the crisis of mid-May 1964, in which the police violated traditional university autonomy in order to arrest students accused of acts of terrorism. When the Rector responded to violent demonstrations against these arrests by announcing that the "no repeating rule" would be strictly enforced, a student strike designed to force the repeal of the rule developed, supported by both communist and Christian democratic student groups. The demonstrations and strike failed, however, when the university administration made it clear that if they continued, all students would be faced with the loss of a year's credit. Much of the success of these efforts to impose more exigent standards depends on the determination of university administrators and the attitude of the public. That students in their opposition to higher standards may be supported by a public which is concerned mainly with increasing the production of university graduates is indicated in Dr. Karve's account from India:

It has happened that when the result of a particular examination was rather strict and a larger number of candidates than usual failed, public agitation in the newspapers and on the platform has been known to have taken place as a protest against the "massacre of the innocents."[66]

Where universities follow the historic Bologna practices of student participation in the government of the university through elections to university bodies, one may expect more political activity among students. In Latin American universities, "generally about one-third of the governing body are students."[67]

The ideal of the university as a republic in microcosm has been central to student ideology in Latin America since the launching of the Cordoba University Reform Movement in Argentina in 1918.... in Latin America the student is used to exercising, or at least demands as his right, a much greater role in the conduct of university affairs than would be dreamed of on a U. S. campus.[68]

University issues such as the quality of teaching, the extent of library facilities, and the character of dormitories are linked in these situations to larger political matters.

Perhaps the best example of the way in which the concern of a student movement for a specifically academic demand, namely, the improvement of the quality of education, may have widespread political consequences is, of course, the famous Latin American University Reform Movement which began in the University of Cordoba in Argentina in 1918. It spread through much of Latin America, demanding a greater emphasis on the social and physical sciences and changes in the university government so as to give increased power to representatives of the staff and students. But regardless of its success in changing the university, the Reform Movement politicized university life in many Latin American countries. Robert Alexander reports: "there is no doubt that after 1918 each generation of students passed on to the next what had become a tradition of intense political activity by an appreciable part of the student body."[69]

The location of a university in or near a capital encourages political activity because national political organizations and personalities are more on the minds of students and are also more available as the foci of thought, agitation, and demonstration. Staff members are likewise more politicized, and students are more accessible to political agitators. Thus it was that Bengal, and particularly Calcutta, became the first center of student political agitation—Calcutta was the capital of the British Raj until 1912.

Latin America, Burma, and Japan testify to a similar relationship. "With few exceptions the only student organisations that historically have had important roles in political life (in Latin America) are those of the major national universities established in the capital cities."[70] Student political activity may soon become as high in provincial as in metropolitan universities, however, since those in the less prestigeous institutions may feel the need to be politically involved to validate their claim to equal distinction. In Japanese student movements

leadership is taken by students of the leading universities (located in Tokyo and Kyoto), and most of the participants belong to them. At the same time students in the minor leagues may feel that they must follow the example set by those in the major leagues in order to assure themselves that they are university students too. Thus the same type of movement spreads easily all over the country, and federation is readily accomplished under the leadership of the students in leading universities.[71]

Earlier it was noted that the larger the university, the greater the absolute number of those with dispositions to political activity and the stronger their mutual support, organization, and resources. Larger student bodies will also heighten the tendency toward the formation of an autonomous student culture resistant to the efforts of the university administration to control it. Large universities in capital cities are, therefore, especially prone to agitation and demonstrative student politics. The massive demonstrations mounted in Tokyo in opposition to the Mutual Security Treaty between Japan and the United States; in Seoul against the treaty between Japan and Korea; in Buenos Aires against a Bill providing for state support of private (Catholic) universities; in Warsaw and Budapest demanding more freedom; in Paris against the Algerian war; and many others in recent years have been associated with the existence of large universities located in major metropolitan centers, often national capitals, in which students have provided an easily mobilizable population available for opposition to authority.

The greater the number of years the student spends at the university, the greater the likelihood of student political activity. Tenure may be determined not only by actual number of scheduled course years, but by rules pertaining to requirements for a degree. Where the university system permits students to "hang around" for years, to finish at their own discretion, one may find the phenomenon of the professional student, from whose ranks political leaders are likely to be recruited. Shils points to those Indians who

live on in the university or college hostels, not registered, not studying, having nothing academic about them except their residence and their associates. Older, tougher, more ingenious, often seductively attractive, these "professional" students are often the catalysts who agitate lambs into lions.[72]

Such a system also permits political parties to maintain paid agents on campus, as occurs in India, Latin America, and elsewhere.

The possibility of making a career of being a student over an extended period by moving from one practically autonomous "faculty" to another, and the extended courses taken by many students, so that the presence of students over 30 years of age does not cause any lifted eyebrows, is a circumstance favorable to the unremarked continuous presence of such agents who have other motives than to get an education.[73]

Whether students live at home with their families, in university halls of residence, or in "digs" will affect their involvement in politics in particular. The common life in a hostel or hall of residence or dormitory enhances the formation of common student attitudes, a consciousness of kind, and the readiness to mobilize for organized activity. The *Cité Universitaire* in Paris clearly has facilitated student political activity in recent years. This proposition assumes, of course, that these common residential arrangements are not attended by strict supervision by adults, where the wardens or other university or college officials stand *in loco parentis*. The relative peacefulness of student life in British and American universities is partly a function of the strength of a tradition in which the teaching staff takes on responsibility for the surveillance and supervision of the students' affairs. The provision of hostels on the continental and Indian styles, where it occurs against a tradition of an almost complete laissez-faire attitude on the part of the teaching staff vis-à-vis the students, only contributes to turning the halls of residence into centers of agitation.

Living in digs and cafés, in the pattern of the major Latin continental countries, France and Italy, is frequently associated with the emergence of an autonomous political culture among the students and that culture is usually agitational and extremist.

Living at home prolongs the authority of the family over the student and tends to insulate him from university influences.[74] The Indian student study cited earlier indicates that the more conservative the political party, the more likely were its supporters to live with parents or relatives while attending university, while a disproportionate number of more leftist students lived in hostels or in a "private lodge."[75] In Japan, with its strong radical student movement, the centers of activity are in the metropolitan areas, especially Tokyo, [which] have the largest proportion of students who are far from home and live either in a dormitory or in a lodging. They are freer as well as lonelier than students who live at home. Their marginality is greater, and they are less controlled—a favorable condition again for student movements.[76]

Similarly, a survey of student political leaders in Santiago, Chile, reports that the "greater freedom of action of students from the provinces, many of whom escape strict parental control for the first time on coming to the university also helps to explain the prominence of provincials."[77]

The quality of the relationships between students and their teachers depends in part on the traditions which have developed within the various university systems and on the student/staff ratio. Where there is a drastic separation between students and teachers, where teachers have other than university employment, or where there is a very great number of students per staff member, the staff will have less direct influence on student behavior than where the relationship is more that of the apprentice working closely with the master. The relationship between teachers and students is, of course, not exclusively determined by the number of students a teacher must teach. The deference accorded to university teachers within their society will to some extent affect their influence on students. The eminence of teachers in the world of science and scholarship, their interest in their own subjects and their academic self-esteem based on their belief in the worthiness of their calling and accomplishment are additional factors which determine whether students become integrated into the structure of the university as an intellectual community connected with the center of its society or whether they will become attached to an autonomous and more or less alienated student community. Frank Bonilla has said that the relatively low level of competence of professors in Brazil and the consequent lack of respect for them by students is one of the factors which "occasionally makes for excesses and for a hyper-politicization of academic issues" in that country.[78] An eminent Indian administrator and educator writing of the sources of student indiscipline attributes much responsibility to the fact that "teachers today do not command the respect and affection of their pupils to the extent they did in the past" and suggests various devices to raise the social status of academics.[79]

The high cost of living in large towns and the lack of financial support or opportunity for employment clearly generate student dissatisfaction and unrest in India and Burma, although this does not determine whether their unrest will take a political form or will express itself in other forms of indiscipline. Student poverty fosters and intensifies resentment which frequently focuses on questions of fees, hostel, and food charges, etc. The main themes of the resentments of impoverished students, particularly in countries without traditions of part-time student employment or without opportunities for it, are easily adaptable to the major themes of conventional extremist political agitation. Part-time student employment does not really fit into the traditions of university life in most countries—students in under-developed countries either come from or aspire to a style of life in which learning and manual work are thought to be incompatible—nor does it fit into the economic situation of those countries. There is, therefore, no remedy for student poverty except further subsidy, or the refusal of admission to indigent students, which is contrary to every assumption of present-day public life and raises serious questions of policy as to how to deal with unemployed secondary school-leavers.

Alternative Activities

Participation in politics is an alternative to other forms of extracurricular activity.

In Colombia and Mexico, where the extracurriculum is virtually non-existent, at least in the public universities, satisfaction of this leadership ambition must focus on participation in university management and in the opportunity to stimulate, organize and inspire student group action.[80]

In the United States, organized sports were expressly introduced into colleges and universities to divert the adolescent energy which in many college communities had gone into brawls and "town and gown" riots. Conscious but unsuccessful efforts to manipulate the situation similarly so as to diminish the energy available for political activity have been attempted by some American-run universities in the Arab world:

American universities in the Near East have tried to reduce their [student] political activity, which takes the form of demonstrations and strikes, by providing more opportunities for extracurricular activities such as athletics and clubs of many kinds. The logic behind this policy has been that such hitherto neglected aspects of Arab campus life might drain off the students' political energies into other channels. But this American technique has not worked. The new activities have only given the students additional stages upon which to play their political roles, more opportunities to disagree with one another, more arenas in which to extend their political attitudes on the campus.[81]

In Japan also, during the 1920's, in a conscious effort to counter the growth of student radicalism, "political societies were banned in the universities, sports were encouraged instead, and the puritanical restrictions on high school love affairs were relaxed in an effort to divert student energies to less dangerous channels."[82] The traditional pattern could not, however, be overcome.

The mere provision of opportunity for extracurricular activities does not, then, guarantee that all or even most students will make a satisfactory social adjustment. In all societies, some, for reasons of personality, inadequate income, or family background, will find themselves to be "outsiders." Political groups simultaneously gratify the resentment of "outsiders" and give them a dignified position in the course of their activities.

Much of the time which male university students in Western countries do not devote to study or to student societies is devoted to attending to young women. Where the tradition of marriage by arrangement prevails, and women are isolated from men before marriage, this opportunity does not exist. Even the small proportion of young women in the student body in such societies live within this tradition. They are more carefully watched over by custodians and the young men are too shy and too gauche. That this is not a minor student concern is dramatically revealed in a recent study of Asian students:

In a series of samples of over 1,500 students in four South-East Asian universities who were asked: "What has been the most serious personal problem which has adversely affected your university studies?", over 80 per cent answered: "Troubles with the opposite sex." This did not mean troubles with females with whom relationships had been established but rather the inability to initiate any relationships at all with them. The stories are legion of Rangoon University male students who for months follow, from a distance, female students they admire in the hope that somehow they might be introduced to them. The initiation of the faintest and least erotic heterosexual relationships in Asian universities is hampered by inhibition and uncertainty.[83]

As a result, students have more time and energy than they can or are willing to use on their studies and they have no satisfactory outlet for them. Their sexual propensities exist in a vacuum.[84] The vacuum is sometimes filled by restless and freely floating hostility and sometimes by the precipitation of that hostility into a political form.

Patterns of Recruitment to Universities

There has been an increase in the proportion of university students in underdeveloped countries coming from lower middle class, village, and even peasant families, although the last are still very rare. Students from these backgrounds tend to be less sophisticated, less at ease in the languages of academic discourse. Despite what seems to be their great seriousness in the pursuit of a "career" through attendance at university, they have more difficulties in settling down. Their pecuniary as well as cultural poverty places them under a great strain. Just what this contributes to the extreme politicization of university students is uncertain. It surely causes distress, but whether distress gives rise to extremist political attitudes is not settled. Bonilla believes that it does have such a consequence, at least for Chile.

... important segments of student leadership come from lower middle- and work-ing-class families, from the provinces and from among first-generation Chileans (though only 3.2 per cent of the population were foreign-born, 31 per cent of the student leaders had at least one foreign-born parent). In an extremely class-con-scious country, all of these are groups with a marked status disadvantage. They are the groups bearing the brunt of existing inequities, the ones with the most to gain from social and political reforms and the individuals most likely to be caught up in the competition for status.[85]

Surveys of Brazilian[86] and Panamanian law students also suggest that lower class origins tend to render students more political. Brazilian students of lower status background were more likely to believe that such activities should be engaged in regularly than were students from more privileged families.[87] A study of student attitudes conducted at the University of Ibadan, Nigeria, in 1960, revealed that students whose fathers had lower status occupations were more likely to be affiliated to a political party, and among the affiliated those from lower status backgrounds were more likely to be politically active.[88]

The study of Panamanian law students, which distinguished between "radical nationalists," those who strongly favored nationalization of the Canal, and "moderates," those who felt less strongly about or who opposed nationalization, supports the hypothesis regarding the class correlates of radicalism. The more radical students disproportionately came from rural or small town backgrounds and low-income families. Their "backgrounds were marginal in a few significant respects which suggest that they may feel relatively deprived in status."[89] And an analysis of Brazilian student opinion in a number of universities reported that lower family income tends to be associated with more leftist views.[90] A survey among college students in various parts of China in 1937 revealed that students in the lowest income group, primarily sons of small landlords and peasants, were most likely to have "radical," essentially communist, political sympathies.[91]

We may wish to distinguish between societies in which admission to university is easy and those in which it is difficult; whether there is mass education, as in the United States, the Philippines, Puerto Rico, or Argentina, in which almost anyone who wants to enter a university may do so; and where education is "elitist," based on the assumption that universities should admit only a relatively small elite who meet stringent criteria and have passed through a rigorous system of elimination in the lower schools, as in Britain and the former British African colonies.

Elitist systems tend to assure those who succeed in reaching university a guaranteed place in the upper levels of society. To enter, remain in, and graduate from systems of higher education is all-important. Relatively few drop out through failure or other reasons. Students may realistically expect to enter the elite and thus they tend to identify with the existing one. One may anticipate, therefore, that elitist systems will be less productive of student political unrest than those which do not offer secure paths to success. A study of Nigerian and Sierra Leonean students attending the University College of Sierra Leone[92] provides striking evidence of elite status expectations in two countries where university students form a tiny minority of their age group. When asked: "By the time you are 45, how active are you likely to be in the political life of your country as a whole?" 49 per cent of the Nigerians said they would be active and 24 per cent expected to be cabinet ministers or members of the legislature (25 per cent). Sierra Leoneans were somewhat less sanguine about high-level political careers, but only 35 per cent of them reported that they did not expect to play any significant political role, as contrasted with 27 per cent among the Nigerians.[93] This is not simply a function of better intellectual and social qualifications on admission or of better prospects after graduation. The pattern of teaching in the "elitist" systems is much more conducive to the incorporation of the student into the university community as a part of the central institutional system. Residence in halls with intimate contact with teachers serving *in loco parentis*, smaller classes, tutorial arrangements, isolation in a part of the country not far from, but not easily accessible to, the capital city, as well as a generally patrician, non-populistic, social and political culture all contribute to this result.[94]

The situation of the Egyptian, Japanese, and Indian students, on the other hand, may be cited to illustrate the consequence of a policy of unlimited admission. In these nations, attendance at university has "skyrocketed" since independence, far outstripping the rise in suitable job opportunities. Malcolm Kerr suggests that in Egypt it is this explosive compound of the high aspirations and self-conscious dignity instilled by university education on the one hand and the frustration and deception imposed by the conditions of the market, that has made university students and graduates a continuing revolutionary force. . . .[95]

Their current support for Nasser rests on his commitment "to provide them with opportunities for successful careers."

In Japan:

Since the end of the war there has been a very spectacular increase in the total number of students enrolled in the higher schools and universities. . . . The proportion of economically poor students has increased at a much higher rate than has the total number of students. . . . The family of the poor student invariably makes a supreme economic sacrifice to get him through college. Nevertheless, only about half of the more than 120 thousand students who graduate annually from the universities are able to find jobs which are in any way commensurate with their level of aspirations and ambitions. With each passing year, it can be anticipated that there will be a steady increase in the number of unemployed or "improperly" employed university graduates who will be dissatisfied with their lot.[96]

The phenomena of increasing university enrollments and a decreasing prospect of access to elite positions for large numbers of university graduates has also occurred to some extent in Latin America. José Enrique Miguens refers to the consequent

deep impression that they are not needed by their societies, that not only are they employed in marginal occupations with minimal [economic] rewards, but they are not accorded gratitude or other forms of social esteem beyond some stylistic flattery in the way they are addressed.[97]

Concluding Observations

This chapter has attempted to analyze some of the conditions under which university students, above all university students in underdeveloped countries, reject incorporation into the university as an intellectual community and refuse to accept the existing political and social order of which the university is a part in the political sphere. It has sought also to account for the radical orientation, usually socialist, of their political outlook and activity. It has considered the factors which help account for variations in the direction and intensity of student political orientations, including cultural and social characteristics of underdeveloped countries, the characteristics of the universities in such countries, and the characteristics of the students themselves.

In general it may be said that where the society, the university, and the student are committed to the fullest development of research and teaching in an atmosphere of academic freedom, and where adequate resources are available in the form of faculty, libraries, laboratories, and financial support, students are less likely to engage in political activities and more likely to allow themselves to be assimilated into the corporate life of the university as an institution devoted to the interpretation of what is inherited, the discovery of new truths, and the training of students to do both of these and to prepare themselves for careers based on these activities. On the other hand, even when these conditions are present, there is an inherent tendency for students to take a critical attitude toward the status quo. This critical attitude is the product of a tradition of criticism and alienation, and of the rebellious attitude of youth toward their elders in modern societies; it is also a product of the application of the presumed standards of advanced countries to the behavior of present elites and the societies they govern.[98]

Many protest movements directed at changes in the university constitution and amenities are not always linked to demands for political changes. Indeed, much of the student indiscipline in some underdeveloped countries has become quite apolitical. Some of it expresses grievances about the conditions of life and study and some of it expresses an amorphous dissatisfaction and hostility with immediate authoritative institutions, without political objects or legitimations. It is particularly important to notice that even though radical and extremist attitudes and actions occur frequently among highly politicized students, many students are not very politicized, and some of them, insofar as they have political attitudes at all, are conservative, moderate, or liberal. Thus, a study conducted among students in twenty-two universities and colleges throughout China in 1937, a period when student radical activity was at its height, revealed wide variation in student ideological orientations. Of some 1,160 students, 10 per cent were "conservative," 14 per cent "fascist," 12 per cent "democratic," 10 per cent "Christian," 19 per cent "radical" (communist), and 16 per cent "nationalist."[99] In India, a sample of students from ten universities, when asked to give their preferred choice of government among a number of alternatives, opted 23 per cent in favor of parliamentary democracy as in England, 15 per cent for democracy as in the United States, 18 per cent for democratic socialism, 6 per cent for the Soviet type of socialism, 21 per cent for people's democracy as in new China, and 10 per cent for "dictatorship."[100] And when asked their views concerning civil liberties for minority groups, 36 per cent of these students indicated agreement with the statement, "Steps should be taken right away to outlaw the Communist party," as contrasted with 52 per cent who opposed such an action and 9 per cent who could not make up their minds.[101]

Other countries in Asia in fact reveal considerable political conservatism among university students. Thus a study of opinions in four universities in the Philippines reports that the overwhelming majority gave very pro-American responses in answer to questions concerning the nature of the American social system or about correspondence of the interests of the Philippines and the United States, while much antagonism was evidenced toward both the Soviet Union and Communist China. Almost two-thirds indicated "satisfaction" with the way American "private companies operated their businesses in the Philippines.[102]

In Malaysia, a study of student opinion at the University of Malaya reported that, when asked to state their preference for government or private ownership of industry, the respondents divided into three almost equal parts, for a mixed system, for private ownership, and for government ownership. Seventy per cent reported having a good opinion of Great Britain and the United States, as contrasted with only 14 per cent favorable to the Soviet Union and 7 per cent to Communist China.[103]

In Thailand similar questions answered by students of Thammasát University resulted in even more conservative responses. Forty-five per cent of the Thai students favored private ownership of industry as contrasted to 25 per cent for government ownership and 27 per cent "mixed" replies. They were also more pro-American than the Malaysians (86 per cent) and more hostile to the Soviet Union and Communist China.[104]

In Latin America too there is substantial evidence that radical and extremist views are far from the only ones to be found among university students. Most recently there has been a decline of the Reformista vote in elections at the University of Buenos Aires, and across the Andes, in the Chilean University elections, a loss of votes for the leftist coalition, FRAP.[105] In Brazil, students, when asked to give their opinions of capitalism, divided almost evenly: 50 per cent answered positively, while 47 per cent were negative. Conversely, 26 per cent stated that communism is "good" while 68 per cent thought it was "bad."[106] A Mexican study based on interviews with students in nine universities also reports considerable ideological diversity, although as a group they seemed much more favorable to socialism than their compeers in Argentina or Brazil. When asked their opinions of socialism, 57 per cent answered "very good" or "good" as contrasted with 10 per cent who had negative answers. A comparable question about "communism" revealed 25 per cent favorable and 40 per cent negative. And "capitalism" as a system was approved by 29 per cent and termed as "bad" or "very bad" by over 40 per cent of those replying.[107]

A recent survey of students in Colombian universities also points to the diversity of political attitudes among students. The large majority expressed dissatisfaction with all parties, including the left-wing liberals and the communists. Of those with preferences, about half favored the parties of government coalition, the official liberals and the conservatives. The communists were backed by 11 per cent of those who expressed an opinion, or 4 per cent of the total sample. But though Colombian students may not identify with any specific reformist or communist ideology, it is important to note that there is a relationship between their satisfaction with their own society and their political opinions. The more dissatisfied students were the least likely to have a preference for any party.[108]

The discrepancy between the image of university students in developing countries as predominantly leftist and the data reported in various opinion surveys points to the existence of large numbers of students who are indifferent to politics or who, whatever their preferences, do not have intense feelings about political things. The Brazilian study, cited earlier, reports that among students who state that they are "very interested" in politics, 60 per cent have negative attitudes toward capitalism, while among those reporting that they "are not at all interested in politics," only 16 per cent are anti-capitalist. However, 55 per cent of the politically apathetic group indicate hostility to communism, as contrasted with but 37 per cent anti-communist among the very interested.[109] The Mexican study suggests a comparable pattern among students in that country.

Whatever the qualifications which have to be introduced into the picture drawn in the preceding pages, the fact remains that university students in underdeveloped countries constitute a significant proportion of the rebellious elements in their respective societies.[110] As such they play an important part in political life. But what happens to their political rebelliousness when they cease to be students?

Writing about what happened to the revolutionary students of tsarist Russia of 60 years ago after they had left university, Bernard Pares raised this question and suggested an answer:

What becomes of the ex-student? In fact, he very often ceases to be a reformer when he ceases to be a student, that is, when he becomes a man. He begins to get experience of life and he leaves his ideals behind him. This ... discounts the political value of the student's ideals. ... Friends of reason and of liberty must be grateful to the universities for offering at least the nucleus of a protest of principle. In a word, one has much less reason to quarrel with the spirit of self-sacrifice amongst the students than with the instinct of self-interest which so many of them have shown when they passed into the ranks of officialdom.[111]

Yet it is doubtful whether Pares was right concerning the adult behavior of student revolutionaries in Russia. Ten years after he wrote, political movements largely led and staffed by alumni of student protest overturned tsarist autocracy. Today in many countries, local political experts agree with Pares about the lack of long-term consequences of student radicalism on participants after graduation. In Japan, where there is general agreement that student socialists turn conservative after securing employment leading to positions in business or government, opinion surveys show that more university graduates vote for leftist rather than for conservative parties and that there is a larger socialist vote among the "management and professionals" category than among manual workers.[112] A Japanese sociologist informed the author that a confidential survey conducted among a sample of young business executives (under 40) reported that a majority voted for the left-wing Socialist party. In India, also survey data show disproportionate backing for the more leftist tendencies among the university-educated.[113] As in tsarist Russia and the China of some decades past, leftist ideologies, socialism, and current varieties of socialism or communism have been strong among the elite because these political tendencies are symbolically associated with modernization, rapid economic development, and ultimately with equality, all of these being objectives favored by the well educated. Capitalism is perceived as being linked to foreign influences, traditionalism, and slow growth. Hence many of the younger and better schooled members of the elites, including business executives, often look with favor on or at least are not hostile to leftist tendencies. Such patterns are more common in Asia and Africa than they are in Latin America, but they seem to exist in most of the nations of the "third world."

The Need for Future Research

It is clear that if we are to understand the effects of modern education on the dynamics of change in these countries, it is important not only to study what happens to the student within universities, but also the way in which those who have had a "modern" education and who have become part of the intellectual classes conceive of their society and its system of authority after they have left university.[114] As yet, however, there are even fewer reliable data concerning the attitudes of the adults of the intellectual classes than concerning students.

Our observations of the political effects of university education, or simply of the political correlates of university education, are still in a very primitive state. Indeed, the entire study of universities and their role in the development of the society, polity, economy, and culture of their countries is still to be undertaken systematically. There are multitudes of questions requiring answers, but there are few answers. We know little about the influence of the patterns of university organization or the types of courses of study best fitted to train young people to become responsible and effective incumbents of elite positions in countries which seek to modernize themselves. The influence of university studies, patterns of recruitment, modes of teaching, on intellectual, professional, political, and cultural standards and aspirations, or the assimilation of students into the various spheres of adult activity is still *terra incognita*. Nor are we better informed about the influence of family background, modes of pre-university education and intra-generational relationships on academic and political performance at the university and after graduation.

One major hypothesis of great practical importance asserts that the intense involvement of students in politics is least likely where their universities have very high standards, adequate study and research facilities, and a teaching staff deeply committed to teaching and research. Still, the factual basis for this hypothesis is very fragmentary and vague. A really scientific answer would require the comparison of institutions which are similar with respect to size, location, pattern of student recruitment, and characteristics of the environing society, but different with respect to their standards, teaching and research staff, library, laboratory provision, etc. Such comparisons between universities within a society should be supplemented by international comparisons, in order to determine the extent to which national variations in culture and in student political traditions account for variations in the extent and character of student political activity.

One could go on multiplying the illustrations of significant research which should be conducted into the role of universities, university teachers, and university students in the life of their societies. In the foregoing chapter, I have taken only one small section of this vast and still uncharted domain and attempted to summarize some of the available historical and sociological studies, some quite rigorously quantitative, some impressionistic, some very general, some very particular, and many of them not readily comparable, bearing on this small section. The illumination brought to it by ordering these data should, I hope, be accepted not only for the substantive insight it affords but as an argument for the necessity of more systematic research into the nature and functions of universities in the modern world.

Notes

1. There are also a number of recent articles, books, and theses concerned with issues of students and politics. Probably the best source for these materials is Philip G. Altbach, ed., *Select Bibliography on Students, Politics, and Higher Education* (Cambridge: Center for International Affairs, Harvard University, 1967).

2. Systematic inquiry into the problems of overseas students has scarcely begun. Some pioneer works are Amar Kumar Singh, *Indian Students in Britain* (London and Bombay: Asia Publishing Co., 1963), and Prodosh Aich, *Farbige unter Weissen* (Berlin and Cologne: Kiepenheuer und Witsch, 1962). These books have been summarized in the following articles: Amar Kumar Singh, "Indian Students in Britain," *Minerva*, I (Autumn 1962), No. 1, pp. 43–53, and Prodosh Aich, "Asian and African Students in West German Universities," *Minerva*, I (Summer 1963), No. 4, pp. 439–452. Cf. also J. M. Meijer, *Knowledge and Revolution: The Russian Colony in Zurich (1870–1873), A Contribution to the Study of Russian Populism* (Assen: Van Gorcum and Comp., 1955); Claire Selltiz et al., *Attitudes and Social Relations of Foreign Students in the United States* (Minneapolis: University of Minnesota Press, 1963); Ralph Beals and Norman Humphrey, *No Frontier to Learning: The Mexican Student in the United States* (Minneapolis: University of Minnesota Press, 1957); John W. Bennett, Herbert Passin, and Robert McKnight, *In Search of Identity: The Japanese Overseas Scholar in America and Japan* (Minneapolis: University of Minnesota Press, 1958); Richard D. Lambert and Marvin Bressler, *Indian Students on an American Campus* (Minneapolis: University of Minnesota Press, 1956); Richard Morris, *The Two-Way Mirror: National Status in Foreign Students' Adjustment* (Minneapolis: University of Minnesota Press, 1960); John Useem and Ruth Hill Useem, *The Western Educated Man in India* (New York: Dryden Press, 1955).

3. Michael Polanyi has best described the nature of this community, particularly the mode by which "tacit knowledge" is communicated. Cf. *Personal Knowledge* (London: Routledge and Kegan Paul, 1958); *Science, Faith and Society* (London: Oxford University Press, 1946; reprinted Chicago University Press, 1964); and "The Republic of Science: Its Political and Economic Theory," *Minerva*, I (Autumn 1962), No. 1, pp. 54–73.

4. Cf. Armad Coquart, *Dmitri Pisarev (1840–1888) et l'idéologie du nihilisme russe* (Paris: Institut d'Études Slaves de l'Université de Paris, 1946), pp.

25–44; Martin Malia, *Alexander Herzen and the Birth of Russian Social-*
ism: 1812–1855 (Cambridge, Mass.: Harvard University Press, 1961),
Chapter IV, pp. 57–68; Valentin Gitermann, *Geschichte Russlands* (Ham-
burg: Europäische Verlagsanstalt GmbH, 1949), Vol. III, Part 8, Chapters
2 and 4, pp. 212–252 and 272–301; Karl Griewank, *Deutsche Studenten*
und Universitäten in der Revolution von 1848 (Weimar: Hermann Bohlaus
Nachfolger, 1949); Carl Brinkmann, *Der Nationalismus und die deutschen*
Universitäten im Zeitalter der deutschen Erhebung (Heidelberg: Carl Winters Universitätsbuchhandlung, 1932).

5. Cf. Edward Shils, "The Intellectuals and the Powers," *Comparative Studies*
   in Society and History, I (1958), No. 1, pp. 15–21.
6. Cf. Robert Waelder, who writes that antagonism between intellectuals and
   the dominant institutions and classes has existed

   "To some degree . . . in all societies in which intellectuals have enjoyed
   the freedom of expression. Since the days of the Sophists, they have been
   in the habit of questioning and challenging the values and the assumptions that were taken for granted in their societies. . . . Intellect tends to
   question and thereby to undermine dogma and tradition. The act of understanding, said the historian of science Charles Coulston Gillespie, is
   an act of alienation. . . . Alienation is an aspect of emancipation."

   "Protest and Revolution against Western Societies," in Morton A. Kaplan,
   ed., *The Revolution in World Politics* (New York: John Wiley, 1962), p. 15.
7. Michio Nagai, "The Development of Intellectuals in the Meiji and Taisho
   Periods," *Journal of Social and Political Ideas in Japan,* II (April 1964),
   No. 1, p. 29. Although Mori favored freedom within the Imperial University
   of Tokyo, "he was convinced that what was taught in Tokyo University
   should not be conveyed to the masses since too much free thought among
   the masses might pose a threat to the regime."
8. Unpublished data from an ongoing American study of student attitudes in
   several colleges and universities in different parts of the United States reveal that students by and large are more likely to prefer the Democratic
   party, and for this preference to increase from their first year in university
   onward. Study of Selected Institutions, Center for the Study of Higher Education, University of California, Berkeley. Many studies reveal the effect
   of education, especially at the university level, in reducing prejudice and
   increasing liberal and tolerant attitudes. See, for example, Charles Herbert
   Stember, *Education and Attitude Change* (New York: Institute of Human
   Relations Press, 1961); and Samuel A. Stouffer, *Communism, Conformity,*
   and Civil Liberties (Garden City: Doubleday and Co., 1955), pp. 89–108.
   Evidence for Britain is provided in a British Gallup youth poll conducted
   in 1959. For Germany, a comparison of party preferences among university
   students, in Jürgen Habermas et al., *Student und Politik* (Neuwied am Rhein
   und Berlin: Hermann Luchterhand Verlag, 1961), p. 290, with those of
   university-educated voters in Wolfgang Hirsch-Weber and Klaus Schütz,

Wähler und Gewählte (Berlin und Frankfurt a.M.: Verlag Franz Vahlen GmbH, 1957), p. 309, reveals a higher preference among students for the Social Democratic party.

9. See Flora Lewis, *The Polish Volcano* (London: Secker and Warburg, 1959), pp. 67–69, 134–135. *Po Prostu* was shut down in October 1957, one year after the demonstrations which had opened the way to liberalization. Students rioted for four days in vain protest; pp. 255–256. See also William R. McIntyre, "Students' Movements," *Editorial Research Reports*, II (December 11, 1957), No. 23, pp. 915–916.

10. The first demonstrations in Hungary in 1956 were those of the university students. Student organizations were also the first groups formed breaking openly with Communist party control. See Paul Kecskemeti, *The Unexpected Revolution: Social Forces in the Hungarian Uprising* (Stanford University Press, 1961), pp. 79–82, 106–109.

11. David Burg, "Observations on Soviet University Students," *Daedalus*, LXXXIX (Summer 1960), No. 3, p. 530.

12. *Ibid.*, pp. 530–531; see also Walter Z. Laqueur and George Lichtheim, *The Soviet Cultural Scene 1956–1957* (New York: Frederick A. Praeger, 1958), pp. 215–220.

13. René Goldman, "The Rectification Campaign at Peking University: May–June 1957," *The China Quarterly*, XII (October–December 1962), 139. For a report by a participant, see Tang Chu-kuo, *The Student Anti-Communist Movement in Peiping* (Taipei: Asian People's Anti-Communist League, 1960).

14. Dennis Doolin, ed., *Communist China; The Politics of Student Opposition* (Stanford: The Hoover Institution on War, Revolution and Peace, 1964), p. 14. This publication contains a verbatim translation of the pamphlet published by the Peking Student Union.

15. See Stefan Nowak, "Social Attitudes of Warsaw Students," *Polish Sociological Bulletin* (January–June 1962), Nos. 1–2 (3–4), pp. 91–103; Stefan Nowak and Anna Pawelczynska, "Les attitudes idéologiques des étudiantes de Varsovie," *Esprit*, XXVI (1958), No. 11, pp. 699–707; Stefan Nowak, "Factors Determining Egalitarianism of Warsaw Students," *American Sociological Review*, XXV (1960), No. 2, pp. 219–231; Anna Pawelczynska and Stefan Nowak, "World Outlook of Students in a Period of Stabilization," *Polish Perspectives*, V (February 1962), No. 2, pp. 38–50; Zofia Jozefowicz, Stefan Nowak, and Anna Pawelszynska, "Students: Myth and Reality," *Polish Perspectives*, I (July–August 1958), Nos. 7–8, pp. 21–28; and "Students: Their Views on Society and Aspirations," *Polish Perspectives*, I (November–December 1958), Nos. 11–12, pp. 31–43.

16. Study conducted by Professor V. Serdar, preliminary results of which were published in Mirko Martic, "Student i Zagrebackog sveucilista u svijetlu jednog anketnog istrazivanja," *Nase Teme* (Zagreb), (1961), No. 2.

17. Socialists and others face the dilemma in the emerging world. In Burma it

may be recalled that it "was from the university students' union that the AFPFL (socialist) government sprang, and that precedent was ironically ominous: for the communists had made inroads among the students. The Rangoon Students' Union and the All-Burma Federation Students' Unions, both of which were captured by the communists, were much stronger than the Democratic Students' Organization sponsored by the socialists. The situation deteriorated to such an extent that the government felt obliged in October 1956 to ban student unions in schools." Saul Rose, *Socialism in Southern Asia* (London: Oxford University Press, 1959), p. 142. Similarly in Venezuela, the social-democratic government of Betancourt and Leoni has been led by men who had themselves entered politics via the student movement and who played a major part as student leaders in undermining reactionary and authoritarian regimes. They are now faced by a student movement in which communists play a significant role.

18. Anatole Leroy-Beaulieu, *The Empire of the Tsars and the Russians*, Part II: "The Institutions" (New York: G. P. Putnam's Sons, 1894), pp. 486–487. He documents these contentions with reference to statistical data on the background of those revolutionists who had been arrested, which showed that four-fifths had received higher or secondary education, most of them in government schools, and that a "statistical list of 1880 shows four-fifths of the agitators arrested by the police to have been nobles, sons of priests, of functionaries and officers, of merchants or city 'notables,' only 20 per cent were small employees, working people, and peasants." See his footnotes on pp. 485 and 486. Cf. also Gabor Kiss, *Die gesellschaftspolitische Rolle der Studentenbewegung im vorrevolutionären Russland* (München: Georg Heller Verlag, 1963). Joseph Conrad, *Under Western Eyes* (London: J. M. Dent, 1955), is one of the classic treatments, perhaps the greatest, of Russian student politics under the *ancien régime*. On the beginnings of the student movement, cf. Franco Venturi, *Il populismo russo*, Vol. I, Ch. VIII, "Il movimento studentesco," pp. 366–385 and *passim*. Alexander Herzen in his *My Past and Thoughts* (translated by Constance Garnett) presents a beautiful account of the political sensitivity of the Russian university students of the 1830's. Vol. I (London: Chatto and Windus, 1924).

19. See George Fischer, *Russian Liberalism* (Cambridge, Mass.: Harvard University Press, 1958), pp. 53–56. Fischer points out that in Russia before 1905, when the lower classes were quiescent, students were the one group which had "the numbers and the hardiness to stand up physically to government force."

20. Jacob Walkin, *The Rise of Democracy in Pre-Revolutionary Russia* (New York: Frederick A. Praeger, 1962), pp. 188–189.

21. *Ibid.*, pp. 129–132. Autonomy was withdrawn in 1911; police broke up meetings within the universities and mass expulsions of students, as well as dismissal of professors, occurred.

22. Bernard Pares, *Russia between Reform and Revolution* (New York:

Schocken Books, 1962), pp. 180–181. This book was first published in 1907. For a detailed discussion of the situation on the Russian intelligentsia and their political roles, see pp. 161–282. As Francis B. Randell, the author of the "Introduction" to this edition, states: "... we read this book because the Russia it presents is so much like so many backward countries today, poor but slowly rising modern economies.... Its *intelligentsia* was a classic example of the nationalist intellectual movement to be found in every backward country. Pares' book is relevant to our many discussions of 'the problem of development' in the many little Russias of the world": p. xi.

23. Wen-han Kiang, *The Chinese Student Movement* (New York: King's Crown Press, 1948).

24. Harold Isaacs, *The Tragedy of the Chinese Revolution* (Stanford University Press, 1961), pp. 53–55.

25. H. Seton-Watson, *The Pattern of Communist Revolution* (London: Methuen, 1953), pp. 190–191.

26. John Israel, *The Chinese Student Movement, 1927–1937* (Ph.D. thesis, History Department, Harvard University, 1963), p. 146.

27. Eduardo Suárez Rivas, *Un pueblo crucificado* (Miami: n. p., 1964), p. 21.

28. Hoang Van Chi, *From Colonialism to Communism* (New York: Praeger, 1964), p. 43.

29. Joseph Broz Tito, *Report to the 5th Congress CPY* (Belgrade: Yugoslavia, 1948), pp. 27–34.

30. Edward Shils, "Political Development in the New States," *Comparative Studies in Society and History*, II (1960), No. 3, pp. 272–277. A similar situation existed even in independent Japan. The early appeal of Marxism to Japanese intellectuals, which underlies its success after 1945, is related to its provision of a universalistic justification for Japanese nationalism. As Yuzuru Okada puts it: "many intellectuals were driven by a desire for Japan to catch up with, or even surpass, the West. For them Marxism represented a system that derived from, and was critical of, the social, political, and cultural systems of the West. It appeared to present them with a model of a society of utopian proportions, far exceeding any society that existed at that time in the West. They felt that if they could create a socialist state in Japan, their nation, at a single stroke, would be ahead of the nations of Europe and America. They were emotionally challenged by the *possibility* of achieving socialism before any nation of the Western world." "Introduction" to special issue dealing with "Japanese Intellectuals," *Journal of Social and Political Ideas in Japan*, II (April 1964), No. 1, p. 4. Joseph Ben-David points out that in eighteenth-century France the model to be emulated was Britain, while Germans later sought to copy France. See "Professions in the Class System of the Present Day Societies," *Current Sociology*, XII (1963–1964), No. 3, p. 273.

31. The "memory" of exploitation by the colonial power is still strong in the consciousness of many of the younger generation, even those born after in-

dependence. Thus there is a tendency for the former colonial power to be viewed with mixed feelings, as the source of intellectual prestige and recognition, as well as the former subjugator of the nation, who still exploits the country economically. In Latin America the United States has played this role for students and intellectuals who have seen her, with considerable justice at times, as an economic exploiter. Recent surveys of students in Iran and Pakistan reveal a negative image of the major former colonial powers, Britain and France, while these students, particularly the Pakistani, are much more favorable to the U.S.A. and Russia. *Student Survey in Pakistan* (Bielefeld: E.M.N.I.D., 1963); *Teheran University Student Survey: Attitudes and Aspirations* (Teheran: National Institute of Psychology, 1963).

32. H. Seton-Watson, *op. cit.*, pp. 8–9.
33. León Cortinas Peláez, "Autonomy and Student Co-Government in the University of Uruguay," *Comparative Education Review*, VII (1963), No. 2, p. 166.
34. See especially Gustavo Lagos, *International Stratification and Underdeveloped Countries* (Chapel Hill: University of North Carolina Press, 1963); Edward Shils, "Metropolis and Province in the Intellectual Community" in N. V. Sovani and V. M. Dandakar, ed., *Changing India* (Bombay: Asia Publishing Co., 1961), pp. 275–294 and R. Waelder, *op. cit.*, pp. 17–18.
35. The general problem has been conceptualized by Edward Shils as part of the general phenomenon of the tension which exists between the intellectual metropolis and province. The writer or scholar in nineteenth-century Eastern Europe sought recognition from Paris or Germany. Then and today, the principal intellectual capitals of Western Europe, and increasingly in recent decades, those of the United States, have "exercised an irresistible fascination on certain strata of the societies outside the European centre, and the situation was not made any easier to bear by the often explicit derogation of their own culture and society which its admirers encountered ... in the works and attitudes of intellectuals of the foreign culture to which they were attracted." Edward Shils, "The Prospects for Intellectuals," *Soviet Survey* (July–September 1959), No. 29, p. 86; see also his "The Traditions of Intellectual Life," *International Journal of Comparative Sociology*, I (1960), No. 2, pp. 180–183.
36. The intelligentsia of the underdeveloped countries are those "who are experiencing internal conflict between allegiance to traditional cultures and the influence of the modern West.... An understanding of the intelligentsia can perhaps most readily be gained by examining the case of the 'returned student.' In China particularly, this term has been used to denote the many thousands of young people who produced a powerful ferment within their country after their return from studies abroad. The same pattern occurred in many other countries. It did not matter whether a student had actually studied in a Western country; many took on the characteristics of the 'returned student' simply after exposure to Western culture in ... schools of

their own country." Klaus Mehnert, "The Social and Political Role of the Intelligentsia in the New Countries," in Kurt London, ed., *New Nations in a Divided World* (New York: Frederick A. Praeger, 1963), pp. 122–123. Cf. also Y. C. Wang, "Intellectuals and Society in China, 1860–1949," *Comparative Studies in Society and History*, III (1961), No. 4, pp. 325–426, and his forthcoming book on the "foreign-returned Chinese student."

37. John Friedman, "Intellectuals in Developing Societies," *Kyklos*, XIII (1964), No. 4, p. 514.

38. *Ibid.*, p. 524.

39. C. Wright Mills, *Power, Politics and People* (New York: Ballantine Books, 1963), pp. 256–259. Mills detailed the many actions by university students as key sources of political opposition and denigrated the political potential of the working class. In discussing the politics of students and intellectuals, he called for "detailed comparative studies of them": p. 257.

40. As Edwin Lieuwen has pointed out in discussing the participation of the Venezuelan students in revolutionary politics on many occasions in the history of the country: "The autonomous status of the universities has provided the students special licence to participate freely in politics, particularly in revolutionary activities." Edwin Lieuwen, *Venezuela* (London: Oxford University Press, 1961), p. 164.

41. Max Weber, *Essays in Sociology*, H. H. Gerth and Wright Mills, trans. and eds. (New York: Oxford University Press, 1946), pp. 126–127.

42. As Talcott Parsons puts it, youth are "inculcated with the major values of the society.... However good the current society may be from various points of view, *it is not good enough to meet their standards.*" See "Youth in the Context of American Society," in Erik H. Erikson, ed., *Youth: Change and Challenge* (New York: Basic Books, 1963), p. 117.

43. For an analysis of both the elements of self-interest and the idealism in student movements in Europe, see Frank A. Pinner, "Student Trade-Unionism in France, Belgium, and Holland," *Sociology of Education*, XXXVII (1964), No. 3, pp. 177–199; and Raymond Aron, "Some Aspects of the Crisis in the French Universities," *Minerva*, II (Spring 1964), No. 3, pp. 279–285.

44. Luigi Einaudi, "The Drama of the Latin American Student Movement" (unpublished paper, 1961), p. 2. Eisenstadt suggests that societies may "evolve an image of youth as the purest manifestation and repository of ultimate cultural and social values." S. N. Eisenstadt, "Archetypal Patterns of Youth," in Erik H. Erikson, *op. cit.*, p. 27.

45. See Eric Josephson, *Political Youth Organizations in Europe, 1900–1950; A Comparative Study of Six Radical Parties and Their Youth Auxiliaries* (unpublished Ph.D. dissertation, Columbia University, 1960).

46. Karl Mannheim has located the concerns of "adolescents and early adults, particularly students" for major political or social concerns beyond their personal interests, in the "uncertainty and doubt" which results when "one's questions outrun the scope of one's inherited answers." This occurs when

the youth learns that there are other values and ways of life different from those urged on him by his family. In seeking distance from his primary environment, "with a sense of liberation ... the adolescent discovers alternative interpretations and new values. Self-assertion and defiance accompany this new experience." This contact with a variety of possibilities not taught within the family is confusing, and rather than remain in a state of doubt, many youths seek a new certainty in beliefs which are opposed to those taught at home. "Intellectual fanaticism is not the product of a tacitly accepted heritage, but the expression of an anxiety to end the wear and tear of a state of suspense by the adoption of a categorical creed." Karl Mannheim, *Essays on the Sociology of Culture* (New York: Oxford University Press, 1956), pp. 163–164.

47. See Seymour M. Lipset, "Political Cleavages in 'Developed' and 'Emerging' Polities," in Erik Allardt and Yrjö Littunen, eds., *Cleavages, Ideologies and Party Systems: Contributions to Comparative Political Sociology* (Helsinki: The Westermarck Society, 1964). For a detailed account of sources of generational conflict between students and their parents in the China of 1935–1937 based on questionnaires filled out by 1,164 university students, see Olga Lang, *Chinese Family and Society* (New Haven: Yale University Press, 1946), pp. 283–296.

48. Joseph Fischer, "Universities and the Political Process in Southeast Asia," *Pacific Affairs*, XXXVI (1963), No. 1, p. 13.

49. Frederick W. Frey writes: "Having spoken of student activities, one can hardly avoid mentioning the very pronounced 'youth culture' which pervades portions of Turkish life. Mustafa Kemal proclaimed youth 'the owner and guardian of the revolution'—a fact which some segments of Turkish youth will let no one ignore." "Education: Turkey," in Robert E. Ward and Dankwart Rustow, eds., *Political Modernization in Japan and Turkey* (Princeton University Press, 1964), p. 235. The conflict of generations and its consequences for politics in Latin America is discussed in Carlos Alberto Floria, "Ideas e ideales políticos de los jóvenes latinoamericanos," *Occidente*, XVII (August 1962), No. 139, pp. 12–17. For empirical research on this topic for Latin America, specifically Uruguay, see Isaac Ganon et al., *Nuestro estudiante contemporáneo* (mimeographed, Instituto de Ciencias Sociales, Facultad de Derecho y Ciencias Sociales; Universidad de la República, Montevideo, Uruguay, 1964), pp. 38-62. Concerning students in Panama, and Latin America generally, as "the only group exerting continuous pressure for socio-economic and governmental reform...", see Daniel Goldrich, *Radical Nationalism: The Political Orientations of Panamanian Law Students* (East Lansing: Bureau of Social and Political Research, Michigan State University, 1961).

50. "The students constituted one of the most modernized groups in Korean society, for they grew up after independence and during the period of the massive American military and diplomatic presence. The older people's attitudes

had been formed during the Yi dynasty and under Japanese colonial rule. Thus the students were more quick than the general public to feel, perhaps only vaguely and unconsciously, that the process of modernisation was at a standstill. They also had a less fatalistic attitude towards the abuse of power by the government. To their more modern minds, Rhee's maneuvres during the election seemed like anachronistic 'absurdities,' as they put it, whereas to the adults, they appeared as merely the most recent manifestations of age-old and inevitable phenomena. The adults suffered more directly from Rhee's repressions than did the students who had no family or economic responsibilities, yet it was the students who acted, not the wage-earners of the professional class." William A. Douglas, "Korean Students and Politics," *Asian Survey*, III (1963), No. 12, p. 586.

51. Hypotheses such as these have been presented to account for the rebelliousness of German youth before World War I, and for Latin American and Japanese students in more recent periods. Walter Laqueur, *Young Germany* (New York: Basic Books, 1962), p. 5; Robert Havighurst, "Latin American and North American Higher Education," *Comparative Education Review*, IV (1961), No. 3, p. 180.

52. The existing data bearing on the subject are fragmentary and inconclusive. Thus a comparison of the student supporters of four Indian political parties —Communist, Socialist, Congress, and the conservative, communal Jan Sangh—reveals, as might be expected, that "commerce" is the subject most frequently studied by those with more conservative party choice, while students in "sociology, economics and anthropology" incline more toward the left. The combined group "philosophy, psychology and education" gives the communists much less support vis-à-vis the other parties than any other. Students in the sciences (about a fifth of the sample) seem evenly distributed among the various political positions. Bureau of Social Science Research, *Political Attitudes of Indian Students* (Washington: The American University, 1955), p. 47. In the National University of Colombia, the students in the Faculties of Law and Economics appear to be much more to the left than those in "education, psychology and sociology," who in turn are more radical than those in the natural sciences. K. Walker, "Determinants of Castro Support among Latin American University Students" (paper presented at the Seventh Latin American Congress of Sociology; Bogotá, Colombia, July 13–19, 1964), and Robert C. Williamson, "El estudiante colombiano y sus actitudes" (Bogotá: Facultad de Sociología, Universidad Nacional de Colombia, 1962), p. 49. On the other hand, in a study of the students in three faculties in the University of Buenos Aires, Silvert and Bonilla indicate that "the economics group stand well below exact sciences in degree of political activity, and most of the details of such participation just a little below even medicine." The science students were much more likely to report having participated in a street rally or having attended a party meeting than the economists. Kalman Silvert and Frank Bonilla, *Education and the So-*

cial Meaning of Development: A Preliminary Statement (New York; American Universities Field Staff, 1961), pp. 127–128. See also Seymour M. Lipset, *op. cit.;* and K. Walker, *op. cit.*, pp. 18–19. In student elections in recent years in Buenos Aires, it has become clear that the most radical faculty by far is letters and philosophy, which includes the large Department of Sociology. In Mexico, a detailed study based on interviews in nine universities indicates considerable variation in political opinion among the different faculties. Within the large National University in Mexico City the economics faculty, which includes sociology, was by far the most leftist, with law second. Commerce, engineering and medical students tended to respond more conservatively. *A Study of Opinions of University Students in Mexico* (Mexico City: International Research Associates, 1964), pp. 16–19, 40–43, 123–132.

53. Justus M. Van der Kroef, "Asian Education and Unemployment: The Continuing Crisis," *Comparative Education Review*, VII (1963), No. 2, pp. 173–180, and Edward Shils, "Indian Students," *Encounter*, XVII (September 1961), No. 3, pp. 12–20. Lorraine D. Eyde, "Characteristics and Problems of Indian Universities and Their Students," *The International Review of Education*, IX (1963–1964), No. 4, pp. 461–476. The classic treatment of this subject is to be found in Walter Kotschnig, *Unemployment in the Learned Professions* (New York and London: Oxford University Press, 1938). See also Philip Altbach, "Japanese Students and Japanese Politics," *Comparative Education Review*, VII (1963), No. 2, p. 182, and M. Shimbori, "Zengakuren: A Japanese Case Study of a Student Political Movement," *Sociology of Education*, XXXVII (1964), No. 2, pp. 233–234.

54. In Egypt, "students were virtually a distinct social class wooed by the government and opposition parties alike." Morroe Berger, *The Arab World Today* (Garden City: Doubleday, 1962), p. 311. ". . . all the major political parties in Venezuela today originated in university groups. . . . Soon after the present Venezuelan political parties came into existence in the 1930's and 1940's, they appointed directors of student activities who recruited supporters not only in the universities but also in the *liceos*, or high schools." S. Walter Washington, "Student Politics in Latin America: The Venezuelan Example," *Foreign Affairs*, XXXVII (1959), No. 3, p. 465.

55. An official communist journal, for example, calls attention to the need "to look at the experience gained in the University of Rome, which, with its enrolment of 50,000, not only is a big cultural centre, but represents the greatest concentration of young people in the country." Giovanni Berlinguer, "In the University of Rome," *World Marxist Review*, VI (February 1963), No. 2, p. 60. "Of all the political parties, the Japan Communist Party has worked assiduously on students, who are very apparently regarded as an important target of the party's activities." Lawrence H. Battistini, *The Postwar Student Struggle in Japan* (Tokyo: Charles Tuttle, 1956), p. 145. Lucien Pye notes that in Asia generally "it is the students and the intelligentsia

who are seen as likely candidates for communism" by the communist parties. See Lucien Pye, *Guerrilla Communism in Malaya* (Princeton University Press, 1956), p. 38.

56. See *Teheran University Study: Attitudes and Aspirations* (Teheran: National Institute of Psychology, 1963), p. 19; and *Student Survey in Pakistan* (Bielefeld: E.M.N.I.D., 1963), pp. 89–90.

57. One study which asked whether the respondent himself was in conflict with his government indicates that two-thirds have such a sense of difference. J.-P. N'Diaye, *Enquête sur les étudiants noirs en France* (Paris: Réalités Africaines, 1963), p. 224. The study which asked whether respondents see a "basic disagreement of aims or interests between the youth of your country and the leaders of your government" reports that 51 per cent see such a conflict. *The African Students in France* (Paris: Institut Français d'Opinion Publique, 1962), p. 48.

58. Although neither study reports on the content of the attitudes of the more critical students, one might hypothesize that the critical students in the more communist-oriented states would espouse a more liberal position, would feel state power as too coercive—much as in the communist states of Europe; while students from other countries should make their criticism from the collectivist extreme, which is more common among politicized students in non-totalitarian countries.

59. Ronald P. Dore, "Education: Japan," in R. E. Ward and D. Rustow, eds., *Political Modernization in Japan and Turkey* (Princeton University Press, 1964), pp. 180–187. He is, of course, writing chiefly of the leading state and private universities.

60. R. Havighurst, "Latin American and North American Higher Education," *Comparative Education Review*, IV (1963), No. 3, p. 180; or as Kalman Silvert has put it: "The Latin American university student is the child of his parents." "Continuity and Change in Latin America: The University Student," in John J. Johnson, ed., *Continuity and Change in Latin America* (Stanford University Press, 1964), p. 225. Parsons argues that the absence of "generalized ideological commitment" among American students reflects "the general political characteristics of the society, which has been a relatively stable system with a strong pluralistic character." "Youth in the Context of American Society," in Erik H. Erikson, ed., *op. cit.*, p. 113.

61. Kalman Silvert, "The University Student," in John J. Johnson, ed., *op. cit.*, p. 217.

62. Edward Shils, "Indian Students," *loc. cit.*, and Myron Weiner, *The Politics of Scarcity* (University of Chicago Press, 1962), pp. 184–185.

63. Chanchal Sarkar, *The Unquiet Campus: Indian Universities Today* (Calcutta: The Statesman, 1960), p. 6; another detailed discussion of the nature and sources of student indiscipline may be found in Margaret Cormack, *She Who Rides a Peacock: Indian Students and Social Change* (New York: Frederick A. Praeger, 1961), especially, pp. 174-212.

64. M. Berger, *The Arab World Today* (Garden City: Doubleday, 1962), p. 333.
65. Justus M. Van der Kroef, *op. cit.*, p. 178.
66. D. D. Karve, "Universities and the Public in India," *Minerva*, I (Spring 1963), No. 3, p. 268.
67. R. Havighurst, *op. cit.*, pp. 176, 178–179.
68. Frank Bonilla, "The Student Federation of Chile: 50 Years of Political Action," *Journal of Inter-American Studies*, II (1960), No. 3, p. 312.
69. Robert Alexander, *Today's Latin America* (Garden City: Doubleday Anchor Books, 1962), p. 199. Perhaps the best collection of materials in English on the University Reform Movement is a book of articles by various Latin American scholars and participants in the movement; *University Reform in Latin America, Analyses and Documents*, published by the International Student Conference; no editor, no place, or date of publication indicated. A basic collection of documents on the movement is Gabriel del Mazo, ed., *La reforma universitaria* (Buenos Aires: Ed. El Ateneo, 1946) Vols. I–III. A sampling of some of the large literature on the university, its problems and the Reform Movement, is the following: Gabriel del Mazo, *La reforma universitaria y la universidad latinoamericana* (Corrientes, República Argentina: Universidad Nacional de Nordeste, 1957); A. Grompone, *Universidad official y universidad viva* (Mexico, D. F.: Biblioteca de Ensayos Sociológicos, Universidad Nacional, n. d.); Luis Alberto Sánchez, *La universidad latinoamericana* (Guatemala City: Editorial Universitaria de Guatemala, 1949); Roberto Mac-Lean y Estenos, *La crisis universitaria en Hispano-América* (Mexico, D.F.: Biblioteca de Ensayos Sociológicos, Universidad Nacional, n. d.); and Lucio Mendieta y Núñez and José Gómez Robleda, *Problemas de la universidad* (Mexico, D.F.: Biblioteca de Ensayos Sociológicos, Universidad Nacional, n. d.); and Foción Febres Cordero, *Reforma universitaria* (Caracas: Universidad Central de Venezuela, 1959). Recent assessments of the Latin American University are found in Abraham Rabotnikov, "Panorama de la universidad latinamericana," *Cultura Universitaria* (April–September 1963), Nos. 83–84, pp. 82–101; and Rudolph P. Atcon, "The Latin American University," *Die Deutsche Universitätzeitung* (February 1962), No. 2, pp. 9–48.
70. Kalman Silvert, *op. cit.*, p. 212.
71. M. Shimbori, "Zengakuren: A Japanese Case Study of a Student Political Movement," *Sociology of Education*, XXXVII (1964), No. 2, p. 232.
72. Edward Shils, "Indian Students," *loc. cit.*, p. 17.
73. E. Wight Bakke, "Students on the March: The Cases of Mexico and Colombia," *Sociology of Education*, XXXVII (1964), No. 3, p. 204.
74. For evidence of this in relationship to Colombia, see K. Walker, "Determinants of Castro Support among Latin American University Students," pp. 16–17, cited footnote 52 above. Cf. also the *Calcutta University Commission 1917–1919 Report* (Calcutta: Government of India Press, 1919), 12 volumes.

75. Bureau of Social Science Research, *Political Attitudes of Indian Students* (Washington: The American University, 1955), p. 46.

76. M. Shimbori, *op. cit.,* p. 233.

77. Frank Bonilla, *Students in Politics: Three Generations of Political Action in a Latin-American University* (Ph.D. thesis, Department of Social Relations, Harvard University, 1959), p. 253. A study of former communists in four countries, the United States, England, France and Italy, points to a comparable causal pattern in describing the conditions under which many joined the party while in university. "It is certainly true that at the time of joining the party their condition might have been accurately described as 'alienated.' In many cases they were away from home for the first time, adapting to a new setting, exposed to confusing impressions, rejective and iconoclastic with regard to their pasts, and confronted with a political world [during the 1930's] in which militance might readily have appeared to be an appropriate attitude." Gabriel Almond, *The Appeals of Communism* (Princeton University Press, 1954), p. 215.

78. Frank Bonilla, "Education and Political Development in Brazil: Growth toward Nationhood" (mimeographed paper, Conference on Education and Political Development, Lake Arrowhead, California, June 25–29, 1962), pp. 13–14. For a general analysis of the way in which large classes, overcrowding, and lack of scholarly resources alienate Latin American students from university life, see Gabriel del Mazo, "La nueva crisis de las universidades latino-americanas," *Panoramas,* II (July–August 1964), No. 10, pp. 95–111.

79. See Humayun Kabir, *Education in New India* (London: Allen and Unwin, 1956), pp. 151–166. Shils has detailed the decline in status, influence and income of Indian academic and other intellectuals since independence. He cites the fact "that in Bombay University more than one-half of the teaching staff had been at one time or another approached by students or friends or kinsmen of students with the intention of obtaining special favors in connection with examinations in return for payment, . . . [as showing] how little respect intellectual life and the standards in which it rests enjoy in the Indian middle classes." Edward Shils, *The Intellectual between Tradition and Modernity: The Indian Situation* (The Hague: Mouton and Co., 1961), p. 107.

80. E. W. Bakke, *op. cit.,* p. 203. "In most Near Eastern universities, . . . students have no organized extracurricular activities and little or no personal contact with teachers. . . . Thus, . . . the excess energy of Near Eastern students is easily sucked into the political vacuum." Dankwart Rustow, "Politics and Westernization in the Near East," in Richard Nolte, ed., *The Modern Middle East* (New York: Atherton Press, 1963), p. 89. An analysis of student life in British universities reports there "are about 200 intercollegiate clubs and societies in Oxford and probably three or four times as many in colleges." Ferdynand Zweig, *The Student in the Age of Anxiety* (London: Heinemann, 1963; New York: The Free Press, 1964), p. 23.

81. M. Berger, *op. cit.*, p. 333.
82. Ronald P. Dore, *op. cit.*, p. 185.
83. Joseph Fischer, "The University Student in South and South-East Asia," *Minerva*, II (Autumn 1963), No. 1, p. 49; and Benjamin Schlesinger, "Student Unrest in Indian Universities," *Comparative Education Review*, VI (1963), No. 3, p. 221.
84. Edward Shils, "Indian Students," *loc. cit.*, p. 19.
85. F. Bonilla, *Students in Politics*, cited footnote 77 above, p. 253.
86. Ronald L. Scheman, "The Brazilian Law Student: Background, Habits, Attitudes," *Journal of Inter-American Studies*, V (1963), No. 3, p. 252.
87. On the other hand, students from middle-class backgrounds were found to be more politically active than those from upper- or lower-class backgrounds. The meaning of these divergent results is obscure.
88. William John Hanna, "Students" in James S. Coleman and Carl G. Rosberg, Jr., eds., *Political Parties and National Integration in Tropical Africa* (Berkeley: University of California, 1964), pp. 419, 421.
89. Daniel Goldrich, *Radical Nationalism: The Political Orientations of Panamanian Law Students* (East Lansing: Bureau of Political and Social Research, Michigan State University, 1961), pp. 7, 9, 19.
90. *Student Study* (São Paulo: Instituto de Estudos Sociais e Economicos, 1963), *passim*. As noted earlier, Gabriel Almond reported that in terms of "class, ethnic or regional origin" European former communists who joined the party while in university in various countries were of relatively low social status (*op. cit.*, p. 215). Within a communist nation, Poland, it is interesting to note that the same variable is associated with support for economic egalitarianism, although the operating communist order and ideology stress the need for inequality of income and university students aspire to the financially more rewarding positions. Thus, a Polish study reports, "the higher the position of the student's parents, the less he is in favour of economic equality." S. Novak, "Social Attitudes of Warsaw Students," *loc. cit.*, p. 100. And in Japan, an analysis of students at the University of Tokyo completed in 1957 found that support for the leftist Zengakuren was associated with lower family socio-economic status. M. Ozaki, "The Third Generation," unpublished translation. It should be noted that almost all students at Tokyo University are from middle-class or higher-class families. There are few children of workers or peasants there. In Iran also, ideological politics is reported to have "its major appeal among students, especially those students of lower middle class connections." Leonard Binder, *Iran: Political Development in a Changing Society* (Berkeley: University of California Press, 1962), p. 215.

On the other hand, a survey of the opinions of students in three families at the University of Buenos Aires indicated that although the differences correlated with mobility are small, the "upwardly mobile elements seem inclined to attach less importance to politics than the stable." K. H. Silvert and Frank Bonilla, *Education and the Social Meaning of Development: A Preliminary Statement* (New York: American Universities Field Staff, 1961), p. 104.

91. Olga Lang, *Chinese Family and Society* (New Haven: Yale University Press, 1946), pp. 317–318.

92. It should be pointed out that Fourah Bay College is the oldest institution of higher education in Africa south of the Sahara. It has produced a larger proportion of older administrators, the cultural, ecclesiastical and political elites of West Africa than any other institution in that part of the world.

93. Dwaine Marvick, "Higher Education in the Development of Future West African Leaders: A Survey of the Perspectives of Students at Fourah Bay College, Freetown, Sierra Leone" (mimeographed paper presented at the Conference on Education and Political Development held at Lake Arrowhead, California, June 25–29, 1962), Table 17, p. 33.

94. At the same time, the students of the University of Ghana, which meets all the criteria of "elitist" education, seem, according to many observers, to be quite alienated from the government of their country.

95. Malcolm Kerr, "Education and Political Development in Egypt: Some Problems of Political Socialization" (mimeographed paper for the Conference on Education and Political Development held at Lake Arrowhead, California, June 25–29, 1962), pp. 25–27; see also M. Berger, *op. cit.*, p. 333.

96. L. H. Battistini, *The Postwar Student Struggle in Japan* (Tokyo: Charles Tuttle, 1956), pp. 141–142.

97. José Enrique Miguens, "Radiografías de las juventudes latinamericanas," *Occidente*, XVII (October 1962), No. 141, p. 20.

98. Although in the main student politics in the underdeveloped societies tend to be "leftist," there are significant variations from this tendency. Despite their education in more modern orientations within the university, many if not most students in such societies have grown up in traditional surroundings, and some of them disapprove of changes which threaten to alter radically the values with which they were raised. Some evidence for this is contained in a report on surveys conducted in Pakistan, Iran, Thailand, and Malaysia, in which students were asked whether a group of nations including Great Britain, France, West Germany, Japan, the United States, and Russia were "too much on the side of reform," "too much on the side of having things as they are," or "about right in their attitudes." The United States and Russia, despite their obvious ideological differences, were seen as excessively *favorable to reform* more often than were the other nations listed. *Student Survey in Pakistan* (Bielefeld: E.M.N.I.D., 1963); *Teheran University Study: Attitudes and Aspirations* (Teheran: National Institute of Psychology, 1963); *Malayan Student Study* (Bangkok: Coordination Center for Southeast Asian Studies, 1963); and *Student Study—Thailand* (Bangkok: Coordination Center for Southeast Asian Studies, 1963).

99. Recomputed from data in Table XV in Olga Lang, *op cit.*, p. 316.

100. *The Indian Student* (Washington, D.C.: Bureau of Social Science Research, 1954), p. 40. One has the impression that since the beginning of the present decade, the proportion in the last two categories has diminished considerably, without any compensating incorporation into the university community.

101. *Ibid.*, p. 43.

102. Private, unpublished survey of student opinion in the Philippines.

103. *Malayan Student Study* (Bangkok: Coordination Center for Southeast Asian Studies, 1963), pp. 27, 32.

104. *Student Study—Thailand* (Bangkok: Coordination Center for Southeast Asian Studies, 1963), pp. 38, 45.

105. On diversity among Argentinian students in the past see Kalman Silvert, *The Conflict Society: Reaction and Revolution in Latin America* (New Orleans: The Hauser Press, 1961), p. 166.

106. *Student Study* (São Paulo: Instituto de Estudos Sociais e Economicos, 1963), responses to question 10 (pages are unnumbered).

107. *A Study of Opinions of University Students in Mexico* (Mexico City: International Research Associates, 1964), pp. 16–19.

108. "En minoría absoluta los universitarios que tienen interés por la política," *El Tiempo* (June 7, 1964), p. 7. This study was done under the direction of Professor Istvan Mustog of the Pontificia Universidad Javeriana, Bogotá.

109. *Student Study* (São Paulo: Instituto de Estudos Sociais e Economicos, 1963).

110. Thus even in the Philippines, students stand out as a group which contribute "many of the active members of the [communist] party and the participants in front organizations." George E. Taylor, *The Philippines and the United States* (New York: Frederick A. Praeger, 1964), pp. 278, 285.

111. B. Pares, *Russia between Reform and Revolution* (New York: Schocken Books, 1962), pp. 197–198.

112. Research Society on Japanese Social Structure, "Special Traits of White-Collar Workers in Large Urban Areas," *Journal of Social and Political Ideas in Japan*, I (August 1963), No. 2, p. 78; Z. Suetuna, H. Aoyama, C. Hyashi, and K. Matusita, "A Study of Japanese National Character, Part II," *Annals of the Institute of Statistical Mathematics* (Tokyo), Supplement II (1961), p. 54; Robert A. Scalapino and Junnosuke Masumi, *Parties and Politics in Contemporary Japan* (Berkeley: University of California Press, 1961), p. 177.

113. See Indian Institute of Public Opinion, *Monthly Public Opinion Surveys* II (January–April 1957), 9–14; IV (June–September 1959), 73; VIII (February 1963), 5. However, it should be noted that the Congress party is dominant among all educational strata. Among those with a "post-graduate" education, 61 per cent favored the Congress party and 11 per cent the communists in 1963. In 1959, before the Chinese War, support for communism among the educated was much higher.

114. It has been suggested that the process of becoming more conservative takes

time, and that it may be concealed in many reports of opinion related to education since the bulk of the well educated in the merging nations are young. An Indian report on communist adherents in Lucknow supports this suggestion. The better educated were the most likely to be communists, but younger college graduates (under 40) gave the communists more support (25 per cent) than did the older (15 per cent). *The Indian Student* (Washington, D.C.: Bureau of Social Science Research, 1954), p. 8.

Roots and Soil of Student Activism

E. WIGHT BAKKE

2

In the years since the end of World War II there are few countries in the world which have not been subjected to revolutionary changes in parts or the whole of their internal institutional structures and in their relations with other nations. These changes have called into question the appropriateness and effectiveness of traditional guidelines to public and personal problem solving and the traditional allocations of responsibility and authority for performing that function. Inevitably this has opened up temptations and opportunities to participate in that function by groups whose participation was formerly not considered important or even legitimate. Among these groups none has been more prominent and more potentially significant for the present and the future than the students.

Activism by students in the affairs of their universities and of their community and nation beyond the universities is no new phenomenon. It is as old as the universities. But the impact of that activism on public affairs, particularly in the countries undergoing rapid and revolutionary political, economic, and social modernization, reached a new intensity and significance. That has been so evident that it has stimulated a greatly expanded research interest on the part of the scientists whose operational field is individual and organizational behavior.

The objectives of these behavioral scientists have focused on varied aspects of this student activism, and they have usually sought for guidelines to its interpretation suggested by the particular disciplines within which they have received their research training. When I turned my attention to this phenomenon in 1961 it was for two reasons. As a labor, or more broadly, a manpower, economist, I was interested in the implications of student activism, and its stimulus from student experience, for the provisions of high level manpower required in rapidly industrializing and modernizing countries. As an organizational theorist I was interested in gaining, from the observation of student movements, fresh insights into the structure and dynamics of social organizations. After four years of study of the literature and documentation relevant to student activism in Mexico, Colombia, Japan, India, Egypt, and the U.S.A. and periods of research in each of these countries it is clear that the tools of my specialized "trade" were inadequate even for making valid and reliable generalizations about causes related to effects specifically of interest to my "trade."

If one were to follow wherever the problem led, even with respect to the interpretation of student activism as a group phenomenon with societal consequences, he would have to be trained at a minimum as a social psychologist, a cultural anthropologist, a sociologist, a political scientist, an institutional economist, a historian, and from time to time as a philosopher. Student activism in particular countries has been investigated by representatives of all of these disciplines. I sense from their reports of their investigations and from personal conferences with many of them that they are aware of the desirability of at least a framework for an over-all theory of student activism by reference to which the contribution of their own results would be more meaningful. Since I share this awareness with them, I would like to suggest for their consideration such a framework, fully aware that when I step outside of my own field of professional competence the results may be considered naïve by those who are professionally competent in those fields.

What Are We Solving For?

The first task of a theorist is to be clear about what he is solving for, that is, about the significant characteristics of his dependent variable or variables. When we use the term "student activism," what do we mean? That phenomenon has certain characteristics common to all the six countries with respect to which I have made first-hand observations. On the whole, however, the differences could very well be more significant than the similarities. (This observation suggests the difficulties in the development of a universally valid theory of student activism, though the predominance of similarities among certain groups of countries may provide the basis for a larger than one-country set of generalizations. The same caveat can be entered with respect to the predominance of similarities or differences as between different geographical areas, or types of educational institutions, or social origins of students within the same country, or other definitions of the universe being studied. At this point, however, I would like to suggest such narrowing of the universe as a method for refining rather than for formulating the original statement of hypotheses.)

The similarities in "student activism" with respect to the six countries are as follows: (1) the rank and file is composed of youth, predominantly between the ages of 16 and 23, give or take a couple of years at either extreme; (2) all examples have some kind of organization (or organizations) with officers and frequently a headquarters office; (3) all engage in group activities the most frequent of which is the mass demonstration in which the activists protest something they don't like or the absence of something they are asserting they would like; (4) all are led by a few initiating activists who propose certain targets for action and the kind of action to be taken, and whose continuing problem is to mobilize a following large enough to make the action effective; (5) all of them raise problems of public order for university and public authorities.

But there the similarities cease. They differ: (1) in the degree to which they can be characterized as a movement; (2) in their organizational structure; (3) in their relationships to other pressure and action groups; (4) in the characteristics of their leaders; (5) in the numbers and characteristics of their members and supporters; (6) in the kinds and characteristics of their activities; (7) in their emphases on particular operational fields (e.g., campus, community or national political); (8) in the objects toward which their actions are directed; and (9) in their ideological orientation.

It can be suggested that theoretical generalizations with respect to the causal relation of the types of independent variables set forth below will be better focused if the nature of the dependent variable (student activism) is defined by reference to the above dimensions.

Why Student Activism?

Numerous hypotheses of causal relationships have been developed in the process of interpreting student activism. In many cases both the dependent variables (say student activism, indiscipline, political activity) and the independent variables (say youthful idealism, generational revolt, post-university prospects of unemployment) have been very general in character, although given rich and suggestive content by descriptive accounts of such effects and possible causes in the countries studied. In other cases it has been possible to give more specific operational definition to both the dependent variables (say activity as leaders in student organizations, activity of students in specific universities or in particular disciplines, with a consistent record of, or absence of, politically oriented demonstrations), and independent variables (say socioeconomic family background, age, sex, labor market prospects upon graduation, political party preferences, specified personality characteristics, experience with specified features of the educational process, etc. of such specified participants).

In both cases a great deal of intellectually honest effort has been given to the development of adequate questionnaire, interview, and survey instruments and to sampling techniques which would provide valid and reliable factual material making possible trustworthy generalizations at least for a specific universe.

A great volume of data has resulted from the efforts of these scientifically oriented researches to supplement, and often to suggest modification in, the impressions of knowledgeable and thoughtful observers who, by reason of their close vocational relationship to the affairs of higher education, or just from a human interest in such affairs, have set forth their ideas about the causes and consequences of student activism today and in the past.

The wealth of data is sufficient so that a discussion of the matter among almost any group of intelligent people will produce a host of propositions of the nature of, "An unusually important factor (or relationship between factors) that has to be taken into account in understanding (or explaining, or interpreting) student activism is . . . "Whether or not particular propositions are sufficiently rooted in reliable evidence and are sufficiently subject to testing to warrant their designation as hypotheses may be open to question. As a non-specialist I will have to leave that matter to the specialists. But they do provide from time to time "insights" illuminating the meaning and significance of the observations and familiar data which have come to the attention of specialist and non-specialist alike.

My problem is to experience a sense of order in all of these "insights" to keep from being intellectually swamped by their volume and variety. What follows is a framework for classifying the insights, or, if you prefer, hypotheses, about the roots and the soil of student activism the elements of which I believe are operationally definable and significant in the six countries with which I am most familiar. The first class of insights which focuses on the relation to student activism of the stage of and problems of maturation faced by those of student age in all countries has greatest claim to being of universal validity. Each succeeding class involves intervening variables that bring into sharper focus the special circumstantial factors conditioning the operation of those variables set forth in the class preceding it, when reported for a particular universe.

Let me briefly, then, define these four classes of insights as to the causes of student activism before discussing each in somewhat greater detail.

1. *Stage of youth in the maturation process.* Student activism is a function of the universal search of adolescent youth for an adult role in society, for self-identity and social integration, and of their predisposition to energetic self-assertion at this stage in the maturation process.

2. *Actualization of the image of the "Student."* The type and degree of student activism, as a particular manifestation of the maturation process, a function of:
a. clues and re-enforcements provided by the image of the Student held by students and others in their countries;
b. the stimulation provided by the frustrations encountered in the university systems in attempts to internalize personally that image;
c. the intensification of that stimulus by the students' perception of inconsistencies between that image and the opportunities for its realization beyond the university;
d. the amplification of active attempts to remove these inadequacies and inconsistencies, produced by both public opposition and permissiveness toward their efforts.

3. *Involvement in societal problems.* Student activism is a function of:
a. student concern about particular societal problems affecting all citizens;
b. their perception of the gap between their own and their elders' ideal premises and what is actually being done about these problems;
c. their predisposition to assert in action their conceptions of the harmonization between premises and action; and, at times,
d. their predisposition to seek new premises;
e. the indications of possible success in their efforts.

4. *Relation to action groups.* Student activism is a function of stimulus and response as between student groups and other action groups with axes to grind, or at a minimum is influenced as to its direction and focus by this interaction.

Now let us consider in greater detail each of these classes of insights or hypotheses.

The Stage of Maturation of Youth

The interpretation of student activism is difficult unless consideration is given to the stage of life at which the individual student is seeking to discover and be sure of himself as a person in relation to those others with whom he associates or anticipates association. This matter is particularly relevant when the experiences through which the country is passing introduce uncertainties and unexpected and unprepared-for complexities into the role of citizenship for all the citizens of the country, as in the cases of Japan, India, and Egypt. The experience of finding and knowing oneself as an adult in relation to a widening group of associates in a widening area of living is one which is common to all people of his age group. (It is also something experienced on occasion by older persons whose maturation has been long postponed or who are suddenly subjected to a radical alteration in their way of life.) The student's experience is differentiated from that of non-students in his age group only by the ambitions which stimulate, and the peculiar circumstances, opportunities, and problems that advance or constrain, his efforts to incorporate in his concept of himself the characteristics of a *student* and to play a role in society appropriate to one who has succeeded in those efforts, and from the relative freedom accorded him as a student.

He shares with all young people, however, a process of maturation in which he interacts with and receives clues to his identity from the reactions of his family, his intimate peers, and the wider public. While all of these associations are simultaneous and normally are experienced to some degree throughout life, the intensity of the change in associations, particularly as between those with the family on the one hand and those with the members of the wider public on the other hand, reaches a very sharp focus at the stage in life that normally coincides with the years as a student. The observation that adolescence is that stage in life in which the person is being transformed from being predominantly a member of a family to predominantly a member of society is related to this changing emphasis. It has also been noted that, at the time of this basic transformation, the importance of the peer group is heightened. Indeed it often appears to those of college and university student age, whether or not they are students, that it is in reaction to their peer group, in gaining a status within it, in being involved in its activities and associations, and in measuring themselves by its standards, that they find the most reliable clues to their personal identity and to a temporary role for them to play in a society governed by more experienced and mature people. It is not that they are not members of a family or of a larger society. But the familiar actions and relationships and codes appropriate within the family are no longer sufficient as an opportunity for the assertion of their changing and growing conception of themselves as near adults. Yet they have not experienced a widely ranging interaction in the affairs of adult society and, indeed, they are not recognized fully as participants in it. It can accordingly almost be said that the young person is passing from dominant association with the members and culture of his family, through association with the members and culture of his youthful peer group, to association with the members and culture of the wider adult society.

The consciousness that this is exactly what is happening to him and that he is capable of and on the verge of entering, but is not yet accepted as a full member of, the third "society," is the major common characteristic of the students in all six countries I have studied. Their actions, both of initiation by student leaders and of response by their followers, appeared to me to be their announcements and assertions, first of all to themselves, then to their intimate peers, and finally to their families and to the public at large, that they felt they had arrived at that point in their development when they were capable of taking their place as thinkers and critics and actors among the adult members of society.

The degree of certainty and security in this conviction varies as between countries and as between individual students in all countries. The degree of stability and dependability of what is required and expected of adults varies. The degree to which they had been trained for adult roles varies. The particular circumstances and events within their universities and their societies which provide them with the specific stimuli to action vary. The alleged purposes and observable character of student actions vary. The degree of their support for or antagonism against the governing authorities of their universities and the nation varies. The degree of discipline, plan, organization, and continuity of their efforts varies. The degree of support of students generally for the program and tactics of the activists varies. The degree of emphasis on what would be labeled by most adults as orderly or as violent and irresponsible behavior varies. But the variations were those of circumstances within which the basic and universal process of maturation became manifest.

The basic process appeared to me then to be one (1) of "coming of age,"

(2) of clarifying, and of gaining certainty in, a conception of their selves that was relevant and significant in the affairs of society they faced, (3) of integrating that self with (or at least inserting it into) the adult world of people, institutions, and affairs, (4) of expressing and symbolizing that "arrival" in *action*, and (5) of assuring themselves, and also gaining a recognition, *first of all from their peers* among students, and then from all adults, that such self-assertion was legitimate and a right to which they were entitled and were predisposed to make manifest in deeds as well as in words.

The manifestations in action of this search and of self-assertion are re-enforced and intensified by the sheer animal vigor and the awareness of constant increase in physical competence characteristic of youth at this age. It is psychologically intensified by the excitement over widening horizons of discovery of what is new to them about their environment, other people, and themselves. The distinctiveness of their identity as youth is sharpened by the observation that they are becoming more closely related to adults whose animal vigor and skills are reaching, if they have not already reached, a plateau, whose *new* discoveries and widening of interests have been diminishing, and whose commitment to what is not normal and customary has been dulled by personal experiences and the repeated compromises with and adaptation to things as they are.[1]

Difficult to explain by reference to any factors other than those internal to the organism of the individual youth himself is the appearance of particular youths who have an abnormal urge to initiate and carry their fellows with them in the direction they are predisposed to take. That urge to leadership among the few will be tempered by experience with foot-dragging associates over time, but at the moment there is ample opportunity for optimistic experimentation among the members of their peer group. It is these individuals who normally "launch" and give focus and direction to student activism.

Personalization of the Image of the Student

While it is desirable to root an interpretation of student activism in factors students experience in common with all others of their age group everywhere, it is necessary to sharpen that experience which pertains to that minority of the population who have chosen to obtain a college or university education. In the effort to bring my observations into a sharper focus upon the ways in which the peculiar motives, circumstances, and outlook characterizing students and student life influenced the activism of students in these six countries, a relationship among three variables appeared to be significant: (1) the "image" or concept of the "student" and his standing and function in society, (2) his university experience, and (3) his perception of the operational field outside the university in which the student lives and would live in the future.

In every country with institutions of higher learning there is a traditional and a developing contemporary "image" of the "Student" in society, that is, a concept of what it means to be a student. This concept is built up out of the expectancies held by students and others about the rights and duties, privileges and immunities, the standing and the function of students. These expectancies are stabilized by popular, cultural, and historical re-enforcements, and by traditions of student life. The concept involves both the student's image of himself and what society owes him, and society's image of the student and what he owes society. There are common features of this image in all countries, but there are also elements peculiar to each country; and the emphasis among even the common elements varies. Unanimity and complete consensus as to the content of this "image" of the student is not to be expected. A foreigner coming into a country, however, soon acquires an impression of a working consensus which distinguishes the elements and the order of emphasis among them in the image of the student there from that in his own country and in the other countries under study.

This image suggests and supports a wide range of degrees of student activism and the forms it should take.

In all the countries visited these elements or operational definitions of the Student fall into six groups. The specific operational definitions are relative to the following six groups:

1. Relative to *career* expectancies and advantages of being a student.
2. Relative to the opportunities for the comparative *freedom* and self-determination of the student.
3. Relative to the *prestige* and social status of the student.
4. Relative to the *intellectual* qualities of the student.
5. Relative to the *idealism* of the students.
6. Relative to *participation* in public affairs of the student.

The rank order of emphasis upon these several types of elements which define what it means to be, and to be thought of, as a student, varies from country to country. As would be expected, variations in emphasis are also to be found among different groups of students when they are classified by reference to such dimensions as university attended, years spent as a student, class origin, area of study, etc.

If one is to define the image of a Student held by a particular national population, by those attending a particular university, by those engaged in a particular field (say law, medicine, the humanities, etc.), it is necessary to go beyond a general characterization relevant to the foregoing types of elements and to develop operational definitions indicating what it means, to the particular population, to be a student. It is not, for instance, sufficient to say, "Students and the general public hold an image of the Student as: A seeker of vocational preparation, a relatively free person, a member of an elite or prestigeful group, an intellectual, an idealist, a participant in public affairs."

As an example of the variations that can be observed in the specific content given to these generalized terms let me set down for each of them operational definitions which could be inferred from the comments on the subject among particular national, university, or discipline populations.

The Varying Content of the Student Image

1. Relative to *career advantages* a student is variously characterized by different populations as:
   a. A person seeking and acquiring more than average ability and competence in a particular non-manual occupation.
   b. The expectant possessor of a degree passport to a permanent and secure white collar job.
   c. A person acquiring influential and career promotion contacts.

2. Relative to *freedom and self-determination* a student is variously characterized by different populations as:
   a. A relatively free person between two periods of life characterized by constraints and regulations, earlier by the family and familiar group and later by the work place and society.
   b. A person unaware of how to use freedom and therefore inexperienced and unpracticed in the constraints and responsibilities essential for corporate living.
   c. A non-conformist.
   d. A rebel without a commonly accepted cause.

e. A playboy.

f. A hanger-on, a "non-student."

3. Relative to the possession of *prestige* and *standing*, a student is variously perceived by different populations as:

a. A successful passer of qualifying examinations.

b. An ambitious upward mobile person.

c. A symbol and pillar of his family's societal mobility and status.

d. A very fortunate beneficiary of public concern for education.

e. A member of the white collar class.

f. A person on the road to acquiring a title or degree.

g. A member (hopefully) of the fraternity of degree-holding and presumably educated persons.

h. A member of a *select* but not necessarily *elite* social group.

i. An actual or potential leader.

j. A highly eligible marriage partner.

4. Relative to *intellectual qualities*, a student is variously perceived by different populations as:

a. A person who knows more about many things than most people.

b. A person familiar with, or in process of learning about, ideas embodied in myths, dogmas, and theories produced by others.

c. A person becoming capable of dealing with and producing ideas.

d. A person developing analytical and problem-solving ability.

e. A person seeking for and capable of making significant, useful, trustworthy, and objective generalizations.

f. A seeker for ideological foundations for personal and societal action.

5. Relative to *idealism* a student is variously perceived by different population as:

a. An admirer if not a follower of moral and social reformers.

b. A sponsor, carrier, and defender of popular ideals of justice and human welfare for the "People."

c. A seeker for (although seldom a finder of) general and universal rather than particularistic and familiar-group-bound ideals.

d. A patriot, but on his own terms.

e. Hopefully, a carrier of some residue of youthful idealism and commitment into the pragmatic adaptation to the responsibilities and constraints of adult life.

f. A cynic with respect to what he considers to be private and public hypocrisy.

6. Relative to participation in public affairs a student is variously perceived by different populations as:

   a. A critic of inconsistencies and contradictions between ideals and practice in public affairs.

   b. A critic and one ambitious to be a codeterminer of educational facilities provided by his society.

   c. A critic of, or an active initiator of change with respect to, the political and economic policies and structure.

   d. A fighter for national self-determination.

   e. A proponent of modernization in social, economic, and political affairs of the nation.

   f. A prospective public servant, but not necessarily a servant of the public.

The University Experience

When a youth decides to devote a number of years as a student in order to internalize in his self this "image," to know himself, and to be recognized and rewarded by others, as a student, he enters into a field of experience which is peculiar to him and others who have made the same choice. He does not by virtue of his attendance at a university miss the difficulties and opportunities of "coming of age." Indeed in many ways the difficulties as well as the opportunities are intensified, and in any case are given a peculiar nature and emphasis which cannot be fully understood by those who have not themselves had the same experience or even have had it at an earlier period. The character and adequacy of the university experience, its impact on his growing conception of himself and his place and function within his peer society and within the adult society he is about to enter (or considers he has already entered), needs to be explored and interpreted as an influence giving stimulus and direction to the thought and behavior which characterize his activism.

The delineation of the characteristics of the university experience affecting positively or negatively the personalizing of this image of the student by students has been exhaustively carried out by a large number of investigators in many countries. Hypotheses pointing to frustrations relative to the factors in those experiences with various aspects of the university environment, as independent variables creating a predisposition toward student activism, are the type most frequently encountered in the literature.

The Societal Opportunities

The *third* important variable in this group of "insights" is the student's perception of the operational field for self-actualization outside and beyond the university, both current and future. This operational field is characterized not only by the kind of human, social, political, technological, and economic opportunities and constraints for life outside and beyond the university, but the traditional and aspired-to methods available for modifying these.

Hypotheses concerning the nature and causes of student activism suggest themselves from a contemplation of the data gathered with respect to the character and relationships among these three variables, namely, the image of the Student, the university experience in personally internalizing that image, and the perception of the opportunities for actualizing that image in the societal environment beyond the university. One is that the traditional image of the Student itself suggests and reinforces the appropriateness of the kind of activism observed. Another is that inconsistencies, incompatibilities, or inadequacies in the three variables create frustrations suggesting the necessity for corrective action which it appears to the students they must themselves undertake. A third is that the circumstances and conditions prevalent in their universities and societies provide the specific occasion, if not the sufficient cause, of action satisfying their predisposition to self-assertion at this stage of the maturation process. A fourth is that their inclination to activism is intensified by the degree of both public opposition and public permissiveness with respect to it.

Student Concerns with and Involvement
in Societal Problems Affecting All Citizens

The third variable referred to in the preceding section, that is, the students' *perception* of the difficulties and opportunities *for them* present in the world beyond the universities is not identical with their *concerns* about such matters, concerns which could well become a stimulus to their activism. But perceptions and concerns are both possible responses to the same national problems. Moreover, it is plausible to suggest that the students are influenced in their interpretations of their world and in what they attempt to be and to do by the same problems faced by all citizens in the nation and that student activism is at least in part one aspect of the response of all citizens to those commonly shared problems.

While the specific nature of these problems varied from country to country, there was a similarity in the general type of the problems most frequently associated with student activism found in all of them. It is therefore possible to organize the discussion of this cause of student activism within a framework of topics which is pertinent to all of them.

Here are the age-old societal problems which came to sharp focus in postwar Japan, in India, Egypt, Colombia, Mexico, and about which we in the United States have still much to learn.

1. The building, or reconstruction of, and the securing of commitment to national goals, national character, and basic values which make individual life and work meaningful. I would call this the building and acceptance of the nation's Organizational Charter.

2. The achievement and maintenance of national autonomy.

3. The integration of public and private interests, that is, the simultaneous achievement of group solidarity and social order and individual liberty.

4. The creation and maintenance of effective government with the consent, support, and activity of all those competent to participate. Several aspects of this task which were and continue to be particularly pressing are:
   a. The legitimacy of the governors to govern.
   b. The division of function between common and uncommon man.
   c. The acceptance of law, judicial interpretation, and official law enforcement as a regulator of the action of both the governed and the governors.
   d. The integration of pluralistic and partisan differences into a working consensus.
   e. The establishment and maintenance of an effective and just channel for public protest.

5. The adaptive reconstruction of economic, political, and social institutions to meet change while simultaneously preserving an ordered society, especially with respect to modernization.

6. The discovery or creation and acceptance of an ideological framework simultaneously suggesting an analysis of problems, appropriate methods of solution, the justification for those methods, and the provision of a symbolic representation of central values.

Students, and particularly those who are engaged in studies in the humanities, the social sciences, the law, have had opened up to them a wider knowledge about these continuing societal problems. What they learn creates in many of them a tendency to observe more carefully and thoughtfully the state of the world about them and what is being done and not done about these problems by those in the adult population. It is not inevitable that this broadened and sharpened knowledge will lead to a deepened concern, but it frequently does. And among many the inconsistency between the ideal premises which professedly furnish the guidelines to action with respect to these problems and the action being taken will be profoundly disturbing. So will the gap between the achieved results of that action and those results which appear to be desirable and possible to youth who have had little experience with the stubborn obstacles in the path of societal change.

In any case the occasion, if not the cause, of the specific focus for student activism will be found in this sensitivity to, concern with, and commitment to doing something about these societal problems which become particularly critical in the life of the people of their countries.

The issues presented to them may involve affairs in society generally or they may become vividly and pointedly manifest in the affairs close to home in their particular universities.

Stimulus and Response between Students and Groups with Axes to Grind

The national problems perceived by and of concern to students are, of course, perceived by and become the subject of concern to other groups in society who have their own axes to grind. The relation between students and these other groups may be one of stimulus or response, and both students and the groups named may perceive the other as an instrument to be used for their own purposes or as an antagonist. The groups most frequently named as relevant to this conditioning factor in student activism are:

1. The faculty and university administrators.
2. The intellectuals, and particularly those committed to social reform.
3. Humanitarian reformers and reform groups interested in the lot of the common people, particularly "the left out" and "the left behind."
4. Student movements in other lands.
5. The "non-students," or hangers-on around or within the student community.
6. Politicians and political parties generally of the left, but also occasionally of the right.

7. Labor organizations and leaders.
8. The "Establishment."
9. The agents of public order, the police, etc.

Summary

These then are the classes of "insights" which appear to me to suggest a number of independent and intervening variables which could be related to the dependent variable of a particular manifestation of student activism in the formulation of hypotheses concerning cause and effect. Arranged in this order, they suggest, I believe, the progressive thrust of factors which would be involved eventually in a theory of student activism, in that each succeeding group of "insights" suggests intervening variables focusing or modifying the operation of those in the preceding group or groups.

1. Youths approaching adulthood in association with their peer group are concerned to find a self-identity and its ultimate integration with others in the adult world and are predisposed to assert that self in action. This process is governed by the experienced preparation for adulthood, the degree of stability or instability in the adult role or roles to which they aspire, and by the criteria for evaluating performance and standing within their peer group. It is intensified by the supply of physical and psychological energy and by the excitement generated by the widening of horizons for thought and action, characteristic of most students, and by the urge to initiation and leadership characteristic of a few.

2. These variables are made more specific for those youths who become students by the image of the Student held in their society (or particular areas of it) by students and others, and by the frustrations or opportunities provided, when they attempt to internalize that image, by aspects of their university experience, and by anticipated frustrations or opportunities perceived to exist in the society beyond the university. The image itself suggests certain clues to and re-enforcement for activity appropriate to students, and the inconsistencies between that image and the opportunities for its actualization in the universities and society provide stimuli to specific manifestations of activism. The activism is amplified both by freedom for and public opposition to its overt expression.

3. But the students are also members of a community and nation and are acquiring an increasing awareness of a wide range of societal problems faced by the people of that community and nation. In many cases a concern develops for the solution of those problems, and, in a smaller number of cases,

a commitment grows for active participation in initiating and carrying through such solutions. That concern and commitment is most likely to arise and be effectuated in action when the actor perceives an inconsistency between publicly declared objectives and results, or between ideal premises for achievement in these problem areas provided by his culture and professed by others and himself on the one hand, and what is actually being done on the other. The areas of concern, commitment, and perceived inconsistency suggest the occasion for, a focus for, and objectives of particular manifestations of student activism.

4. Students and student groups come in contact with other action groups, and in interaction with them receive a modifying stimulus to the determination of the scope, the focus, the direction, the methodology, and the intensity of their activism. In the course of this interaction the students may perceive and react to the other action groups as supporters or as antagonists, and may use or be used by these action groups for their respective purposes. In the light of the operation of the other independent and intervening variables set forth above, however, this "cause" of their activism can plausibly be considered as a modifying rather than as an originating or controlling variable.

What of It?

William Graham Sumner in discussing the results of their research with his graduate students and colleagues is said to have posed to them three questions: "Is it true? How do you know it is true? What of it?" That last question is important for all of us who are given the high privilege of devoting our lives to study, analysis, and generalization about areas of human effort and experience which are interesting to us. In order to maximize our satisfaction in the utilization of that privilege it occurs to most of us that it is essential, in choosing the areas for our attention, to select those that are not only possible and interesting for us personally, but are also significant from the point of view of the interests and concerns of a wider public.

That wider public is composed in the first instance of our colleagues engaged in the same field of scientific endeavor as ourselves, psychology, sociology, cultural anthropology, political science, economics, philosophy, etc. Since this article is addressed primarily to those whose life work is carried on in association with colleagues in these fields of study, and since we have presumably chosen to cultivate this field because of the promise it offers, not merely to learn more about student activism, but to contribute to the empirical foundations and the theoretical structure of our particular disciplines, it is unnecessary to elaborate upon the significance of our studies in this respect. Not only have we for the most part set up our studies with the objective of advancing the body of empirical and theoretical knowledge in our particular disciplines, but it is clear that we have focused on an area for study in which there is ample opportunity for contribution to an understanding of the relationship of ideas and methodology in all of those disciplines to each other.

That there is a wider interested and concerned public than that composed of colleagues in our own and related disciplines, however, is clear from the numerous articles, reports, and books on the subject of student activism which have come from non-academic sources and which have been directed toward a readership which we often refer to as the general public. Another indication of the interest of a wider-than-academic group of concerned people is the number of conferences called on this and closely related subjects by government and foundation and educational agencies concerned with the problems of youth, especially those which involved the maintenance of a nation's educational and manpower facilities.

It is possible to suggest that those who are engaged in the scientific study of student activism may find the significance, i.e., the "What of it?" aspects of their efforts increased by setting their minds to work on the possible consequences of the fact of and causes of student activism for national development in the political, economic, social, and educational areas. Certainly their familiarity with the factors involved in interpreting student activism puts them in a position to bring the results of their studies to bear on issues of concern to a large number of non-academic members of the society.

Let me suggest three foci for such a contribution.

1. *The direct impact of student demands, pressures, and activities on current economic, political, and social affairs.* This impact is normally hard to distinguish from other impacts, particularly when the focus of attention is on national problems which are the object of active attention by others than students. This is not the case to the same degree when the object of attention is unsatisfactory circumstances or arrangements or people within the university. But here also there are other forces at work simultaneously with the students' efforts. Nevertheless, in view of the varying degrees to which student activism in the several countries has appeared to be among the *effective* instruments of change, the elucidation of the circumstances and times and conditions which are associated with their activism would ap-

pear to be important not only for understanding the past, but for anticipating the future course of national events.

2. *The direct or indirect influence of participation in student activist affairs on the predispositions and qualifications of students related to their positive future contributions.* Judgment on this matter will involve setting forth the kinds of predispositions and qualifications experience has shown to be essential or helpful, or at least relevant, to economic, political, and social development. These are dangerous assumptions to make, for such development has taken place utilizing varieties of human stuff under great variations in the quality of its training for participation in public affairs. Nevertheless the estimate of the possible impact of participation or nonparticipation in the kind of activist effort observed in each country on those particular human qualities assumed to be relevant provides a framework for a discussion of the *possible* significance of student activism from this point of view.

3. *The direct relevance of the kind of higher education available and experienced on the development of the essential capabilities in those students hoping to become leaders in the nation's affairs.* In the study of student activism it is inevitable that a large volume of data should be gathered with respect to the nature and operation of the several aspects of the universities as instruments for the production of present and future leadership in the nation's affairs. In all countries, but especially in those experiencing rapid development and modernization, universities are charged with the responsibility for the orientation and development of youth who shall form the reservoir of talent from which that leadership shall come. Studies of student activism have not necessarily focused upon variations in effectiveness in the performance of that function as a dependent variable, but the data gathered can normally be analyzed from the point of view of their impact upon the effectiveness with which that responsibility is likely to be discharged.

Note

1. In the statements above I have made use of the phrase "appeared to me" to indicate that they are not conclusions supported by a lifetime of study and research in this matter. Such behavioral tendencies and predispositions have been the operational field of social psychologists concerned with the development of personality and the socialization of individuals. In these matters I am a layman. But a student of societal phenomena and organizational behavior ex-

periences an ultimate formlessness and lack of significance in his data, however systematically organized, unless it can be related to what is happening in the experience of the human beings who are both the initiators of, and the persons affected by, those phenomena and that behavior.

It therefore appeared desirable not only to explore with the students I interviewed in these countries what they were doing, their perception of the overt circumstances and affairs that provided the occasion for, if not the cause of, their actions, their expressed reasons for doing it, and the attitudes that accompanied the doing, *but also to explore* with them their experiences related to the task faced by all young people everywhere, of understanding their selves and of bringing those selves out into a dependable and satisfying relationship with the society of their time.

Students and Politics

PHILIP G. ALTBACH

3

For more than a century, student movements have had an important place among the agents of social change. In some nations, students have succeeded in toppling governments or changing policies. In others, they have been instrumental in various kinds of cultural revivals. In the new nations of Asia, Africa, and Latin America, students are often instrumental in political, social, and cultural development. Students have provided inspired leadership to national liberation movements, political parties, and on a more local level, labor organizations and cultural groups. Not only have the leaders of the new states frequently come from student ranks, but the ideological base of many of the new societies has been influenced by the student movement.

While the organizational manifestation of student concern is the most dramatic indication of the power and importance of the student community, the day-to-day life of the student in these societies is also crucial to their development. The values which are obtained during the process of higher education and the quality of that education will inevitably have an impact on nations which have a very small reservoir of trained manpower.

While students in the industrially advanced nations of the West are important, their numbers are large and the society is sufficiently well developed so that the fate of an individual student or even fairly large group of students is not crucial. In most new nations, however, students often form an "incipient elite." In many of these societies, students assume political responsibility even before finishing their studies, thus bringing national politics onto the campuses in a very direct way. Governments are therefore conscious of the student population, trying to influence it or perhaps repress

74

some of its leaders. It is hard to imagine that the head of a Western nation would engage in a protracted debate with student leaders in order to ensure the loyalty of the student union. Yet, the President of the Ivory Coast recently engaged in just that kind of dialogue with student leaders, arguing with them, and finally threatening to suspend their government scholarships in order to ensure the loyalty of the student organization. Because the government has financial and political power at its command, it can usually impose its will on the students. If all else fails, governments can, as has happened in Burma, close the universities for extended periods. The fact that governments in many of the new nations must either argue with or force the students to accept their policies is an indication of the potential power of the students.

The student population in many of the developing nations is numerically small, and is often very much cut off from the rest of its peer group by vastly differing experiences, "Western" ideas, and educational opportunities. This alienation from the peer group, as well as from the mainstream of the traditional society in many cases, often makes the student community self-reliant and at the same time unsure of its roots. In addition, students often have to develop their own traditions, since established patterns of "modern" educational, political, and social behavior in many new states have not as yet evolved.

Although substantial attention has been given to the student organizations and higher education in the new nations, much of what has been said has been little more than uninspiring exhortation or political rhetoric. Obviously one must carefully analyze the student community, a vital segment of the population of the new states. Moving beyond the clichés of the politicians and the limited proposals of educators should enable us to apply historical and sociological principles to the consideration of the student population and its organizations.

Characteristics of Students and Student Groups

While the concept "student" has existed in the modern sense of the term since the Middle Ages, the individual student lost much of his importance in the West in an era of mass education. In medieval Europe, the student had something of an elite status with its accompanying freedom and prerogatives. Now, in the new nations, modern Western systems of higher education are being grafted onto traditional societies, re-creating, in some aspects, older patterns of student life.

Studentship is a transitory state, usually lasting only three or four years, though perhaps extended by graduate study. While some student leaders have prolonged their affiliation with the student community, for the vast majority academic life is a short, although often highly intensive period. This makes the existence of on-going organizations and sustained leadership almost impossible. The problem is further aggravated by the fact that student participation in a movement is sporadic, for extra-curricular activity becomes difficult to pursue when the pressure of examinations grows intense, or when official disapproval is manifested. Moreover, because the student feels he is in a period of transition, he often does not develop deep ties to the student community. Academic life is seen as a brief way-station on the road to economic advancement by many, while for others it is a time of unparalleled freedom. The important difference in orientation between the generally career-minded and therefore apolitical science and professional students and the more intellectual orientation of many liberal arts students has had vital implications. A number of studies have pointed out that, in many nations, liberal arts students constitute the key element in political movements.[1]

The student days are one of the few times in the life of an individual when he is not burdened by financial or social responsibilities or subject to outside control. The concept of adolescence does not exist in many traditional societies; there is simply an abrupt transition from childhood to adult life. The young person anticipates with pleasure the freedom of his student career; however, he is often unprepared for this freedom. Relative freedom from parental and familial control, from financial responsibility (in some cases), and from outside work combine to make the academic environment a heady experience for many young people. Furthermore, many realize that the student years mark the end of youth and that adult responsibilities will necessarily follow graduation from the university.

Because of their freedom, students can often afford to take risks which others in the society, saddled with family and other responsibilities, cannot take. It is partly for this same reason that the student community is considered less corrupt than any other segment of the society. In the public image, student politics are supposedly unmarred by considerations of partisanship or personal material gain. In many nations, students have attempted to take upon themselves the leadership of the working classes, who are often unable to speak for themselves and have no tradition of organization. Students also have the reputation, perhaps justified, for having greater ideological "purity" than other elements in society, and it is true that they can often approach society without the biases of vested interests or social constraints and with a relatively high degree of intellectual honesty. They are relatively free agents in their thought and actions, often having the security of future employment because of their education in the elite class.

It is no coincidence that students have often been in the vanguard of revolutionary movements in various countries. The Russian student movement provided an important impetus to revolutionary activity, and students in Burma, India, Korea, and other nations have been a leading element in independence movements. Participation in revolutionary movements is often part of the generational conflicts which are so often evident among students. Advocacy of drastic social reforms is often seen as a means of fighting the authoritarian influence of the traditional family.[2] Because of their lack of outside responsibility, their openness to modernizing ideologies, and their desire to create a better society, students are often involved in social movements.

Because students deal with ideas and intellectualized concepts in their academic work, they are better able to understand abstract ideological systems than are persons who regularly work in concrete "non-intellectual'" situations. As a result, students are often more receptive to ideologically oriented movements and causes. Having little or no experience in practical politics or the problems of economic development, they are often more naïve about the key issues facing their societies, and are more likely to seek all-encompassing solutions to societal problems than are their elders. Because of this intellectual interest and urge to systematize, students seek an ideological system which will provide them with a *Weltanschauung*, a guide to thought and action. Both left- and right-wing ideological movements have traditionally found strong student support, although in the developing nations the left far outweighs the right in popularity and influence.[3] This natural interest in intellectualized ideological systems has been an important factor in stimulating the growth of student movements and in providing them with some enduring impetus. In the non-student world, organizational initiative can help keep a movement alive. On the student level, ideological convictions among succeeding generations of students must suffice because of the rapidly changing nature of the student population.

In addition to the freedom which is naturally a part of student life, many societies, both traditional and advanced, have taken a permissive attitude toward student values and activity. Political acts which would be subjected to severe government repression if performed by labor unions or other groups often go unheeded if done by students. The concept of "sowing wild oats," restricted to pranks in the United States, extends to politics in many nations, where it is assumed that students will make an active and often volatile role in politics. This tradition of intellectual, political, and physical freedom which students enjoy in many societies acts as a reinforcing element to the student movement, permitting it to act with relative impunity. Understandably, the student community often has very little in common with other young people. For many college students in the developing nations college life is the first non-family experience. Physiologically and psychologically, the period of adolescence is one of adjustment and change, and this cannot but have repercussions on the educational, social, and political attitudes of the students. The need for independence and self-expression is great during this period, and the tendency toward rebellion against authority, particularly that represented by the father, is marked. Studies of youth in Japan and in India indicate that many of the same factors which have been documented in the West also operate in non-Western societies.[4]

In addition to the factors which lead the individual student in a political direction, there are various pressures on the student population which also drive in this direction. The existence of a large number of students at one location, with similar interests, and subject to similar stimuli from the environment, gives a powerful impetus to organizational activities of all kinds. It is difficult to imagine a more cohesive community from which to recruit members. The intellectual ferment which takes place as a natural result of the academic setting is also influential in moving students to action. While only a minority of any given group of students is likely to be interested in politics (or any other extra-curricular subject), the presence of substantial numbers of students in a single location tends to create a numerically significant group of dedicated and committed politicized students, even though the percentages involved may remain relatively small.

Communications within the student movement are usually quite good, especially when the majority of the students in a given area are congregated on one campus. Thus, when external conditions or ideological issues move students to action, it is easy to create a substantial movement in a relatively short time. Expensive and complex newspapers, radio programs, etc., are unnecessary; all that is needed is a mimeograph machine and a few strategically placed posters. It is difficult to overestimate the value of good communications in the development of student movements. Even in totalitarian societies, the students are one of the most difficult groups to control partly because of the ease with which they can communicate among themselves.

The sense of community which is often built up by the students because of their similarities in background and outlook and their common environment provides a basis for a student movement or organization. Without this sense of community the students would be unable to participate in political and cultural affairs to the extent that they have in the new nations. Indeed, there are indications that as the student population becomes larger and less homogeneous, it is more difficult to organize large scale student movements. In India, for example, as higher education became available to young people from middle and lower middle class backgrounds and the educational institutions expanded at a rapid rate, the student community lost its cohesive quality and it has been more difficult to organize the students.

Students have often been united by a common alienation from traditional patterns of society. Students are often one of the few representatives of "Western" culture and ideology in their societies. The structure and content of their educational institutions are largely imported, and many of their teachers are either foreigners or foreign-educated. There is much vacillation between tradition and modernity in the student community.[5] Intellectual trends often push the students further from traditional cultural and social patterns. As a result of these factors, the students feel alienated from and superior to their families and the society at large, but at the same time they feel guilty because of their rejection of the "true" values of their culture. While this alienation often disappears as the student takes his place in his society, it is an important factor during the student period.

This very sense of alienation serves to unite the student community. Alienation also has a politicizing effect, in that the values of the "modern" Western ideologies are often combined with elements of traditional culture to form the basis of new ideological movements. Elements of "African Socialism," nineteenth-century Indian revivalism, and other ideological tendencies are part of this phenomenon. Regardless of the result of the sense of alienation, it is true that it is a powerful force on the students of the developing nations. Notions of deracination and cultural regeneration are recurrent themes in student discussions in many of the new states. Thus, regardless of the truth in the notions, they are important influences on students' thinking, and hence on their actions.[6]

The student population also provides an organizational base for student political and social action. Student unions and other organizations which have been set up by educational authorities or governments often provide a meeting place for students interested in ideological discussions or cultural activity. Often, more radical groups grow out of these "official" organizations. Even in totalitarian societies, the "official" youth movements often provide the basis for dissenting groups of various kinds. Much of the impetus for the political ferment in Poland in the late 1950's came from the Polish student movement and its publications, which were officially sanctioned by the government.[7]

Despite the fact that students in the developing nations are usually privileged people and have a much higher standard of living than the average citizen, the student is often under severe pressure during his academic career. Sometimes economic, but more often academic or social, these pressures help to determine the scope and intensity of student social action. The most direct pressure on the student is from the educational institution itself. The need to pass the periodic examinations, to keep up with course work, and to achieve a high academic status are some of the main worries of any student. The educational institution often demands an outward show of loyalty from its students and occasionally asks for ideological and social conformity from them. In nations where university graduates are threatened by unemployment, and the quality of the instruction is perceived by the students as inadequate, there is likely to be a good deal of underlying discontent. There is often a substantial difference in student attitudes and involvement in politics from faculty to faculty within a university. In India, for example, academic standards and employment prospects are much better for science and technological students than for those in the liberal arts, and it is true that science students are not often involved in student "indiscipline." Where the academic program is challenging, the pressures of the university on the students (in the direction of academic excellence, for instance) are usually seen as justified. In faculties where there exists a good deal of ambivalence about the future and a realization that standards of education are inadequate there is likely to be discontent.

Academic standards and methods of university administration vary greatly in the developing nations. While some nations have worked hard to maintain educational standards and limit enrollments, others have engaged in rapid expansion of educational institutions with an accompanying lowering of standards. It is clear that educational policies imposed by governments have an important impact on the students and that the nature of student organization is often determined by educational standards in various faculties, employment prospects, and other external factors.

Most traditional societies are family-oriented; the individual may be primarily a member of his family rather than a citizen of the state or nation. The family can and often does apply pressure on the student. Representing the traditional values in the society, the family may influence the student toward social conformity, adherence to traditional social and religious ideas, and retention of traditional values. In any case, the pressure from traditional elements within any society is often one of the major sources of stress in the life of the student.

While the government usually exercises a rather nebulous influence on the individual student, it can on occasion become a major force in his life. Government educational policies, particularly in the developing nations, have a profound impact on the educational system and, consequently, on the lives of individual students. Government pressure for political conformity, censorship, and suppression affects the students. Since the latter are often impatient with the slowness and ineffectuality of government efforts in economic development, there is often opposition to the established regime. Government also represents the older generation and in many cases provides an obstacle to ambitious student leaders seeking quick advancement.

Politics exercise a strong attraction and a potent pressure among students. As a general rule, the political groups cannot apply the kind of direct pressure of which the educational authorities and the government are capable. In many of the developing nations, political issues have caused student uprisings and agitational campaigns. Students have sacrificed their educational future in order to participate in political movements, and such organizations on university campuses consume a great deal of time and energy. While it is difficult to include politics as another "pressure," it is often a major preoccupation of the student community.

Ideology attunes the student not only to the broader issues of his society, but makes him more willing to participate in campus-based movements. It is often true that an agitational campaign against an increase in university fees, ostensibly a campus-based issue, will be led by ideologically committed students. During the various struggles for independence and national liberation, students left the universities in substantial numbers to participate in labor and peasant movements as well as directly in the independence struggle. While not consisting of direct physical pressure on the student community, ideology and political movements provide the pressure and stimulus of ideas and all-encompassing answers to some of the important questions facing the developing nations.

The environment of the individual student usually provides pressure. Indeed, much of his behavior, and his ideological views as well, are shaped by his environment. Many students suffer from financial hardship during their educational careers and have to live in poor conditions. In many cases, college facilities are poor and do not provide even the basic necessities for higher education. Inadequate libraries, badly trained staff, and outmoded buildings mark many colleges in the developing nations. The impact of these conditions cannot but have an important influence on the student, his attitudes, and naturally his educational attainment. Students from the working and new middle classes, whose experience with Western values is shorter and whose families can ill afford the expense of a college education, are usually affected by these factors most. The threat of unemployment hangs over the heads of many college students in the new nations, and this fear naturally has implications for the individuals involved.

Student Organizations and Movements

Before discussing the "student movement" one must adequately define the term. It is not a fraternity, a social club, an academic society, or an extra-curricular cultural group, although under certain circumstances it may encompass the activities and functions of such groups. We may define a student movement as an association of students inspired by aims set forth in a specific ideological doctrine, usually, although not exclusively, political in nature. A student movement may be generated by emotional feelings often associated with inter-generational conflicts, although it may also be motivated by positive goals; the members of a student movement, moreover, have the conviction that, as young intellectuals, they have a special historical mission to achieve the goals which the older generation failed to achieve, or to correct imperfections in their environment.[8] A student movement is a combination of emotional response and intellectual conviction.

The student movement is almost invariably expressed in organizational terms, although not all student organizations are "movements." It is true that almost every student community has a nexus of organizations which involve individuals in various activities. These organizations exist regardless of the political composition of the student community or the form of government or educational authority which exists in the society. There are, furthermore, numerous types of student organizations, many of which have overlapping memberships. Groups range from large officially sponsored organizations to clandestine informal study circles.

Almost every college or university abounds with various "official" student organizations, devoted to manifold causes. In many institutions, officially recognized student unions are an integral part of the university community and in some places, notably Latin America, students have a constitutional voice in academic affairs. Extra-curricular social, cultural, or service organizations also involve many students. These groups provide a potentially valuable adjunct to the education of the participants, and it is common for them to be financially aided by the university administration or by the governments concerned. These groups are often formed by the university authorities for specific purposes and are subjected to strict supervision. The popularity of such groups varies, and it is a fact that many of the "official" student groups have minimal support or participation.

In many nations, an attempt has been made to create movements on the basis of the official student groups; however, such efforts have usually been unsuccessful. It is also true that educational administrators or government officials frequently try to use these groups to forestall or compete with student protest organizations which oppose the authorities. Almost without exception, the official student organizations become a natural and logical training and recruiting ground for political leadership. Occasionally, the official student groups develop into militant student movements, sometimes opposing their patrons. At different periods, the influence of these groups has varied from country to country; nevertheless, through sheer size and power, the official student organizations usually constitute an important part of the organized student community.

In addition to the official groups, most universities support a multitude of voluntary extra-curricular organizations. These are often recognized by the university authorities and may be required to have a faculty member as advisor, but they are usually student administerd. Because they have no official patronage, they stand or fall on their own merits; the average life-span of many of them is very short. These organizations range from purely social gatherings to those devoted to politics, social service, discussion and debate, athletics, dramatics, and culture. Many are organized by the members of a particular religious or linguistic community as social and cultural centers.

These organizations do not as a rule constitute movements, although they sometimes inspire more militant and massive organizational efforts. Students from a particular religious minority may, for example, in the course of discussions within an approved student group, formulate a broader religious or political creed which leads them to collaborate with or to form a mass movement. Similarly, the political ideas which are discussed in such an organization can easily lead to more radical organizational activity.

Finally, there are often various kinds of unofficial and unapproved student organizations existing at a given university. Student movements are more often started by such groups than by the official organizations. Such unrecognized groups are often devoted to political issues or ideologies and are often militantly opposed to the power structure of their society. Some, however, may be of purely social nature, such as fraternities in the United States. The student "underground" may never reach an insurrectionary or an active stage; yet it undeniably plays an important part in influencing its membership even at the discussion-group stage.[9]

The membership of such unapproved student groups is in general much smaller than the approved organizations, although this is often compensated by a high level of commitment from the membership, and a great deal of loyalty to the peer group. These associations are sometimes, but not always, affiliated to or under the influence of outside organizations, such as political parties or larger student movements. Members of highly disciplined clandestine student groups may hold high offices in "respectable" groups, thereby enhancing their influence.

All of these types of student organizations can be important in specific situations, and it would be a mistake to overlook aspects of seemingly respectable groups in any evaluation of a student movement. There is often a good deal of interaction between these various elements of the organized student community, a fact of primary importance in investigating the web of personal contacts and ideologies within the student community. The overlap of membership in various types of organizations is often substantial, and there is often an accompanying overlap of ideas. Infiltration of official student groups by the student "underground" is not uncommon and often accounts for the radical nature of ostensibly respectable organizations. Thus, the ideology of the unofficial student organizations can permeate the entire student community without much difficulty regardless of the wishes of university officials.

A student movement need not have as its goal violent political change; it can, for example, press for a "cultural renaissance" within a society. It may also be concerned solely with educational or campus issues, without involving individuals or issues from the broader society. Thus, in searching for the roots of a student movement or agitational campaign, it may be fruitful to examine all organizations, not only the militantly politically motivated student groups, bearing in mind, however, that movements of a militant nature more often than not arise from ideologically committed groups.

Regardless of the type, function, or size, student groups are notoriously unstable. This is due mainly to the rapidly changing nature of the student population, but also to the changing interests of the students themselves. Even the large groups with lavish government support often lose much of their leadership and support in a short time due to changes in the interests of the students or the loss of key leaders. The clandestine organizations are still more vulnerable to changes in the winds of the student community or of the society at large. It is possible with intelligent student leadership and by careful planning and leadership training to ensure a relatively long period of organizational continuity. In the last analysis, the transitory nature of the student groups is one of their dominant characteristics and a key element in the understanding of the student community. Even seemingly stable and militant student movements can lose their popular support in a short period; internal disputes and factional disagreements can destroy the core of leadership in a matter of days, and administrative restrictions can cause serious difficulties. Other factors, such as a university examination, a diverting event in the broader society, or the arrest of key student leaders, can temporarily destroy a student organization or movement. Yet, it is entirely possible for a movement to recoup its losses in a very short time, thus suggesting that its ideology and program have survived a temporary organizational setback.

In recent years, there has been a growing realization of the importance of student activity in both educational and political development in many of the new nations.[10] Because of the fact that student political movements have had a dramatic influence in some of these nations, attention has been focused on them. It is possible to state, in capsule form, some of the general causes for student action which have been pointed out in recent studies, as well as those which have been observed in various student movements. Such an enumeration will help give an idea of the causes of student action.

It is almost a truism that the university is greatly dependent on its environment. The student community may be aroused or swayed by events in the outside world. Political leaders often take a direct and active interest in the students, occasionally guiding or exploiting student movements. It has been mentioned that the various national liberation movements received substantial support from the students. The struggle for independence influenced the university campus and transformed many universities into battlegrounds for extended periods of time. Cultural trends in the society can also have an impact on the students, as can international events, economic crises, or religious strife. The student is also influenced by his future prospects for employment and prestige in the society.

A tradition of independent political and social action among the students can help to determine the nature and direction of the student movement. Where the student community has few traditions to fall back on, its response to external events is unpredictable and inconsistent; where there is a tradition of apoliticism among the students, even severe social crisis often fails to move the students to action. Thus, the historical roots of the system of higher education and the student population itself both play an important part in the development of the student movement.

It is unlikely that movements stimulated by specific or isolated events will be able to sustain themselves over a long period of time. One would expect to encounter less ideological sophistication or broad political concern in them than in movements founded by politically conscious students with long range goals in mind.

These "spontaneous" movements may arise when the student movement feels directly threatened or challenged. The cause can be an imposed fee increase or an unusually difficult examination. In the past, administrative censorship, suppression, or condescension have instigated demonstrations. Once students have taken action on some issue, it is difficult for them to quietly return to their routine academic life after having experienced the exhilaration of political agitation and contact with the centers of power in the society.

In the recent past much student unrest has been collectively described as "indiscipline," as the result of immaturity or the ever-present generational conflict. While it is true that much of the violence which takes place on the campus is a result of one or the other of the above factors, students often have legitimate grievances, and are capable of expressing their concern in a disciplined and at times effective manner. They are often in the vanguard of the political and social movements of their nations, and their actions frequently reflect sensitivity to social reality rather than immaturity.

Students are driven by many motives, some of them contradictory. By using a variety of approaches, it may be possible to define these motives. Psychological examination and depth interviews will reveal facets of student behavior which an historical analysis of student activity could not, and sociologically oriented attitude surveys have much relevance. Yet, it would be a mistake to suggest that psychological and sociological methods are the only valid means for analyzing student movements, just as a sole dependence on historical analysis would be inadequate.

An examination of the student movement alone is insufficient to obtain a total picture of the student population. The social class background of the students will in part determine their attitudes toward education and occupation. Caste or tribal affiliations also influence student attitudes. The relationship between the student and society can also have an impact on the nature of the movement, since students will not tend toward political activism when there are few external causes for discontent. Where the society is marked by generational tension or by economic discontent, student political activism is more likely.

These are various types of student political activity which have been important in the new states. Each type is a response to a specific grievance or aimed at a particular goal. One important distinction is the difference between norm- and value-oriented student political action. Norm-oriented student movements generally aim at the correction of a specific grievance or at a particular goal, and do not often have broader ideological overtones. The norm-oriented movement is unlikely to maintain itself after its goal has been attained, although, as has been noted, such movements often provide an impetus for further activity.

Orientations of Student Groups

While the norm-oriented movement is concerned with specific goals and is more likely a product of an emotional response to a specific limited issue, the value-oriented movement is concerned with broader ideological issues, and, when it is involved in concrete actions, this activity is usually linked directly to a broader concern.[11] Most revolutionary political movements are value-oriented, and most of the on-going student political organizations, particularly "underground" groups, are value-oriented. A value orientation does not prevent students from participating in limited campaigns or agitations, although such participation is usually done for reasons transcending the specific objective. In the student community, a value-oriented movement has a more important influence in the long run and is often a leading element in apparently norm-oriented actions. Both types of groups, the norm-oriented "cause-group" aimed at reducing fees or securing a change in college administration, and the value-oriented political organization committed to doctrines of Marxism, Hinduism, or other ideological concepts, exist side by side in the student community. Naturally, there is some overlap between these two types of groups, and it is often difficult to make a clear distinction between them, since the leadership of a group which is seemingly norm-oriented may be ideologically sophisticated and able to turn the attention of the participants to broader issues.

What starts as a limited protest against some isolated issue may easily turn into a sustained movement, with concerns extending to the broader society. The leadership of the student movement is notably fluid, and it is very possible for a norm-oriented leadership to be supplanted by students interested in capitalizing on a particular movement for their broader political purposes. Thus, while the norm and value orientations offer some convenient models to work from, student movements often defy a tight definition of either category and care must be taken in applying these labels to various student movements and organizations.

In addition to the distinction between norm- and value-oriented movements, there is a related series of factors which can influence the direction of student organizations. A student movement may be concerned only with "campus" issues and have relatively little interest or impact on the external political situation. Such movements have been called "etudialist" because of their primary student orientation. They are often quite militant over issues of student welfare, fee increases, and administrative harassment of students. They are occasionally interested in the broader issues of educational policy and reform, although generally student interests are confined to more limited areas. Contrasted to such movements are society-oriented student movements, which are concerned with societal issues—usually political, although occasionally social or cultural.[12]

There are similarities between the norm-value distinction and the etudialist-society orientation of the student movement. It is usually true that student organizations or movements interested in broader social issues are motivated by value orientations, although this is not always the case. Student groups affiliated with political parties usually have a value orientation and are often concerned with broader political issues. Yet, it is important to keep these two sets of criteria clear, since it is possible for student movements to manifest differing orientations over a period of time. The Zengakuren, Japan's militant student organization, is clearly a value-oriented student organization, adhering to extreme leftist ideological views.[13] Yet, this organization has alternatively taken part in etudialist and societal activities during its postwar history. Thus, while its orientation has been value directed, it has switched its tactics on a number of occasions to meet the needs of the students and/or of its political ideology. The Indian student movement shows similar examples of this relatively facile change of tactics. The Communist-sponsored student organization, the All-India Students' Federation, clearly a value-oriented movement, has alternatively taken part in broader political issues under the direction of the Communist party and has participated in campus-oriented activity when such action has served its needs or has become of importance to the students. It is also possible for norm-oriented student groups to take part in societal activity. At various Indian universities, students have taken part in outside politics when such action has been deemed necessary to fulfill a student demand. Pressure on political leaders often can lead to amelioration of a campus problem.

These distinctions are often blurred and are hardly ever clear in the minds of the students themselves. Yet, they are valuable tools for gaining an understanding of a specific student movement. The issue is further complicated by the fact that the orientation and direction of student organizations can and often do change rather radically in a short period of time. These changes usually occur in a relatively disciplined manner, and a knowledge of the general orientation of the movement can help to predict its direction, or can lead to a further understanding of its motives and goals.

Student political activity often contains an important non-student element, which sometimes provides direction and ideological sophistication to the movement. In most societies, the student community consists not only of students currently enrolled in institutions of higher education, but also of ex-students or part-time students who wish to remain on the periphery of the student community. While a student per se may remain at an institution for only four years, non-student elements in the student community often remain for longer periods of time, providing something of an historical sense to the student movement. Political parties often assign young activists to the student work and seek to expand their influence in this way. Part of the "underground" of the student population, these elements cannot be overlooked as they are often of crucial importance to student movements.

Functions of Student Movements

The student movement, in addition to meeting certain emotional and intellectual needs of the students, also has a number of important functions within the framework of education and political development in the new nations. Student cultural and social organizations are often important sources of academic knowledge, since they sponsor well-attended lectures and other programs. These organizations provide the student community with one of the few opportunities for serious discussion and a chance to meet informally with professors and other academic persons. University authorities often try to include the "extra-curriculum" as an important part of the educational experience of the students, although quite often these groups are left to student initiative. In some cases, Western ideas are engendered through the activities of such groups. The various debating societies which are popular give valuable training in parliamentary methods, public speaking, and often in politics as well. The religiously based student groups often give the student a new insight into and perhaps identification with his religious tradition. Literary groups are sometimes as effective as formal courses in literature in providing the students with a background in this field.

One of the most important educational aspects of the student organizations is concerned with politics. Where they are permitted, most universities have active political discussion groups. Where there are constraints on student organization, such discussion groups often operate underground on a smaller scale. Such groups are usually the main source of political education for the students involved in them, and often have a vital and lasting effect on those involved. Student cultural organizations often provide training in drama, dancing, and other arts to students who go on to become well known in the cultural realm. Students who are active in the movement often have an advantage in such mundane affairs as business and commerce because of their training in human relations and organizational techniques. Indeed, it has been said that the alumni of the militant leftist Zengakuren in Japan often make very good businessmen after their revolutionary careers come to an end.[14]

The socializing role of the student movement has been implicit in much of the foregoing discussion. Student groups are often a primary element in the political socialization of whole student generations, thereby playing an important although indirect role in the shaping of the political life of the broader society. Even when students lose much of their youthful radicalism in later years, they retain something of the training they received in the movement. In India, for example, the organizational training provided by the Communist student movement has proved a valuable asset to the many former Communists who have achieved high business or government positions. Students occasionally make career choices on the basis of their experiences in the student movement, and many choose politics as a career because of their experiences in the student movement.[15]

Student organizations of all types often shape student attitudes. This is a particularly important consideration in societies in which the student community is surrounded by traditional value orientations. In such societies, the student movement is one of the few modernizing elements and can go a long way toward breaking down caste, religious, and linguistic rivalries and building a sense of nationality. Thus, social views as well as political outlooks are shaped by the student movement. And again, when students leave the universities, they often retain something of the attitudes which they learned in the movement. In rigidly administered educational systems, the more informal structures of the student movement can be even more important.

The student movement has been a stimulus for nationalism in many of the new nations. Much of modern Indian nationalism was developed by individuals with Western educations, many of whom had studied in Europe. Many of the first generation of African nationalists were trained in the London-based West African Students' Union. Student groups in other areas have also been important training centers for nationalist leaders, and some nationalist ideology was developed within such organizations.

The student movement has occasionally achieved direct political results from its activity. Governments in Korea and Turkey were toppled by militant student movements although the military soon took over the reins of government. Students in Japan forced the Kishi government to resign as a result of massive demonstrations. Students exercised an important influence on the Russian revolutionary movement and on the nationalist movements in India, Burma, and parts of Africa. Thus, the student movement can have a direct political function as well as a more diffuse educational impact. Students have never been able to successfully control a revolutionary movement, even in those instances when they have been primarily responsible for it.

The student movement is often a primary contact between the student population and the educational authorities, thus functioning as a means of communication between the two key elements in any system of higher education. Students have often taken a direct role in educational affairs by suggesting changes and reforms, which have occasionally been accepted. When the students feel strongly about an educational issue, they can force the hand of the authorities by demanding reforms and enforcing their wishes by agitational campaigns.

The student movement does not always play a radical role in the community, pressing for progressive reforms and backing left-wing politicians. It can also act as a reactionary force, supporting traditional elements in the society. Although it would seem that leftism is a more pervasive influence, strong conservative student organizations exist in many nations. As in politics, the cultural influence of the student movement can be conservative as well, and can help to build an identification of the students with traditional cultural patterns after an initial rebellion from them.

That student movements, political and non-political, have played an important and at times crucial role in the developing nations is clear. Generalizing about the nature of such movements is more difficult, since there are many differences between nations. One of the difficulties in analyzing student movements is their transitory nature—the student community as well as the interests of the students change rapidly. Organizations are often temporary, and leadership fluctuates. The emphasis of the movements shifts from campus to society and back again at rather regular intervals, and the movement itself can disappear for extended periods of time.

Interaction between the educational system, the broader political and economic situation, and the socio-psychological nature of the student community is complex, making any thorough understanding of the role of the students in politics and on the educational establishment difficult. Yet, it is of crucial importance that the student movement be thoroughly analyzed if an important aspect of economic and political development in the new nations is to be understood.

Notes

1. See Metta Spencer, Chapter 14, this book.
2. See Seymour Martin Lipset, Chapter 1, this book.
3. See Glaucio A. D. Soares, Chapter 5, this book.
4. Lewis Feuer, "A Talk with the Zengakuren," *New Leader*, XLIV (May 1, 1961), 17.
5. Edward Shils, "Indian Students: Rather Sadhus than Philistines," *Encounter*, XVII (September 1961), 15.
6. Robert Jay Lifton, "Youth and History: Individual Change in Postwar Japan," *Daedalus*, LI (Winter 1962), 179.
7. See Lipset, *op. cit.*
8. Lewis Feuer, "Patterns in the History of Student Movements" (mimeographed, Berkeley, University of California, 1965), p. 4.
9. Calvin Trillin, "Letter from Berkeley," in Michael Miller and Susan Gilmore, eds., *Revolution at Berkeley* (New York: Dell Books, 1965), p. 261.

10. Dwaine Marvick, "African University Students: A Presumptive Elite," in James S. Coleman, ed., *Education and Political Development* (Princeton, N.J.: Princeton University Press, 1965), p. 491.
11. Neil Smelser, *Theory of Collective Behavior* (New York: The Free Press, 1963), p. 275.
12. James Petras, "General Remarks on Politics and Students" (unpublished paper, Berkeley, University of California, 1964), p. 2.
13. Feuer, "Patterns of Student Movements," *op. cit.*, p. 17.
14. Philip G. Altbach, "Japanese Students and Japanese Politics," *Comparative Education Review*, VII (October 1963), 184.
15. Sagar Ahluwalia, "The Student Movement in India" (unpublished manuscript, Delhi, 1963), p. 20.

Comparative Perspectives
on Students and Politics

PART II

Student Unrest on Four Continents:
Montreal, Ibadan, Warsaw, and Rangoon[1]

GEORGE Z. F. BEREDAY

4

Student unrest has now assumed the proportions of a world phenomenon and the speculation as to its causes continues to be lively. Many discussions are concerned with what could be described as "horizontal" causes, that is to say, cleavages between viewpoints of generations, between parents and children, or between members of the gerontocracies, the older groups in power and the "angry young men" of the "new frontier." This chapter will attempt to deal with "vertical" cleavages, which could best be described as tensions not between generations but between groups, not as unrest derived from the sense that something is wrong with the world, but a sense of threat from other contemporary groups to one's interests within this world. When Berkeley students condemn the war in Vietnam, they are in the former, "cosmic," category; when Alabama students protest racial integration, they are in the latter category.

The distinction between horizontal and vertical alienation, however, cannot always be as neat as might be wished for. Often the two appear together as part of the same student explosion. It is impossible in most instances to avoid fuzziness and overlapping. Thus some students may protest the war in Vietnam not because they think their elders morally wrong, but because they fear being drafted, a narrower, personal reason. Others may resist integration not because they fear the immediate Negro contact and competition, but because race equality violates their wider historic notions of what is just and right, a "horizontal" reason. Such overlaps make discussion difficult, but in a sense also justify it. The question that this review will ultimately lead to is: Are the "big wrongs" in themselves sufficient to cause active student unrest? Or are there frequently "little wrongs," personal threats or scores to settle which act as a trigger to student activism, hidden under the big words and rationalizations? In other words, the concern of this discussion is to catalogue forms of unrest that are primarily apolitical or incidental to politics and thus to supplement the growing literature concerned with the activism of students that is primarily political.

Four different illustrations of conflict have been selected from random countries as typical. The 1965 maneuvers between French-speaking and English-speaking students in Montreal, Canada, supply an example of unrest based on ethnic cleavage. The 1957 upsets at the University of Ibadan in Nigeria furnish a distant documentation, in other forms well familiar to Americans, of racial cleavage. Student demonstrations in Warsaw in 1957, though primarily political in nature, bring forth little discussed animosities due to social class and interuniversity prestige. Finally, the Rangoon disturbances of 1953, a less known example of many similar riots in Burma, suggest a purely educational unrest, representing a cluster of cases all over the world in which students rebel against university authorities because they object to some educational provisions rather than because of some specific grievances of a social or political type.

Ethnic Cleavage: Montreal

Tensions built on aspirations and fears of different national groups appear sporadically in stories of student activities. Thus, the revelation of Stalin's crimes by Khrushchev in 1956 caused student demonstrations in Tbilisi in defense of the late dictator, the most famous product of that city. A somewhat more broadly conceived ethnic conflict was illustrated by one of the rare demonstrations of Thai students which occurred in Bangkok in 1962 to protest the World Court decision giving Cambodia sovereignty over Phra Viham Wat (district) on the Thai-Cambodian frontier. Animosities between the Chinese and Malays in Singapore or between Tamils and Singhalese in Ceylon sooner or later find their echo in student affairs in the relevant universities.[2]

The case of Montreal is the contemporary example of this type of tension. For some years or, indeed, for some decades the politics of the province of Quebec in Canada have been affected by a strong revival of French regionalism. French-English animosities in Canada have deep-rooted historical precedents dating back to the time before the British North American Act. It is probably the independent stance taken by de Gaulle against the Anglo-Saxon community of nations that has fanned anew the flames of smoldering

French resentment. In 1965, the General officially received a delegation from Quebec, and several statements made sounded as if the province were a sovereign state, a member of the French community of nations. Accordingly, the sentiments for political independence of Quebec have been revived. They dovetail with the long-standing feud between Catholic and Protestant interests which are, of course, drawn along ethnic lines. They coincide, although to a somewhat lesser degree, with the economic differences which are also correlated with national origin. There is even an educational cleavage related to ethnic divisions: high academic and selective standards being equated with French education, and more diversified, more technological, more mass-oriented school career profiles being tied to Anglo-Saxon, specifically American, education.[3] French Canadians, when they view themselves within the confines of the province of Quebec, see themselves as a political and cultural majority. In the perspective of Canada as a whole, they are forced to change roles from a dominant group to a minority which is threatened by the overwhelming Anglo-Saxon power and interests of the Federation.

Politically, French-speaking student activists are identified with syndicalism, and so extreme a position has caused internal splits even within the French group. The behavior and activities of the students in Montreal can be taken as an example. On October 28, 1965, a demonstration occurred on the campus of the University of Montreal, the largest French-speaking university in North America. A group of students from the polytechnic school of the University seized a truckload of 10,000 copies of the University's student paper, Le Quartier Latin, and ceremoniously burned it. The involved students published a communiqué (in the next number of the same Quartier Latin) stating that they disapproved of the socialist, syndicalist stand openly taken in the name of all the students of the University by the editorial staff and by the sponsoring organization, the Association Générale des Étudiants de l'Université de Montréal (AGEUM). They blamed the editors for "morbid negativism and anarchism, intransigent and unrealistic," called them "a band of poets in the worst sense of the term, and paper revolutionaries," accused them of having turned the paper into "a vulgar pamphlet of propaganda at the service of movements for independence and socialism, external to the university and alien to the great majority of its students."[4] Thus the issue of syndicalism contributed to the unrest of French Canadian students even internally. A month later it was destined to emphasize the lines of division also between French and English students.

Student syndicalism began in a tangible form in 1962 when a meeting of the politically active students and student journalists was convoked in Montreal by the *Presse Étudiante Nationale* (PEN). In February 1963 the legislative assembly of Quebec passed a law extending suffrage to persons eighteen years old and over, thus lending tremendous political force to the student movement. In March of that year, the full-fledged Canadian version of student syndicalism appeared in a conference organized by AGEUM. Other student organizations comprising students of the region of Montreal, students of Laval University, and students of Sherbrook University participated in the meeting and a provisional committee of *l'Union Générale des Étudiants du Québec* (UGEQ) was formed. This committee was strengthened in April and May by several new organizations of students of the classical colleges of Quebec, of student nurses, of students in normal schools, and other already existing unions. A year later, on April 1, 1964, on the occasion of a federal and provincial fiscal conference held in Quebec, the joint student associations organized a demonstration march upon the City of Quebec. Thus strengthened, UGEQ came formally into being in November 1964.[5]

Through a variety of activities, such as the publication of pamphlets and of a special newspaper explaining its aims,[6] the support of labor disputes and strikes, and through political lobbying, the institutionalized student movement became a force in Montreal politics. Their most recent triumph consists of breaking historical precedents as regards the secularization of the government of Catholic universities.[7] In December 1965, for the first time in history, a lay rector was installed as the head of the University of Montreal. As of 1965, twenty-two consulting committees had been formed to assist the Senate of that University, some *ad hoc*, others on a permanent basis. Each of these committees is made up of students, faculty, and administration. In December 1965 the student organizations requested that a student representative be appointed to the nine-member University Senate, thus embodying the suggestion put forward by the Royal Commission on Education.[8] By June 1966, there were indications that the request would be acquiesced to, thus introducing the principle of student co-government in North America.

This show of strength by the French-speaking students could not and cannot leave unaffected the English-speaking students in Quebec. At the time of its formation the UGEQ demanded from the joining organizations as a condition of admission that they secede from the Canadian Union of Students (CUS), the federal organization of all Canadian students. This was justified by "different language, cultural needs and aspirations" of the French Canadians; UGEQ is a unilingual French organization. Immediately the English-speaking but Catholic student organization of the University of Ottawa had difficulty with this rule and requested permission on behalf of its Quebec students for a double affiliation with CUS and UGEQ. This request was rejected for the present. As a result, although the march on Quebec was joined by a small group of *étudiants anglais libres* only a few minor English-speaking universities have joined UGEQ. This posed a problem for both ethnic groups involved. The French *Québécois* are anxious to have the English-speaking inhabitants of the province drawn into collaboration provided this is on French terms. The English-speaking Quebecquers seek to propitiate the French in order to retain their position in Quebec. In view of this, accession of English-speaking universities to UGEQ became important. Most important was the question of the accession of McGill University.

McGill is the most prominent Canadian university—Protestant, Anglo-Saxon, and in the middle of Montreal. As such, it is an object of perpetual French Canadian suspicion, especially by students of the University of Montreal. *Le Quartier Latin*, in particular, not infrequently publishes anti-McGill if not outright anti-Anglo-Saxon sentiments in editorials and articles.[9]

In spite of attacks upon them, the English-speaking Quebecquers seek to pacify the French; hence there was a strong desire within McGill's Student Council to join; provisionally, the organization participated in the activities of UGEQ. A referendum on the question of joining was, however, forced by the opponents of such collaboration. The date was set for December 1, 1965. The McGill Council was lukewarm to the president of CUS when the latter sought to enter the McGill campus presumably to take part in the campaign. The *McGill Daily*, the student newspaper, also came out in support of McGill's joining UGEQ.

Yet, when a referendum was taken among McGill students, only 47 per cent (2,548) voted for joining UGEQ, while 53 per cent (2,859) were against it. The motion was lost and the results represent an example of the operation of ethnic cleavages in interstudent relations. Despite the cooperative attitude of the Student Council, a majority of McGill students have demonstrated a strong feeling of separate ethnic identity. A small journal, entitled *Resistance*, was organized to act as spokesman against the Union. Its reasons for the majority's hostility to the motion were given as follows:

1. no more professional private practice
2. active unquestioning solidarity with labor unions
3. unilingualism and the prospect of condoning a separatist Quebec

4. silencing of McGill delegates through regionalization
5. withdrawal from CUS
6. forcing social change through general student strike
7. compulsory adherence to a single ideology
8. involvement without effective representation.

The majority of McGill students were clearly against socialism and French independence and nationalism inherent in the UGEQ movement.

There were many accusations and disclaimers of racialism (as an Anglo-Saxon feeling of dislike for French Canadians is called) on both sides, and some heated exchange of passion, but on the whole the issues were squarely defined. The case for those opposing the merger is best expressed by Saeed Mirza, Chairman of the anti-merger organization called Committee for a Rational Approach to UGEQ at McGill. In a letter to the *McGill Daily* on November 29, 1965, he wrote as follows:

The undemocratic manner in which the members of the executive committee have forced UGEQ on McGill is extremely lamentable. However, it is gratifying to see that a referendum has been forced on the issue and I would like all students to bear in mind the following facts about UGEQ before they vote. . . . McGill sent observers to the founding convention, but after sizing up the entire situation, the students' council last year decided *not to join* UGEQ. The basic reasons were the avowed UGEQ policies on unilingualism, restriction of membership to either UGEQ or CUS, and student syndicalism. We know how McGill students feel about this last ideology by the negligible turn-out last week for the "La Grenade" strike.[10]

The French response to the outcome of the McGill referendum was expressed in another letter in the *McGill Daily*, excerpted as follows:

How can you now ask French Canadians to remain in a country in which they are a minority and where they are "silenced through regionalization" (provinces) and where they are "involved without effective representation." . . . The break with CUS was a bad move on the part of UGEQ, but this could have been remedied when the emotions caused by the attitude of CUS towards French universities disappeared. . . . When English Quebecquers learn how hard it is to be a minority, maybe they will make the effort to explain to the rest of the country what the real problem is.[11]

The president of the defeated Council, Sharon Sholzberg, submitted her resignation which was not accepted by the Council. She summed up the defeat by stating that the average man in the street may feel that "once again McGill has proven to be the bastion of the Anglo-Saxon aristocracy."

The struggles in Montreal reflect wider social issues, but have a quality of regionalism that is decidedly ethnic. Even the coupling of socialism with Quebec independence is ethnic in a sense since, as stated, national lines coincide with economic lines and to soak the rich means to soak Anglo-Saxons. The rise of the French in national aspirations and economic wealth has produced a generation of activists, the youngest of which now try out their wings in the University. Their hostilities are against other groups of students. The disenchantment with the general state of Quebec and with the older generations which built it that way serves only as a background cause of the unrest. It is because Montreal posits an intergroup rather than an intergeneration cleavage that the situation is explosive. Time only can tell at which point peaceful activity is capable of erupting into open disturbances.

Racial Cleavages: Ibadan

Racial tensions are illustrated by several cases of university unrest in the United States and elsewhere. In the United States, riots following admission of Negro students to Southern universities, at the University of Mississippi in 1962 for instance, received international headlines. Demonstrations on the opposite tack, to protest the discrimination against Negroes, are nationwide and on the increase. In fact, as Lipset and Altbach have remarked, most of the leading rioters at Berkeley in 1964 seem to have received their training and developed their style in civil rights demonstrations.[12] The race-based outbreaks against the students of the University of the Friendship of the Peoples in Moscow also received publicity. To illustrate race-conditioned conflicts the less known (and less momentous) case of the Nigerian students against the authorities of the University College (now University) of Ibadan in 1957 is presented.

The racial tensions in Nigeria are couched in nationalist rather than in racial terms but, before independence at any rate, the racial ingredient in anticolonial tensions and British-African animosities was unmistakable and is thoroughly documented. The resident British elite in Nigeria was always small. But it was also temporary, ultimately intending to return to Britain and thus somewhat more British, more Anglo-Saxon, and perhaps more snobbish than are the British groups which plan a permanent settlement in colonial areas, especially after such areas achieve independence. In addition to a native clerical group and a lower-level middle class which all colonial administrations bring into being, the British in their colonies pursued the policy of creating a fully educated, upper-class native elite.

Even though such an elite in Nigeria was very small in numbers and many appeared to be very eager for assimilation as "black Englishmen," there was evidence of racial discrimination against them not only in terms of physical restriction of public facilities, but in the sphere of emotions. "With many notable exceptions, the characteristic attitude of resident Europeans towards the educated African was one of contempt, amusement, condescension, or veiled hostility."[13] In addition, racial segregation by physical factors in residential neighborhoods, in cinemas, in hospitals, and in social clubs (often in practice if not in principle) served to identify social class and national barriers with racial barriers.[14]

In education as a whole, and at the University College in Ibadan in particular, racial tensions were ever present in spite of some attempts to alleviate them. The actual degree of racial discrimination is disputed. J. T. Saunders, the second principal of Ibadan, makes hardly a mention of race in his book.[15] More realistically, Ibadan's first principal, Kenneth Mellanby, devotes considerable place to race animosities, reproducing even cartoons which appeared against him in the Nigerian press with accusations that he discriminated against Africans. This Mellanby denies.[16] Whatever actual discrimination there was, the image of inequality at Ibadan in the minds of Nigerian faculty, students, and the press is unmistakable. The Nigerians resented the fact that European faculty were paid additional allowances which made their salaries about one-third higher than those of the Nigerians of corresponding rank. This policy, an implementation of the recommendations of the Asquith Commission, was remembered and bitterly resented long after it had been abolished in the early 1950's. Equally resented was the small number of Nigerians asked to serve on the Ibadan faculty in comparison to the number of Europeans. As late as 1958 only 42 out of a 170-member faculty and 12 out of 39 administrative staff were Nigerian.[17] Most resented perhaps was the persistence with which senior posts were denied to Nigerians. As stated by Mellanby, "I always believed that for junior posts we should give preference to Nigerians, and hope they would thus receive training to fit them for the higher posts, but this preference would be fatal if it applied to senior positions."[18] Thus the road to professorial appointments as well as to higher administrative posts seemed closed to Nigerians. The point at dispute seemed to be the qualifications deemed appropriate to these levels. The fact that expatriate professorial appointees, in the manner of the English, held often only M. A. degrees did not help matters. Substantial faculty turnover from abroad was interpreted as not flattering to Ibadan administration and conditions. Finally, as commented upon by a foreign observer, the British connection made the University less responsive to the need for economic and political development of the country, and thus somewhat out of touch with Nigerian national aspirations.

It must be held in the favor of the University College that its hands were narrowly tied in certain decisions by the close union with the University of London. But a university in a developing country that begins work with 55 students (January 1948) with the help of a strong contingent of "Alt-philologen," must at once at the beginning fall under suspicion of being an ivory tower, even if it is housed in old military barracks.... It is a farce when the "Alt-philologen" invite one to a lantern lecture on agriculture in Ancient Greece, while no one can tell why the Red Chinese try unsuccessfully to establish collective farms in Guinea.[19]

Complaints against importations of foreign professors and their low qualifications, about uninteresting and unrelated lectures, and about denial of their due to Nigerian faculty or the implication that they were of lower intellectual caliber formed part of the tensions evinced not only by adult Nigerians, but also by the students. Destined for the new elite, and eventually housed in quite sumptuous single room dormitories, the students were a particularly ambivalent group, Westernizing and elitist in the British sense on one side, and nationalistic, touchy, and anti-British on the other. Students complained that all successful holders of the Matriculation Examination of London University were not automatically admitted to university study (the ratio of selection was in fact one out of seven), that the University course of studies was set at four years and not at three as in Britain, and that disciplinary requirements were too strict and getting stricter with the University attempting between 1947 and 1957 to introduce "moral tutors" to supervise the behavior of students. In spite of the good progress in the University and several efforts by the administration to alleviate conditions of race inequality, the general feeling of alienation at the time of the 1957 outbreaks seems to have persisted.

The actual disciplinary problems that caused an eruption and led to the closing of the school on November 12, 1957, are best presented in the words of an eyewitness.

Underlying factors had been smoldering for some time on the campus, such as student resentment at failure to appoint qualified Nigerians to the faculty and assigning those appointed to lower faculty rank; dislike of all top administrative posts being held by non-Nigerians; feeling that much of the teaching staff is of inferior quality; lack of confidence in top administrative officers; irritation at what they regarded as increasingly stringent disciplinary regulations; all added to the unrest at UCI. For some time students also had been complaining about the quality of food, certain regulations governing their use of electrical equipment in their rooms (radios, teapots, hot water kettles, etc.), unwillingness of the administration to meet with their representatives to discuss certain student problems, etc.

This resentment boiled over into a full-fledged strike when the school authorities, acting out of a sincere concern for the students and institution, decided to place heavy wire screens around the corridors of all dormitories in order to control traffic into them. This was done as a precaution against repetition of an unfortunate incident involving the death of a girl student in a male student's room as a result of an attempted abortion. Irritated by the erection of these "cages," as the screens were called, some students removed them. When the authorities were unable to get the students themselves to single out those responsible for this act, they called on the Nigerian secret police whose agents tried to pose as servants and circulate among the student body to gather information. In addition, regular members of the Nigerian Police Force also were called to the campus to grill certain students suspected of being the leaders of the rebellion. All of this, of course, only served to arouse student resistance still more until things reached an impasse when faculty members of the University Senate were unable to agree among themselves on what steps to take to handle the situation.

Without prior consultation with the Federal Minister of Education, under whose jurisdiction the institution falls, the principal of UCI closed the school. Public response to this action was quite strong and for weeks letters poured into the local press and there was much private discussion both pro and con, although sentiment ran against the action as extreme, precipitate, and unwarranted. The press took a moderate stand calling for a full investigation of the facts but criticized the Ministry of Education for failure to keep abreast of developments at UCI.

It had been feared by students that the administration would pursue a punitive policy of screening in accepting returning students. But mindful of an interested and critical public opinion for its opening on Jan. 6, 1958, the administration decided to admit all students who had applied for readmission by mid-Dec., and more than 95% of them took advantage of this procedure.[20]

The outward appearances of the Ibadan disturbance would seem to place it in the category of educational rather than racial cleavages. Students protested against the University, against bad food while money was spent on wire fences and other remodeling. Resentment and action of the students was caused directly by the University's use of police on campus. Yet it may be inferred that the riots were social and national in nature and hence racial in a Nigerian frame of reference. The placing of the "cages" in the corridors and the use of police were more likely to hurt racial pride in an environment in which the African felt inferior and resented being treated like a child. The fact that the University closed its gates before consulting the government suggested an anxiety of its Senate. Probably it was feared that a racially tense situation would cause the University to lose face had they asked and been officially refused such permission. The readmission of students without victimization is also typical of a racial "situation" without the presence of which the University might embark upon a more severe form of punitive repression. At the time of the strike as well as before and after, complaints against racial discrimination at Ibadan continued in the press. In May 1958, to cite one instance, the Prime Minister of the Western Region condemned faculty appointment policies in a public address in Calabar. Within three weeks an appointment of two Nigerians, one to a Vice-Principality and another to a Deanship, was announced at Ibadan.[21]

The 1957 outbreak made the British very angry, more angry perhaps than they would have been if it had been a minor and purely educational occurrence. Apparently the disturbance is a subject of serious differences in interpretation. When the eyewitness account presented above was summarized in 1959 in another publication,[22] a distinguished British academic authority was led to condemn it:

A paragraph purports to describe events, called "student riots," which took place at Ibadan University College in 1957. This description is false in almost every particular. It is stated that the students resented "the inadequate provision of university posts for Nigerians" and that the college was forced to re-open "under pressure of public opinion." All these statements are false, and moreover damaging to the reputation of the college. It is most regrettable that the authors should have given currency to rubbish which reflects adversely on a young and flourishing college which is in special relation to the University of London, many members of which are well aware of the true course of events in 1957.[23]

The unrest in Ibadan did not rest squarely on racial issues but it seems to support the main argument of this discussion. It supplies a profile of disturbances which erupt over a small pretext if a long-standing intergroup grievance exists to support it. Such a grievance, when it is a racial grievance, affects the students personally. It is related to the prestige and careers of students as well as to some social wrong at large. Not dissimilar disturbances have occurred in Southern Negro colleges in the United States (Tuskegee) or in South Africa (Fort Hare). In each case, the presence of a personally embittered group made the difference between action and lack of action by the student body at large when a controversial political issue emerged to warrant such action.

Social Cleavage: Warsaw

Social class is an important source of student antagonism and one of its expressions is the pattern of hostilities based on interuniversity prestige. The celebrated relationship between the English Oxbridge and Redbrick universities has been dramatized, especially by Alison Peers.[24] The difference in prestige between the University of Tokyo and other Japanese universities is also well known and colors the style of student demonstrations by the Zengakuren.[25] In the U.S., the rivalries around the Harvard-Yale or Army-Navy football games are only a faint reflection of more deep-seated divisions. In 1965, for instance, the Harvard Chapter of the Students for a Democratic Society (SDS) did not vote in favor of civil disobedience while the Berkeley and Michigan groups did.[26] In reverse, Irish-Catholic boys from Boston College resent, even hate, Harvard, but their favorite week-end hangout is the Oxford Grill in Harvard Square; Harvard students stay away from the Grill preferring Jim Cronin's, a little off the Square.

We quote the Warsaw riots in 1957 following the suspension of the magazine *Po Prostu* as illustration of such cleavages. Poland, for centuries a society of virtual castes, emerged into modernity as a strongly class-conscious country. The richest *szlachta*, the land-owning gentry, was not entirely dispossessed until the Communist takeover. Poorer gentry in alliance with the rising professionals from other classes quickly became an alloy, a bourgeois intelligentsia to use the appellation of Poland's present sociologists. This socio-intellectual class administered Poland between the wars. It attempted to meet but on the whole it postponed the growth of the aspirations of the expanding working class and of the enormous landed peasantry. The Communist takeover has changed things, but not entirely. Poland remains past rather than future oriented,[27] hence old buildings are lovingly reconstructed, museums assiduously visited, heraldry and knowledge of the lines of descent and blood relationships discreetly but persistently maintained. The intelligentsia of Poland continue to evince an almost built-in dislike of manual labor, in spite of the fact that it is being revolutionized by the accession of the able sons of workers and peasants. Marxist philosophy *à la polonaise*, in contrast to the Russian, encourages a lively and sociologically scientific interest in social classes and class behavior. Things are being talked about freely and *eo ipso* consciousness of class exists and persists.

In education, the major weapon of equalization, the social class situation reflects itself, by prewar standards, somewhat strangely. Emphasis is, as in all Communist countries, on social rise and equal opportunity for the underprivileged classes. But Poland is one of the first countries in the world to be also affected by a reverse phenomenon: a refusal by many sons of peasants and workers to take advantage of that opportunity. Education is still influenced by the traditions of the old intelligentsia and academic standards remain conservative and exacting. An unusually large proportion of the almost forcibly impressed sons of workers and peasants become thus discouraged and quit long before graduation.

Within the world of the educated a re-evaluation of the distinction between scientists and humanists is taking place in favor of the former. The Soviet vogue for science was passed on to Poland, further reinforcing an older tradition. In most prewar European countries there was a recognizable prestige distinction between humanists trained as civil servants, publicists and literati, and those in sciences and technical skills who ranked somewhat below. By contrast, in Poland, similar to Germany, there was always less social distinction between the humanists and the technologists. The tradition of the *Politechnische Hochschule* meant that technological occupations enjoyed equivalent, if not equal, prestige. Under Communist tutelage the prestige of the scientists has tended to soar even further. This has forced the humanists to adopt techniques and defenses characteristic of the underprivileged groups.

Given these atypical features, the "usual" class structure in Polish society and education cannot be denied. The basis of it is ascription rather than achievement. What matters is not so much what a person does or even what his income is, but indirectly his blood line and circumstance of birth and directly his life style as a cultivated even more than as an educated man. Set in this way the field of higher education is ripe for a strong operation of intellectual snobberies. Feelings of inferiority and superiority persist in spite of the communization of the country. It is the contention of this discussion that social class tensions, especially illustrated by the relation between the two leading higher education institutions in Warsaw, were present on the occasion of the October 1957 riot, which followed upon the suspension of the magazine *Po Prostu*.

The basic theme of the riots was, of course, political. After the October unrest of 1956 Poland became the scene of a bid for power by two groups of Communist leaders. One, known as the Natolin group, advocated the modernization of Polish Communism, de-Stalinization and greater accommodation to the historical heritage of Polish freedom. The other group, supported by old-line Stalinists and later known as "Pulawianie," attempted to maintain Poland on more conservative Communist lines. The key person in this struggle was, of course, Gomulka, who was brought into power thanks to the pressure of the Natolin group, but who within a year found himself forced to make more and more concessions to the "Pulawianie." The weekly magazine, *Po Prostu*, an organ of youth and university students, was one of the main weapons in the hands of Natolin. On its pages a young and idealistic editorial committee over and over again expressed its concern for what they regarded as an uncontaminated liberal construction of the Communist experiment. As time went on their voice became steadily more critical and in the first days of October, a year after the Polish October Revolution, *Po Prostu* was suspended, causing a four-day outbreak of major youth riots.

The details of the riots are fairly well known. On October 3 the rumor of the suspension of the magazine caused a group of students from Warsaw Polytechnic, numbering about two thousand, to assemble for a protest meeting in Warsaw's Narutowicz Square, outside the largest student hostel in the city. Before any speeches were made the students were charged by police armed with sticks and tear gas. For the space of some three hours, the police battled the students. Some bystanders coming out of the nearby church service also became involved, causing an even greater public outcry against police action and forcing the Commissioner of Police, a few days later, to issue a public apology. Late in the evening the government requested directors of all the institutions of higher education in Warsaw to issue a communiqué warning the students "against too hasty efforts" and bidding them to refrain from illegal action.

A new rally was scheduled for the next evening, October 4, in the Central Courtyard of the Warsaw Polytechnic, the same place where the protest meetings in 1956 had been held. Four thousand students appeared and were addressed by a member of Parliament, who was elected not as a Communist, but as an Independent. An attempt was made by the speaker to pacify the students by declaring that the suspension of *Po Prostu* was only temporary. Following the address a resolution was drawn up requesting the government to order the continuation of the magazine. The leader of the meeting, having conferred with officers of the police massed outside, assured the students of safe conduct upon leaving. When the students streamed out of the building, however, new outbreaks and police violence occurred and again lasted for several hours. About twenty students were injured and thirty student leaders were arrested. All but eight were released the next morning.

On that morning, October 5, *Trybuna Ludu* (People's Forum), the official organ of the United Workers' party, published its decision to close *Po Prostu*. The statement indicated

that its editorial team, including party members working on it, for many months acted counter to the resolutions undertaken by the Central Party organ and thus sank to the level of barren negation, representing falsely the political and economic reality of the country, disseminating lack of faith in the feasibility of building Socialism, and in many cases advocating bourgeois concepts.[28]

The events of the previous two days were later described as defensive action of the police being forced to tackle some "adventuresome students who yelled anti-government slogans."

On that day and on the following day, October 6, the riots broadened to include working class youths and others described as "hooligans and dregs of society." A motorized police column was attacked during the afternoon of October 6 in the center of town. The attack was fought off, reputedly, by three battalions of police. In other parts of town, militia cars were attacked and stones were thrown at cars and at house windows. A sign "Freedom of Word" was placed on the student hostel building where the earliest disturbances occurred, but was later taken down. Earlier that same day, a three-member student delegation called on Prime Minister Gomulka to present its petition. That student delegation was later arrested at the student hostel. Disturbances continued for another day but became almost entirely non-student in character. The issue of the magazine *Po Prostu* was forgotten, and one by one different intellectual groups disassociated themselves from the riots. In one of the statements issued by the House Committee of the Narutowicz Square student hostel, the following was stated by the Polytechnic students: "We want to stress that the large majority of academic youth did not take part in the incidents, nor did they instigate any demonstrations that would dishonor the name of the students."[29]

It is the disassociation of the intellectuals from the demonstrations once they became working class in character that is a significant social class component in an otherwise political riot. At the height of the student disturbances during the first and second day, factory meetings of workers were held to condemn "street brawls." Now that the lower class youths appeared in the riots the intelligentsia in turn were in retreat. The journal

Sztandar Mlodych (The Banner of Youth) published an article on October 7 entitled "Enough," demanding that the authorities put an end to the disturbances. Even more interesting was the fact that the students of the University of Warsaw had not taken part in the demonstration at all and according to one source, actually assisted the police in quelling the riots.[30] On the subject of the intellectuals' withdrawal one eyewitness has written as follows:

Beginning with the third day, the riots became unpopular. The participation of the intelligentsia in the two last demonstrations was minimal and even those who took an active part in previous ones, from the third day, stayed aloof and condemned further demonstrations. . . . I will not forget a conversation with a man who at the outbreak of the demonstrations took a vital part and who told me later that the demonstration in Constitution Square was a "raid of hoolligans from Targowka, Mlocin, and Powisle" (working class districts of Warsaw). He probably was of the opinion that the revolution was good only as long as it was led by the intelligentsia. The reader may not know that on Constitution Square are located the most luxurious shops of Warsaw among them two large jewelry stores. It is a fact that during the entire demonstration not one window in these shops was broken, not one person could be found coveting the gold and diamonds and thus giving the reactionary press a chance for a display of moral indignation. The stones flew only at the policemen.[31]

The internal social class tensions within the groups of intellectuals can be stated in this case only in the form of a hypothesis. They are analogous to the broader animosities between the intelligentsia and workers. There is class tension in a political contest in which the Natolin group refers to the "Pulawianie" as "Zydy" (Jews) and is in turn referred to as "Chamy" (Peasants). These terms are hard to translate into English because in Polish they carry definitely derisive social class connotations, implying perverse intellectualism or cleverness on one side and vulgarity and uncouthness on the other. But these analogies do not adequately answer the question why the students of the University of Warsaw refrained from participation in the riots. One can only offer conjectures. Both the University of Warsaw and Warsaw Polytechnic are modern creations with a system of respective ranking that is not distinctly drawn. The University concentrates on humanities and thus enjoys cultural pre-eminence. The Polytechnic on the other hand, as already indicated, has an old and respected German tradition. Still there is a distinction made between the arts and the sciences, between the Latin and the German. It is accentuated by the fact that in Communist Poland the Polytechnic, which trains engineers, guarantees better salaries and a better share of power and voice in the management of government enterprises. It thus creates envy toward and rejection of the Polytechnic students by the students of Warsaw University. It is interesting to note that the oldest Polish university, Cracow, where Copernicus studied, prides itself as much on its scientific as on its humanistic tradition. Cracow students are reported to have staged a demonstration in favor of the Warsaw rioters after the *Po Prostu* suspension.

That social divisions between the University of Warsaw and Warsaw Polytechnic exist can be further deduced from different attitudes which the students at these two institutions display toward economic equality. According to a series of studies carried out by a group of Polish sociologists, it appears that, taken as a whole, for students of all the institutions of higher learning in Warsaw "acceptance of social ideological values is to be found more often in the lower regions of social stratification."[32] If we break down that group into respective universities the students of the University of Warsaw show themselves consistently more egalitarian.[33] In a manner reminiscent of the reversed prestige between the French universities and the *Grandes Écoles*, the students at the University of Warsaw appear now to be of humbler origin, more careful as to the chances of future employment. Open rioting, as indeed any excessive activity of a political nature, is considered less appropriate by these more academic and economically less privileged students. It is at the more self-assured and more independent Polytechnic that reform movements crowned by the October 1956 revolution arose. And it is students of this institution that set out to keep and to consolidate the political relaxations and achievements then won. The device of the *Stodola* (Barn) has been used not only to provide places for dancing and social gatherings, but also to present the now famous student political skits which became the major conveyors of political caricature. Another device was the magazine *Po Prostu*. Its demise had goaded the Polytechnic students to fury.

Just as the participation of non-students put the riots beyond the pale of any university student, so the participation in the riots by students in technology put them beyond the pale of students in the academic faculties. We see here a parallel to the animosities between academic and technological students in Montreal resulting in the burning of the student journal *Le Quartier Latin* alluded to previously. It is a rare educational system that can escape reflecting the distinctions of social class prevailing in society. Even in the heat of political struggle for and against Stalinist communism the students of Polish universities prove to be no exception.

Educational Cleavage: Rangoon

In addition to cleavages of ethnic, racial, and stratificatory nature there appears a fourth type which for want of a better name might be called educational. This is the type of unrest to which clearly defined outside grievances cannot be ascribed. Rather, the students exhibit discontent brought about by the educational process and as a result of the institutional situations in which they find themselves. The comparative panorama does not lack examples of unrest caused by such educational grievances, although usually social and political reasons can be found to be lurking in the background. A riot in Morocco, in Casablanca in 1965, for instance, was brought about by what appeared an arbitrary ruling of the authorities that students over certain ages may not take the *baccalauréat*, a measure which hit hard those who were retarded in their studies by war. Demonstrations and unrest have been frequent in France for a variety of educational reasons, of which best known are the student marches in Paris demanding that the government assign more liberal funds for the maintenance of the universities to relieve overcrowding. Last October there were disturbances in Kabul, Afghanistan. This was the occasion of the opening of the first popularly elected Parliament and students who overflowed the building as public spectators proved themselves unruly. Ultimately they had to be ejected, thus triggering off a three-day riot. In Scotland the outburst involving the throwing of flour bags during Chancellor Butler's inaugural lecture at the University of Glasgow in 1958 illustrates the traditional though curious pattern of attitudes of Scottish university students who to this day have the right to elect their university rectors and then haze their appointees.

We have selected the 1953 riot at the University of Rangoon as an example of this type of unrest. A newly independent country, Burma is almost by definition destined to a life of anti-colonial overtones. In reaction to the rankling inheritance from the British, the new national leadership emerged largely socialist in character. This raised the problem of left-wing reforms in general and Communism in particular to the forefront of national politics. These modern concerns were in-grafted upon a population which, if we are to believe the psychologists and anthropologists, was happy, carefree and easygoing on one side, and touchy, quick-tempered and opportunistic on the other.[34] The result was a somewhat unregulated political process, and by consequence, somewhat chaotic and uneven educational provisions.

This situation had registered itself from the beginning upon the educational life of the University of Rangoon. "The University of Rangoon was founded under conditions of virtual siege and appears to have remained in that state for 43 years."[35] Already in December 1920, two days before its official opening, the University was a victim of a strike by students, outraged by a purely educational requirement that the freshman year should be a year of probation. The celebrated student strike in 1936, in which the Burmese national leaders including the late Prime Minister U Nu had their apprenticeship, resulted from causes "so trivial that the participants are generally embarrassed at their mention."[36] There was a strike in 1953 and again in 1956.[37] As late as July 1962, the Student Union building at the University of Rangoon was blown up by the government forces in reprisal for what were considered to be irresponsible student actions.[38] This was the last of several riots to date.[39]

The September–October 1953 riots at Rangoon began with registration As related by an eyewitness, whose account will be chiefly relied upon in the entire survey of the strike:

Registration had been unusually heavy and the hostels were inadequate to meet the needs of the expanding student body. In competition for space, a large number of students had simply pre-empted hostel beds without leave from University authorities, and occupied them on squatters' rights. Repeated pleas and mild directives from the administration, requesting the squatters to relinquish their quarters and be assigned properly, along with the rest of the applicants, were ignored. Nevertheless, the authorities were loath to create an incident by taking a more forceful action. This vacillation encouraged among the students a vogue of contempt for authority which eventually brought disrepute on the whole university body, and became a subject—both the vacillation and the vogue—of severe censure from the newspapers and the general public.[40]

The registration incident was soon to be topped by another incident connected with the mid-semester student union elections. The contest was between two political parties, a Democratic Student Organization, a government-supported Socialist group, on one side, and the Progressives, a Communist-supported party, on the other. In the nature of the contest of political parties in the country at large, the relations between the two parties on campus were calculated to be bitter. Prior to election day, groups of students roamed the campus on foot, in old trucks and jeeps and in motorcades, shouting slogans, waving banners and singing long into the night. On election day the riotous behavior continued and in the afternoon, sensing impending defeat, the Progressives invaded the polling station, seized the ballot box and destroyed it. Thus, the election did not come to pass at all. The University authorities chose to ignore this incident again, thereby further contributing to the students' feeling of impunity.

The actual strike took place when the time for mid-year vacation was announced. Toward the end of the first semester the University decided that the usual one-month vacation would be shortened to two weeks. The student body, now united by so unpopular a measure, rose instantly in protest. A Full-month Vacation Implementation Committee was formed, which delivered an ultimatum to the University administration. A token strike was called for September 29, 1953, and successfully carried out by almost the entire student body, thus rendering ineffective the University's threat of the expulsion of the strikers. Even though the students of the Faculty of Education were originally out of sympathy with the main body of students, the strikes now spread to teacher training institutes and secondary schools.

Faced with a total debacle the University appealed to the Prime Minister in his capacity of honorary Chancellor. The meeting between the Prime Minister and five elected student delegates received wide press coverage. Emboldened by this recognition, the students did not obey U Nu's demand that they call off the strike. The Prime Minister was forced to appeal to the nation in a radio appearance. He revealed that he himself had ordered the shortening of vacations. He claimed that only 118 days or four months out of the year were occupied by instruction time, and that such time should be expanded in view of the need for trained personnel. He blamed student unrest on Communist leadership on this occasion and censured the students severely for having caused disturbances outside the building in which the University Council was in session—disturbances which included attacking police cars sent to the rescue.

In spite of the Prime Minister's appeal the strike went on as scheduled and was not disturbed for twenty-four hours. It was on the following day that military police, fully armed, and the fire brigade invaded the university campus and cleared it of the strikers. Shots were exchanged as the police charged with fixed bayonets, but no one was killed and few students were injured seriously. Most of the leaders of the strike were arrested, others fled. Two thousand students applied for special leave to go home and were permitted to do so without adverse consequences. Only a remnant of the strikers supported by secondary school students paraded through downtown Rangoon with signs demanding the release of their imprisoned leaders and later attempted to raise money on the campus for their legal defense.

Having broken the strike, the government again assumed exceedingly lenient methods. U Nu again addressed the nation committing the government to pay legal fees to defend the arrested leaders of the strike. Actually no penalty except expulsion from the university was imposed upon them. Others prominently involved in the strike had their scholarships canceled. All other students were re-admitted to the University provided they submit a statement undersigned by the parents promising henceforth to obey university regulations.

The story of this riot is a story of unruliness and rebellion for no good cause. The incident had plenty of political overtones to be sure, and there is some suspicion of an organized Communist participation, but the significance of Rangoon in comparison with other cases is that the causes of the disturbance were if anything educational. In spite of efforts at broadening the intake, the students are still recruited primarily from Burma's upper classes[41] and are in a sense accustomed to be unruly with impunity. As one authority put it, "they fail to distinguish between a university and a school."[42] On the other side, lack of firm handling by the University authorities had clearly encouraged riotous activity among the students. In addition, historical precedents for settling grievances through strikes was for, rather than against, upheaval. The Rangoon riot is thus one model of a student unrest directed internally against the institutional milieu in which they live.

The educational types of unrest are multiple and await a job of systematic classification. First, as indicated for Burma by a recent study, sexual limitations and cultural difficulties attendant upon meeting young women play an important role.[43] Problems connected with the sexual life of students are a frequent source of irritation in many universities. Restrictions on visits in dormitories, whether at Harvard or at the University of Moscow, may result in tensions released through "climbing in" or brawling at student dances. Second, when university education is restrictive, for instance when entrance examinations are very severe, students who succeed in passing them may experience a sense of release which sometimes generates unrest. This is the reason behind the impetuosity of freshmen in the universities of France and Japan. Third, in mass education the appearance of students of a wide spread of ability may present the university authorities with student demands for more tutoring and more classroom attention. In the U.S.A. such demands were presented to secondary schools in the last century, causing a revolution in curricular offerings. The demands for more attention to teaching now presented to American universities, at which research-mindedness and frequent absences of faculty are notable, are portents of the arrival of mass education at the university level. More students now demand that universities behave like a school instead of a community of scholars. Fourth, rivalry between different groups of students which occasionally causes unrest need not be political, economic, or social. Student factions form to win sport competitions, to control beauty contests or editorial policies of student newspapers. In German universities, for instance, as in American, animosities between different fraternities may have a casual or traditional rather than social character. Fifth, good or bad lectures condition student attitudes toward universities. The strain of hard study for harsh examinations in Russia, or contempt because of the absence of such severity in India, may trigger student restlessness. Some considerable inroads have been made toward understanding educationally conditioned disturbances.[44] But more work is needed to ascertain the conditions potentially capable of embroiling the students in activity against the university.

Discussion

The four illustrations presented are an attempt to classify types of student unrest which contain elements other than *Weltschmerz* of a general nature. These inter-group tensions add fuel and often act as a trigger to student demonstrations. The broader dissatisfactions of students with the adult world are always present below the surface. But since such alienation extends across whole generations, it would seem to be a necessary but not a sufficient cause of open student rebellion. Intergeneration tensions cannot adequately explain in any one country the extremes of discontent which prompt some groups of students to take the law into their own hands. Such groups are usually small proportions of the entire student body and an infinitesimal proportion of the age group. While some do not, many others peacefully pursue their studies and many others outside the universities establish families and have gainful employment as full-fledged adults.

The conflict between generations, the process of alienation of young people that begins in adolescence, is at the base of student unrest. A search for a separate place in the adult world naturally extends into college days. The insistence on "being left alone," on "being allowed to be oneself," ends up at that age level as an uncompromising idealism of the student and his yearning for a better world. But these are simply ways by which fledgling adults establish the identity of their own generation. As states of mind they seldom have significant and immediate consequences in the form of incitement to riots. Historically some societies, the English and the American as instances, have been for at least a hundred years singularly devoid of student demonstrations. Until the riots for or against civil rights were ushered in a decade ago, the history of American universities registered hardly more than a sequence of panty raids. In England too, until recently, nothing more momentous than an occasional ducking of an occasional "fairy" has ruffled the serenity of academic quadrangles. By contrast, in other societies, for instance in Latin American universities, students riot regularly as if by ancient tradition. In several countries, Argentina, Uruguay or Bolivia, the constitutional *cogobierno* provides for active participation of students in university councils. Yet discontent and disturbances flare up continuously. The psychological maturation and integration of youth into adult society does not express itself in the same way in the two Americas. In world perspective it is not consistently responsible for youth ferment of a violent nature.

Having seen the students of earlier generations unaroused on one continent by the United States' betrayal of the League of Nations, the great depression, or McCarthy's inquisitions and on the other continent by famine, collectivization, and Stalin's purges, it is hard to attribute an exclusive role in arousing unrest to the civil rights struggle and war in Vietnam here, and to the refusal of the authorities to publish symbolic poetry there. Intergenerational conflict arises because epochs and conditions change. Youth of America, born after World War II, were born after the racial integration of the Armed Forces and after court victories in Southern universities assured an admission of a future elite of Negro civil rights lawyers. They simply have no "feel" for "the American dilemma" of the older generation raised in an age of harsher race divisions. To Western generations that lived through the age of Stalin and the era of the American abandonment of China to Communism, the war in Vietnam appears a logical link in a chain of efforts to contain Chinese influence in Japan, in Korea, in Taiwan, in Malaysia, in the Philippines. A generation too young to remember Stalin is more likely to think in terms of people-to-people contact, the Peace Corps, and the atom bomb, rather than be moved by the specter of Communism. Similar splits affect the Soviet Union. All those born before the revolution could be brought to heel by the government and made to abide by its interpretation of Communism either because of the memories of how bad the times were before the revolution and how they have improved, or through the threat of being accused as *radiski* (radishes), red on the outside but white inside. No weapons of this kind can be used against youth, born under Communism, raised under Communism, and only too apt to blame the older generation, their mentors, for their own deviations. Intergenerational conflicts are a potent force and can topple governments as did Turkish students in the case of Menderes and Korean students in the case of Syngman Rhee. But conflict along age lines seldom appears by itself; intergroup tensions usually reveal themselves at some decisive point sooner or later.

Student disturbances most frequently seem to be the doing of a small, determined, and tightly organized group with a grudge, not so much against the world as is, as against some of its vital components. What changes is the temperature of the student feeling at large which gives these leadership groups a chance to place themselves at the head of "liberation" movements. All universities train the elites. In all appear sons of the elites firmly and securely bound to succeed their fathers. In all appear also some sons of the "have nots" aware that their talent will carry them into the ranks of the elite. Such students seldom riot. The activists are rather a coalition of the splinters of these groups: sons of the elite who for some reason or for the time being don't want to join it, who instead want "to get even with their fathers"; and sons of the "have-nots" whose prospects of absorption into the elite are not secure or not attractive and who instead of "joining" elect to "lick" it. The coalition of these two groups is usually unbeatable. The rebel sons of the elite supply the know-how of how to operate and to rock the establishment. The rebel "have-nots" supply the fury and the determination to forge ahead which only those who feel "left out" can muster. Whenever and wherever the students are not bound for the ranks of the Establishment, either because they do not want or cannot expect political power or economic well-being, that youngest and very vigorous age group among dissatisfied intellectuals lets its weight be felt throughout the system. The immediate and often unpredictable incidents on the basis of which riots flare up have behind them more long-term inter-group dissatisfactions which are more predictable.

Such a thesis is disenchanting. The view that students riot not that right may prevail, but because they have not been bought off by the social system, may appear cynical. But at bottom ancient truths may be vindicated or new justice forced even by such lowly motivation. Values apart, the "vertical" approach to student riots improves predictability. In a rapidly expanding spectrum of higher education, knowledge of all symptoms of the coming student "malaise" may help to prevent it in the interest of preserving general felicity.

Notes

1. Thanks are due to Karlann Puerschner, Barry Laffan, and Mary Bereday who assisted in the preparation of this chapter.
2. There were disturbances at Nanyang University (Chinese) in Singapore on October 31, 1965, one of several riots in Malaysia. For references to ethnic problems in the University of Ceylon see, among others, Joseph Fischer, "Universities and the Political Process in Southeast Asia," *Pacific Affairs*, XXXVI (Spring 1964), No. 1, p. 10; and Bryce Ryan, "The Dilemmas of Education in Ceylon," *Comparative Education Review*, IV (October 1960), No. 2, pp. 90–91.
3. Paul Nash, "Quality and Equality in Canadian Education," *Comparative Education Review*, V (October 1961), No. 2, p. 120.
4. *Le Quartier Latin*, LVIII (November 2, 1965), No. 15, p. 3. (My translation from the French.)
5. "Qu'est-ce que l'UGEQ" (mimeographed, n.d.). Received through the courtesy of Michele Beauchamp, Secretary General of UGEQ. Thanks are also due to other Canadian referents: Magdelhayne Buteau of McGill University and Edouard Cloutier, Secretary General of AGEUM.
6. *Etudiant Citoyen*, Numéro spécial (October 1965).
7. See also Roger P. Magnuson, "Secular Trends in French Canadian Education," *Comparative Education Review*, VII (June 1963), No. 1, pp. 43–46.
8. "A considerable number of universities include the president of the alumni association as a member of the central administration board; no one has had the daring to grant students the same privilege. Many difficulties would be averted if the students felt themselves more closely associated with the administration of the various levels of the university and if they were kept informed of the difficulties and problems confronting their institutions." *Report of the Royal Commission of Inquiry on Education in the Province of Quebec*, Part II: "The Pedagogical Structures of the Educational System, A. The Structures and the Levels of Education" (1964), pp. 242–243.
9. The following are a few recent quotations: "To become a master of its destiny Quebec must disengage itself from the political-economic stranglehold of the Americans and the Anglo-Saxons. *Le Quartier Latin*, LVIII (November 13, 1965), No. 18, p. 2.
   "McGill University is a menace to the Quebec nation. It is, therefore, imperative to destroy it. . . . It is masochism to maintain a foreign and luxurious institution in our country when we lack resources for ourselves." *Ibid.* (November 4, 1965), No. 16, p. 4.
   "Not to be naïve, one has to admit that Anglo-Saxon capital more generally

tends to help an institution like McGill rather than the University of Montreal or Laval University. This is not raising the cry of racism but rather a question of the just distribution of the funds of the community for its universities." *Ibid.* (December 9, 1965), No. 21, p. 2. (My translations from the French.)

10. *McGill Daily,* LVI (November 29, 1965), No. 51, p. 4.
11. Jacques Dupuis in *McGill Daily,* LVI (December 3, 1965), No. 55, p. 4.
12. See Seymour Martin Lipset and Philip G. Altbach, Chapter 7, this book.
13. James S. Coleman, *Nigeria, Background to Nationalism* (Berkeley and Los Angeles: University of California Press, 1960), p. 145.
14. Hugh H. Smythe and Mabel M. Smythe, *The New Nigerian Elite* (Stanford: Stanford University Press, 1960), p. 52.
15. J. T. Saunders, *University College, Ibadan* (Cambridge: Cambridge University Press, 1960).
16. Kenneth Mellanby, *The Birth of Nigeria's University* (London: Methuen, 1958).
17. Smythe and Smythe, *op. cit.,* p. 64.
18. Mellanby, *op. cit.,* p. 245.
19. Willfried Fenser, "Die Universitäten in Nigeria und ihr Beitrag," in Hans N. Weiler, ed., *Erziehung und Politik in Nigeria* (Freiburg im Breisgau: Verlag Rombach, 1964), pp. 211–212. (My translation from the German.)
20. Hugh H. Smythe, "Disturbances at University College, Ibadan," *School and Society,* LXXXVI (April 12, 1958), No. 2130, pp. 175–176.
21. Smythe and Smythe, *op. cit.,* p. 187.
22. George Z. F. Bereday and J. A. Lauwerys, *Higher Education: The Year Book of Education, 1959* (New York and London: World Book Company and Evans Bros., 1959), Editors' Introduction, p. 21.
23. Sir Alexander Carr-Saunders, *The Sociological Review,* VIII (July 1960), No. 1, p. 145.
24. Alison Peers [Bruce Truscot], *Red Brick University* (London: Faber and Faber, 1943). (This was the first of several on the subject.)
25. See Herbert Passin, *Society and Education in Japan* (New York: Teachers College Press, 1965), especially pp. 113 ff.
26. See Lipset and Altbach, *op. cit.*
27. George Z. F. Bereday, *Comparative Method in Education,* Ch. 3, "Education and Indoctrination in Poland" (New York: Holt, Rinehart and Winston, 1964), p. 66.
28. Cf. *Kultura i Spoleczenstwo* (Culture and Society), I (October–December 1957), No. 4, p. 182. (My translation from the Polish.)
29. *New York Times,* October 7, 1957, p. 8.
30. *Keesing's Contemporary Archives 1957–58,* p. 15872.
31. Witold Jedlicki, *Klub Krzywego Kola* (the Club of the Crooked Wheel) (Paris: Institut Literacki, 1963), p. 47. (My translation from the Polish.)
32. Stefan Nowak, "Social Attitudes of Warsaw Students," *The Polish Sociological Bulletin,* Nos. 1–2 (3–4) (January–June 1962), p. 99.

33. Stefan Nowak, "Egalitarian Attitudes of Warsaw Students," *American Sociological Review*, XXV (April 1960), No. 2, pp. 225–227.

34. Lucian W. Pye, *Politics, Personality and Nation Building, Burma's Search for Identity* (New Haven and London: Yale University Press, 1962), p. 178.

35. Joseph Fischer, *Universities in Southeast Asia, An Essay on Comparison and Development* (Columbus, Ohio: Ohio State University Press, Kappa Delta Pi International Education Monographs, 1964), No. 6, p. 84.

36. Pye, *op. cit.*, p. 260.

37. The 1956 riot is described in J. Silverstein, "Politics, Parties and National Elections in Burma," *Far Eastern Survey*, December 1956, pp. 177–184.

38. Fischer, *op. cit.*

39. The 1962 riots are described in J. Silverstein and J. Wohl, "University Students and Politics in Burma," *Pacific Affairs*, XXVII (Spring 1964), No. 1, pp. 50–65.

40. George Mannello, "Student Strike at an Asian University—A Case History," *AAUP Bulletin*, XLIII (June 1957), No. 2, pp. 249–262.

41. Joseph Fischer, "Education and Political Modernization in Burma and Indonesia," *Comparative Education Review*, IX (October 1965), No. 3, p. 286.

42. Cf. Fischer, *Universities in Southeast Asia, op. cit.*, p. 87.

43. Joseph Fischer, "The University Student in South and Southeast Asia," *Minerva*, II (Autumn 1963), No. 1, p. 49.

44. See, for instance, Seymour Martin Lipset, Chapter 1, this book.

The Active Few: Student Ideology and Participation in Developing Countries

GLAUCIO A. D. SOARES

5

The emphasis in the press on student street demonstrations, riots, and the like may have given a distorted picture of student political opinion in developing countries. These demonstrations constitute a relatively small part of student political life, and only a small percentage of the total student body actually participates in them.

The main purpose of this chapter is to specify the ideological characteristics of student political activists and to differentiate them from the whole student body, that is, discerning how activists differ from the larger mass of apathetic students.

Political participation is a broad concept which has been used rather loosely by sociologists and political scientists alike. But political participation is not a monolithic concept, as it embodies different *forms, levels, and degrees of intensity*.[1] Thus, reading about politics, voting, and stoning embassies are different forms of participation. By the same token, reliance on survey data tends to obliterate these differences by simply treating them as varying forms of political participation. However, not only are they different actions, but they also involve different degrees of *intensity*. This intensity differential is not without consequences. Many more are likely to read about politics than to go and participate in a street demonstration. Conceiving various forms of political participation as having different degrees of intensity is in itself a good justification for analyzing those forms separately.[2] However, there are other reasons that justify this separation, the most important of which is that there is no inherent reason to assume that participants in a more intense form of politics are simply a random sample of the larger group of participants in a less intense form.[3]

Studies of political participation among national populations indicate that it is correlated with factors such as socio-economic status,[4] family structure,[5] and personality traits.[6] Embracing people of sharply different socio-economic levels, ages, and so on, such general research necessarily emphasizes broad differences within the population. University students, however, are a relatively homogeneous population. There is little variation among them in age, education, or class or status levels. Consequently an examination of participation differentials among them should point up the influence of factors which are difficult to isolate in studies of much more heterogeneous total populations.

Our efforts in studying the political behavior of students in many countries indicate that the principal correlates of participation differentials among university students are ideological variations. To be more explicit, *within* the universities studied, leftists tend to participate more than conservatives. The differential between them is greater in more intense forms of participation.

Any conclusion drawn from a study of student political participation is necessarily limited by the possibility that the factors correlated with being politically active in school may differ widely from those associated with local, regional, national or international politics. This point is particularly relevant to an analysis of the differences between leftist and conservative students, since, as we shall see, conservatives are more likely to deny legitimacy to *student* politics. To be explicit, *within* each of the universities studied, the radical student tends to participate more than the conservative student.[7]

Political Ideology and Student Role Image

Radical and conservative students have different role images. A radical orientation seems to be connected with an *integrated* role image, in the sense that the student role is not separated from the citizen role. Student life is seen as *part* of national political life.[8]

Conservative students, on the contrary, tend to see themselves as full-time students preparing for a career. They are more likely to think of the student days as a long-term investment leading toward a well-paid occupation. They are more concerned with technical professional problems than with national issues. They feel unhappy when university life is interwoven with national politics. A conservative orientation seems to be closely associated with a *compartmentalized*[9] and more professionalized student role image.[10]

Actually, these differences in the degree of compartmentalization of academic and political roles may ultimately reflect differences in the frame of reference that limits self-image. These factors may, in turn, reflect important cognitive and personality differences which may be linked to childhood experiences.

If the above assumptions are correct, conservative students should be more likely to oppose the political involvement of student movements and organizations. Consequently, conservative students should also be more critical of a direct relationship between student politics and national political parties.

Radicalism and Participation: A Nondirectional Approach

Logically, the relationship between "radicalism" and political participation should be nondirectional in ideological terms, i.e., radicals whether of the left or right are more likely to be active than conservatives. In this sense, both far leftists and far rightists should be more active politically than moderate students. However, to test these assumptions is difficult under contemporary political conditions. Since the defeat of Nazism in World War II, the far right has become very unfashionable in academic circles and its numerical strength is extremely small.[11] Thus, it is very difficult to test the nondirectional radicalism theory. In the data available to us, all the numerically significant radical groups are leftist. It is difficult therefore to test whether participation is associated with radicalism per se or with *leftist* radicalism.[12] Data from non-university populations do suggest that it is radicalism per se, not simply leftist radicalism, that is associated with heightened political interest and participation.

One possible test of this hypothesis at the university level is given by Indian data. The radical left is represented in Indian politics by the Communist party of India, and the moderate left by the Praja Socialist party.[13] The Congress party, in spite of its early socialist leanings, is nowadays at best a left-of-center party, and the Jan Sangh is a rightist group.[14] The proportion of the respondents preferring each party who declared that it is highly important that a job allow them to participate in political affairs before they consider it ideal, declines from 26 per cent among the Communists, to 22 per cent among the Socialists, to 13 per cent among Congress supporters, and then goes up to 22 per cent among those preferring the Jan Sangh.

Another question indicates that the percentage which gets as excited about politics as about something that happens in personal life declines from the Communists to the Socialists, goes further down among Congress party supporters and then recovers, reaching its peak among those preferring the Jan Sangh.[15]

Although admittedly one may legitimately disagree with a particular interpretation given to one of the various indicators of political radicalism in this section, data generally tend to confirm the hypothesis that the more "radical" the student, the more likely he is to be interested in and to participate in politics. In the few instances where data covering supporters of far right politicians and political parties were available, this tendency is borne out. Radicals are more interested and more likely to participate than middle-of-the-roaders. Campbell and associates, using U. S. data, found that "the stronger the individual's sense of attachment to one of the parties, the greater his psychological involvement in political affairs."[16] They show that interest in the 1956 campaign, and concern with its outcome, is higher among strong party identifiers than among weak party identifiers. These findings were confirmed by Berelson and associates[17] and Agger,[18] and suggest that the *intensity* of the partisanship and the belief *strength*, in addition to party preference, are associated with high participation.[19]

Evidence from applicants to the ITA (Air Force Technological Institute) in Brazil also indicates that high political interest and participation is associated *not* with a leftist ideology per se, but rather with the *strength* of the ideological beliefs, regardless of their directions. The percentage of the applicants who declared to be very interested in the next presidential elections is higher among those holding extreme attitudes toward Fidel Castro and Carlos Lacerda (an ultra-conservative Brazilian politician). Both those who agree completely and those who disagree completely with Castro's actions and ideas are more interested than the middle-of-the-roaders, the percentages being 46 among those who strongly agree, 32 among those who agree somewhat, 29 among those who disagree somewhat, climbing to 41 among those who strongly disagree with Fidel Castro. The same is true of Carlos Lacerda: 55 per cent of those who are completely in agreement with Lacerda's actions and ideas are very interested in next elections; this percentage drops to 31 per cent among those who agree a little with Lacerda, does not change significantly among those who disagree a little with Lacerda (33 per cent), and then increases five percentage points, up to 38 per cent, among those who strongly disagree with Lacerda.[20]

Radicalism and Participation
in National Politics

The previous reasoning may now be formalized in order to formulate a testable hypothesis, as follows: Radical (leftist) students are more interested and participate more in national politics than other students.

Data from several studies provide a test for the above hypothesis. Thus, a carefully drawn random sample of the philosophy faculty of the University of Brazil[21] shows that a positive attitude toward the legalization of the Brazilian Communist party (*Partido Comunista Brasileiros*, PCB) is positively related to interest in the last national elections.[22]

The percentage of Brazilian students claiming to be very interested or interested (*Muito interessado* or simply *interessado*) in the previous electoral campaign decreased from no less than 96 per cent among those who are completely in favor of the legalization, to 72 per cent among those who are moderately in favor (those who simply answered *a favor* or *mais ou menos a favor*) down to no more than 68 per cent among those who claimed to be completely against the legalization.[23] The same pattern appears when attitudes toward the Cuban blockade and the Alliance for Progress are used.

However, it may be argued that these findings may be idiosyncratic of the philosophy faculty, undoubtedly one of the most radical and politicized educational institutions in Latin America. In order to discuss this possibility, data from another Brazilian study, which covered several universities in four states, also showed that interest in political affairs is positively related to a leftist ideological position: whereas 52 per cent of those very interested in politics had a positive opinion of Fidel Castro (very good or good), only 29 per cent of those moderately interested, and 17 per cent of the slightly interested did so. Among those who were not at all interested in political affairs, only 12 per cent had a positive opinion of Castro.[24]

Similarly in Uruguay a study of students, which included a small sample of student leaders and followers, shows that radicalism is positively correlated with various forms of political interest and participation, as shown in Table 1.

Table 1 shows that radicals are consistently more active than conservatives. From heated discussions with a friend down to attendance at political meetings sponsored by political parties, radicals are more involved than conservatives.

This correlation between radicalism and political participation is not limited to one given form of political participation, such as discussing pol-

TABLE 1.

Percentage of Uruguayan Students Who Answered "Yes" to Four Questions on Political Participation (1963)[25]

Questions	Political Orientation	
	Radicals	Conservatives
Have you had any heated discussion with a friend?	91 (43)*	82 (28)
Have you taken part in a public manifestation?	86	54
Have you attended any meeting sponsored by a political party?	60	39
Have you worked actively in politics?	35	18

* Number in parentheses indicates size of sample from which percentage was computed. The totals are the same for all questions.

itics with friends, but it persists throughout the intensity continuum of different forms of political participation. Actually, as will be shown later on, the more intense the form of participation at hand, the greater the participation differentials between radicals and nonradicals are likely to be.

A study of Panamanian law students shows similar results. Using attitudes toward the nationalization of the Panama Canal as an indicator of radicalism, Goldrich found that nationalists (those who strongly agreed that the Canal should be nationalized) are more involved than moderates (those who agree, but not strongly, and those who disagree). Although nationalization of the Canal probably is accepted by the majority of the population, covering a wide political spectrum, many conservatives disagree with nationalization. Thus, although the nationalization question at best distinguishes between conservatives and the left-of-center groups, the findings do conform to our expectations, in the sense that those holding an *extreme* position toward the nationalization (those who strongly agreed) are more interested in national politics, are more likely to intend to participate in politics after graduation, discuss politics more, are more likely to have participated in street demonstrations, etc.[26]

Argentinian data[27] give further support to our position. Using a battery of three questions dealing with identity of interests with workers and industrialists, and with trust in workers holding government jobs, an index of radicalism was built.[28] Those answering all three questions in an extremely pro-worker, anti-industrialist direction were labeled "radicals."

Table 2 shows that radicals are more participant than other students, even
after the family's socio-economic status is allowed for.

TABLE 2.

**Percentage of University of Buenos Aires Students Who Answered "Yes"
to Three Questions on Political Participation, Classified According to
Political Orientation and Socio-Economic Status (1964)**

		Family Monthly Income in Pesos		
Questions	*Political Orientation*	*Less than $20,000*	*$20-49,999*	*$50,000 and over*
Do you often talk politics with your friends?				
	Radicals	61 (59)*	68 (37)	86 (22)
	Liberals	30 (153)	43 (155)	41 (133)
Do political events interest you as much as those of your personal life?				
	Radicals	66	62	55
	Liberals	28	35	34
Do you read newspapers and magazines about politics in general?				
	Radicals	95	95	95
	Liberals	74	72	74

* Number in parentheses indicates size of sample from which percentage was computed.
The totals are the same for all questions.

Table 2 shows that at each income level radicals are more participant.
Radicals are more likely to talk politics with friends, to read newspapers
and magazines about politics in general, and are as much interested by political events as by personal ones. All relationships are significant at .05
level, and are one-tailed. Actually, all except one are significant at the .01
level.

Data from the aformentioned Indian study supply further support to the
contention that political participation is higher among radicals even after
socio-economic status is controlled for. Taking the parent's or guardian's
monthly income in rupees as an indicator of socio-economic status, we see
that *within* each income category Communist party supporters are more
likely to claim that they "get as excited about politics as about things that
happen in their personal lives" in comparison to middle-of-the-road Con-

gress party supporters. All four differences are statistically significant at the .10 level, and their combined probability is less than .005. Thus, it is apparent that in India radical university students are politically more participant than Congress party supporters after socio-economic status is controlled for (Table 3).

TABLE 3.

Percentage of Indian Students Who Answered "Yes" to the Question, "Do You Get as Excited about Politics as about Things That Happen in Your Personal Life?" Classified According to Political Party Affiliation and Socio-Economic Status (1952)

| Party | Parent's or Guardian's Monthly Income in Rupees | | | |
	Less than 100	101-300	301-500	501 and more
Communist	70 (77)*	71 (146)	65 (81)	62 (113)
Congress	61 (141)	60 (327)	56 (183)	48 (298)

* Number in parentheses indicates size of sample from which percentage was computed.

On the other hand, it may also be seen that socio-economic status continues to influence political participation *after* ideology is controlled for. Interestingly enough, it is the student with *lower* socio-economic background who is the most likely to be motivated toward politics. This finding is not consistent with the Argentinian data.

The findings relating ideology to interest and participation in national politics receive further support from Brazilian data. The study of applicants to the *Instituto Tecnologico da Aeronautica*—ITA (Air Force Technological Institute), a renowned engineering school financed by the Brazilian Air Force, leads to similar conclusions.

The ITA data have the advantage that several other variables are also controlled, due to the nature of the population studied. Thus, sex (all males), age (all between 17 and 23), educational background (all high school graduates, applicants to a highly vocational engineering school), type of education (96 per cent went to scientific high schools) and marital status (98 per cent single) are either invariant or have very limited variance. Thus, demonstrating that the association between ideology and concern with politics remains even after so many possible relevant factors are controlled for, will give a greater weight to our hypothesis.

It is seen in Table 4 that those agreeing with Fidel Castro's ideas and actions are more likely to be concerned with national problems than those

TABLE 4.

Percentage of ITA Applicants Who Answered "Frequently" or "Sometimes" to the Question "Do You Think about National Problems, Analyzing Them and Elaborating Plans Mentally in Order to Solve Them?" Classified According to Their Socio-Economic Status and Their Degree of Agreement with Fidel Castro's Action and Ideas (Brazil, 1964)

Attitude toward Fidel Castro's Action and Ideas	Father's Highest Educational Attainment		
	Elementary or less	Secondary*	University*
Agree	73 (68)†	74 (95)	76 (38)
Somewhat Disagree	69 (83)	70 (73)	71 (38)
Totally Disagree	59 (240)	64 (320)	66 (180)

* Includes those who did not complete the full secondary or university course.
† Number in parentheses indicates size of sample from which percentage was computed.

who disagree with them. This relationship holds within each of the three socio-economic levels considered. Thus, in an extremely homogeneous population, the association between ideology and political participation subsists.

On the other hand, within each ideological group it is the student from middle and upper class origins who is most likely to be concerned with national problems. These results are congruent with the Argentinian findings and incongruent with the Indian ones, thus suggesting that there may be interesting differences in patterns of recruitment and in the academic structure between Latin American countries, on the one hand, and India, on the other.

So far the data presented in support of the radicalism-participation hypothesis have been limited to underdeveloped countries. The question immediately appears as to the extension of this generalization to more developed countries. Data for the United States suggest that the relationship between ideology and participation is also valid in developed countries. Using a battery of six questions dealing with attitudes toward labor, the role of government, welfare state, war against communism,[29] etc., we divided a population of college students in three categories: the consistent right, the consistent left, and a center block which includes a large variety of political positions. Only those whose answers in all six questions pointed to the right were included in our consistent right group; the consistent left was composed of those who answered all six questions in a pro-labor direction.

By conventional scaling techniques we separated the highest and the lowest possible scores from the larger group of intermediate scores. It is in this sense that our respondents occupy extreme positions in the ideological continuum. In a statistical sense, those groups are also extreme, for together they represented less than 5 per cent of the total number of respondents.

TABLE 5.

Percentage of U.S. Students at Eleven Universities Who Answered "Yes" to the Question "Do You Get as Worked Up about Something That Happens in Political or Public Affairs as about Something That Happens in Personal Life?" Classified According to Ideological Preference and Socio-Economic Status (1952)[30]

Ideology	Family Income in Dollars		
	Less than $5,000	$5,000–10,000	More than $10,000
Consistent Left	43 (14)*	67 (42)	58 (26)
Center	39 (1405)	38 (1429)	42 (1148)
Consistent Right	68 (41)	50 (20)	47 (38)

* Number in parentheses indicates size of sample from which percentage was computed.

Table 5 shows that those holding extreme views, both left and right, are more politicized. This gives further support to our initial contention that it is radicalism per se, and not only leftist radicalism, that is associated with heightened political participation and interest.

In the lower income group, the percentage corresponding to the "participants" (those who "get as worked up about something that happens in political or public affairs as about something that happens in their personal lives") drops from 43 per cent among leftist radicals to 39 per cent among right radicals. Taking the middle income group, the curvilinearity is also present: from a high of 67 per cent among the radical leftists, to a low of 38 per cent among the middle-of-the-roaders, the percentage of participants goes up again among the radical rightists, reaching 50 per cent. Finally, in the case of the higher income group, the same trend can be observed, the corresponding percentages being 58, 42, and 47. The pattern, therefore, is a consistent one.

An Italian youth study also suggests that Neo-fascists (MSI supporters) and Communists are more interested in national and international political developments than Christian Democrats or Socialists. Furthermore, their degree of party and electoral commitment and decisiveness is also greater.

In response to the question, "If elections were held tomorrow, would you know for which party to vote, or would you still be undecided?" 85 per cent of both Communists and Neo-fascists answered that they would have decided, as opposed to 80 per cent of the Christian Democrats, 76 per cent of the Socialists and 50 per cent of those preferring other parties.[31]

Data from a Communist society also support our hypothesis. Nowak, in a careful study of Polish youth, shows that there is a cluster of attitudes which the author entitles the "socio-economic syndrome" that is characterized by acceptance of socialism, a positive attitude toward Marxism *and* a need for political activity. This syndrome is, as Nowak puts it, an attitudinal cluster "in which the three items (i.e., attitude to Marxism, socialism, and the need for political activity) occur together consists of the fact that they are located in the context of far-reaching acceptance of a nationalized economy and its management by the workers' councils. . . ."[32]

Thus, the relationship between ideology and participation seems to cut across developmental and political lines. It is a valid generalization for Latin American countries, such as Argentina, Brazil, and Uruguay, and for a culturally distinctive underdeveloped country—India—as well. It holds in a semi-developed country, such as Italy, and in a developed one, the United States. Furthermore, the little available evidence from a Communist society also supports our hypothesis.

Radicalism and Extreme Participation: Strikes and Demonstrations

In the preceding sections we have shown that various forms of political participation, interest and involvement are related to political ideology. In all these, however, there was no systematic evidence of a clear "cutting point" that would separate the active participants and the extremely motivated from others on the basis of political ideology.

However, active participation in strikes and demonstrations provides a sharp ideological cutting point. The radical left is outstanding in providing a large share of the demonstrators, entirely out of proportion with its actual support in the whole student body.

Brazilian data show a sharp drop in active participation from those who *completely* favor the legalization of the Communist party in Brazil, to those who just favor it. In the indicators of active participation, attendance to *comicios* or political rallies, attendance to other political meetings, and participation in the last strike, there is a sharp drop of 30 percentage points or more, when we move from the position of full support for the legalization of the Communist party to less radical positions. Thus, although extreme supporters of the legalization of the Communist party represented only 32 per cent of the philosophy faculty student body, they represented 89 per cent of those who always attended political rallies and 73 per cent of those who always attended other types of political meetings. Furthermore, participation in the last student strike is clearly associated with radicalism: taking only sophomores and up (the strike was in the preceding year, therefore most freshmen did not attend), we find that 67 per cent of those completely in favor of the registration of the Communist party participated actively in the strike, as opposed to only 31 per cent of those moderately in favor of the registration, and to no more than 4 per cent of those who opposed the registration.[33] Therefore, it is exactly in the more *extreme* forms of student political participation that the differentials between radicals and other political groups are magnified.

Japanese data fully confirm this point. A random sample of the University of Tokyo shows that 63 per cent of the Communists had a positive participation in the student movement, as opposed to only 8 per cent of the socialists and 1 per cent of the liberal democrats (conservative). Conversely, no less than 41 per cent of the liberal democrats declared to have had no participation whatsoever in the student movement, as opposed to only 9 per cent of the socialists and a mere 2 per cent of the communists.[34]

Not only is a radical ideology associated with broader interest and participation in political affairs in general, but radicalism is closely linked with party membership and active participation in meetings, demonstrations, rallies, etc. Therefore, if one tries to estimate the real extent of student radicalism by mass demonstrations, severe distortions are bound to appear as the radical leftist groups are likely to be greatly over-represented among demonstrators.

Radicalism and Extreme Participation: Mobilization by Political Parties

Higher mobilization by political parties is, of course, related to higher participation. Thus, one would expect that the more active students are more likely to belong to political parties, by comparison with the less active ones. As radicals are more active than liberals or conservatives, the obvious conclusion is that more radicals have been mobilized by political parties. Using Argentinian data we see that although the proportion of party members in the whole student body is relatively small, 10 per cent in the University of Buenos Aires, it is clear that radical students are more likely to be party members than students with other political orientations. The crucial test is given by the proportion of party-affiliates among students with different political orientations. The data clearly support our reasoning: among those in the low-income group, 20 per cent of the radicals belong to a political party or group; but only 7 per cent of the controls do so; among those in the middle income group, differences are reduced but they still point to the predicted direction: 16 per cent and 9 per cent; finally, among the high income group, radicals continue to be more likely to belong to a political party (18 per cent as opposed to 8 per cent).[35]

Thus, it seems justifiable to claim that radicalism is conducive to extreme participation. The implications of this finding are clear: other things being equal, radical political parties have an influence on the student life that is out of proportion with the numerical support that they receive from the student body at large. Not only do radical political parties have among their followers the most active and participant students, but they have also been able to mobilize through formal affiliation a higher proportion of their ideological supporters.

Intensity of the Form of Participation and Ideological Differentials in Participation

The sections dealing with participation in strikes, demonstrations, etc., and with mobilization by political parties suggested that the radical/non-radical participation differentials are larger in these extreme forms than in less extreme forms of participation such as reading about politics in the papers or simply being interested in national and international affairs. In this section we will try to present systematic data in support of the contention that the participation ratio between radicals and non-radicals increases with the intensity of the form of participation.

The intensity of each specific form of political participation will be measured simply by the proportion of each sample which actually participated in each one of them. Thus, the greater the proportion, the *least* intensive the participation.

Using data from the 1962 study of the philosophy faculty of the University of Brazil we see that in the least intensive indicator of political activism, interest in the next presidential elections, differences between radicals and non-radicals are relatively small; 96 per cent of the radicals are "very" or "a lot" interested, as compared with 70 per cent of the non-radicals. Taking the percentage who go to political meetings, the differences increase considerably, as 83 per cent of the radicals answered affirmatively, but only 46 per cent of the non-radicals did so. Finally, participation in the last student strike maximizes the differentials: 42 per cent of the radicals participated, as opposed to 13 per cent of the non-radicals. Dividing the corresponding participation percentages, we obtain a participation ratio. Plotting this ratio against the intensity measure, we can see very clearly that the ratio increases with the participation intensity (Table 6).

TABLE 6.

Ideology and Participation Differentials, University of Brazil (Philosophy Faculty), 1962

	Radicals	Others	Participation (Radical/Non-radical) Ratio
% interested in presidential elections	96	70	137
% attending political meetings	83	46	180
% participating in last student strike	42	13	323

Thus, the participation ratio increases from 137 in the interest question to 180 in the political meetings question, jumping to 323 in the strike question. This increase seems to substantiate our point.

However, in the most intense item—participation in the last student strikes—we combine *two* factors which are related to the ideological differentials in political participation. On the one hand, strikes rank high in the *intensity* scale and, on the other hand, they belong in the realm of *student* politics and one cannot separate the influence of the one from the other. Although unquestionably the trend is toward an increase of the participation ratio with participation intensity, when the question dealing with student strikes is included, an uncontrolled element is introduced.

Nevertheless, the Argentinian study throws further light on this point. This time, in order to use behavior rather than attitudes as an indicator of ideology, we reclassified the student population in accordance with their voting behavior: those who in the last two student elections *consistently* voted for liberal parties were classified as radicals; those who voted in *both* elections for liberal parties entered as liberals, and those voting for conservative parties in the last two elections entered as conservatives. Those who only voted once and those who changed their voting orientation were excluded, with the purpose of controlling the possible variations due to political consistency or inconsistency. Both in terms of national *and* student politics, intensity is positively associated with the radical/non-radical participation differentials.

TABLE 7.

Ideology and Participation Differentials, University of Buenos Aires, 1964

	Radicals	Others	Radical/Non-radical Ratio
I—*Student Politics*			
% who read about university politics in magazines	86	67	128
% who voted in last student elections	72	55	131
% who attend student political meetings	49	31	158
II—*National Politics*			
% who read about politics in general in magazines	90	70	129
% who belong to a political party	15	8	188
Number of cases	(176)	(232)	

Looking at Table 7 we see that the decrease in the degree of participation among radical students is not as sharp as among non-radical students. This can be moderately sensed in the student politics section, as the radical/non-radical participation ratio increases gradually as intensity increases, starting with a low of 128 in the least intensive question (read about university politics in magazines), increasing slightly to 131 when it comes to actual voting, and increasing further to 158 in the political meeting attendance question. Thus, it is clear that the over-representation of radical students is itself a variable with higher values in the more intensive forms of political participation. This over-representation is particularly strong when it comes to membership in national parties as the ratio is 188.

Radicalism, Political Legitimacy, and the Compartmentalization Hypothesis

It could be argued that these differences could be explained in terms of participation styles, that radical students are more likely to emphasize street and mass demonstrations as a matter of political strategy. Obviously, this argument has to be taken into account. For one thing, since the overwhelming majority of university students come from the middle and upper classes, which are politically conservative, radical students are more likely than conservative students to disagree politically with their family and therefore look for other outlets for political participation. It could also be argued that radical students are usually at odds with the governmental ideology and that this forces them into different strategies, such as strikes and mass demonstrations. However, unsystematic impressionistic evidence from Nazi Germany, Fascist Italy, and Communist societies still points to a higher participation of radical students especially in the more intense forms.

I feel that the participation styles hypothesis may contribute to the present theory, but that it in no way replaces it. The compartmentalization hypothesis received substantial factual support which cannot be accounted for by the styles hypothesis. Thus, data dealing with the *legitimacy* of student politics and of its relations with national politics systematically point to the fact that radical students are more likely to give legitimacy to student politics and to accept a direct link with, say, national political parties.

The degree of legitimacy given to student organizations and movements is an important point which has to do with the compartmentalization hypothesis.[36] Although legitimacy is usually given to student organizations by large majorities of the student body, a significant few oppose the very existence of such organizations. This opposition must be understood in its own context. Conservative students wage a permanent war against student interference in politics. As most large scale student organizations are usually politically active and ideologically committed, some conservative students may come to believe that student organizations will inevitably end up politically involved. It could also be predicted that a larger group will recognize the legitimacy of student organizations, but oppose their involvement in politics. These students probably do not perceive student organizations' political involvement as inevitable. Thus, whereas only 9 per cent of the students at the philosophy faculty thought that UNE (National Students' Union) and UME (Metropolitan Students' Union) are not necessary to protect the students' interests, a much larger group, comprising 24 per cent of the sample, expressed the belief that students should not have political activities. This meant that *more* students are likely to oppose students' political involvement than to oppose student organizations per se.

The over-all relationship between ideology and support for student organizations is clearly seen as support for UNE (National Students' Union) and UME (Metropolitan Students' Union) goes from a high of 98 per cent among those who are completely in favor of the "legalization" (registration) of the Brazilian Communist party, to 85 per cent among those who are in favor (but not completely, including those who answered in favor and more or less in favor), to a low of 55 per cent among those who are completely opposed to the registration.

Japanese data obtained from a random sample of the University of Tokyo also support the above position: no less than 80 per cent of the Communists support the student movement (political and social) wholeheartedly, as opposed to only 33 per cent of the socialists and no more than 10 per cent of the liberal democrats.[37]

The ITA (Air Force Technical Institute) study provides us with further data bearing on this hypothesis.

TABLE 8.

Percentage of ITA Students Who Stated That Students Should Not Participate in Politics, Classified According to Their Socio-Economic Status and Their Attitude toward Fidel Castro (Brazil, 1964)

Student Attitude	Father's Highest Educational Attainment		
	Elementary	Secondary	University
Pro-Fidel	9 (67)*	9 (95)	11 (38)
Somewhat against Fidel	24 (82)	21 (68)	19 (37)
Totally against Fidel	27 (234)	30 (315)	31 (173)

* Number in parentheses indicates size of sample from which percentage was computed.

Table 8 shows that the association between leftist values and the degree of compartmentalization between student life and politics holds even after socio-economic status is held constant. In all three socio-economic levels, the differences are in the predicted direction. One should re-emphasize that, due to the characteristics of the population studies, sex is invariant, and age, educational background, type of education, and marital status have little variance. Even so, radical students are clearly more likely to think that students should engage in political activities.

The high legitimacy attributed by radicals to student politics can also be seen in what different political groups define as legitimate *areas* of student political activity. Nasatir's study included questions on the accepted degree of student participation in university life, by contrast with the faculty members' participation. Systematically, radical students are more likely to believe that student participation in university administration life should be equal to or greater than that of the faculty.

TABLE 9.

Percentage of Students at the University of Buenos Aires Who Believe That the Participation of Students in the Election of University Administrators Should Be Equal to or Greater than That of the Faculty, Classified According to Socio-Economic Status and Political Orientation (1964)

	Family Monthly Income in Pesos		
Political Orientation	Less than $20,000	$20,000–49,999	$50,000 and over
Radicals	82 (59)*	79 (37)	86 (22)
Others	60 (153)	61 (155)	57 (33)

* Number in parentheses indicates size of sample from which percentage was computed.

Table 9 shows that at each socio-economic level, radicals are more likely to think that the participation of students should be equal to or greater than that of the faculty.

Notice that this question refers to the election and appointment of high university officials, an area in which North American students would never have dreamed of having a say. Nevertheless, we see that even among non-radical students acceptance of student participation is very high, thus suggesting strong national differences in the degree of legitimacy of student participation in university politics. Actually, differences are also institutional, for in the Catholic University located in Buenos Aires, throughout the ideological continuum legitimacy is much lower than in the University of Buenos Aires. All differences are significant at the 5 per cent level, and at the highest and lowest income groups, they are significant at the 1 per cent level. Q coefficients suggest that this association is a fairly strong one, as they vary from .66 at the top income level to .39 at the middle level, with a coefficient of .44 at the lowest level.

Uruguayan data from the aforementioned study directed by Van Aiken lead to similar conclusions, as the same question used in the Argentinian study was also applied to Uruguayan students: 75 per cent of the radical students agreed that students' participation should be equal to or greater than that of the faculty, by comparison with 70 per cent of the non-radicals. In both countries differences between the ideological groups persist when questions dealing with faculty appointment, preparation of bibliographies and course outlines, admissions policy, regulations affecting library and laboratories, regulations affecting the university administration, organization of courses and study programs are concerned.

The compartmentalization hypothesis is further supported by Uruguayan data, as 95 per cent of the radicals strongly agreed with the statement that "the university as an institution should analyze national political and social problems and actively publicize its positions about them," by contrast with only 36 per cent of the non-radicals.

Conclusions

A substantial part of the literature dealing with students' and intellectuals' politics in developing countries concentrates on the more *visible* forms of participation, such as strikes and demonstrations. Amidst the many possible forms of political participation, the focused forms tend to be placed at the more intense end. This discussion suggests that data dealing with intense political participation cannot be used as a basis for estimating ideological parameters in the total student population in a given area. Estimates based on participants in a strike or a demonstration will result in a gross overestimation of the proportion of radicals in this population, as radicals are over-represented in the more active forms of participation.

This has some interesting implications which are only of side interest here. For instance, to what extent is public opinion about university students distorted as a consequence of the selective character of mass information which concentrates on the more visible, and thereby more extreme, aspects of student political life? To what extent is policy, both university and national, more sensitive to the more visible forms of participation, rather than to the ideological parameters of the total student population?[38]

It seems legitimate to conclude that although university students in developing countries seem to be generally less conservative than their counterparts in developed countries, especially the United States, the extent of leftist radicalism in student politics in underdeveloped countries may have been over-emphasized. Nevertheless, thinking in terms of power, it is exactly the higher participation of radical students which allows radical ideologies to have a numerical strength. When student participation in university administration is widely accepted and taken for granted, relatively small radical student groups may attain an amazing share of influence in national life. This influence is further facilitated by the fact that being a radical increases the likelihood of an integration between academic life and national life and that, from this standpoint, it is perfectly natural to use the student's union or the university as a means to attain ideological ends in society as a whole.

Further research is needed in order to examine further the relationship between ideology and participation. Does this relationship reveal the existence of a personality type with a need for activism, intensity, radicalism, etc.? Or is it simply a consequence of ideology itself, in which case integration and compartmentalization would simply act as conflict-avoiding mechanisms? These are the types of questions which should be answered next.

Notes

1. For analyses of correlates of various forms of political participation, see Robert Lane, *Political Life* (Glencoe: The Free Press, 1959); on electoral participation, see Angus Campbell, Phillip Converse, Warren Miller, and Donald Stokes, *The American Voter* (New York: Wiley, 1960), Chapter V. On the universalization of formal political and electoral rights in a historical perspective, see Stein Rokkan, "Mass Suffrage, Secret Voting and Political Participation" *Archives Européennes de Sociologie*, II (1961), 132–152. See also Herbert Tingsten, *Political Behavior: Studies in Election Statistics* (London: P. S. King and Sons, 1937), and Seymour Martin Lipset, *Political Man* (New York: Doubleday, 1960), Chapter VI.

2. Political participation is an area which has been extensively studied by scholars from various countries using a variety of different approaches. However, there is a considerable amount of terminological and conceptual confusion in this area. The past few decades have witnessed a mass production of intercorrelated concepts which have been customarily related to outside variables. However, the study of their interrelationships and of their *differential* relationships with outside variables has been neglected.

3. Angus Campbell has given a theoretical treatment to the characteristics of passive and active citizens. See his "The Passive Citizen," *Acta Sociológica*, VI (1962), Nos. 1–2, pp. 9–21.

4. Several studies have shown that political interest and participation are higher at the upper socio-economic levels. For a presentation of these studies, see Lane, *op. cit.*, and Lipset, *op. cit.* Brazilian data can be found in Glaucio Ary Dillon Soares, "Interesse Político, Conflito de Pressoes e Indecisao Eleitoral" *Síntese Política, Economica e Social*, IX (janeiro–março de 1961), 5–34. Bernard Berelson, Paul Lazarsfeld, and William McPhee, *Voting* (Chicago: The University of Chicago Press, 1956), presented one of the most systematic studies of political interest and its correlate.

5. A study of youth participation in the United States 1952 presidential election shows that the percentage *not* following political conventions and speeches

increases sharply as parental income declines. See Herbert Hyman, *Political Socialization* (Glencoe: The Free Press, 1959), Table I, p. 35.

6. See Campbell et al., Chapter 18, for a discussion of this problem. See also Hans Jurgen Eysenck, *Political Psychology* (London: Routledge and Kegan Paul, 1954); Milton Rokeach, *The Open and Closed Mind* (New York: Basic Books, 1960); and Sven Rydenfelt, *Kommunismen i Sverige* (Lund: Universitetsbokhandeln, 1954).

7. Although radicalism is a symmetric concept, i.e., it applies to both far right (Nazism, Fascism) and far left (Communism) ideologies, since the end of World War II far right ideologies have been demoralized, especially in academic circles. Thus, in this article radicalism usually refers to the left end of the political continuum.

8. This integration is well exemplified in the following excerpt from a paper by Rodolfo Guioldi: "Today more than ever the problems of the university are inseparable from the problems of society as a whole, and it is clear that it would be utopian to conceive of a progressive university within a regressive society." See "Contesta Rodolfo Guioldi," in Carlos Strasser, ed., *Las izquierdas en el proceso político argentino* (Buenos Aires: Editorial Palestra, 1959), p. 65.

9. In the context of the present analysis, compartmentalization is to be understood simply as the act of keeping things separate, assigning separate functions to different roles, keeping communications between these roles at a minimum. The concept is derived from Freud's original concept of isolation. See Sigmund Freud, *The Problem of Anxiety* (New York: Norton, 1936).

10. I feel tempted by the hypothesis that compartmentalization is keen to a cognitive style which places emphasis on focusing. On focusing, see H. J. Schlesinger, "Cognitive Attitudes in Relation to Susceptibility to Interference," *Journal of Personality*, XXII (1954), 354–374. See also Riley Gardner et al., "Cognitive Control," in George Klein, ed., *Psychological Issues* (New York: International Universities Press, 1959).

11. This, of course, is not to say that the far right has disappeared from academic circles. Fascist students still exist in Italy today and the *Tacuara* group in Argentina is well known. However, their relative *numerical* strength is small.

12. Actually, unsystematic evidence points to the higher participation of radical students, including far-right students, in different periods. In 1955, members of the *Alianza Libertadora Nacionalista* resisted the revolution to the point of having their see demolished by cannon fire. *Tacuara* and its splinter group, *La Guardia Nacional Conservadora*, have been known for their activism and their violent methods. And, perhaps with the sole exception of the Frondizi election, Argentinian communists have been exceptionally active. On student and intellectual support for Nazism, see Karl Bracher, *Die Auflösung der Weimarer Republic* (Stuttgart: Ring Verlag, 1955); Calvin Hoover, *Germany Enters the Third Reich* (New York: Macmillan, 1933); Konrad Heiden, *Der Fuehrer, Hitler's Rise to Power* (Boston: Houghton Mifflin, 1944); and Walter

Kotschnig, *Unemployment in the Learned Professions* (London: Oxford University Press, 1937).

13. For a description of Indian political parties, see Myron Weiner, *Party Politics in India* (Princeton: Princeton University Press, 1957). The Communist movement and the Communist party of India are dealt with in M. R. Masani, *The Communist Party of India* (New York: Macmillan, 1954), and Gene D. Overstreet and Marshall Windmiller, *Communism in India* (Berkeley: University of California Press, 1960).

14. The Bharatiya Jan Sangh is a Hindu party opposed to Westernization, to the India-Pakistan sub-division, and to what its leader Syama Prasad Mukerjee consistently called "The Politics of Muslim Appeasement." It was strongly backed by members of the Rashtriya Swayamsevak Sangh (RSS), an authoritarian Hindu nationalist organization. Although both the Jan Sangh and the RSS do not seem to have had any direct ideological influence from Nazism and Fascism, in the Indian context they can safely be characterized as far-right organizations.

15. Data computed by the author from cards pertaining to the aforementioned 1952 study and by the SRC's International Data Library Service.

16. See Campbell et al., *op. cit.*, pp. 142–145.

17. See Berelson et al., *op. cit.*, pp. 24–26.

18. See Robert Agger, "Independents and Party Identifiers: Characteristics and Behavior in 1952," in Eugene Burdick and Arthur Brodbeck, eds., *American Voting Behavior* (Glencoe: The Free Press, 1959).

19. It can be legitimately argued that these results refer not to radicalism, but to extremism. From a conceptual standpoint, radicalism is defined by the *position* that one takes, by its opposition to gradualism. Extremism is defined by the intensity with which *any* position is taken. However, although there is adequate theoretical support for the contention that both radicalism and extremism have independent effects upon participation, in practice extremism and radicalism are intercorrelated and sometimes hard to separate, in the sense that most radicals are extremists, although many extremists are not radicals.

20. Data collected with the collaboration of the Instituto Technológico da Aeronáutica (ITA) located in San José dos Campos, São Paulo, Brazil. Respondents were 1964 ITA applicants who were scattered around the country. The majority, however, came from the State of São Paulo proper.

21. Data collected in 1963 by Sulamita A. de Britto. The research was sponsored by the Centro de Estudos e Pesquisas Sociais do Curso de Ciencias Sociais and by the Diretório Academico da Faculdade Nacional de Filosofia (F. N. Fi.). The present author is indebted to the investigators and sponsors for use of the data.

22. The Brazilian Communist party (PCB) was outlawed in 1947. The "legalization" of the PCB, i.e., its return to a legal status, has been an issue ever since.

23. The scales used in the F. N. Fi. study were often asymmetric. In the above

question there was no "moderately against" answer, and one wonders how many students who would otherwise check the "moderately against" category were forced to check the "completely against" category.

24. See Instituto de Estudos Sociais e Economicos, *Student Study* (São Paulo: INESE, mimeographed, 1963). We collapsed the "very good opinion" and "good opinion" responses in a single positive category. Other data from the same survey emphasize the same point: active students are more likely to be favorable to Khrushchev, Francisco Juliao, and Leonel Brizzola (two Brazilian leftist leaders) and less likely to have positive attitudes toward Kennedy and Carlos Lacerda (a Brazilian conservative leader). Furthermore, when asked which country they would choose to study in if they had the opportunity to do so, 17 per cent of the very interested chose the Soviet Union, as opposed to less than 4 per cent in the other categories. Thus, although the sampling methods of this study do not ensure randomness, the *internal* differences within the sample are impressive enough.

25. We are indebted to Mark Van Aken, who conducted this study, for permission to use the cards and for detailed information on the study's methodology.

26. See Daniel Goldrich, *Radical Nationalism* (East Lansing: Michigan State University, 1961). See also, from the same author, "Requisites for Political Legitimacy in Panama," *Public Opinion Quarterly*, XXVI (Winter 1962), 664–668; and "Panamanian Students' Orientations toward Government and Democracy," *Journal of Inter-American Studies*, V (July 1963), 397–404. See also Daniel Goldrich and Edward Scott, Jr., "Developing Political Orientations of Panamanian Students," *Journal of Politics*, XXIII (February 1961).

27. The study was conducted by David Nasatir. See David Nasatir, *Estudio sobre la juventud argentina: Introducción* (Buenos Aires: Universidad de Buenos Aires, Trabajos e Investigaciones del Instituto de Sociología, publicación interna n. 69, n.d.) and "University Education and Political Orientation: The Argentine Case" (paper presented at the meetings of the American Sociological Society, Montreal, August 1964).

28. Radicals were those who thought that "workers have interests which are common with my own," who believed that "big industrialists have interests opposed to my own," and who stated that they "would trust *very much* that if workers had a top government job they would place national interests above their own."

29. The items were: (1) Do you think it worth while to fight an all-out war to stop communism? (2) Labor unions in this country are doing a fine job. (3) The laws governing labor unions are not strict enough. (4) If people are sure of a minimum wage they might lose their initiative. (5) The best government is the one which governs the least. (6) The welfare state tends to destroy individual initiative.

One might argue that the consistent left group is not necessarily radical, for the battery of tests had no question which dealt strictly with communist ideology (e.g., ownership of the means of production, etc.). It can also be argued that one does not have to be a communist in order to answer all questions in the "radical-left" direction, and I am willing to grant this. In this sense, the "consistent left" group may include a number of consistent extreme liberals, besides socialists and communists.

30. The author is indebted to Rose Goldsen for permission to use the cards. The data from this study has been extensively analyzed in R. Goldsen, M. Rosenberg, R. Williams, Jr., and E. Suchman, *What College Students Think* (New York: Van Nostrand, 1960).

31. Data computed by the author from cards provided by the International Data Library Service of the University of California at Berkeley. The original study was conducted in 1958 by the Italian Center of Market Study and Research.

32. See Stefan Nowak, "Social Attitudes of Warsaw Students," *Polish Sociological Bulletin*, I–II (January–June 1962), 97.

33. Data computed by the present author from cards kindly supplied by Sulamita Almeida de Britto.

34. See M. Osaki, *Daisan no Setai* (Tokyo: 1957).

35. Data computed by the present author from cards kindly supplied by David Nasatir.

36. For a work stressing the relevance of political legitimacy, see Seymour Martin Lipset, "Algunos Requisitos Sociais da Democracia: Desenvolvimiento Economico e Legitimidade Politica," *Revista Brasileira de Estudos Politicos*, XIII (January 1962), 7–68. See also *Political Man*, Chapter III.

37. Data from M. Ozaki, *op. cit.*

38. However, this is *not* to say that students in developing countries are as conservative as their own middle class or as students in developed countries. Thus, whereas one study of American college students reports that 59 per cent of the interviewees believed that the welfare state tends to destroy individual initiative, a study of Indian university students reports that only 23 per cent expressed a similar belief. The same studies report that 62 per cent of the American students believe that democracy depends fundamentally on the existence of free business enterprise, as opposed to only 29 per cent of the Indian students. Notice that in the *Faculdade Nacional de Filosofia*, only 1 per cent of the students declared that the government should not intervene in economic life and let private enterprise take care of it. Looking at it from another point, no less than 73 per cent of the F. N. Fi. students expressed the belief that the government should own all the basic industries.

A Comparative Study of Academic Freedom and Student Politics [1]

JOSEPH BEN-DAVID

RANDALL COLLINS

6

Difficulties concerning academic freedom are usually considered as interference in the teaching and research functions of a university, to be resolved by recourse to formal authority or brute force.[2] The most blatant of such interferences occur in the purges of universities that follow the ascent to power of autocratic regimes. But this is only a single aspect of a broad attack on freedom of all kinds, and rarely a specifically academic issue. Why certain regimes are opposed to freedom may be a sociological question, but it will not teach us anything about the sociology of universities or intellectual life in general.

We propose, therefore, to treat academic freedom as a set of institutional arrangements designed to facilitate teaching and research on the most advanced level. It is the same kind of thing as the freedom or autonomy of doctors, lawyers, or other professionals; it is one of the necessary conditions of the efficient and effective performance of a job which requires specialized knowledge, ability, intellectual integrity, and, preferably, creativity.

This, of course, is not the only approach to academic freedom, nor even the most important one. Like all freedom, that of academic teachers, researchers, and students is first of all a moral question. That aspect, however, requires a discussion of basic principles and ultimate goals. Here, we shall restrict ourselves to the discussion of means-ends relationships; given the goals of teaching and research, what are the means of attaining them, and what are the conditions facilitating or impeding their attainment. Besides, defining academic freedom as one kind of professional freedom makes it possible to include under the heading not only authoritarian interference from the outside, but also abuses and misuses of the arrangements by the academic community itself.

It makes little difference whether academic freedom is violated by a ruler refusing to appoint persons to university positions who belong to the political opposition, or whether self-governing academic cliques refuse to appoint people whose scholarly views they do not like. In fact, the latter may be more harmful to intellectual advance, since it is more likely to be aimed at the suppression of specific intellectual arguments, or even truths, than the former. Finally, this perspective makes it possible to compare specific arrangements of academic freedom both as the result of different conditions, and as causes of distinct consequences.

Let us first define the institutional arrangements of professional freedom in general:

1. Monopoly rights over the performance of certain functions, namely teaching and granting recognized university degrees (as treating patients is a monopoly of doctors or pleading before the courts is a monopoly of lawyers).

2. Maintenance of its standards of talent, erudition, and as a result, of its status, by control of admission into the profession.

3. Authority of the professional community (organized for the purpose) over the ethical conduct of its members, thus avoiding lay interference by convincing the public that the profession itself protects the public interest; and the regulation of competition among members so as to maintain their economic security and not to compromise their professional judgment under the pressure of material circumstances.

4. Strict limitation of the contractual obligation of the professional toward his client or employer, to the performance of only those services which are approved by the profession, and to their performance in a manner approved by it. A doctor cannot be charged with malpractice for not doing what the patient asks him to do, as long as what he does is in accordance with the standards of practice. Similarly, an academic can choose to teach, study, or write whatever he thinks is relevant to his subject matter and to do it in whatever manner he wants, as long as he remains within the accepted framework of the standards of his specialty.[3]

If professions were to be ordered on a scale according to how fully they realize these conditions, academics would come out on the top (cf. Table 1).

They are the only profession which, at least in principle, possesses all the characteristics of professional freedom. All the rest, including doctors and lawyers, have to share the control of admission into their profession with the academics, or sometimes surrender it to them entirely.

TABLE 1.

Professions by Presence or Absence of Principal Characteristics of Professional Freedom

| Professions | Characteristics of Freedom | | | |
	1	2	3	4
Academics	+	+	+	+
Doctors and Lawyers	+	+ −	+	+
Engineers	+ −	+ −	−	−

Infringements of academic freedom by outside interference can be seen as violations of various of these professional norms. Interference with the content of teaching infringes on the monopoly rights of academics over the teaching function; political criteria for appointment or promotion violate the profession's control over admissions to its own ranks and its disciplinary authority over the ethical conduct of its own members; attempts to ban or dictate research or publication violate the autonomy of the profession's limited contractual obligation to those who employ it.

On the other side, there is a completely parallel set of abuses, or failures of the members of the academic profession themselves to live up to these norms. The monopoly rights over teaching and the control of admission into the academic profession may be used, not to keep up standards, but to keep out competition or new ideas; disciplinary authority may be used, not to uphold legitimate professional standards, but to enforce extraneous political, class, or racial criteria; contractual autonomy (and such safeguards as tenure) may be used, not merely to do what work one is interested in, but to do slipshod work, political propaganda, or nothing at all.

The norms, then, can be violated on both sides, from within and without the profession. Academic freedom depends, therefore, on the balance between factors within the academic community and those outside of it. As will be seen, abuses on one side tend to lead to abuses on the other, with a resulting decline in the force of the norms themselves.

In the following pages we shall first describe and trace back to their origins the main types of conflict which usually accompany the realization of these norms. Later, we shall examine national differences in the conflicts about academic freedom and their solutions, and relate them to the different uses made of the university in different types of societies.

Conflicts Concerning Academic Freedom

Academic freedom became a controversial issue as soon as there emerged a full time academic profession attached to independent university corporations during the Middle Ages. The most usual type of conflict was the clash between "town" and "gown." The gathering of several thousand young men in cities with a fighting population of perhaps an equal size gave rise to a great many disputes and often to violence. To increase their mutual protection and power, the scholars sought to incorporate themselves as an *universitas* (at the time, a term applied to any guild), basing their claims for corporate privileges and exemption from the public jurisdiction on both the general rights of corporations and on the traditional rights of the individual scholar in Roman and Canon law.[4]

Furthermore, the universities became politically very important, also due to their size and privileges. The University of Paris played a decisive role in the conciliatory movement that ended the Great Schism, and the universities were a natural center for the different religious movements preceding and during the Reformation.[5] In them were concentrated the experts, as well as much of the intelligent and active public concerned with these religio-political issues.

This concern, on the one hand, had led to the decline of their intellectual importance, since those interested in true scholarship and science could not find the necessary tolerance among colleagues engaged in bitter doctrinal fights; while on the other hand, it provoked political interference with their liberties.[6] These two things mutually reinforced each other: the moving of the intellectual elite from the universities reduced the legitimacy of their claim for rights, while political interference induced more scholars to seek other places of work for themselves. As a result, starting from the fifteenth century and lasting until the nineteenth, the stature as well as the freedom of the universities was greatly reduced.

This change, however, does not imply the elimination of either the academic role or of academic freedom. What occurred was simply that the universities, or, to be more precise, their arts faculties, came to be regarded increasingly as secondary schools are today. Creative intellectuals were not usually expected to work there. Instead they were accorded greater freedom and new privileges in the academies founded all over Europe.[7] Besides, some faculties of arts, and all the advanced faculties of law, medicine, and theology had maintained their autonomy and status. Thus even in these ages which are usually considered the nadir of academic freedom—roughly between 1400 and 1800—the continuity of the autonomy of the academic role and community had not ceased (and was in fact extended to new fields of learning); its seat was merely transferred from one institution to another, and distinctions were made—not so dissimilar to those existing today— between teachers of undergraduates and those of graduates. To some extent, therefore, it was merely a change in the definition of the groups to which the freedom was extended, and not a change in the principle of the freedom itself.[8]

This development had been connected with the emergence of a problem concerning the limits on the contents of academic freedom. This may seem a more basic matter involving not only the freedom of the profession, but the philosophical principle of freedom itself. In fact it can—and has—been argued that the ancient and medieval autonomy of the learned was not academic freedom in the modern sense, since the scholar was free to teach and write only within the framework of an accepted doctrine and was always liable to charges of heresy and subversion. Even if he had felt subjectively free, having been in agreement with the basic tenets of the existing religious and social order, he was not objectively so, since he could not go beyond those limits.[9]

This view is true, yet the usefulness of identifying academic freedom in general is questionable. There is a whole world of difference between the medieval and the modern conceptions of freedom of thought, speech, and political activity. But academic freedom is a much more limited affair than the freedom of the ordinary citizen in a liberal country. It is conferred on only a few, at the end of a prolonged period of instruction and—whether one likes the word or not—indoctrination, on the basis of extensive and intensive evidence that the person is fit and properly prepared for the academic role in the judgment of the established authorities in his chosen field. In fact, even his choice of a field is limited by whatever the established authorities consider as worth choosing from, and the difficulties of getting new fields recognized are well known. Once admitted to the professional fraternity, he still has to play the game according to the accepted rules (which may well be stupid and restrictive), and innovations of a revolutionary kind may embroil him with his fraternity, even if they are scientific by accepted standards. Objective academic freedom is therefore a myth, since there are always some people who authoritatively define what its limits are. The stupidity of Aristotelian professors of philosophy opposing Galileo's discovery has been matched by the stupidity of modern natural scientists in the mid-nineteenth century who opposed Semmelweiss and Pasteur, and was of precisely the same kind.[10] They were also similar in their staunch adherence to "academic freedom."

It can still be observed that this is a different kind of problem than opposition to some teaching on the basis of extraneous religious or political criteria. The disputes between the Aristotelians and the new philosophers of the seventeenth century, or those concerning the bacterial causation of illness, one may say, were controversies; while the interdiction of the Church on the teaching of Galileo was a suppression of intellectual freedom, since instead of arguments force was used. This is true, and is precisely the reason why the action of the Catholic church was considered scandalous at that time even by many a good Catholic.[11] But the problem involved was not the enunciation of a new principle of academic freedom, but rather the extension of this freedom to new fields—physics and astronomy—which had not been regarded previously as separate fields justifying the recognition of the autonomy of those specializing in them. The difficulty in making distinctions between external and internal criteria becomes clear concerning an earlier controversy, that about Averroism and other philosophical doctrines. The interference of Bishop Tempier in this controversy in 1277, condemning the view that matter is eternal (and denying thereby creation from nothing by God); the belief in the unity of the "active intellect" which casts a doubt on the survival of the individual soul; and astrological determinism leading to a negation of free will, was regarded by the academic community as a violation of its freedom. Yet by criteria of our present day knowledge, Tempier was in many ways right, and even by the criteria of his own times, he was perhaps not more bound doctrinally than the masters of the university.[12] Thus while his attempt to use his authority was an interference with academic freedom—and was so regarded by the academics—his invocation of the authority of the Bible against Aristotle and other philosophers cannot be considered as a recourse to external criteria. The Bible and religious doctrine were considered scientifically relevant truths and admissible evidence at that time.

It should not be forgotten that even today there are very different standards of admissible evidence in different fields.

Thus, instead of defining the difference between academic freedom in the Middle Ages and the present day as a difference in the idea of freedom, asserting that the Middle Ages had a bound and the modern times an unbound view of that freedom, we suggest that academic, like all professional freedom, is linked to certain topics and methods, but that the range of topics and methods in which this professional freedom is applicable has been gradually extended. The advantage of this approach—which is, in a way, a choice between two alternative languages—is that it makes possible a wider range of comparisons and, more importantly, enables us to include in the discussion of academic freedom the question of how the fields where this freedom applies are defined. As will be seen, this is a crucial question. There is a whole series of conflicts about academic freedom which are closely related to certain fields. The absence of such conflicts in some academic systems may, therefore, simply be a result of their exclusion from the academic world, a worse curtailment of professional freedom than any attempts at influence.

The origins of still another kind of problem concerning academic freedom are even more recent, being the result of the combination of large scale research with large scale teaching. Most types of creative intellectuals today work in universities maintained by public or private philanthropic funds primarily for the purpose of teaching and training. The autonomy of the academic person has to be accommodated, therefore, with the needs of the students as well as the purposes of the supporters. In a free society in which all these groups are permitted to fight for their own interests, as they conceive them, there is a great likelihood of conflicts. Many of these would simply not exist if teachers and students made their own arrangements, if research were a matter of private enterprise, and some would be avoided if research were, as a rule, separated from teaching. This is not to say that these alternatives would be preferable to the present state of affairs, only that as things are today, the maintenance of academic freedom presents a complex problem of the relationships between groups and categories of people and difficult matters of organization.

These, then, are the principal issues, inherent in the relationship of the university and society, which give rise to conflicts about academic freedom: the potential involvement of the university in political conflict as a participant or interest group; the definition of the group to which academic freedom should be extended and the determination of the limits of the professional competence of the university within which academic freedom should prevail; and, finally, the division of authority and powers between donors, administrators, faculty, and students. We shall now examine international differences in the development and solution of these conflicts.

Academic Freedom in the Principal Types of Modern University

The political problem presented by the size, physical strength, and wealth of the university corporation to the medieval city had—as it has been shown—disappeared in the fifteenth century with the emergence of centralized states. Within these the universities had become a politically negligible quantity. They had become purely educational institutions, where young people, dependent on their parents and politically inactive, had spent three or four years preparing for a career. Starting from the nineteenth century this situation changed again. Universities in some countries became concentrations of politically conscious intellectuals playing very important roles as ideologists and organizers of political movements. Unlike in the Middle Ages, however, the university as an organization did not play a role in the struggle for power on its own behalf; only its students and/or its teachers joined as individuals, or organized groups, broadly based social movements and political parties.[13] Lately with the tremendous growth in size of university enrollments, and the rising age of full-time students for many of whom the university and its attached institutions provide a long term—if not life-time—career, the situation may change again in a direction similar to the Middle Ages. The universities' population may become again a politically conscious group, fighting for causes of its own and not merely acting as elites representing the causes of others. For the time being, however, these are only possibilities about which one can only speculate. To the extent that we are concerned with conditions which have actually existed either in the recent past or in the present, the political involvement of the universities has been a secondary phenomenon, depending on the relationship of its members—faculty and/or students—to the leading groups in society. This in its turn has been —as will be shown—to a large extent a function of the definition of the educational aims and the goverance of the universities, or, in other words, of the difficulty of finding a satisfactory definition of the fields and the levels within which academic freedom should prevail, and the allocation of authority to decide in these matters.

Concerning the definition of fields, the questions which pose themselves daily are: whether certain subject matters should be considered as science or scholarship, or rather as ideology or politics; or whether certain other subjects should be considered as properly academic—thus conferring upon its teachers and students academic privileges and titles—or whether they are merely vocational studies in which case the issue of academic freedom does not pertain to either. If a kind of study is declared in advance as non-academic, teachers need not be autonomous in planning their research and teaching; students need not have a choice between different courses, and will not receive academic degrees. These two questions are quite closely related. As has been noted, by defining certain subjects, e.g., social sciences, as not sufficiently scientific, one can eliminate a great source of potential friction between faculty and whoever are the "owners" of the university, without any formal violation of academic freedom. Similarly, by separating a great deal of professional education from the university, one can restrict the numbers of students and academics so drastically as to make their freedom quite unimportant, or to make their scrutiny and selection very easy. Both measures can be taken in a way which is perfectly consistent with the principle of academic freedom. If certain studies are not sufficiently *Wertfrei,* or if they are directed to the acquisition of a specific practical technology, it means that they are bound to ulterior, non-intellectual ends, and, therefore, it is neither justified nor useful to treat them the same way as the unbiased and non-utilitarian pursuit of knowledge is treated. Controls and restrictions on teachers and students can be justified in ideological and technological instruction even if rejected in "pure" science and scholarship.

The criterion usually employed to decide whether there is or is not an infringement of freedom in such cases is whether the decision to exclude or include new fields is taken by the academic body. This, however, is a poor criterion. Academics, like everyone else, are not too anxious to share scarce resources or power and honor with others, and they may be the hardest to convince that a new specialty should be given full recognition.

Closely related to this issue is the problem of admission to practice. What distinguishes freedom from privilege is that in the former people have equal chances to attain scarce ends and there is no doubt that those are allocated according to relevant criteria. As Max Weber has shown, it did not take much to destroy this sense of equality and equity in Germany, one of the systems known as an ideal case of academic freedom.[14] Another example of such a change—less well known today—occurred within the French Academy prior to the Revolution.[15] The *Académie des Sciences* had been at the height of its success in terms of integrity and autonomy. One of the ways this elite institution had succeeded in strengthening its autonomy versus the king and his ministers was by making standards of admission so strict and unequivocally scientific as to make appointments on any but purely scientific grounds so glaring an abuse that they would not even be attempted. This implied putting all the burden of the proof on those considered for co-optation and the rejection of all the cases in which there was the slightest doubt. This, as in the later case of Germany, was enough (1) to create an invidiously great social distance between people whose attainments were only slightly different in quality; and (2) since even the best men are not infallible, nor is the quality of intellectual creation of people over time constant—some decline and others improve—there were a few cases of mistakes. The bitterness and recrimination aroused by these were compounded by the high status and restrictiveness of the institution. Thus the very safeguards of freedom—an autonomous body of impeccably qualified people controlling admission by recourse to impeccable standards —may create a sense of injustice and authoritarianism. This will be a particularly great danger in scholarly and philosophical fields in which the ranking of excellence is more equivocal than in the exact sciences.

These are issues which, though rarely identified as problems of academic freedom, lie in fact nearer to its heart than many spectacular cases which have little to do with specifically academic matters. Their neglect is partly the result of the tendency to be concerned with the infringements of existing privileges, but to leave unnoticed the cases where privileges have never been granted. Partly, however, it is the result of semantics—academic freedom is defined as a right of recognized scholars, working in academically recognized fields; those not appointed to an academic position, even though equally qualified, do not appear under the same heading. These semantics have concealed a great many problems of restraint and authoritarianism in science and scholarship in some places, but have highlighted them elsewhere. Thus authoritarian supervision of teaching in German or French high schools; the illegitimate exercise of authority by "experts" over fields in which they were not expert—anatomists over physiology, philosophers over psychology, strict direction of research in university research institutes—have not usually been considered infringements of academic freedom,[16] but restrictions on nineteenth-century American college professors, engaged in less creative work and often less qualified, were so considered.

This problem is compounded by organization. Due to their very complexity, academic research and teaching need large investments, planning, and organization. In response there arises a university which—in this respect like private or governmental bureaucracies—is owned by others rather than those who work in it, or who are the main direct users of its services. There is a potentially vicious circle here; the more the scope of academic activities expands—and freedom of research and teaching is supposed to expand them—the more frequently financial and administrative decisions have to be taken, and therefore the greater the likelihood of clash between governing bodies and academics.

Students are affected by these developments in several ways. Where academic freedom is safeguarded by restrictive policies concerning admission of new fields and new men to the universities, the main sufferers will be the students, or at least some of them. Because of the narrowness of academic study they may be prevented from learning what they want, or even what is up to date, and they may feel blocked in their aspirations by lack of opportunity. On the other hand, where development is rapid, they may be caught up in the conflicts and uncertainties accompanying change. Furthermore, the extension of research at universities may place them in a somewhat similar position to patients in advanced research hospitals. On the one hand they enjoy the services of creative researchers, often of unique accomplishment; on the other, they have to pay for this privilege by scant attention paid to some of their needs which do not require original solutions. The greater, therefore, the freedom of the teachers, the greater the need for freedom of the students. There have to be safeguards concerning practicability of the requirements—which may impose a limitation on the discretion of the teacher—and students have to have some freedom in the organization of their studies, choice of courses and institutions to protect themselves against the inevitable vagaries of a system which at best is a compromise between the requirement of research and teaching and is altogether very loosely coordinated.

Among the *dramatis personae* of academic freedom, the students will be treated as a group which reacts to, rather than acts independently in, the situation. The problem around which the different solutions of university government have so far crystallized is then defined as a search for an optimal division of labor between academics, considered as free professionals on the one hand, and governing bodies and administrations who are financially responsible for the university on the other, in a situation which necessitates frequent decisions about the proper fields and levels of academic study and research. The solutions arrived at determine the way students can fit themselves into the university and eventually into society. If this turns out to be unsatisfactory, students may be led to political action which—in its turn—may affect academic freedom in various ways.

The usual aim is an administration without any coercion and with a great measure of active participation by those administered. An essential requirement for this is mutual trust. This is presumably established on the basis of the same considerations we generally use in making individual decisions. Where the risks are unknown or great, general trustworthiness becomes decisive; where the risks are small—either because of the triviality of the affair, or because the odds are known to be low, personal acquaintance will be less important.

Translated to the problem of academic freedom, these considerations manifested themselves partly in attempts at the restriction of the academic privileges to a very small number of people, amounting to the definition of the academics as an elite rather than a profession; and partly in attempts at the restriction of the functions of academic institutions to fields in which patterns and outcomes of training and research were known well enough to regard the risks as negligible. Different academic systems have chosen different ways to minimize their risks. Some have preferred to create a restricted elite, failing to take advantage of extending the uses of the university. Others, starting out somewhat later, have tried to exploit fully the potentials of the university. Since this made the establishment of personal trust such as can exist among small circles of people rather difficult, they have tried to reduce their risks by specifying as far as possible procedures and results. Whether the one or the other course is taken, trust is more easily established in situations which are reasonably well known to both parties. Such is the case where people and roles of the same kind as the universities are expected to produce have existed for a long time, and where the intellectual activities engaged in by the university are continuous with activities engaged in outside the university. On the other hand, misunderstanding is likely to arise in the absence of concrete models so that agreement has to be based on abstract principles. Besides, the absence of role-models in society makes it difficult to adjust the supply of graduates to the demand for their services. As the exact size and nature of this latter are unknown, the expectations concerning the rewards for university studies will be unrealistic, and frustration will be inevitable. The tensions resulting therefrom may seriously jeopardize academic freedom.[17]

We shall therefore expect different kinds of conflicts about academic freedom, and different kinds of outcomes in four types of university systems (cf. Table 2).

TABLE 2.

Types of University Systems by Aim and the Availability of Models

		Model	
Aim		*Available*	*Unavailable*
to employ and train {	elite	Type I	Type II
	expert	Type III	Type IV

Theoretically an eightfold classification would be required, since there may be systems where professors are considered as an elite, but not necessarily the students, and vice versa. Since, however, in practice the two tend to go together, it is preferable not to complicate the scheme. It must be made clear that the dichotomization of the components is arbitrary. All university systems, as well as the majority of the individual universities, try to turn out an elite and at the same time train experts who are not necessarily destined to become an elite. These are only differences of emphasis which form a continuum. A scale of reasonable validity can be established by simply taking the ratio of students to population. These ranged in 1958 from 185 per 10,000 of general population in the United States to 19 per 10,000 in Britain and less than that in most of the Latin American and Middle Eastern countries. Continental Europe is much nearer in this respect to the lower than to the upper end. These differences have been, with few exceptions, stable since the beginning of this century.[18] These variations reflect differences of purpose: the European systems had started out and were meant to be first and foremost elite intellectual institutions, providing positions for the leaders in scholarly and scientific fields. At the same time they were responsible for the training of an intellectual and political elite, as well as some of the higher professions which, to some extent, share in the elite status. Leading lawyers, physicians, and clergymen have been traditionally part of the central elite of European countries, while the rank and file, alongside of teachers in the European *gymnasia* and *lycées*, have had a respected place among local notables. To perform this function, it was not necessary to have large numbers of teachers or students. These people were not expected to make very important direct contributions to the economy; they were only supposed to contribute to it indirectly by creating new knowledge and providing excellent leadership for the country. Restriction of admission, as long as it was done according to impeccable standards, was considered an advantage, it safeguarded quality.

In those countries, on the other hand, in which the ratios are high—the prototype of which has been the U. S.—the system as a whole has been designed to train experts and to extend research into fields which, partly perhaps because they had not been considered worth specialized attention, promised to yield useful results quickly. This is not to say that the elite function of education was lost sight of. The universities do train the elite in these systems too. Besides, expertise and research which produce new knowledge are a kind of leadership. The difference between these and the previously discussed elite systems is that the expert systems do not regard it as a debasement of the university also to train people for positions which are not elite roles.

The difference is not limited to the range of fields taught at universities, but extends also to the way they are taught. The elite type of university, even when it requires high technical standards from its staff, does not care much about the technical training of the students. This, it assumes, will be acquired by trial and error, or through inpractice training and not necessarily in the university. It suspects professional schools—the ideal solution is that of English medical schools, in which the university medical schools concentrate on the basic fields, whereas clinical training is provided in teaching hospitals possessing considerable autonomy and only loosely tied to the university.[19] Ideally this type of university is an academy, the staff of which also does a limited amount of teaching, but has practically no responsibility for training.

The prototype of the expert university, on the other hand, is the professional school. Even if it teaches pure science or humanities, it endeavors to impart to the students the actual tools for his research. Thus, the most original innovation of the American universities has been the graduate school which is an extension of the techniques of training in professional schools to all the arts and sciences.

The distinction between countries in which models are available and those in which they are not is also a matter of a continuum. In most countries there are fairly clear-cut models of physicians or engineers, and in few is it clear what the model is for a young man studying for an arts degree. The situation also changes through time: where there is no model to-day there may be one tomorrow. At the same time, a distinction can be made between systems in which the university trains and educates for roles which are well known and accepted in the society, and systems which are created by a traditional, or at any rate uneducated, elite for the purpose of eventually reforming themselves or increasing their efficiency through training new and better qualified people of a kind that do not yet exist in the country.

In England, France, the U. S., and probably some other countries, modern higher education developed in the nineteenth century, shortly after the changes in occupational system and the rise of an educated class. The universities of Oxford, Cambridge, or Paris, at least since the sixteenth century, have not had the privilege of intellectual leadership. For a long time, in fact, they were followers rather than leaders. In both countries during the eighteenth century, and in England the nineteenth as well, many of the most outstanding scholars, intellectuals, and scientists did not hold academic positions. The change was instigated partly by this non-academic intelligentsia, who were civil servants, politicians, professionals, or—especially in England—simply wealthy people often of noble descent.[20] The kind of people who should form the academic elite, as well as the nature of the products, were not in question. There was consensus between those who taught at the universities and those who decided about the fate of university budgets as civil servants, donors, or politicians. They all belonged to the same class and spoke the same language. Similarly there had been a long non-university tradition in higher education, scholarship, science, and technology in the U. S. before the country seriously embarked on the reform of its higher education. Although this has been true for the north-eastern part of the country, elsewhere the situation has often been one of the "non-model": governments and/or philanthropists of pioneering and educationally backward states setting up institutions to bring their own areas up to the standards of the East.[21]

The best known examples of non-model systems are Austria, Prussia, and Russia in the eighteenth century, and the latter also in the nineteenth century (or the reformed system of the U.S.S.R. in the twentieth). In all of these cases the universities were established by a minority of educated rulers and officials with the purpose of creating a new educated elite of the Western type, not to replace landed aristocracy as the mainstay of the respective regimes, but to educate the latter and selectively introduce into it able people of non-aristocratic origin. Apparently, similar conditions prevailed in Japan and China at the end of the nineteenth and early twentieth centuries, when their modern systems of higher education were established, as well as in the Eastern and Southern European, Latin American, Asian, and African countries at various times in the nineteenth and twentieth centuries. Obviously, there is a great deal of variation here concerning the efficiency and determination of those in power to carry through their attempts at modernization, and thus change a situation of "non-model" into one in which the model becomes available. Still the two categories are clearly enough distinguishable.[22]

Clearly, these types present separate and distinct problems for the maintenance of academic freedom. We shall try to explore these by taking each type in turn. We shall not give a detailed account and classification of the existing academic systems, but seek to present models of the working of those which seem to be most representative of each type.

Type I: Elite Systems with Accepted Models. There is a nearly perfect example of this type in the English academic system. Germany, the Scandinavian countries, and France presumably also belong to this type, but the workings of these, especially that of France, are much more complex. We shall, therefore, describe the model mainly with reference to England.

The governing of this type of system is effectively shared between the academics who have complete autonomy in running their own affairs, and the government which has effective means of letting its views be known and seriously considered without openly interfering with the universities. This is so because there are no basic differences between the two sides involved. The exchange of opinion between the higher civil servants and the leadership of the universities takes place either through a formally constituted body (like the University Grants Commission in Britain, or the Chancellor of the Universities in Sweden), as well as informally since the people know each other quite well. The civil servants are of similar education and background as the university professors, so that there are no barriers to communication between them.

One of the important effects of this situation is that the civil servants form an effective buffer between politics and the universities.[23] Certain parties may have opinions about the necessity of making the universities more representative, or they may want to look into the finances of the universities. In these cases some solution is worked out informally which then makes the execution of the policies acceptable to the academics as well as to the politicians.

Thus, even though there may be a good deal of public discussion and criticism of the universities, there is no attempt to interfere with their autonomy. It is taken for granted that, whatever changes may prove to be desirable or necessary, they will be carried out autonomously by the universities. The consensus necessary for such a degree of trust is the result of keeping the academic system exclusive, small, and so highly selected as to command universal or near-universal respect. Conservatism is the price paid for this: academic innovations, whether in education or research, have to be relegated to peripheral parts of the system, since the elite cannot take chances without endangering its status. An example of this in England has been the great hesitancy of Oxford and Cambridge (particularly the former) in making provision for the social sciences: economics was introduced only in the 1920's, and then without adequate library facilities or sufficient staff; psychology achieved its first chairs in 1931 and 1947 at Cambridge and Oxford, respectively; sociology was introduced only in 1961, and still does not have a chair at either institution. There have been similar lacks in medical science, particularly in the integration of basic and clinical research.[24]

At first sight this delay does not seem too inefficient. It is logical to develop new things by trying them out on a small scale in a peripheral setting, and then decide on the basis of experience whether to pursue or drop the matter. The trouble is that this kind of wisdom only occurs retrospectively in the pages of official histories. For a new field to succeed, those who believe in it have to be given a chance to fight for it with as good resources as they can possibly muster, and to vie for as good students as they are capable of attracting. By being shunted to a third-rate university, or to some kind of more gilded academic ghetto where there is no chance of getting disciples or support for research, the novelty is doomed to failure.

This, however, is beside the point here. The purpose of this discussion is not to investigate the innovative capability of different systems, but to study academic freedom. From this point of view, the important thing is that the situation is not perceived as an unjust limitation of the opportunities by a privileged clique, but as a fair, if not perfect, system. The possibilities for this lie in the efficiency of selection and allocation. Limitations and restrictions are perceived as just, if their rationale is reasonable and their administration equitable. As long as the elite does reasonably well what it is supposed to do, people have a good grasp of what the criteria of admission into the elite are and the elite does not make life too difficult for the rest, there will be a feeling of justice. This is assured by the existence of what we have called a "model," that is, when academic systems have been shaped by successful people in their own image. The image is well reflected throughout the educational system, and children from a very early age are made aware of it, and learn what their chances are. Expectations are geared to reality, and there are no (or insignificantly few) aspirants for academic careers, especially for top positions, who will have to be frustrated. Since, therefore, much of the envy is taken out of competition—or disposed with at an early age before the personality is formed in its final shape—there is no vindictiveness on the part of the elite, and no aggression on the part of those professionals and intellectuals who are not academics.[25] To the extent that some of the latter feel that the definition of the academic fields and roles should be broadened, they will be listened to and often given a chance "to prove" themselves. They will rarely succeed, although they will be treated fairly enough to end up blaming only themselves.[26]

Another way of bringing the educational system in accord with available social models has been the conscious attempt to make the composition of the academic elite representative of all the important political and social groups. Universities may make (and have made) efforts to find a person of working class origin for a position, or to have a communist or two on their staff. Such steps, if taken before the emergence of a frustrated group of alienated anti-establishment intellectuals, lend to this type of system an air of generosity and limitless tolerance and freedom. In fact, however, when combined with the selective, elite-oriented process of education, this policy has the effect of giving the system maximum stability and of enhancing to the limit its conservative tendencies. Since selection is thorough and efficient, and consensus about important things great, the likelihood of individual dissent having any disrupting effect on the system is negligible. The effectiveness of scientific policy-making by a small group which knows itself to be the best in a certain field in the country, and is recognized by the relevant others as such, will not be affected by one of its members publicly advocating communism or free love. The same member, when it comes to professional policy-making, may be the "soundest" or even the most conservative of all. And, if members of the group, possibly including even the dissenter, have been known for a great many years to the civil servants who advise the minister (or, perhaps, to the minister himself, too), then no one will come to suspect them of being politically or morally unsound, and therefore not to be supported by public money. Paradoxically, the tolerance probably also reduces the dissenter's effectiveness as a propagator for his subversive non-academic interests. Having been admitted to the establishment and not being victimized by it for his views and activities, his activities only confirm the fairness of the system. The rebel himself will usually feel so and his revolutionary fervor will be blunted.[27] But even if he does not feel this, his public will. A brilliant scientist and scholar victimized for his views in his academic career makes a very good agitator. As a martyr he is a living indictment of the system. But the same person, treated fairly, is living propaganda for the status quo.

Such a system is in near perfect balance, with a minimum of conflict and a maximum feeling of freedom. Compared with more enterprising systems, it may seem too restrictive both in its expansion of scope and its selection of personnel. But for those within it, it provides a stable, fair, and predictable system. Lack of innovativeness is counterbalanced by flexibility and openness for suggestions of reform and innovation coming from outside the society, or—in principle—even from within.

The French system, operating in a much more impersonal way, achieves similar results. There is an elaborate system of selection and allocation which produces a somewhat similar elite as in England, but instead of reducing conflict and effective dissent through group consensus, the same end is achieved there, though probably accompanied by qualitatively different emotions through careful isolation and delimitation of spheres of influence.[28]

Type II: Elite Systems without Models in Society. While Type I tends toward a more or less stable balance, this second type is the most likely to be out of balance. This is implied in its very purpose, since it is founded in order to foster social change. Simply because these systems were all instigated by more advanced examples, they were initially built so as to create conflict. Historically, the line of educational reform leading to social conflict (and often culminating in revolution) can be traced back as far as the seventeenth century. The enlightened circles of France propagandizing for the establishment of the Academy of Sciences and Baconian educational ideas and supported by such "modernizing" civil servants as Richelieu or Colbert, had English models before their eyes. The movement which arose as a result eventually played an important role in the overthrow of the old regime. The reforms of Austrian and German higher education at the end of the eighteenth and early nineteenth century were first an imitation and then a reaction to French models; Russian higher education, established mainly in the nineteenth century, took its model mainly from Germany; the even newer systems of higher education in Latin America, Asia, and Africa have usually followed one of those three models.

The common characteristic of all these imitations has been that they are not mere adoptions of innovations in education and research made elsewhere, but deliberate attempts at facilitating a change in the character and/or composition of the ruling elite, and/or the creation of entirely new secondary elites, by means of the educational reform. This distinguishes the present type from such cases as the adoption of certain features of the German academic system in the nineteenth century by English, French, and American universities. In these earlier cases the "models" for educated administrators, politicians, professionals, or even scientists and scholars had existed prior to the adoption of the foreign pattern. The innovation was a means of producing more and better of the same kinds of people as already existed in society. This, of course, might have led eventually to unexpected political problems. But the replacement of existing elites with a new one, or the introduction of a new stratum in society, is bound to lead to direct conflict. No existing elite will put up gracefully with an open attempt to transform and replace it, and even less will young men reared as future elite according to models of more advanced societies admit to the authority of a traditional ruling class. One can postulate, therefore, that at some point attempts will be made by the authorities to regulate the university and tell professors what to teach and what not to teach, and what in general should be the model they present to their students. It is nearly inevitable that under such circumstances students, and at least some of the teachers, will become politically rebellious.

Since, therefore, this is a system which by definition starts from imbalance, no single case can be regarded as representative of it. Some systems never attain balance, so that the universities become permanent centers of intellectual and political conflict over a long period of time; others manage to establish some kind of a balance which may be more or less precarious depending on conditions to be specified. We shall, therefore, attempt first to describe a model of chronic disequilibrium, based mainly on the nineteenth-century Russian and twentieth-century Latin American cases, and then referring to the well-known case of Germany in the nineteenth and early twentieth century, we shall treat an example of a temporarily successful establishment of balance.

One of the distinguishing features of these systems, compared with the previous type, is the high degree of formalization of the rights and privileges of the academic person and the academic corporation. In principle these may appear as not too different from the arrangements of the first type—both are designed to ensure the autonomy of the profession—but in the first type of system there are few or no laws to define these rights, so that in principle it would probably be quite easy for any government which so desired to impair them without any change in the legal situation. The necessity of spelling out the rights in the non-model systems is the result of lack of communication and mutual trust between the academics and the rulers. Almost immediately after the establishment of the new University of Berlin in 1809, which was to serve as a model of academic freedom, there arose conflicts in Berlin and elsewhere about a variety of issues concerning the freedom of teachers to participate in opposition politics, present religiously heterodox views, and a variety of major and minor issues concerning freedom of publication, academic self-government, and honors. Such difficulties were, however, prevented wherever the minister of education was a cultivated person with good connections with the academic world. Since, however, the majority of the politicians and higher civil servants at that time were not people who valued intellectual achievements nearly as much as they valued noble birth or political and military excellence, the autonomy of the profession was constantly in danger and, therefore, required formal safeguards.[29] In countries such as nineteenth-century Russia, or Latin America today, where military dictatorship is always an imminent possibility, these needs have been even greater.[30]

How effective are such formal safeguards in preserving, or—since there are often countries where civil freedom is very limited—creating academic freedom? Of course, no safeguards help against a government which wants and has the power to disregard them. But, as has been noted, most governments most of the time do not want to tamper with the universities and the academic profession. Formal safeguards, therefore, have some value since violating them will be regarded as a breach of legitimacy which governments can ill afford. The problem, however, is to what extent the formal safeguards, even if more or less honored by the government, will ensure that the autonomous academic community will use its power to promote an ever-growing freedom of enquiry. The assumption that by granting to the academic community visibly high status and responsibility the norms of scholarship and science will prevail is based on some kind of concept of *noblesse oblige*. Unfortunately what is true of other cases of privileged nobility is true of the academic case as well, namely that the rule has been abuse of privilege. Only under circumstances where the privilege was rather limited, have such groups lived up to their obligations of their own free will. The conditions of "non-model" societies, however, are usually such that the privileged academic community will be corrupted sooner or later.

Even minor matters of chicanery and honor will have their effect. Where lack of personal power means subjection to arbitrary authority and lack of special honors means dishonor, university professors will fight for these, and, since they fulfill an important function and are able people, will sooner or later succeed. They will become part of, or at least friendly with, a corrupt ruling group, which inevitably involves a measure of corruption. Such corruption which replaces academic standards with nepotism and subordinates scholarship to politics had been widespread in nineteenth-century Russia and is said to be even worse in many Latin American countries today. The tragic thing is that many who do not want to be corrupted by the rulers, and oppose the falsification of the purpose of the university through turning it into one of the fortresses of personal privilege, often end up by similarly falsifying these objectives by using their privileged position as a lever for opposition politics. Morally their stand may be impeccable. There is an excellent argument for giving priority to the larger interests of defending freedom and justice over academic duties. But the line between a temporary situation of emergency in which the professor and the student, as well as the doctor, the lawyer, the merchant, and the worker, must leave their places of work and study to man the barricades and fight for justice and a situation in which one has to go on working and to use one's spare time for discharging one's political and civic duties has to be clearly drawn. If everyone else works, but professors (and/or students) supported by public funds and special facilities and immunities conferred upon them to pursue their studies use those facilities and immunities for political activity, they may come dangerously near to abusing their privileges. There are situations in which this is justified. But one should not include those under academic freedom; these rather involve a deliberate abandonment of the professional concerns of the academic in order to engage in something much more important than any professional obligation. This seems to have been the case in many individual instances in a great many places. But where—as it seems to be the case in some of the Latin American (and Southern European) countries—professors have come to regard their positions conferring on them high status, public visibility, immunities and income (or access to income), as sinecures provided by the State to engage in politics, then whatever the worth of those politics, they are abusing academic freedom.[31] Not only because freedom and facilities meant to be used for the advancement of knowledge are thus diverted to other ends, but because almost inevitably such actions will be justified by an ideology which identifies intellectual activity with activist politics, and thus opposes or even suppresses free and unbiased enquiry in all ideologically sensitive fields. What starts out (and in individual cases may continue to be) as a justified subordination of intellectual freedom to the cause of freedom in general may then turn into a threat to the principle of freedom of inquiry.

Even more serious problems arise because of the difficulty in controlling the students. Since models are non-existent, criteria of student selection cannot be too efficient. Besides, since the society is backward relative to the educational model it adopts, it will tend to lack a similar range of alternatives as the model for useful and respectable non-elite professional jobs for those who cannot make the elite. Finally, even those who are suitable in every respect to enter the elite will usually find that they are admitted by the ruling class only with very specialized qualifications and on sufferance, and then only to positions of secondary importance. It is almost inevitable, therefore, that many are admitted to universities and their aspirations raised without any hope of realizing them. Even those who due to exceptional ability and/or the fact that they come from upper class families should expect elite status will also encounter difficulties for a number of reasons. Almost inevitably, the system will be fairly inefficient, since the country will usually lack enough people of sufficient qualification to teach at a university, and even those qualified will lack experience and know-how to run such an institution. Worse yet, where the faculty has been corrupted, the able students will become very cynical; where the faculty is honest, students will learn to despise even more that kind of authority to which they are expected to subordinate themselves when leaving the university; and when the faculty is partly corrupted and partly honest they may conclude that the whole existing adult society makes no sense. In any case they are likely to be in a situation of the type Durkheim called *anomie*, where norms of conduct are unreliable and do not lead to their expected ends. Thus the students become alienated from the very ruling class which had created the university. The honeymoon period with enlightened absolutist rulers is followed by absolute disillusionment on both sides.

This general pattern, which has a great many variations, is most clearly discernible in nineteenth-century Russia and in present-day Latin America. The sequence of events in Russia was somewhat like this. The modern university started out as an institution to which Messianic hopes for social improvement were attached. After a very short time, however, the hopes went sour. Instead of preparing themselves for entering the slots in society which they were intended to enter, the students grew impatient with both society and the slots, and organized themselves for (or at least threatened) subversion. This was followed by government attempts to restrict entrance into universities and to control what happened in them. This action caused even more dissatisfaction. The restrictions were perceived as injustices by those who were now prevented from entry, and their sense of injustice was incensed by the corrupt and erratic way admission was administered. Those who were admitted became alienated nonetheless, since they were made to suffer from the usually stupid attempts at controlling instruction, speech, writing, and thought. Eventually the futility and injustice of the restrictive measures were recognized, and a new liberal era began, starting a new cycle of the vicious circle. This is in a schematic way what happened in Russian higher education starting from early in the nineteenth century with the reforms of 1804 and lasting until World War I. The cycles were: first, a liberalization under Alexander I with the reforms of 1804, followed by a reaction after the Napoleonic War of 1812, and culminating in the Decembrist Revolt of 1825. The restriction of admissions to an ever-smaller elite and the tightening of controls over the teachings and the curriculum followed in the reign of Nicholas I, 1825–1855. Alexander II brought a new period of liberal reform, approximately during the years 1856–1866, but conflicts led to spasmodic repressions throughout the remainder of the reign, ending with the assassination of the tsar in 1881; Alexander II instituted a severe reaction until 1894, but student strikes and other forms of defiance continued; reforms were attempted in 1901, but without quelling the tide of disturbances. Revolution broke out in 1905, and liberal and reactionary policies fluctuated rapidly thereafter until the Revolution of 1917 ended forever the tsarist educational experiments.[32]

As a result student culture became overwhelmingly politicized, and students came to regard academic freedom as equivalent to freedom of speech and agitation. The intellectual atmosphere which resulted from this was one of doctrinaire adherence to ideologies and the spread of ideological intolerance.[33] If all this did not completely exhaust Russian intellectual creativity, it was probably due to proximity to Western Europe. The best Russian intellectuals, irrespective of their field of activity, had studied in France and Germany, or Switzerland, published in German and French, and/or were exposed to publications coming from those countries. This counteracted the tendencies for intellectual corruption and complete politicization inherent in the internal conditions.

The parallel between nineteenth-century Russia and present-day Latin

America is particularly interesting, since this latter area has had some revolutions. As a result individuals and groups from the alienated intelligentsia have found their way to supreme power. Due to the existence of many independent states in the area, there has been no period of time since the second half of the nineteenth century, without the existence in some of the countries of relatively liberal regimes respecting the independence and autonomy of the universities.

What, however, these countries have in common with pre-World War I Russia has been their social structures. These latter have been left virtually unaffected by political change: there is everywhere a very narrow and conservative stratum of extremely rich and conservative landowners; an overwhelmingly large and abjectly poor and backward peasantry and urban *lumpenproletariat* and in between a small, economically insecure mobile and relatively educated middle class.

Since the universities have been modeled on elitist European examples— Spanish traditions going back to the Middle Ages and the universities of Continental Europe—they imbue the students with aspirations for leadership. But in these economically backward and unstable countries the only way to obtain positions of economic security and honor (for those who were not born into such position) is through political power or patronage. Therefore, even though the proportion of university trained people in positions of responsibility is among the highest in the world, this remains an extreme non-model situation nevertheless. The professionals in high positions are there not as a result of their training, but of political success or connections. There are no models in society of the kind of elite roles for which the universities are supposedly training their students—creative scientists and scholars, high grade professionals, or broadly educated intellectuals with a keen sense for practical affairs whose services are rewarded because of their superior intellectual training and abilities.

The very high degree of legally safeguarded freedom (which is actually observed in some of the countries) is used deliberately and consciously to secure for those connected with the university far-going privileges to engage in politics. Furthermore, this freedom is often used to prevent improvements of academic standards, or to suppress the expression of views unpalatable to an important political faction, or simply to victimize certain individuals.

This case is particularly important since unlike the Russian failure which could be attributed to the insufficiency of the safeguards of academic freedom and to constant interference by bumbling autocratic governments, the failure of the Latin American university must be blamed on the actions of relatively autonomous scholars and students. If nevertheless the results have been similar or worse than those in Russia, they have to be attributed to the dynamics of elite non-model systems.[34]

In contrast to these failures of elite non-model systems Germany, or rather the system of German language universities, in the nineteenth century is considered a great success. Here autonomy was used wisely and responsibly. The universities had not been deflected from the pursuit of the highest standards of science and scholarship for a period of more than one hundred years. The people appointed were generally of a high caliber, the quality of the lectures, seminars and research was among the best in the world, the graduates were well trained, and the German universities attracted many of the best students from all over the world. Much of this success has been attributed to the specific arrangement of academic freedom prevailing in the German universities.[35]

We should like to suggest, however, that those formal arrangements were not a sufficient condition for the scientific success of the universities. An abuse of these freedoms in a manner similar to Latin America (or their suppression similar to Russia or under Perón, in Argentina) was only prevented by a set of circumstances which had nothing to do with these formalities.

We shall trace now the way the system had worked. The first effect of the new freedom of the Prussian universities was indeed an attempt to politicize them on the one hand, as in present-day Latin America, and to regulate them authoritatively as in Russia, on the other. One of the first and most famous manifestations of the newly won freedom of the academic profession and of the students was the Wartburgfest in 1817—a festival arranged by the student organizations to commemorate the Jubilee of the Reformation. One of its features was the burning of books which were not in accordance with the taste of one of the principal ideologists of the "youth" movement, Professor Massmann. Several other professors were active in fomenting extremist nationalist movements among the students, and their agitation led amongst other things to the murder of the Austrian playwright Kotzebue and to several anti-Semitic outbursts.[36]

The authorities started reacting to this by restricting entrance to the universities so as to prevent the admission of students from popular backgrounds who might be insecure and potentially subversive. There were also attempts to discipline academic teachers with an ineptness similar to the tsarist government.[37] But the worst, nevertheless, did not follow. In addition to the fact that the German ruling class contained a much greater minority of enlightened and educated people than its Russian counterpart, German universities had the advantage of decentralization. Whenever one of the governments decided to interfere high-handedly with a university, the academic elite of that university usually had the choice of resigning and finding a haven in another state which happened to have a more enlightened ruler at that time, or just taking an opportunity of the occasion, so as to benefit its own university. As a last resort there was also democratic Switzerland with its German-language universities. Moreover, reactionary measures against the universities were never general, so that the system developed by the initiative taken first in one place, and then in another. This decentralization could have such a favorable effect, of course, only because of the unevenness of the situation; the lack of "models," of sympathetic, educated men in society, was not completely general throughout German society; thus, it was less in a position of "non-model" than Russia or Latin America.[38]

The outcome was a strengthening of genuine research and learning, since this was in the long run the most useful strategy from the point of view of the profession. Playing autonomous politics, as in Latin America, was not tolerated anywhere in the area, and would not have been feasible anyway due to the greater differentiation of society. Becoming martyrs for freedom in general, as in Russia, was not necessary. There was a third and respectable possibility of practicing professional freedom efficiently. Although in the beginning the inefficiencies of a "non-model" situation caused considerable damage, competitive pluralism prevented complete bankruptcy and brought about rapid improvement.

The balance which emerged and the conditions under which it eventually broke down between World Wars I and II precisely reflect these various forces. The political freedom of the academic profession as well as of the students was limited. It was assumed that the academic teacher as a civil servant had to have political and ideological convictions acceptable to the rulers. Even though the majority of the academic profession opposed the *Lex Arons*, passed by the Prussian legislature in 1898, requesting positive identification with the government, they would have preferred Arons to resign his position as a *Privatdozent* in physics, believing that activity in the Social-Democratic party was inconsistent with the "civil service" position of the member of a university.[39] Political prejudice and extremism of the kind acceptable to the ruling class (extreme chauvinism, incitement to war, anti-Semitism) were on the other hand quite frequent among university professors. It went without saying that Jews were discriminated against in appointments and that the appointment of Catholics and Protestants was often influenced by considerations of religious politics. Liberal academics did not accept these things. But apart from being active in liberal politics outside the university, as some of them were, the only thing they could do about it within the university was to try to keep the institution on as high a level, and as far above and away from topics which might open it to contact with the outside world, as possible. They opposed everything that might have implied value judgments or technological application, arguing that those were matters to be discussed and taught elsewhere. In principle, of course, this attitude is impeccable, and everyone would accept Paulsen's statement that "Ein gebundener Unterricht ist kein wissenschaftlicher" (a restricted education is not a complete one), and it probably was the best way to reduce attempts at controlling the university, or corrupting the integrity of the staff. But it should be clear that it was a compromise, and not a clear and simple criterion of what is academic and therefore what should be free. This is evident from the actual decisions made. Theology was an acceptable discipline, but sociology was usually not; medicine and law were traditional subjects, but engineering and business administration were kept outside the universities. The principle, therefore, cannot be taken too seriously. It was an adjustment to a precarious situation. Academic freedom could be maintained only in limited subjects which were old and venerable so that they became part of the unquestioning routine and in those which either because of their highly abstract nature, or, at times, because of their complete remoteness from any practical application or social implications were absolutely certain not to produce any friction.[40]

Thus academic freedom, as it actually existed, was a Janus-faced institution and none of its faces represented that ideal of beauty which had been so often attributed to it. On the one hand, academics shared the honors, emoluments, and privileges of the ruling classes in an authoritarian society, and only a negligible minority felt any pangs of conscience. To the extent that violations were "localized," the majority tolerated abuse and corruption, such as has been enumerated (right wing bias, etc.), and often actively participated in them. On the other hand, they were good enough professionals not to want the system to be totally corrupted into one of the domains of ascribed privilege reflecting the exercise of bureaucratic power. In this concern they agreed with the liberal minority. Building up the university into a kind of holy shrine, and establishing impressive rituals to symbolize the elevated status of the place and the profession, were acceptable to all. They added even more status to those who were corruptible, and they could be used by the honest academics as weapons against corruption.

Thus the successful institutionalization of academic freedom in this elite non-model setting has to be attributed to the effective decentralization of the system. The academic profession was able to maintain a decent measure of autonomy and freedom in a relatively authoritarian society, because it had been able to opt out easily from oppression. The establishment of German unity did not change this situation, because (1) it did not include the Austrian lands and Switzerland, and (2) because by that time the German system, which had started out as "international" in the German language area, had already become a center of a new cosmopolitan world of universities. German universities had trained most of the academic elite of Eastern and the rest of Central Europe, much of that of England and the U. S., and practically all the new academic elite of Japan. Thus the German university professor had a role of international significance and influence which no German government could attack without hurting its own international standing.

This outcome was a more or less satisfactory solution only for those who had been admitted into the academic profession. The majority of the students, however, had to find their way within German society, and face its general authoritarianism. From their point of view the privileges of the established academics, strictly restricted to a few lucky incumbents of positions and a limited number of recognized academic fields, appeared as arbitrary intellectual authoritarianism. They reacted to this situation by the creation of a variety of what might be described as intellectual sects. Marxism with its tendency to build up a whole intellectual establishment parallel to the universities, psychoanalysis with only slightly more modest aims at intellectual self-sufficiency, and a variety of less well developed instances, such as that of Nietzsche and his followers, were all, at least in part, expressions of discontent and alienation by scholars and intellectuals who felt that they had been driven out into the wilderness by the academic establishment.[41] There are obviously limits to who can and cannot be absorbed in an academic (or any other) establishment which exist everywhere. But it makes all the difference whether these limits are perceived as legitimate means to the purpose of the university, or whether they are seen as illegitimate monopolization of scarce opportunities and honors for intellectual work. In Germany there was a widespread feeling of this latter kind, resulting from the defensive conservativeness of the academic profession, wary of moving out of time-tested precedents into intellectual fields which might have involved them in conflict with the ruling elite, or undermined the justification of their high privileges and immunity from control.

The intellectual movements which arose in this situation were often connected with extremist politics of the left, or the right. The question is how these onsets of student-intellectual unrest resembling those in Russia and Latin America were prevented from politicizing the university to the extent of seriously interfering with the quality of studies, as it happened in those countries. This was achieved by (1) emphasizing reasonably high and honest academic standards; in this respect there was much less room for feelings of cynicism and normlessness than in Russia, or in Latin America; (2) the "non-model" situation was mitigated by numerous exceptions: for the intellectual elite of the students there existed at different times reasonably good prospects for suitable careers at the universities, secondary schools and professions; and for those coming from the upper and upper-middle class—who formed a considerable part of the student body—there were good and intellectually quite acceptable careers in the civil service or the military. The potential alliance of these student elites with the insecure and subversive part of the student body was further prevented by the existence of exclusive student organizations which kept these higher class students apart from the others and placed them in a separate environment within the university which closely resembled in its social structure, if not necessarily in human values, the English and French elite institutions.[42] Thus finding themselves in a framework of interlocking elites, including part of the faculty and important sectors of the ruling class, the elite student culture was politically innocuous. This pattern explains why the crises of the system occurred in the beginning, before these new elite frameworks were consolidated. After World War I when, as the combined result of attempts at democratization and inflation, these frameworks broke down, the way was opened to extremists skillfully using the dubious symbols of valor and virility of the old upper classes to unite their descendants with many of the hopeless mass of students from the lower middle classes in a movement promising to make them all into an elite, not at the expense of the lower classes, but of so-called lower races.[43]

The success of the German universities cannot, therefore, be attributed to the institutions of academic freedom and the freedom of students. Similar institutions elsewhere did not prevent deterioration; there was a considerable measure of political and ideological corruption in German universities too. As in Latin America the decentralization of the system enhanced the formal autonomy of the universities. Unlike Latin America, however, the decentralized system was much more pluralistic, with some parts of it very near, and all parts of it closer to the model end of the continuum than either Latin America or Russia. Because of the much greater mobility of staff and students, the German system was also much more competitive than the other two systems dealt with here. Thus academics had not only rights and privileges, but also an opportunity to prove the value of real excellence.

In this context a word should be said about the formal freedoms of the students, which have not been dealt with yet. These consisted of an agreement to transfer enrollment credits from one university to another and to reduce the formal requirements for attending classes and passing intermediate examinations to a minimum.[44] Interestingly, these freedoms have not been imitated elsewhere, and have rarely been mentioned as a desirable model. Indeed they are of a quite different kind than those of the academic body. They are not privileges of a traditional, corporate kind, but freedoms in the liberal-democratic sense. They have probably contributed a very great deal to the competitive nature of the system, serving as a check on the professors—if students did not like the way a part of their subject was taught at one institution they could go elsewhere; and they must have increased satisfaction by allowing the students to find the most congenial place for themselves by trial and error. Finally, they served to correct some of the shortcomings of the elite system. As said, such a system makes no point of training the student. The university staff is small. The most important thing is that they should be excellent. No particular care is taken that every aspect of the field should be covered, and even less that the actual techniques of research should be taught. This, of course, greatly enhances the insecurity of the student in a "non-model" system, since he cannot safely look forward to a place of work or professional practice with traditions of technical excellence and socialization of the novice. By allowing the students to move from one place to another they could make up for some of these deficiencies. Thus while the structure of the individual university definitely places this system in the elite category, the working of the system as a whole pushes it along some way toward the "expert" end of the continuum.

The validity of this explanation can be tested by reference to more recent parallels. The most interesting of these is Japan. Its academic system had been in many ways the best and most successful imitation of the German system. The possibility and value of granting complete academic freedom to a highly selected intellectual elite of international standing was clearly recognized by the leaders of educational reform, though they were aware of the problems which might result from this for the maintenance of the stability of an otherwise authoritarian system. Great care was taken, therefore, to isolate the university system, to justify and legitimate the isolation by true adherance to high standards, and to ensure the loyalty of the graduates to the system by linking them through informal cliques to the elite (reminiscent of the function of German student corporations). Having linked its universities from the outset into the most advanced international academic network and possessing a considerable educated and honest administrative class, as well as a potential middle class—like Germany—Japan had avoided in the beginning the instabilities attending the Russian and the Latin American systems. Yet after World War I a class of unemployable and increasingly radicalized intellectuals emerged as in Germany, which was open to ideologies of national superiority like their German counterparts.[45]

A parallel to Latin American developments may emerge soon in Africa. Prior to independence there had arisen in most places a conflict between the colonial ruling class and the embryonic native educated class possessing English or French education, spearheading more or less broadly based nationalist movements. With the attainment of independence these educated groups found themselves in a situation where they had easy access to power, and great potential influence on educational policies. Individuals or, as in the case of the Mobutu administration in the Congo, groups attained actual power. But despite their progressive intentions, they have not been able to change the class structure. Apart from those having very great wealth, politics remains the main avenue to comfort and security. Those who are in the educational system have retained a completely and usually unrealistically elitist view of education. The expectations of the students concerning their futures as educated members of their societies are so unrealistic, in view of the actual opportunities which those societies can offer, that they are bound to become hopelessly frustrated. The relative success of some of the local universities in actually living up to the British or French ideal of a university and maintaining ivory towers of almost European academic standards, and more than European standards of living in splendid isolation from their environments, is apt to lead within a generation or two to a situation resembling Latin America.[46] The existence of culturally coherent, but politically decentralized, areas (particularly in English-speaking Africa), and extreme economic backwardness coupled with unstable, revolutionary politics, is closely parallel to the situation prevailing in Latin America. On the other hand, both the English- and the French-language African universities are closely attached to effective, high-standard European academic systems, which has not been the case in Latin America. This is a circumstance favoring the maintenance of international academic standards and preventing such far-reaching politicization of the university as occurs in Latin America. If other things remain unchanged, the situation may then develop somewhat in the same direction as in India, where a few institutions and individuals oriented toward the outside world struggle for high standards amidst a flood of academic pettiness, decadence, and politicization.[47]

There is finally the possibility that these elite systems will turn into expert systems. This actually occurred in the more or less recent past in the U.S.S.R. and in Japan. In both cases the transition took place under extraordinary conditions: revolution in Russia, and defeat followed by foreign occupation in Japan. Otherwise the transition from an elite to an expert system of universities is very difficult, since it is inevitably opposed by the only experts available. These are necessarily the products of an elite system, and they will perceive the transition to an expert system as a threat to their status as well as to their values.

This resistance notwithstanding, it is possible that the Russian and Japanese example will eventually be followed. This may occur not because of the immanent instability of the elitist system in developing societies—this could just as well become chronic as in Latin America—but because the internationally most influential system—the American one—is an expert system, as are the two others next in size and potential influence, those of the U.S.S.R. and Japan. Since the African systems are linked to international networks they may re-orient themselves—especially the English-language ones—to the U. S. pattern.

Types III and IV: Expert Systems. Whereas in the elite systems the model and non-model types are poles apart, the distance between these two in the expert systems is not so great. The reason is that where the role definition of the academic is that of an expert, the differences between various fields and institutions within the system become relatively more important than in the elite type. Professors of engineering will always tend to be different kinds of person than their counterparts in modern English poetry. But in the elite type they will have more contact and more identification with each other and less with engineers on the one hand and poets on the other who are not academics than in the expert system. As a result, in expert systems, a situation of model may prevail in one field (e.g., medicine) and of non-model in another (e.g., mathematics). Transition from a non-model to a model state will, as a result, be easier. In elite systems such transition implies a change in the ruling elite, in practice, often amounting to revolutionary upheaval. In the expert system this may be a more gradual process, such as the decision to hire certain kinds of new experts by government or business. We shall therefore treat these two types together, especially since the information of academic freedom in Type IV, the major representative of which is the U.S.S.R., is not sufficient nor easily comparable with that existing for other systems. It is hoped, nevertheless, that the few comparisons which can be made at this point will make further research on the subject better focused and more useful.

Taking the U. S. academic system as an example of the expert type of university may seem misleading, since the American undergraduate school is anything but a school for experts. The word coined by Clark Kerr for the largest and most representative units of the system, the "multi-versity," seems to be a much more fitting description of this combination of liberal education, training of experts and large scale research.[48] The very fact, however, that many of the individual units, as well as the system as a whole, try to do all of these things, defines the role of the academic teacher as a specialized expert. The variety of the tasks and the size itself prevent the development of an *esprit de corps* such as is possible within communities of some one hundred professors each regarded as the outstanding man in his field, comprising for all intents and purposes the university corporation. Furthermore, the variety of tasks also provides a variety of facilities for the full realization of one's scientific and scholarly capacity, and for the advancement of one's career. An able chemist, or political scientist, will probably work either simultaneously or at different stages of his career, both as the member of a department and of the staff of a research institute and will be engaged at one time or another primarily in undergraduate teaching, in the training of graduates, or in full-time research, and in administration. The opportunity for such changes and variation is a very great advantage for the professional person, since it makes it possible for him to try out and develop his capacity under a variety of conditions and thus make the best use of them. The effect of this is that the career and the role pattern is defined more in terms of professional expertise than of academic elite position.[49] From the point of view of the teachers, therefore, this type of academic consists of organizations employing experts, and designed to create optimal conditions for the utilization of their knowledge and skills for a wide and expanding variety of teaching and research tasks, provided that these do not fall below the level commensurate with their qualifications, and do not limit the unfolding of the creative potential. This is not to say that there are no elite academic institutions in the U. S. Their elite position, however, is due to the ability and willingness of each of their departments to compete with all other similar departments in the country and only to a much smaller extent to the personal relationship of the members of the university to members of a generalized elite, or to the inherited fame and symbolical importance of the institution.

This type of university becomes a workplace. Professors in America have "offices"—elsewhere "rooms"; and in America they work in them regularly, whereas elsewhere they may only visit them. Whatever the function is—teaching undergraduates, training graduates in research or doing research—there is an expectation that the academic will do a finished job. Even in the liberal arts college the part of the university system which has a diffuse educational aim, the outline of each course, the requirements and the testing of achievements are much more clearly defined than in the European systems. At the graduate level and in research the aim is to turn out finished products, and at all levels there is a conscious attempt to measure quality and quantity of production.

All this necessitates much higher levels of professional staff employment as related to the number of students, and much greater coordination of different kinds and levels of skill than in the elite systems. Such tasks need full-time administrative experts, so that the functions of academic self-government become necessarily much more restricted and partial than in the elite systems. It is quite inconceivable that this "multiversity" should be governed by temporarily elected representatives and assemblies of the faculty, or that curricula and examinations be handled in quite the same informal way as in Europe. Even in Europe—with the growth in size and functions of the university—the informal system becomes increasingly inefficient. If it were adopted by American universities, they would probably not become freer, but simply more chaotic. The university in the U. S. is not and never has been a corporation of teachers (and/or students). Self-government there is partly an administrative device for organizing the work of individual departments, and using the faculty as staff experts on committees, and partly a union type of activity defending the interests of the faculty against the administration by bargaining for agreed-upon principles of hiring, firing, promotions, tenure, and conditions of work and participation through representatives in all these processes. The professional freedom thus obtained may be much greater than any which a truly self-governing institution can confer. No one will be so tolerant of individual differences or helpful in catering to a variety of individual tastes as an efficient university administration which knows that the standing of the university depends on its ability to attract and keep the most sought after experts in the world. On the other hand, the power of the administration to make life difficult for academics where and when their bargaining position is weak, is considerable. The only way to fend off such an eventuality is by good, legally enforceable contracts and union type protection.

This explains the different and more endemic nature of conflicts concerning academic freedom in the American and—potentially—the Soviet systems, from those in the European elite systems.

Let us take the clashes which have actually occurred. These were basically centered around three issues: the theory of evolution, anti-monopoly and Keynesian economics, and questions of loyalty in times of war. Surprisingly, although there were famous controversies about the teaching of evolution in secondary schools, problems of academic freedom in the American universities in regard to this issue were quite mild. The most famous case was the demand of President Noah Porter of Yale to William Graham Sumner in 1879 that he withdraw the use of Spencer's *Study of Sociology* in his classes. The question here, however, was not the teaching of biological evolution, but its extension to the field of social philosophy. Thus, the controversy centered around a new area which lacked the precedents and the clear methodological criteria of the natural sciences. The outcome was something of a draw: the Corporation of Yale University refused to accept Sumner's resignation, due to his powerful support among the faculty; on the other hand, Sumner withdrew the text on the grounds that the publicity had impaired its usefulness.[50] In the long run, the principle of academic freedom was extended to this area as well, and Sumner's stand contributed to its victory.

There were two main periods of attacks on economics and economists at the American universities. The first came in the "Progressive Era" of the 1890's and 1900's. Among these cases were the dismissal of Henry Carter Adams from Cornell in the 1880's for having delivered a pro-labor speech; of J. Allen Smith, political scientist, from Marietta College, in 1897, for "anti-monopoly teaching"; of Edward W. Bemis, Chicago economist, in 1895, for holding anti-monopoly views; and of Edward A. Ross, economics professor at Stanford, in 1903, and John S. Bassett, history professor at Trinity (later renamed Duke) in 1903.[51] There were other cases, including the trial of the famous economist Richard T. Ely at Wisconsin in 1894 for believing in "strikes and boycotts," justifying and encouraging the one while practicing the other.[52] However, Ely won his case and retained his position, and the principle of academic freedom was upheld.

Thus, not all of the cases were lost, nor was it unequivocal that some of the cases may not have concerned personality conflicts and personal antagonisms as well as issues of principle. All of these, it should be noted, involved professors of economics or of social science, who took public positions on political issues. In other words, the conflict took place in relatively uncertain fields which lacked the secure position of the natural sciences; moreover it was not merely a question of the political views of professors, but of professors who might lay claim to a special expertise in politics because of their academic positions. Similarly, the attacks on Keynesian economists during the New Deal era of the 1930's and the period of the 1940's were directed toward academic specialists whose views might be given special weight in public policy, and furthermore who held a relatively new point of view within their field. But this time, although there was considerable noise, there was little concrete action; the only major case known of economists resigning under pressure of such attacks took place at the University of Illinois, when Dean Bowen of the College of Commerce and Business Administration resigned in a general controversy about the appointment of new professors, along with the Chairman of the Department of Economics, Everett Hagen, and seven other economists.[53]

Finally, there is the issue of the loyalty of academic personnel which takes place in every war-time period. The charge of pro-Germanism led to a number of dismissals from American universities in 1917 and 1918, but led as a direct result to the rapid expansion of the AAUP in its efforts to protect academic freedom.[54] There were similar attempted purges during World War II and the Korean War. But in all of these cases, the attacks on academics were not specifically an issue of academic freedom, but comprised part of general attacks on freedom in the society. Even in these cases, the same general principle applies: physicists were less likely to be harassed by the McCarthy-type probes than were Chinese experts (or State Department officials); the greatest attacks were always delivered on those fields with the greatest consequences for policy and which were most vulnerable due to the lack of a clear criterion of purely scholarly evaluation.[55]

The places where conflicts are most likely to occur have generally been in the less prominent universities; with the exception of Pennsylvania, Yale, and Smith, none of the major private or state universities were censured by the AAUP from its founding in 1915 to 1953. Otherwise, those censured included approximately random proportions of universities and colleges of every size, geographical location, and form of control.[56]

This shows that in no cases has there been a general clash about principles of academic freedom in the society as a whole. The clashes occurred in new fields, or in fields which were put to a new type of use. These new enterprises were suggested either by the outside community, or by the scholars and scientists. Hence, they could not count on having experts in the area in crucial civil service or other elite positions to serve as an effective buffer between the academics and the politicians. When a new kind of enterprise crops up, such a class of people in the new field simply cannot exist yet. They may be produced within a generation or two; until then the two sides to the enterprise may very well collide. In Europe this type of conflict was prevented by (1) a much greater apprehensiveness and caution in introducing such potentially "dangerous" fields as economics and social sciences into the universities; (2) the fact that where introduced, they were defined in a sufficiently abstract way as to make the drawing of practical conclusions out of place (after all academics were defined as intellectuals who should keep away from practice) whereas in the U. S. the academic is constantly challenged to do something practical; and (3) universities being elite institutions controlled by a central elite, and appointments being few, so that "unsuitable" persons are usually screened out in advance, especially in new and risky fields, or are put into positions where—as shown above—they constitute a harmless minority of one.

The second kind of factor contributing to conflict in the expert system is that the line between what is and what is not a university cannot easily be drawn, since the burden of the proof is on those who want to exclude something from it. They would have to prove why research and training in a new field can not produce desirable results, or why giving freedoms usually given to creative people would harm the level of teaching of a faculty which had never attempted to create very much. Thus, there is a constant extension of academic freedom to categories of institutions which in elite systems would never be considered as academic institutions. Where the burden of the proof is on those who want to be admitted to the academic rank, and the question typically posed is whether the new field or the school lives up to the highest standards, exclusion is the legitimate procedure in case of doubt. The German universities resisted the granting of academic status to institutes of technology (they were granted this status by the government in spite of the universities) and much of the engineering and professional training in England has taken place in schools or in apprenticeship programs which were not considered academic at all.[57] The "expert" universities, therefore, are under pressure to expand and enter into risky marginal fields, and thus are more in danger of getting into situations of "non-model," where either some of the research activities and/or the character of the expanding teaching and student body is such that it impresses the legislatures and/or the public as going beyond the accepted aim and character of the university.

The background of the conflicts between politicians and universities about military secrecy and diplomatic interests is of the same kind. These conflicts did not lead to attack on academic freedom in Europe because there this type of work has not been performed in the universities (whether the work concerns the manufacture of the hydrogen bomb or the policy toward China), but in properly constituted, centrally-controlled civil service establishments. Thus the taking of chances was to a large extent prevented in advance, and such problems as still arose could be dealt with as a civil service rather than an academic affair. In the U. S., universities and other independent academic institutions have been charged with these tasks, and have in fact suggested most of them. Some of these tasks involved the creation of new types of specialists, others, the use of old ones in tasks with which there had been no previous experience and in numbers which created a scarcity. To organize matters so as to ensure in advance proper control and communication between the experts and the politicians through an elite capable of serving as mediators—and to repeat this on the different local levels of a decentralized system—would have greatly retarded or entirely prevented developments. This is not to justify the stupidity and cruelty of the attacks on scholars and scientists. On the other hand, academic freedom cannot be used to prevent the legislature or the donor from making up their own minds even at the risk of committing a mistake. Such situations, even given the best intentions and maximum wisdom, involve legitimate conflict, controversy, and trial and error which may represent an interference with academic freedom. But it is a moot question whether a situation in which the academic has the opportunity to pioneer new fields, at the risk of getting involved in undignified conflict, means more or less freedom than where he is prevented from such conflicts by being confined to a closely guarded ivory tower.

Some of the interference with academic freedom in the U.S.S.R.—though not the barbaric methods which were applied to resolve the issue—arose under comparable conditions. The Lysenko controversy was originally the result of dissatisfaction with the failure of geneticists to find a way to eliminate a potato disease which was of very great importance for the economy. Support given for applied research was—justifiably—used for the solution of basic problems, and the researchers were accused of dishonesty and of deliberate sabotage of the economy. The accusations were supported by a disgruntled old-fashioned member of the profession, in a field of study which had undergone revolutionary change shortly before the events.[58] In every respect the situation is comparable to what happened at the University of Illinois concerning Keynesian economics. Both cases were scandalous, and the Russian case was a much crueler scandal than the U. S. one. But controversies of this kind are inevitable. Had the result been temporary rescinding of funds, it would have been part of the risk that enterprising research, like all other enterprise, always has to take.

As all these instances show, the typical problem of freedom in the expert university is limited at one time to a certain selected field, connected with a specific topic or method in that field (statistical genetics, anti-trust theories, Keynesian economics, Chinese specialists in political science, etc.) and arises as a result of an academic innovation or of drastic changes in the economy or politics involving the applications of those specific studies. Thus, even though there may be political conflicts, they are too specific to become ideological ones. They do not involve the principle of free enquiry, or even the basic organization of the university. The attacks are on selected members of the faculty, or on selected departments, or research institutes, concerning issues which are in some doubt, and the greater the doubt the more likely there will be conflicts. They may result in the victimization of certain people or the reduction of funds for some kinds of research or both. The danger resulting from this for the academic profession as a whole and the advancement of science in general is that it tends to introduce an element of incalculable and unpredictable risk in the work of the scientist, thus making the profession unattractive, and suppressing, both as a result of short-term fear and long-term selection, creative pioneering.

The typical means of fighting this danger has been through defensive legal measures of collective agreements and contracts about tenure. An important role in the promotion of academic freedom in the United States has been played by the AAUP, which is, in everything but its name, a kind of trade union. It has not been engaged in salary negotiations, but it has brought pressure on universities to raise salaries; it has no collective contract, but it tries to enforce common patterns of contracts safeguarding the professional autonomy of the academic profession.[59]

The working of the market is probably an even more important safeguard. Where academics are an elite, they are treated like a luxury, and their professional freedom is a privilege. Where they are widely used, they are a necessity and command a price. Attacks on them making the profession riskier are bound to be counteracted by raising the pay and status— and in consequence the autonomy of the scientists. It is quite likely that in the not even so long run American scientists in general have benefited economically from the McCarthy attack, and those at the University of California in particular from the loyalty oath controversy. (This may also explain the extremely high pay and extraordinary privileges of scientists in the U.S.S.R., relative to the rest of the populace.)

The conflict in the expert type university between those supporting the university and the professionals working in it is therefore of the same type as that occurring in governmental or industrial organizations which employ scientists. Although the fact that the principal product of the universities is what the scientists do, so that their interests are more likely to be given priority over other interests, their specific output is often supposed to be useful for practical purposes, and, therefore, to some extent subject to outside scrutiny and criticism. Professional autonomy has therefore to be constantly re-defined. Twenty, thirty, or fifty years ago the claims of the economists for professional autonomy were challenged, partly because the subject was less developed, and partly because the outsiders who had to form an opinion about it received conflicting guidance about it. Today such conflicts about economics in America are inconceivable, since professionally trained economists abound in business and government thus creating a model, and serving as effective mediators between academics and politicians. A similar change has probably taken place in Soviet genetics during the last ten years, and is not unlikely to take place in the near future in Soviet economics.

The basic problem of students and nonacademic intellectuals in the elite systems, namely that they face an authoritative elite—in intellectual and other spheres—which may block their advancement and restrict the scope of their enterprise, does not exist in the expert systems. Since the intellectual situation is not defined in terms of a unidimensional hierarchy it is unlikely to generate a sense of oppression such as may arise where an official body of intellectuals controls and restricts opportunities for other intellectuals. It is unlikely, therefore, that any discontent arising in such a situation will be formulated in terms of generalized ideologies.

Discontent which may arise will tend to center about problems of instruction and other conditions prevailing at the university, or about the share of the students, a growing and distinct social group, in political power. The specificity of the training may turn into pedantry of a not very inspiring kind. This is a distinct possibility, and quite widespread in the lower grade American and Soviet institutions. Since, however, this will be serious only in the weaker institutions, it will not affect the totality of students. Besides, these are technical matters which can be dealt with locally and in an open competitive system are unlikely to reach very serious proportions. There may be an acceptance of a great deal of regulation in this system without being justifiably considered as a violation of the freedom of the student.

One would not expect in these systems the existence of widespread resentment or even of a significant politically conscious student movement. Student dissatisfaction with the relative deprivation of undergraduate teaching would generally manifest itself in such things as riotous behavior, which is a problem of discipline, but not of academic freedom. Of course, where there is general political oppression students and intellectuals may show greater sensitivity and display more activity for reform than others irrespective of the type of university, but these will not be generated by conditions prevailing at the university, nor will they be directed toward changes in the university.

Conclusion

Academic freedom is, on the one hand, a professional role pattern implying that those engaged in higher learning and creative research use their personal discretion and initiative to determine their work subject only to standards accepted by their own profession. In this sense academic freedom is a widespread phenomenon, known in all literate societies. On the other hand, the term refers to the organization of specialized institutions engaged in teaching and research in an expanding range of fields. Organization implies certain constraints in exchange for gains in efficiency. And an expanding range involves a procedure for the granting of facilities for new kinds of work and new types of people. The method originally adopted to administer the organizational facilities and make the decisions consistent with the autonomy of the professional pattern was a guildlike corporation. It has been shown that in the best case this created conservatism and some inefficiency in the expansion of the uses of learning and research, and in the worst cases it resulted in abuse or misuse of privilege.

It seems, therefore, that development toward some kind of an expert system is inevitable. The loss of freedom involved in this is deceptive: it is like the loss of "freedom" of the guilds which was inefficient privilege enjoyed at the expense of others. The means appropriate to protect the freedom of the role pattern in the new system are not corporate (i.e., faculty) government, but contract, some kind of unionization to resist organized pressure, and the opportunities and responsibilities of a market.

With the rise of this type of university, the crucial role of students and intellectuals in ideological politics will probably pass. Emerging student politics are likely to be concerned with the re-definition of the rights and duties of a student body which is greater in relative size, older in age, and spending more of its life at universities than previous generations of students, and which both studies and, increasingly works, at universities which perform more productive work. Of course, with the growth of the proportion of students among the voting-age population, their political influence is bound to grow. But again, this is not likely to result in a particular brand of ideological student politics, but in the kind of pressure that other well-defined and able social groups exert on politics.

Notes

1. We are indebted for comments on the first draft of the manuscript to Professors Reinhard Bendix, S. M. Lipset, Talcott Parsons, Gerald Platt and Norman Storer. The research was supported by the Comparative Student Project of the Institute of International Studies of the University of California, Berkeley.
2. On academic freedom cf. R. Hofstadter and W. Metzger, *The Development of Academic Freedom in the United States* (New York: Columbia University Press, 1955); Robert MacIver, *Academic Freedom in Our Time* (New York:

Columbia University Press, 1955); *Law and Contemporary Problems—Special Issue; Academic Freedom*, XXVIII (Summer 1963).

3. For definitions of professionalism in general (not only of professional freedom) cf. A. M. Carr-Saunders and A. P. Wilson, *The Professions* (Oxford: Clarendon Press, 1933); Bernard Barber, "Some Problems in the Sociology of Professions," *Daedalus* (Fall 1963), pp. 669–688. Joseph Ben-David, "Professions in the Class System of Present-Day Societies," *Current Sociology*, XII (1963–1964), Chapter I; Harold L. Wilensky, "The Professionalization of Everyone?" *American Journal of Sociology*, LXX (September 1964), 137–158.

4. Pearl Kibre, *Scholarly Privileges in the Middle Ages* (Cambridge, Mass.: Medieval Academy of America, 1962), pp. 20–21; Hastings Rashdall, in *The Universities of Europe in the Middle Ages* (Oxford: Clarendon Press, 1936), Vol. I, p. 164, T. M. Powicke and A. B. Emden, eds.

5. Rashdall, *op. cit.*, Vol. I, pp. 540–584; Friedrich Paulsen, *The German Universities: Their Character and Historical Development* (New York: Macmillan, 1895).

6. Rashdall, *op. cit.*, Vol. I, pp. 541–543, 580; Mark H. Curtis, *Oxford and Cambridge in Transition, 1558–1642* (Oxford: Clarendon Press, 1959), pp. 278–280; G. F. Kneller, *Higher Learning in Britain* (London: Cambridge University Press, 1955), p. 18; Paulsen, *op. cit.*, p. 545.

7. M. Ornstein, *The Role of Scientific Societies in the Seventeenth Century* (Chicago: Chicago University Press, 1938), pp. 73–197, 257–263.

8. This statement refers only to the freedom of the full-fledged academics. The change had affected the freedom of students for whom there were no alternative institutions.

9. Hofstadter and Metzger, *op. cit.*, p. 16.

10. Joseph Ben-David, "Roles and Innovations in Medicine," *American Journal of Sociology*, LXV (May 1960), 557–568.

11. Giorgio di Santillana, *The Crime of Galileo* (Chicago: University of Chicago Press, 1963), pp. 344–347.

12. Pierre Duhem, *Le système du monde* (Paris: Herman et Cie, 1954), Vol. VI, pp. 20–29; Jacques Le Goff, *Les intellectuels au Moyen Age* (Paris: Seuil, 1957), pp. 123–127; Guy Beaujouan, "Motives and Opportunities for Science in the Medieval Universities," in A. C. Crombie, ed., *Scientific Change* (New York: Basic Books, 1963), pp. 224–231.

13. For a recent survey of student politics containing references to nineteenth-century material as well, cf. Seymour Martin Lipset, Chapter 1, this book.

14. Max Weber, "Science as a Vocation" in H. H. Gertz and C. W. Mills, eds., *From Max Weber: Essays in Sociology* (New York: Oxford University Press, 1958), pp. 129–156.

15. Joseph Fayet, *La Révolution Française et la science* (Paris: Marcel Rivière, pp. 17–21.

16. Joseph Ben-David and A. Zloczower, "Universities and Academic Systems in Modern Societies," *European Journal of Sociology*, III (1963), 45–85.

17. Joseph Ben-David, "Professions in the Class System of Present-Day Societies," *Current Sociology*, XII (1963-1964), No. 3, pp. 273-275.

18. *Ibid.*, p. 263.

19. "Elite" as opposed to "expert" is a distinction between diffuseness and specificity. The academic in the elite systems has to be an expert too, but that is not a sufficient condition. His expertise itself is judged according to criteria of diffuseness. Such questions typically asked as, "Is his specialization broad enough, or important enough?"; "Is he not merely a good technician?" (1) that the academic person has to cover a broader segment of fields than those who are merely "experts"; and (2) that he must possess qualities of leadership which are not easily defined, only intuitively distinguishable when compared with those who do not possess those qualities.

20. D. S. L. Cardwell, *The Organization of Science in England* (London: Heinemann, 1957), pp. 46-51.

21. Hofstadter and Metzger, *op. cit.*, pp. 413-414.

22. It should be possible to define them in quantitative terms by relating the numbers and kinds of students at the early stages of modern university growth to the numbers of trained and qualified people in the ruling elites, or in the country in general.

23. Don K. Price, *Government and Science* (New York: New York University Press, 1954), p. 122; Lord Chorley, "Academic Freedom in the United Kingdom," *Law and Contemporary Problems*, XXVIII (Summer 1963), 647-671.

24. A. Flexner, *Universities: American, English, German* (New York: Oxford University Press, 1930), pp. 289-296; E. G. Boring, *A History of Experimental Psychology* (2nd ed.; New York: Appleton-Century-Crofts, 1950), p. 494; Howard Becker, *Social Thought from Lore to Science* (3rd ed.; New York: Dover Books, 1961), Vol. 3, p. xcviii.

25. Glen H. Elder, Jr., "Life Opportunity and Personality: Some Consequences of Stratified Secondary Education in Britain," *Sociology of Education*, XXXVIII (Spring 1965), 173-202. In addition we are indebted to Professors Max Gluckman and Hilde Himmelweit for information about different enquiries showing the decisive effect of the ranking system within and between schools on the self-perception and level of aspiration of students in England.

26. Cf. Michael Young, *The Rise of Meritocracy: 1870-2033* (London: Thames and Hudson, 1958), for a semi-literary presentation of this atmosphere and its imagined consequences.

27. On the general point of the cooptation of dissenters by controlling elites, cf. Philip Selznick, "Foundations of the Theory of Organizations," *American Sociological Review*, XIII (February 1948), 25-35.

28. Michel Crozier, *The Bureaucratic Phenomenon* (Chicago: The University of Chicago Press, 1964), pp. 238-244.

29. Franz Schnabel, *Deutsche Geschichte im Neunzehnten Jahrhundert* (Freiberg: Herder, 1934), Vol. 3, pp. 140-141; Frederic Lilge, *The Abuse of Learning* (New York: Macmillan, 1948), pp. 20-23, 30-34; Richard Graf du Moulin

Eckart, *Geschichte der deutschen Universitäten* (Stuttgart: Enke, 1929), p. 350.

30. This is not to say that they actually obtained such safeguards. In Russia they never have. In Latin America, on the other hand, they did. Cf. Luigi Einandi, "University Autonomy and Academic Freedom in Latin America," *Law and Contemporary Problems, Special Issue: Academic Freedom*, XXVIII (Summer 1963), 636–646.

31. Frank Bowles, *Access to Higher Education* (Paris: UNESCO and the International Association of Universities, 1963), Vol. I, pp. 147–152; Rudolph P. Atcon, "The Latin American University," *Die Deutsche Universitätszeitung*, XVII (February 1962), 9–48.

32. Nicholas Hans, *History of Russian Educational Policy* (London: P. S. King, 1931); Hans-Eberhard Müller, *State, Society and Education: The Russian Case in the Nineteenth Century* (Unpublished M.A. thesis, Department of Sociology, University of California, Berkeley, Calif., 1966).

33. Richard Pipes, ed., *The Russian Intelligentsia* (New York: Columbia University Press, 1961), p. 10.

34. Gabriel del Mazo, *La reforma universitaria (1918–1940)* (3 vols.; La Plata: Edición del Centro Estudiantes de Ingeniera, 1941), and his *Estudiantes y gobierno universitario* (2nd ed.; Buenos Aires: El Ateneo, 1956); Roberto MacLean y Estenos, *La crisis universitaria en Hispano-América* (Mexico, D. F.: Universidad Nacional, 1956), pp. 51–56, 73–75; Foción Febres Cordero, *Reforma universitaria* (Caracas: Universidad Central de Venezuela, 1960), pp. 65–68; Arthur P. Whitaker, *The United States and Argentina* (Cambridge, Mass.: Harvard University Press, 1954), pp. 67–74, 152–153; Frank Bonilla, "The Student Federation of Chile: 50 years of Political Activity," *Journal of Inter-American Studies*, II (July 1960), 311–334; Kalman H. Silvert, *The Conflict Society: Reaction and Revolution in Latin America* (New Orleans: Hauser, 1961), pp. 162–182; and his "The University Student," in John J. Johnson, ed., *Continuity and Change in Latin America* (Stanford: Stanford University Press, 1964), pp. 206–226. On the general setting of the problem cf. S. M. Lipset, "Values, Education and Entrepreneurship in Latin America," in S. M. Lipset and Aldo Solari, eds., *Elites and Development in Latin America* (New York: Oxford University Press, 1967), pp. 3–49.

35. Friedrich Paulsen, *The German University: Its Character and Historical Development* (New York: Macmillan, 1895), pp. 85–86; Flexner, *op. cit.*, 1930, pp. 317–320.

36. Du Moulin Eckart, *op. cit.*, p. 222; Carl Brinkmann, *Der Nationalismus und die deutschen Universitäten im Zeitalter der deutschen Erhebung, Sitzungsverichte d. Heidelberger Akademic d. Wissenschaften*, Philosophisch-historische Klasse (1931–1932) 3 (Abhandlung, Heidelberg: Carl Winters, 1932). Cf. especially pp. 72–78 for parallels with late nineteenth-century Russia and p. 72 for social background—insecure, downwardly mobile parents—of alienated students.

37. After the number of students in Prussia had increased from 3,311 (or 29.3/100,000 of population) to 15,751 (52.5/100,000) between 1820–1830, measures were taken to restrict entrance. The figures for the following decades were 1841: 11,593; 1851: 12,314; 1861: 13,248 (34.0/100,000, 34.2/100,000; 33.8/100,000). These figures and the description of the measures are based on Volker Eisele, "Democratization in German Higher Education" (unpublished seminar paper, Department of Sociology, University of California, Berkeley, 1965).

38. Schnabel, *loc. cit.*

39. Friedrich Paulsen, *The German Universities and University Study* (New York: Longmans Green, 1960), pp. 228–231.

40. Ben-David and Zloczower, *op. cit.*

41. For the invidious atmosphere concerning university honors cf. Samuel and Thomas, *op. cit.*, pp. 116–117. The ideologies of the period are described in Karl Löwith, *Von Hegel bis Nietzsche* (Zürich-New York: Europa Verlag, 1941); for some of the sociological aspects of the psychoanalytic movement cf. J. Ben-David, *op. cit.*, *American Journal of Sociology.*

42. Paulsen, *op. cit.*, 1895, pp. 189–194; Samuel and Thomas, *op. cit.*, pp. 120–121.

43. W. Kornhauser, *The Politics of Mass Society* (New York: Free Press, 1959), pp. 187–192.

44. Paulsen, *op. cit.*, 1895, pp. 187–188, 201.

45. Michio Nagai, "The University and the Intellectual," *Japan Quarterly* (Autumn, 1964), 46–52; Herbert Passin, "Japan," in James S. Coleman, ed., *Education and Political Development* (Princeton: Princeton University Press, 1965), pp. 272–312.

46. Cf. James S. Coleman, ed., *op. cit.*, articles by Coleman, pp. 35–50; Francis X. Sutton, pp. 51–74; Michel Debeauvais, pp. 75–91; Ayo Ogunsheye, pp. 123–143; Coleman, pp. 353–371; Anthony H. M. Kirk-Greene, pp. 372–407; Dwaine Marwick, pp. 463–497.

47. Cf. Edward A. Shils, *The Intellectual between Tradition and Modernity: The Indian Situation* (The Hague: Mouton, 1961), and his "Towards a Modern Intellectual Community in the New States," in Coleman, ed., *op. cit.*, pp. 498–518.

48. Cf. Clark Kerr, *The Uses of the University* (Cambridge, Mass.: Harvard University Press, 1964).

49. The mobility from university to university characteristic of German academics could not achieve quite the same effect, because of the formalized distinction between the academic and non-academic careers (the former requiring Habilitation) and the very limited opportunities in the former career.

50. Hofstadter and Metzger, *op. cit.*, pp. 335–338.

51. *Ibid.*, pp. 419–451.

52. *Ibid.*, p. 426.

53. Robert MacIver, *op. cit.*, 1955, pp. 132–134.

54. Hofstadter and Metzger, *op. cit.*, pp. 495–505.
55. Price, *op. cit.*, pp. 109–110.
56. Hofstadter and Metzger, *op. cit.*, p. 493.
57. A. Flexner, *op. cit.*, pp. 330–331.
58. David Joravsky, "The Lysenko Affair," *Scientific American*, CCIX (November 1962), 41–49.
59. Hofstadter and Metzger, *op. cit.*, pp. 468–506.

Students and Politics in Western Countries

PART III

Student Politics and Higher Education in the United States[1]

SEYMOUR MARTIN LIPSET
PHILIP G. ALTBACH

7

In recent years, American students, previously noted more for their political apathy than their interest in governmental issues, have received worldwide attention for their political activism. Starting with the Berkeley "revolt" of 1964, the American campus has seemingly exploded with political and social action, and the "new student left" has become the subject of much analysis—by educators worried about the tranquility of their institutions, government officials concerned about "subversive" influences on the campus, social scientists interested in political movements, and by the mass media. The number of articles, books, and dissertations on the new student movement in the United States is substantial.[2]

In the past decade, various events have taken place which have emphasized the importance of students in politics and higher education in many of the developing areas. These areas are discussed in more detail in other chapters. Spurred by student demonstrations which have succeeded in toppling governments in such nations as Turkey, South Korea, and South Vietnam, both academic observers and government officials have taken an increased interest in student political activities and movements. The historical role of students in various independence movements, in India, Burma, Vietnam, Algeria, and other nations, and their potential as "incipient elites" in many new nations, have also been the subject of analysis.[3] In Spain and Portugal, students have played a major role in demanding more academic and political freedom. More recently, students in the industrially advanced nations have also taken a politically active role, and have obtained their share of newspaper headlines. Student strikes in France, Italy, and West Germany demanding better educational facilities and the recent upsurge of American student activity seem to indicate a new political consciousness on the part of the students.

This chapter will examine the American student movement in an effort to analyze some of the causes and effects of student political involvement in the United States, and to link this activity to trends in the developing nations. We are convinced that students are, in certain circumstances, an important political element and that, in any case, political activity is often a vital means of socialization for students. As the other chapters in this book indicate, in many nations where the student population is small and mostly composed of the offspring of the various elites, student activism has been of crucial importance in national politics.

At the outset, it should be made clear that we recognize that the scope of the American student "revolution" has been greatly exaggerated by the mass media, which have seized upon dramatic forms of student political activity and have devoted substantial attention to them. Student political organizations involve only a tiny minority of the total student population in the United States. The *National Guardian*, a left-wing newspaper, has estimated that there are perhaps 12,000 members of *all* of the various "new left" organizations in the United States, with a similar number of sympathizers.[4] Representatives of the "new left" Students for a Democratic Society claim 20,000 members and supporters. When it is remembered that there are about 6,000,000 students in American colleges and universities, these figures are not very significant. Most American institutions of higher education have not been affected by the "new left." A comprehensive study of student activism during 1964–1965, based on replies to questionnaires from the Deans of Students in 849 institutions, reports the total absence of student radicals in 74 per cent of them. In the remaining group, those who filled out the questionnaires checked the lowest possible category of response other than "none," i.e., "less than 5 per cent," in all but .5 per cent of the cases. Student leftism, involvement in civil rights activities, and opposition to the Vietnamese war, are largely associated with size and quality of university.[5] The smaller private and denominational colleges, many state universities, and almost all technological schools, teachers' and junior colleges, have seen no demonstrations, have no chapters of left-wing or civil rights groups, and their student bodies do not exhibit much political awareness.

Yet, if the press, the educational community, and the public believe that there has been a student revolution in the United States, then there has indeed been one. The fact that only a small minority of the students have participated in radical politics, or have criticized the workings of the university has not prevented many conferences and meetings concerning ways to deal with the "new student." Thus, even in the United States, where the student population is large, heterogeneous, and generally not considered a politically crucial factor, a vocal student minority has been able to attract a good deal of attention and has stimulated much thought on political and educational issues. The effects of the new student left on the larger polity are still being felt, and it is clear that while the movement has been unable to change the nation's Vietnam policy, it has been a source of pressure for educational reform and has given a voice to the student community.

There are three different sets of events which are related to the mass media's interest in student activism since 1964 and to the considerable publicity which it has received. The first, the rise of the student-based civil rights movement has continued for about seven years, and in many ways made the other two, the Berkeley revolt and the aggressive movement against the Vietnam war, possible.

The involvement of white students in the fight for civil rights grew slowly but steadily in the years following the desegregation decision of the Supreme Court in 1954. By 1960, it was organized into two groups, the Student Non-Violent Coordinating Committee (SNCC), and the Congress of Racial Equality (CORE). Both organizations, the first operating primarily in the South and the other more concentrated in the North, came to accept civil disobedience against unjust laws as the most effective way of gaining the supremely moral end of equal rights. Although only a small minority of students were willing to engage in acts of civil disobedience, there can be little doubt that the overwhelming majority of the academic community, both student and faculty, agreed with the objectives of these groups, and admired their courage in risking jail to fight for equal rights. The proportion of students nationally who reported to pollsters that they had taken part in picket lines, presumably mainly to enforce a civil rights objective, is rather large, 18 per cent.[6]

Participation in such activities has often had the effect of radicalizing the students involved, particularly among those who went South for summer work, or those in the San Francisco Bay area, who during 1963–1964 had engaged in many acts of civil disobedience, including sit-ins at major business firms, which led to many being arrested. To such students, civil disobedience became the primary means of bringing pressure on community leaders. The analysis of student activism in 849 schools reported higher correlations between a record of past involvement by students in civil rights activities in the South and the incidence of a variety of campus protests than between the presumed proportion of the student body belonging to leftist organizations and active demonstrations. As Richard Peterson comments:

Civil rights experience in the South could provide students with a set of proven techniques, a kind of tactical style, that could be used in protesting a variety of situations—both on the campus as well as off campus.[7]

The lessons and experiences of the civil rights movement made the Berkeley revolt of 1964 possible. The action of the Berkeley administration in denying to political groups the right to use the one small part of the campus on which they had previously been allowed to collect funds and recruit participants for off-campus activities, including civil rights demonstrations, was widely interpreted as a result of the University's yielding to pressure from institutions which had been attacked by campus-based civil rights groups. A study of the participants in the effort to prevent the arrest of a CORE leader by keeping a police car surrounded indicated that over half of the students involved had taken part in at least one previous civil rights demonstration; 17 per cent indicated that they had taken part in seven or more.[8]

The Berkeley revolt, which witnessed the siege of a police car holding an arrested CORE leader for over 30 hours by over 600 students, the occupation of Sproul Hall, the campus administration building, by 700 students who had to be pulled out bodily one by one by the police and were arrested, and a strike which closed down much of the campus for a few days, was probably the most militant series of student demonstrations in American campus history. It was clearly newsworthy in its own right. Once Berkeley had impressed university administrators and the mass media with the potential for student action, many insignificant protests, some involving a handful of students, on other campuses around the country suddenly became potential Berkeleys. In a sense the Berkeley Free Speech Movement became the massive locomotive behind which many toy trains were hooked by the press, frightening deans and college presidents. In retrospect, it is clear that the Berkeley revolt was an isolated event caused by very specific local factors, that it did not foretell any national upsurge of student protest against the evils of the "multiversity," the isolated nature of Berkeley however was not clear during the academic year 1964–1965.

Much more important than the Berkeley revolt in determining reactions to the student movement has been the nature of opposition to the Vietnam War. Following the decision by the U.S. government in February 1965 to escalate American participation by bombing North Vietnam and pouring in hundreds of thousands of American troops, campus opposition, both faculty and student, grew rapidly. At the University of Michigan, in March, a faculty group sought to emulate Berkeley by calling for a campus-wide strike against the War. This proposal, which brought down the wrath of politicians, business leaders, and the press on the University, was dropped in favor of an alternative, presented to the University administration: the teach-in, a twenty-four-hour meeting to discuss the issues of the War involving both faculty and students.

The teach-in tactic and other forms of protest against the war spread to many campuses and soon gained widespread publicity, which made some observers think that they were witnessing the birth of a mass campus radical protest movement. To oppose an on-going war is clearly a much more radical act than to press for more civil rights for Negroes, an objective favored in principle by almost everyone. Campus opposition to the war has remained extremely important in the eyes of the press.

The escalation of the war effort between 1965 and 1967 has lent strength to the more extremist elements among the student opposition, since desperate measures seem warranted as the only means of impressing the country and its leaders. A number of student anti-war groups, led by those based in Berkeley, have engaged in various acts of civil disobedience against the war, including efforts to stop the movement of troop trains, the demonstrative burning of draft cards, and the passing out of anti-war leaflets at military bases urging soldiers not to fight. The role of foreign policy opposition assumed by the campus critics of the war, both faculty and students, has given them access to the mass media, which focus on the inherently attention-worthy acts of civil disobedience. They sometimes give the impression that a large proportion, if not the great majority, of American students are in revolt against the war. Thus a British visitor to the United States reporting on the B.B.C. on the academic year 1964–1965 stated that

American academic life is in turmoil. . . .Over Vietnam, the academics . . . have flexed their muscles, gained considerably in morale, and are ready for the next round. In this, they have the wholehearted support on the students who . . . on various campuses are in fighting trim.[9]

The campus Vietnam protest movement has involved a number of small national left-wing groups, which have supplied the militant spark and aggressive leadership. On the extreme left was the May 2 Movement, which dissolved in 1966 due to insufficient support and internal factional problems. This organization was established by the pro-Maoist Progressive Labor party. The Trotskyist Young Socialist Alliance has also been active on the left wing of the protest movement, as has the New York based Marxist Youth against War and Fascism. The Communist oriented (pro-Russian) Du Bois Clubs have been the largest (2,500 members) and also the most moderate of the "old left" groups descended from the Leninist Movement. The Young People's Socialist League (YPSL) is also small and has tended to ignore the other leftist groupings in favor of cooperating with the Young Democrats and ADA. The most important organization of the "new left," the Students for a Democratic Society (SDS), is also the biggest (7,000) and most effective radical group. It, however, has continued to devote much of its energy to domestic issues, such as poverty and civil rights.

At Berkeley, the Vietnam Day Committee (VDC) and the Peace Rights Organizing Committee (PROC) have spearheaded the anti-Vietnam agitation. They have stimulated militant activity elsewhere. These groups involve many who were active in the Free Speech Movement. The Berkeley opposition has engaged in publicly planning and occasionally carrying out various acts of civil disobedience against the war. It is indicative of Berkeley's importance in setting the pace for the wider movement that the two International Days of Protest of the 1965–1966 school year involving demonstrations around the world from Montevideo to Tokyo were determined by the Berkeley academic calendar. The first protests, October 15 and 16, coincided with Berkeley's Family Day, the occasion on which thousands of parents of students visit the campus. It is inherently the day on which radical political demonstrations are most embarrassing to the University. The second set, March 24 to 26, included Berkeley's Charter Day, the celebration of the University's founding, to which it has always invited internationally famous personalities, on this occasion the Ambassador to the United Nations, Arthur Goldberg.

At other less-engaged schools many radical and pacifist groups have been actively involved in somewhat less militant anti-war meetings, marches, and petition campaigns. A small number of faculty have joined with the student groups on various campuses. Nationally, the different groups have been somewhat divided as to the extent to which they should use civil disobedience tactics such as the public burning of draft cards. A referendum in 1966 within the largest left-wing student organization, SDS, voted down reliance on such methods by 56 per cent to 44 per cent. The Berkeley and Michigan chapters strongly backed civil disobedience, while the Harvard affiliate opposed it.

An attempt to found a national anti-Vietnam coalition in November 1965 failed. At a conference in Washington on November 26, 1965, the various political factions of the "old left" (mainly the Communists, Maoists, and Trotskyists) fought each other for control and succeeded only in producing a sense of increasing alienation and despair among many of the young SDS and SNCC activists who were present.

In evaluating the extent of student politics, it is important to differentiate between the leftist groups, which are committed to some form of socialism, or, like many members of SNCC and CORE, basically reject American society as inherently evil, corrupt, and unreformable except through a major social change, and those more numerous politically concerned students who favor liberal reforms. A number of religious student groups, for example, have supported the revival of student activism, particularly as it involves support of civil rights and responsible criticism of American foreign policy. The magazine *Motive*, which is published by the Board of Higher Education of the Methodist Church, has consistently stressed the importance of student political action. Similarly, the student branches of the YMCA, and the Young Christian Students, a Catholic group, have sent many students to the South to work on civil rights projects and have provided a forum for discussion of political topics.

A study of the attitudes of the volunteers with the largest civil rights project in the South during the summer of 1965, the Summer Community Organization and Political Education Program (SCOPE), indicates that most of this group of committed student activists are *not* radicals. As the authors of the study report:

On most . . . issues, their [the activists'] position is little left of the stated policies of the Johnson administration and its pursuit of the great society. Fully 60 per cent [of about 300 volunteers] are confident that the current political system is competent to cope successfully with the problem of discrimination. . . .Only 10 per cent of the volunteers agree strongly with the current maxim of the left that "American culture is sick and moving along the road to destruction." [Less than 60 per cent strongly agree that the United States should try to initiate negotiations in Vietnam.] Clearly these are not in the main radical revolutionaries.[10]

Perhaps the largest student political organizations are the university affiliates of the Young Democrats and Young Republicans. Estimates of their memberships have ranged up to 250,000 students, and it is probable that they may have approached this figure around the presidential election of 1964. At the moment, however, 100,000, or 2 per cent of the total student population, is probably a more accurate figure. Much of this figure, however, only exists "on paper." Few YDs or YRs attend meetings or do more than pay nominal dues. These groups do sponsor campus political meetings from time to time and are quite active during election campaigns. Many local branches, particularly of the Young Democrats, have supported civil rights campaigns, and a number have been active in criticizing the government's Vietnam policies. Some of the active members of these groups, for example many law students, are reputed to have an interest in making politics a career.

Right-wing student activity, though less noteworthy than in the late 1950's, as far as the press is concerned, probably still includes many more students in its membership than does the organized left. The president of the most significant such group, the Young Americans for Freedom (YAF), claims that as a result of the Goldwater campaign his group now has organized support on 200 campuses. It reports a membership of over 30,000 students and young adults in support of essentially very conservative policies. The YAF, like its left-wing opponents, has devoted much attention to the Vietnamese war. Right-wing student groups have been active in organizing mass meetings, petitions, blood donor campaigns, and the like in support of the war. Groups like the YAF have also applied pressure on the Administration, through their demonstrations of support, for a "harder" line, in favor of increased bombing of North Vietnam and other forms of escalation of the conflict in order to achieve an American "victory" in Southeast Asia. While the conservative groups are well represented in the large universities, they differ from the left-leaning ones in having much of their backing in schools outside the "mainstream" of American student politics—schools which are not leaders in intellectual life, such as church-affiliated institutions, southern universities, and locally oriented colleges outside of the metropolitan areas. The organizational stability and strength of the conservative student groups are enhanced by substantial financial support from interested adults. This relative financial affluence permits groups like the YAF and the Intercollegiate Society of Individualists (ISI) to hire full time organizers, publish slick magazines, and service a large (and often apathetic) mailing list. The left-wing groups, in contrast, find themselves chronically in debt and have often had to curtail their activities due to financial problems.

The student conservative movement is not generally aimed at substantial social change in the society—even in the direction of the libertarianism of Locke, Burke, and others who are popular among YAF members. Theirs is a movement of education, to limit the influence of liberalism and collectivism which they see as the dominant trend on the American campus. In direct contrast to the student left, campus conservatives are pessimistic about human progress and decry the "naïve optimism" of the liberals. The relatively simple and straightforward program of the conservative movement appeals to these students.[11] While the "new left" often feels that American society is controlled by a reactionary establishment, the student conservatives strongly believe that liberalism and collectivism pervade both the campus and the society.[12]

The orientation of the campus conservative movement, which has generally condemned student activism and expressed support for college administrators, has not generated much attention from the mass media, which find the dynamic actions of the "new left" more newsworthy. Furthermore, conservative students do not engage in the forms of non-conformist social behavior found among some supporters of the "new left"— i.e., use of narcotics, "beatnikism," etc. The conservative student organizations, despite their impressive financial and organizational backing, have not been notably successful in building a movement which has much commitment from its membership, nor have they made any real impact on the campus. They do, however, constitute a larger organized minority than the radical left. At the summer 1966 Congress of the National Student Association, a YAF leader, Danny Boggs, received over one-third of the votes for President.

Variations in Support: The Mood of the Faculty

The support for more radical student political actions may be analyzed in terms of types of institutions in which such activity is more common, and of the traits which characterize the individuals who participate. On the whole, as we have noted, radical student political activity has been limited to a relatively small number of colleges and universities, predominantly large schools with good faculties (as indicated by proportions with Ph.D's among them).[13] Three universities appear to stand out as centers of organized student activity in recent years. These are the University of California at Berkeley, the University of Michigan (Ann Arbor), and the University of Wisconsin (Madison). These three institutions are the leading state universities as judged by national rankings of faculty scholarly eminence, are quite big (close to 30,000 students each), have a very large graduate student enrollment including many who remain around campus for many years, are located at some considerable distance from the national centers of political power and influence, and have a largely non-local student body. Sheer numbers mean that a relatively small percentage of the total student population can mount a large demonstration. (For example, the sit-in at Sproul Hall, the administration building, which was the high point of the Berkeley revolt, involved close to 700 students or less than 3 per cent of the student body.)

Since other equally large state universities—if less eminent from the scholarly point of view—have originated less potent political protest, some have argued that the tensions reflected at these three institutions arise in part from aggrieved faculty members, whose conditions of work and sense of a lack of proper intellectual style create resentment against both the university and the larger society and polity.[14] Berkeley, of course, stands in a class by itself since the two largest and most noteworthy campus protests in a fifteen-year period both occurred there, the fight against the non-Communist Loyalty Oath in 1949–1950, and the Free Speech controversy in 1964–1965. While both of these conflicts were initiated by stupid, reactionary, and restrictive changes by the Regents or administration, these precipitating events cannot be regarded as the primary "causes." One can point to comparable attacks on academic and political freedom at many other large state universities and at some distinguished private ones which did not result in comparable faculty reactions. Clearly, the Berkeley social system has been more unstable than those of other institutions. As the most successful "upwardly mobile" institution in American academe, it has endured many of the tensions inherent in growth and development comparable to those faced by the state of California generally. And it may be suggested that just as the latter facilitate larger extremist movements of the left and right in the state, the exacerbation of social relations among faculty, students, and administration, inherent in the successful pursuit of academic eminence, has contributed to making possible the considerable political unrest and attacks against the university from within.

As most discussions of sources of student unrest have ignored the possibility that student attitudes reflect the mood of significant sections of the faculty, we would like first to discuss faculty dissatisfactions at the prestigious state universities. It is difficult to pinpoint the sources of these resentments, but some of them would seem to reflect institutional and personal status insecurities. These schools, though having large numbers of distinguished faculty, lack the sense of permanent traditional eminence which is possessed by the older private universities of the East. In a sense the major public universities resemble in their position and behavior the *nouveaux riches*, who constantly worry about their status and who seek evidence that they have really arrived. The more ancient prestigeful schools, like aristocratic old families, can ignore external opinion. The insecurity of these state universities is directly reflected in their lesser willingness to appoint their own graduates to faculty positions; they would rather rely on the judgment of others. It also shows up in the greater concern evidenced for the national rankings of departments, and for the number of awards achieved by faculty. This institutional concern results in an internal salary and reward structure which is largely geared to the market; invidious salary differentials of large magnitudes become a mechanism to recruit and retain eminent or highly promising scholarly "productive" faculty. And these differentials, in turn, create considerable resentments among faculty toward the institution.

Intellectual life is inherently very competitive, but the structure and values of the distinguished public universities magnify the factors making for competitive resentments, while some of the older major private universities are able to follow policies which somewhat reduce these pressures through the fact that they can rely on institutional prestige to secure and hold faculty, many of whom are their own former students. As one Yale professor who had also taught at Berkeley put it, an Ivy League professor is much less likely to find himself "trumped" by a younger man than he would be at Berkeley. At less distinguished and less ambitious public institutions, administration and faculty aspirations are presumably lower, and consequently there is less pressure for invidious internal differentiation, and less resentment at institutional failings. The significant difference is not whether an institution is public or private, but whether it aspires to academic eminence, and can or cannot rely on ascriptive prestige. Thus a private school which appears to fall into the same category as the big three of the state universities, Brandeis University, seems to have some of the faculty political resentments found at Madison or Berkeley. The University of Chicago, which has been in the forefront of private university student protest in 1966, also has been characterized recently by a sharply invidious internal reward system. Whether consequent strains help account for the faculty minority which encouraged on-campus civil disobedience is not known. Unlike Berkeley, a large majority of the Chicago faculty strongly backed the administration's refusal to negotiate while under pressure.

Institutional differences between public and private universities can, however, play an important role in determining the professional self-image, attitudes, and performance of the faculty. Public institutions are intrinsically under greater external pressures than their private counterparts. Dependent on public authorities for a large proportion of their budgets, and under the often careful scrutiny of legislators, journalists, and others who feel that the state university is within their domain of competence, these institutions must always be on their guard against outside political and other pressures. This fact has acted in subtle ways to diminish the status and security of the faculty, as well as to make administrators more careful in their actions. Interference with largely academic matters by publicly appointed or elected university trustees, who are necessarily more involved in their own non-academic concerns than in higher education, has had bad effects at Berkeley, and is an important problem for many state universities. In contrast, the major private institutions have few such worries. Their presidents usually have only to report to distinguished trustees, who are almost invariably alumni, and who see one of their main roles as the defense of the university from outside pressure. It is, after all, much easier to appeal to the institutional loyalties of the alumni than it is to appeal to the state legislature.

The fact that state university professors are often made aware of substantial outside control encourages the feeling among them that they are not "trusted" to make their own decisions, thus creating a sense of low status. The faculty is affected in more subtle ways by public scrutiny. Faculty members are encouraged by the administration and senior colleagues to impose a kind of self-censorship on their activities or statements for fear of public condemnation of the university. This vulnerability of public universities to outside pressure and scrutiny has had some important effects on faculty and administration. In an effort to protect their academic independence and freedom, public university faculties have attempted to achieve the maximum degree of academic self-government. Decisions which at first-rate private institutions are usually made by administrators must be dealt with by faculty committees at major public universities. The proliferation of committees has meant that professors at California, Wisconsin, and Michigan spend a good deal more time in meetings of various kinds than do their compeers at Harvard, Yale, and Princeton. It has also increased the potential for intrafaculty factionalism and dispute, since professors at the more "democratic" institutions are more likely to blame each other for unpopular decisions. A common complaint at public institutions is the large amount of time taken up in committee meetings. At the University of California, one of the explicit criteria for faculty advancement is "service to the university," which usually means participation in various committees. To this extent, the system is institutionalized.

Elaborate mechanisms of academic self-government may provide the faculty with the institutionalized means of resisting high authority in periods of crisis. They also, however, make for institutional conservatism, since as Martin Trow suggests, "Deans are usually more hospitable to experiments and innovations than are faculty committees."[15] And administrators in academic polities which involve considerable consultation with such committees tend to be weak, chosen for their ability to get along, rather than for their scholarly eminence or leadership qualities. Ironically, the very faculty which demand as much self-government as possible often bitterly criticize their administrators for lack of leadership abilities, lack of foresight in anticipating problems, and inability to cope with external pressures, liabilities which are inherent in the weakness of the role.

The greater size of the faculty and student body at the major public institutions compared with the private schools creates other frustrations and tensions. With larger departments and faculties, more meetings become necessary and more formal rules must be imposed. And in accordance with some Parkinsonian law, these factors tend to create more factionalism, to limit the freedom of the individual professor to pursue his own interests without interference from others. (The issues arising over the role of student activism at Berkeley exacerbated intra-faculty tension, and seemingly led to a sharp increase in the number departing for other positions. During the academic years, 1964–1965 and 1965–1966, approximately sixty tenured faculty resigned from Berkeley. The "normal" rate per year in more peaceful times had been much less.)

The differences between the elite private schools and the best state institutions which affect the attitude of the faculty to the university and polity are not solely a consequence of the strains of achieved as compared with the security of ascribed institutional status, or to differences which may be attributed to variations in size or type of external control. Variations in the quality of the student body are also relevant. Even the best state institutions have a student body which is quite heterogeneous in intellectual quality as compared with a rather consistent high level in the top private schools.[16] Although concern for research and other forms of intellectually creative activities is great among the faculties at all major universities, whether public or private, it seems evident that those at the elite private institutions take their teaching activities much more seriously, secure more intrinsic rewards from feeling that they are good teachers, than do those at the big three of the state schools. In a recent article on American students, Martin Meyerson, former Acting Chancellor at Berkeley, who taught for many years at Harvard, eloquently summed up some of the sources of these distinctions.

> At Oxford and Cambridge, Harvard, Yale, and Princeton, the rewards of teaching included the faculty's sense—even if not articulated—that their students were the sons of the famous or were themselves apt to be famous in the future. It is more attractive for teachers to spend time with the well-prepared and potentially powerful, than with the mediocre student of humble origins. The professor's frequent preference is to devote intellectual and leisure energies to colleagues or in some cases to men of affairs; he can be motivated to attention toward his students by a sense of duty, but this sense functions best when duty is reinforced by pleasure. And the pleasure the teacher gets seems to increase with the intellectual and social standing of his pupils.[17]

These factors encourage the active and distinguished scholars at the major private institutions to devote greater energies to teaching, and also give to those who are less competent and unrecognized as scholars a greater sense of achievement, of satisfaction with their jobs as teachers, than their equivalents secure at comparably eminent public institutions. This assumption concerning the lesser commitment to teaching of faculty at major public universities is reflected in the opinions of the faculty themselves.

> When a sample of Berkeley faculty was asked recently "What proportion of the faculty members here would you say are strongly interested in the academic problems of students?" only a third answered "almost all" or "over half" as compared with 85–90 per cent giving those responses among the faculty at three selective liberal arts colleges. The faculty's judgments of their colleagues is closely reflected in their students' judgments of them.[18]

These comments on the institutional variations between the leading public and private universities, which adversely affect faculty morale and values at the better public institutions, assume that faculty attitudes and behavior are a major source of influence on the political stance of students.

At both Berkeley and Michigan, members of the faculty have shown a willingness to attack the university as a means of attaining political ends in ways that would be unthinkable at the older major private universities.

Variations in Support: Student Reactions

The thesis that heterogeneity and size contribute to discontent may also be argued on the student level. The three major state schools recruit an intellectually much abler student body, particularly for their massive graduate student programs, than do the other public universities; yet they have many more students per faculty member than the high ranking private schools.[19] The difference in favor of the prestige private universities would increase greatly if one computed the student to distinguished faculty ratio. A recent survey of Wisconsin student opinion found that 80 per cent felt that the institution is "depersonalized." Over half of the students (59 per cent) expressed agreement with the statement that "Generally speaking, students in today's large university are no longer treated as individuals; instead they have become IBM cards, numbers, cogs in a sort of educational factory."[20] Similar attitudes have been expressed by Berkeley students in a number of different survey studies.[21] That this type of frustration is specific to the large public universities, and not to college life generally, may be seen from the results of a 1966 national survey of freshmen across the country conducted by the American Council on Education. Forty per cent of the first-year students at public universities expressed agreement with the statement that students at their school are like numbers in a book. The corresponding percentage for private universities was 20, while only 6 per cent of freshmen at four-year private nonsectarian colleges felt the same way. Reliable statistical data indicate a very high drop-out rate among undergraduates in the three high ranking public institutions (50 per cent of those who enter Berkeley as freshmen *do not* graduate.[22] Less than 5 per cent of those who enter Harvard fail to graduate; the corresponding figure for Stanford across the Bay from Berkeley is under 10 per cent). The success record among graduate students is also poor. Those who secure their doctorates there, particularly in the social sciences, often take close to a decade to do so. The figures at the major private schools are clearly better on both the graduate and undergraduate levels. The complexity of the large public institutions gives rise to substantial frustrations, among both students and faculty. It is not surprising that there seems to be social and political alienation among a significant and often the most capable minority within them.

The major state universities remain extremely heterogeneous in their student bodies, not only in terms of intellectual caliber, discussed above, but also in student sub-cultures; they still include large numbers involved in the so-called "collegiate" or fraternity—athletic—social culture; many who are narrowly vocationally oriented, viewing the university solely as a means to attaining a well-paying job; the academically-intellectually inclined; and the "non-conformists."[23] The best private schools, on the other hand, have become increasingly *homogeneous* in the caliber and traits of their students. As Martin Trow has put it:

> In liberal arts colleges and leading private universities, the enormous growth in demand for college places since World War II and the increased selectivity that has resulted have led to . . . a predominance of able, academically oriented students, the great majority of whom are going on to graduate and professional school; even their "non-conformists" and political activists are more cautious, more aware of what they have to lose.[24]

The best public institutions are large and attractive enough to support a "non-conformist" sub-culture which is sufficiently large in absolute terms to ignore social or intellectual pressures from the more purely "academic" or "collegiate" sub-cultures. The fact that they are not commuter institutions, that the great majority of their students come from outside the area also contributes to their ability to sustain a "non-conformist" culture. Various studies of student leftists, drug-users, and academically competent "drop-outs" agree that these groups draw heavily from students who are living away from home in off-campus housing, i.e., not in dormitories, houses, or fraternities.[25] The distinguished private schools are also not commuter institutions, but almost all their undergraduates live in university housing and are necessarily immersed in a primarily university environment.

Another group of large public universities, those which are located in urban centers, and draw from a less well-to-do student body which lives at home, tend to be much more vocationally oriented, and hence are less supportive of political or social non-conformism. Such institutions were major strongholds of political protest during the 1930's when many of their students feared a lack of opportunity as a result of the Depression. Today, however, upwardly mobile students from less privileged backgrounds can anticipate economically rewarding positions upon graduation. Institutions characterized by large numbers of such students tend to be relatively politically quiescent. (One seeming exception is composed of urban schools with a majority of Jewish students who are disproportionately liberal and left for other reasons.)

The best private institutions, on the other hand, possess a student body which is predominantly academic and intellectual in orientation and which works hard to accomplish the goal of an academic or other type of intellectual career. Such students are usually quite liberal in their political outlook and are sympathetic to many of the objectives of the student activists. The overwhelming majority of them desist, however, from participation in the more militant activities of the student movement, if for no other reason than that they do not have the time to engage in politics and also secure the grades necessary to get into a good graduate school.

The increasing number of graduate students, particularly in the large state universities, provides a major source of encouragement, and more important, continuity in leadership for the activist student movement. There are currently over 500,000 graduate students in the United States. Graduate students, in general, resemble the more academically oriented undergraduates in their political behavior. Although they are relatively sympathetic to activist causes, they are disinclined to participate, given their commitment to scholarship and their clear-cut career orientations. Since many of them are "teaching assistants" in close contact with lower-division undergraduates, they are in a position to communicate the sense of grievance which many of them have to first and second year students who, less involved in scholarship and careerist activities, are freer to act. As Kenneth Keniston has pointed out: "[T]he plight of graduate students is probably more dire than that of any other student group. . . . The graduate student . . . is often pressured, judged, graded, endentured and exploited."[26] Teaching assistants are obligated to devote a considerable amount of time to teaching (for only a small stipend), while at the same time they must demonstrate their competence as scholars. Graduate students in the liberal arts field are in an especially tension-ridden situation, since their research-minded professors are constantly on the outlook for brilliance. They give their graduate students the sense that they are constantly being judged for their scholarly potential by criteria which are often imprecise and highly subjective. To view the larger society as a competitive "rat-race" is but to project the situation of many graduate students onto the total system. Many "drop-out" for shorter or longer periods to escape these pressures, while often continuing to live near the campus. Some become available to serve as the "non-student" leaders of campus protest. In groups like SDS, many of the older leaders, who provide the ideological flavor of the organization, are present or former graduate students. A number of the major figures in the various forms of protest at Berkeley fall in these categories.

If we turn to an examination of the traits which seem to differentiate those who support the new student activism, it may be worthwhile to examine the assumption that the movement represents an expression of generational conflict, in which those who seek to separate themselves from their conservative elders move to the left for shock effect. Studies of the backgrounds of activists indicate that the opposite, if anything, is true. They are much more often students who are acting out in practice the values which they have been taught by ideologically liberal parents in much the same way as the members of the YAF who tend to come from conservative Republican backgrounds. A comparative study of activists in SDS and YAF, largely based on questionnaires administered to delegates at the 1966 conventions of each group, reports significant differences in the cultural-political backgrounds of activists on the right and left:

SDS members generally came from liberal, Democratic, Socialist, and secular-oriented homes which condition their attitudes toward society in general. . . . YAF members who tended to come from conservative, Republican, and highly religious backgrounds maintain a different Weltanschauung.[27]

The conclusions drawn from reports of students concerning the values of their parents which point to the similarities between generations are reinforced in a detailed comparison of the backgrounds of activist and non-activist students in Chicago in 1965, which involved interviews with the students *and* their fathers. Richard Flacks reports that 16 per cent of the fathers of activists classified themselves as "socialist," 50 per cent checked "highly liberal," and 30 per cent "moderately liberal." Not a single father saw himself as even a moderate conservative. Among the control group of the fathers of non-activists, only 6 per cent classified themselves as "socialist" or "highly liberal," while 40 per cent identified their politics as conservative. The differences were equally striking with respect to attitudes on specific issues. Thus only 27 per cent of the fathers of Chicago activists favored the bombing of North Vietnam as contrasted with 80 per cent approval among those with non-activist student offspring.[28]

Given these findings, it is not surprising that the study of civil rights activists in SCOPE indicates that they were not

rebelling against parental wishes in becoming civil rights participants. Almost two-thirds reported that their parents supported their work in the summer program.

About one-half felt that their participation would actually enhance their relationship with their parents, . . . only five per cent of the volunteers reported that they didn't get along with or were hostile toward their parents.[29]

Almost identical conclusions have been reached by Keniston after examining the results of various studies:

Indeed, if there is any single psychological thread that runs through student activism today, it is this "identification with parental values." When parents and their activist offspring disagree, it is usually not over principle but over practice; and when these students criticize their parents, it is not for what their parents believe, but for their failure to practice the beliefs they drummed into their children's ears from an early age. . . . [Most of the activists] . . . get along moderately well with their parents, and most of their parents feel compelled—at least in principle— to support their children's activism.[30]

It is worth noting also that some statistical evidence suggests that a visible number are the children of former radicals. Samuel Lubell reports that those "with radical family upbringing represent a sixth of all the leftists who turned up in my random sample." He comments that "the sons and daughters of one-time Socialists, Communists and other leftists . . . provide the organizing leadership for demonstrations at many campuses."[31] This is not as surprising as it first appears. The Communist party of the U.S. had about 100,000 members between the mid 1930's and the early 1940's. It also had, according to former leaders, an annual turnover of close to 90 per cent. Consequently the number of former American communists, many of whom are currently middle class or higher, is well over 500,000. Former members in the American Socialist party and the larger number of "splinter" radical groups add to this number, as do the many "fellow travellers" of both the communists and socialists. Many of these people, particularly the former communists, appear to carry an internal stigma, they fear exposure and have remained on the left in many of their opinions. Moreover, they often feel guilty about their political inactivity and retain a sense of alienation from the mainstream of society. Although now outside of the radical movement, many of them have repeatedly impressed on their children the evils of American society which they see as denying them some part of their rights as citizens.

The issue of past radical politics apart, a variety of studies suggest that the modal family background characteristics of the left-oriented student activists are intellectually oriented, relatively well-to-do homes, where the "parents maintain a libertarian viewpoint in matters of politics, human relations, and religion . . . [rather than] from the economic and socially deprived. . . ." The parents of the left activists are strikingly better educated than those of conservative or non-activist students. Thus 35 per cent of the SDS convention delegates reported that their fathers had attended graduate school, compared to 16 per cent among YAF delegates. Almost half the fathers of YAF leaders did not enter college; the comparable figure among the SDSers was 27 per cent.[32] At Berkeley, a study of a sample of the 700 students arrested in the Sproul Hall sit-in indicates that 26 per cent of them had fathers with academic graduate degrees as contrasted with 11 per cent among the student body as a whole.[33] The Chicago study reports 40 per cent of the fathers of activists with graduate training, significantly more than the 27 per cent among others. Even more striking are the differences reported in Chicago between the mothers of activists and non-activists. Only 16 per cent of the former did not attend college, while almost half (49 per cent) of the mothers of non-activists did not enter college.[34]

The findings that the parents of left activists tend to be disproportionately highly educated leads us to anticipate the findings of two surveys that left activists in Berkeley and Chicago were much more likely to report their parents as having been more permissive in their child-rearing practices, less insistent on discipline, than were non-activist or conservative students.[35] These reports were confirmed in the Chicago study by direct reports from the parents themselves.[36] Looking at these data, the psychologists Jeanne Block, Norman Haas, and M. Brewster Smith comment:

Many young activists in contemporary America were reared under the influence of Benjamin Spock who, as an articulate pediatrician, led a revolt against the more authoritarian, rigid, constraining child-rearing practices. . . . It may be argued that the emergence of a dedicated, spontaneous generation concerned with humanitarian values and personal authenticity is a triumph of Spockian philosophy and principles. Others have suggested, in a less benign interpretation, that activism is the consequence of excessive parental permissiveness, a failure to teach respect for authority, and an unfortunate submission to the needs and feelings of the child.[37]

Curiously, given the evidence that the parents of leftist activists are "milder disciplinarians than those of non-activists" or conservative activists, the study of those who participated in the national conventions of Students for a Democratic Society and Young American for Freedom finds that "significantly more YAF than SDS members . . . felt a close relationship with one or both of their parents and indicated they could communicate with the latter concerning personal and emotional problems."[38] For example, 60 per cent of the SDS delegates *disagreed* with the statement: "I feel that I can always go and talk with my parents about personal and emotional problems," as contrasted with 39 per cent among the conservative YAFers. More YAFers (54 per cent) reported a close relationship with their mothers involving "much communication and mutual understanding" than did SDSers (41 per cent).[39] Seemingly, the greater permissiveness and reluctance to apply strict discipline of liberal or leftist well-educated parents do not make for closer affective ties with their children. Whether they make for lesser respect for adult authority and opinions cannot be determined from the available data.

Given the seeming linkage between parental higher (post-graduate) education and political liberalism among the parents of university students, it may seem logical that various researchers also conclude that "intellectualism" and high academic aptitude are characteristics of the left activist student group. Studies in various emerging nations reported by Metta Spencer and Glaucio Soares elsewhere in this volume also find that those who are favorably disposed toward an "intellectual" rather than a professional or vocational academic style are more likely to "devote great energy to political and social causes." Lubell indicates that among every ten American radical students whom he interviewed, "four thought they would like to teach at the college level; two wanted to work as psychologists, one as a journalist or artist, while three were undecided what to do." A study of involvement in the 1966 University of Chicago sit-in against the draft policies reports that 52 per cent of a sample of participants in the sit-in indicated a preference for college teaching as a career, while another 15 per cent looked forward to employment in the "arts." Conversely, among a sample of those who signed a petition opposing the objective of the sit-in, only 26 per cent had college teaching as a career goal, and none opted for "the arts." The second group was primarily disposed toward the professions and science.[40] Those inclined toward the vocational and professional world tend to come from lower socioeconomic backgrounds, or from conservative business-managerial families. Lower status origins are conducive to concentration on upward mobility, which many of the activists regard as careerism. Both low status and conservative well-to-do family environments are associated with relative disinterest in politics or with support of right-wing politics.[41] The study of the backgrounds of SDS and YAF convention delegates indicates that the leftists come from much higher occupational and educational backgrounds than do the rightists. Fifty-eight per cent of the fathers of the former hold middle- or upper-level business or professional positions as compared with but 29 per cent of the conservatives. Conversely, 19 per cent of the YAF activists are of manual working-class origin, as compared with but 7 per cent of the comparable group of SDSers.[42] A study of student conservatives at Harvard, however, found that many of them came from wealthy conservative homes,[43] as did an analysis of the members of student conservative clubs at various Eastern colleges.[44] One possible source of the discrepancy among these data is that the convention delegates came from around the country, and as studies drawn from deans' reports at over 800 colleges cited earlier would suggest, the YAF delegates as compared to the SDS ones "were more prone to attend smaller and church-affiliated colleges."[45] That leftist activists are more likely to be well-to-do than conservative ones, holding other factors constant, is also indicated by the analysis of involvement at the University of Chicago sit-in. Almost four-fifths (78 per cent) of those sitting in reported family incomes of over $15,000 a year, as contrasted with 50 per cent among those who signed a pro-administration statement.[46]

A somewhat different linkage between personal experiences and student activism may be found in the hypothesis which suggests that students as a stratum are disproportionately drawn to such movements because a campus population inherently contains a large number of socially dislocated individuals, those who have shifted from one social environment to another, and are consequently predisposed to find new values and possibly commit themselves to activism. Berkeley data again are relevant. The faculty Select Committee on Education stressed this factor as contributing to unrest. They point to the large number of Berkeley students who normally drop out and are replaced by transfers, as undermining the potential for a "community." As they comment, "it is hardly surprising that many students feel alone in a community of strangers. In the April 1965 survey, almost two-thirds of the students felt the University to be an 'impersonal institution. . . .' "[47] The study of the police car demonstrators reports that, as a group, they had spent much less time as students at Berkeley than the student body as a whole.[48] A second survey of a sample of those arrested in December 1964 for sitting in at Sproul Hall yielded similar results. This study found that half of the undergraduates arrested were transfer students, many from out of state, i.e., had not begun their college careers at Berkeley or in California. Among the leaders of the FSM, "transfer students were in evidence in significantly larger numbers."[49] More recently, reports on the Spring 1966 anti-draft sit-in at the University of Wisconsin indicate that the three leaders of the demonstration came from metropolitan New York.

There are many factors which seem to correlate with liberal attitudes and support of activism among American university students. While student activists are more irreligious than the campus population as a whole, certain religious backgrounds, mainly Jewish and liberal Protestant, tend to produce a large proportion of them.[50] The differences in the religious backgrounds of the SDS and YAF convention delegates are striking. Twenty per cent of the former as compared with three of the latter report no religious preference. Among SDSers with a choice, the proportion of Jews and Protestants is the same, 46 per cent. Only 8 per cent are Catholics. Among the YAF, on the other hand, 69 per cent are Protestants, 26 per cent are Catholics, and only 5 per cent are Jewish.[51] The Chicago study reports that 60 per cent of the left activists have Jewish fathers, 36 per cent Protestant, and 4 per cent Catholics. Among the non-activists, the corresponding percentages are 33 Jewish, 41 Protestant, and 23 Catholic.[52] (Unfortunately, none of the studies compare the traits of leftist and conservative activists and non-activists while controlling for religious background. It is quite possible, given the magnitude of the religious differences among these categories, that much of the variation among them is associated with religious-culture differences. That is, if one compares Jews, Catholics, and Protestants in each political category for academic abilities, family child-rearing background, social class origins, and so forth, the differences may turn out to be much less significant.)

Within the university, social science and humanities majors seem to be much more involved in the student movement than those in other fields. A comparison of those who participated in a peace demonstration in Washington compared with "counterpickets" representing student conservative groups indicates clearly the relevant patterns found in a number of studies:

Of those who gave answers to questionnaire items pertaining to academic vocational areas, two-thirds (66 per cent) were majoring in the humanities or social sciences, with relatively few in the physical or biological sciences, and very few in pre-professional courses. . . .Career plans were often indefinite and were predominantly centered in teaching, social service, and research. This finding stands in marked contrast to the career goals of the "counter-pickets" from student conservative groups. These young people were typically very definite about careers in business or law, and were taking appropriate pre-professional courses.[53]

The data linking subject studied in university with political values and activity correspond generally with the information available concerning the politics of university faculties and intellectuals generally.[54] Presumably students in humanistic and social science courses are exposed to more liberalizing and politically activating experiences than those in other fields. Some evidence, however, suggests that the correlations between subjects studied and political beliefs may be more a consequence of self-selection of certain fields by students who are already liberals or conservatives, rather than of influence from their education as such. Thus in one panel (repeat interview) study of student attitudes, Morris Rosenberg found that among freshmen, conservative students were more inclined than others to study business, a not unexpected finding although some non-conservatives made the same choice. When the same students were canvassed two years later, it turned out that their original political beliefs were a good predictor of which students would change their career orientation. The more liberal among those who had initially chosen to be businessmen changed to another career, while the bulk of more conservative business majors remained faithful to their original objective.[55] Further evidence suggesting that the correlation between beliefs and major subject is a product of student selection rather than accumulated learning may be found in a Berkeley study of entering freshmen in 1959 which

showed a distinct correlation between their attitudes and their intended majors, especially among men. The men students who most frequently gave answers indicating their opposition to existing social and political conditions were those entering the humanities and fine arts. The groups which found existing conditions most acceptable were the potential engineers.

Lubell reports that students who

plan to go into the professions, business, engineering or the sciences range from 70 to 90 per cent "in favor of the Vietnam war," while among students who talk of teaching, . . . only 47 per cent support the war.[56]

While a clear-cut pattern seems to exist between various background factors, liberal social and political attitudes, and involvement in student activism, it is important to note that these relationships, particularly as they relate to activism, lack certain important comparisons with other types of students. As Barry Metzger points out, while

it appears evident that the radical minority is more middle class, more concentrated in the study of the humanities and social sciences, and more academically distinguished than the campus majority . . ., these generalizations might also be true of *non-radical student activists*.[57]

And the two available studies of the leaders in student government and campus service activities generally indicate that they also differ from the student population at large along the same dimensions as the radical activists.[57] The most comprehensive report on the characteristics of student government leaders, based on a questionnaire survey at the 1966 National Congress of the United States National Student Association, indicates that this group of student "activists," one-third of whom voted for a YAF leader as their next president, tended to resemble those involved in various campus demonstrations, or in organizations like SDS. As contrasted with a national sample of the student population generally, the NSA delegates were disproportionately from large metropolitan centers, from relatively well-to-do families, from highly educated backgrounds (26 per cent of their fathers had attended graduate school as compared with the national average of 14 per cent), from families of Eastern European and Jewish origin, majors in the social sciences (51 per cent among the delegates as compared to 11 per cent nationally) or the humanities and arts (21 per cent as compared to 16), and had a history of high scholarly achievement in high school and college.[58]

When we compare students active in conservative groups or demonstrations with those participating in left-wing causes, certain clear differences emerge, some of which have been mentioned earlier. The conservatives, on the whole, seem to come from relatively poorer, less educated, more provincial, more Anglo-Saxon, and more Protestant backgrounds than the more liberal activists. And while a study of conservative counter-demonstrators during a Washington peace march found that they came largely from pre-professional, engineering, and business students, the most comprehensive survey of the members and leaders of campus conservative clubs in a large number of universities reported that they resembled the leftists in their college major. Almost half of them (47 per cent) were majoring in the social sciences, with another 18 per cent in the humanities, much like the student government and liberal social-action group participants.[59] The comparative analysis of SDS and YAF convention delegates also reported that social-science majors were overrepresented in both groups (63 per cent in SDS and 45 per cent in YAF).[60]

A variety of data have suggested that students active in liberal and left social-action groups have better academic records than the campus population as a whole.[61] There is, however, evidence which indicates that student government leaders (see above) and those involved in conservative activities are also disproportionally drawn from the intellectually superior part of the student population. Thus the study of Chicago sit-in participants indicates that 73 per cent of those involved in the protest had grades of B or better, as contrasted with 69 per cent among those who actively supported the university's draft policies.[62] And a 1965 survey of Pennsylvania State University students which compared members of SENSE (Students for Peace, a liberal activist group), and those belonging to the local chapter of YAF, also reports similar grade averages for each.[63] These findings point up the need to keep Metzger's caution in mind, to compare different ideological varieties of activists with one another, rather than to form conclusions about the sources of liberal and left involvement, by contrasting liberal activists with the general student population.

The fact that we can locate some of the factors associated with student protest in terms of types of institutions and traits of participants does not, of course, account for the rise and fall of activism, nor explain why certain issues or patterns of behavior emerge at given points in time. One of the main attributes of American student organizations—particularly those concerned with politics—has been instability. Not only do the interests of the "non-conformist" students shift quickly from experimentation with drugs to advocacy of complete sexual freedom, from peace to civil rights, from alienation with any aspect of the real world including revolutionary politics to deep political concern—but a "generation" of students lasts only a relatively short time, three or four years at most, thereby making it difficult to have continuing leadership and long-term programs. The very commitment of student radical movements to generally non-conformist styles of life in terms of attitudes toward sex, drugs, literature, philosophy tends to give each generation of activists a unique style which cuts it off from those which preceded it and those which may come later. One of the major problems faced by student activist groups is that their participants become such an "in-group" that recruitment from other "generations" becomes impossible, and groups which appeared to dominate a campus' political life seemingly disappear a year or two later.

The instability of student activism in the U.S. is even more transient than indicated here. It is increased by the vagaries of the academic schedule, and even by the weather. Student protests are particularly successful in the spring, when the pressure of examinations is not so great, and the weather helps stimulate mass meetings and demonstrations. The periods just before examinations almost always see a sharp decline in student activity of all kinds. The summer has traditionally been a time of quiet on the campus, although in recent years many student activists have gone to the South on civil rights projects or have devoted themselves to various kinds of full-time social action work. Administrators have often been accused of announcing tuition increases or other unpopular measures during the summer or at other times when protest is difficult to organize.

Styles of Current Action

Student political activity has almost never developed as a purely campus phenomenon, isolated from trends in the larger society. Not only has it been very much dependent on broader issues in the society and in the educational system, but American student organizations have traditionally been closely associated with, and often guided by adults. The current student "new left" is perhaps the first to insist openly on the alienation of student militants from adult life. One of the rallying cries of the Berkeley revolt was the notion that anyone over thirty was untrustworthy (although much of the success of the movement was due to the strong support and even stimulation from segments of the University of California faculty). In the past more student political organizations have been directly associated with adult organizations. The left-wing student groups have almost always been directly affiliated to an adult party, such as the Americans for Democratic Action, the Socialist party, or the Communists. Adult financial and ideological support has been of key importance to student movements. During the heyday of the 1930's, some left-wing organizations had full-time staff devoted to "student work."

The situation has, however, shifted somewhat. The student "new left" has often rejected adult support and has reacted negatively to "guidance" from non-student organizations. Groups like the Student Peace Union in the early 1960's and more recently the Student Non-Violent Coordinating Committee and Students for a Democratic Society have remained independent of adult affiliation. The SDS, which started as the student affiliate of the social-democratic League for Industrial Democracy, split from the L.I.D. after a long and often bitter dispute, in large part precipitated by attitudes toward cooperating with Communists. SDS, like other sections of the "new left," opposes making judgment about the morality of working with Communists. They insist that all those who support a given good cause should cooperate on the basis of a single issue. SNCC has also been at odds with the moderate leadership of the civil rights movement concerning degrees of militancy which are required in various situations. They, too, insist on total autonomy from the control of adult groups.

The reasons for this alienation from adult politics are complex. On the one hand, they involve a rejection of the "old left" of the socialists and communists as committed to outmoded ideologies and internecine warfare derived from the issues of the 1930's. The old left is also seen as having compromised too easily with the liberal establishment. On the other hand, the rejection of the politics of the adult world reflects the disillusion of the student radicals with the reformist approach of ADA and the liberal Democrats. The latter are seen as basically unfeeling about the misery of poverty and racial inferiority, and as willing to defend American national interests abroad at the expense of efforts of local populations to make revolutionary changes. To attack the status quo of the affluent society seems to require defining it as an essentially corrupt and sick society which cannot be reformed. All those willing to work within it, whether socialists, communists, or liberals, are essentially supporting the system. In their efforts to locate groups outside the system, the new left students have rejected the traditional longed-for ally of radical intellectuals, the labor movement, and have sought potentially honest and revolutionary groups in the truly dispossessed—the poverty-stricken and the Negroes. They are glorified as the only uncorrupted elements historically. Such behavior is not uncommon among student radicalism. As David Matza has pointed out, populism, the belief in the superior morality and worth of the poor, has been characteristic of such movements:

Among students, the appeal of populism is not simply an outgrowth of traditional radical propensities, just as the apocalyptic mentality has a special appeal to youth, so, too, does populism. Students have a special liking for populism because it is a vehicle for an effective attack on the professional authority and a way of defending against unflattering assessment of themselves. For the radical, and bohemian, too, a belief in populism allows students who perceive themselves as avant-garde to deflect the contrary judgments of academic elders.[64]

Much has been made of the new "style" of the student left. There is considerable continuity in the kinds of students who are attracted to radical movements as well as in the concerns of the campus movement. The disillusionment with traditional ideologies and conventional "legal" methods of protest, and with many of the adult leaders of the liberal and radical movements in the United States by the new student left is, perhaps, the most significant change. Yet, the continuity with the past is probably greater than the differences which have been so widely discussed.

Despite the fact that the student movement necessarily functions within the context of American higher education, student activists have never had very much interest in the broader educational issues which confront them and their institutions. Even the Berkeley student revolt offers no real break from this tradition, since few students showed any concern with the various proposals for academic reform despite the fact that many, both within and outside the student movement there, suggested that the revolt was stimulated at least in part by a conscious discontent with the quality and methods of undergraduate instruction at the University of California. Even in this campus-oriented struggle, neither the leadership nor the rank and file of the movement took a sustained interest in these matters, preferring instead to concentrate their attention on more purely political issues.

The Berkeley students followed a time-honored tradition within the American student movement; academic issues have never been very popular among American radical student organizations. After an initial protest against a specific injustice, the students are unwilling to devote sustained thought to the complex problems of educational reform, even when administrators might welcome such consideration. David Riesman pointed out a number of years ago that students could have a more influential role in academic policy making if they took a real interest in such matters.[65]

The Berkeley revolt has probably had some effect in increasing the sensitivity of both students and faculty to problems of educational reform and of academic policy. The demonstrations in favor of a popular philosophy professor at Yale who was not given tenure because of his poor publication record indicate that there may be a growing concern for these issues. In this controversy, the students raised the issue of publication versus teaching in their unsuccessful efforts to keep the professor. Yet, it remains true that while students can be mobilized for the dramatic issues of academic freedom, they have rarely taken responsibility for implementing educational proposals.

In the recent past, one can see two conflicting tendencies in the student movement. Efforts of the University of California faculty and administration to involve the students in educational reform have proved unsuccessful. Only thirteen students showed up at a discussion with the new Chancellor on these matters. Few came to public sessions of the special faculty committee on educational reform. The attempts of the Free Student Union (successor to the Free Speech Movement, which spearheaded the revolt) to maintain an active program directed at campus issues failed and the group dissolved. It may be, however, that the new "free universities" which have been started in some major academic centers indicate that the student movement is determined to avoid collaboration with the educational "establishment" at all costs. These "free universities," which have received a good deal of publicity, involve, however, only a tiny fraction of the student population, perhaps a few thousand in all, and have proved only a moderate success. Their courses, which range from Marxist philosophy and revolutionary theory to discussions of erotic literature and the social use of narcotics, vary greatly in quality.[66] The institutions have had a difficult time keeping alive financially and have not attracted substantial student support, even among the participants in the student political movements. Thus, while the educational impact of the new student left has been felt in increased faculty and mass media discussion of educational issues and a new awareness of the problems of students in the emerging multiversity, the students themselves have contributed little to the discussion itself, and have been instrumental only in stimulating the debate in the first place.

Interestingly enough, the more moderate segments of the student movement have taken a more active interest in educational problems than has the left wing. The tutoring projects which have been set up by various colleges to help Negro children in urban slums have been undertaken at the initiative of relatively moderate student organizations. The Northern Student Movement, a little publicized but very active group, has stimulated this kind of social service program in many colleges in the North. Various student government committees, often working in cooperation with university authorities, have undertaken studies of educational issues, as well as direct social service work. An example of this trend in the student community was a recent "manifesto" drawn up by students in Harvard's Graduate School of Education. The students claimed that their preparation was aimed primarily at teaching in upper class suburbs, and they demanded that the school focus more on the problem of urban ghetto education. The Dean, in welcoming the students' suggestions, asked them to make more sweeping criticisms, and suggested that an on-going student-faculty-administration committee be set up to plan innovations in the school. Although clearly not a direct result of the Berkeley revolt, this initiative and others like it at various universities are an indication of another trend in the student population which has received much less publicity than the "new left," but is perhaps of equal or greater importance.

A recent emphasis on the notion of "student power" may change the predominant off-campus orientation of the American student left. Activists in such groups as the Students for a Democratic Society, as well as in more moderate organizations such as the National Student Association, have been pressing for increased student participation in university government. Demonstrations at the City College of New York and at other schools have demanded that students be given a voice in academic policy making. The model for the "student power" slogan has been the Latin American ideal of co-government, a system under which students have a constitutional right to participation in academic decision making, and often in the selection of professors. (This system is discussed in more detail in Chapter 10 by Orlando Albórnoz.)

It is important to note that much of the student "new left," in its desire to escape from the clichés and sterile ideologies of the old left, has found itself without any guide lines for continued action either on or off campus. The largest group, SDS, has tried to build a movement without a coherent organization or program. In this way, it has achieved a great deal of spontaneity and creative innovation, but it has failed to maintain a stable structure in all but a few areas. Its "community union" projects, which have brought college students in direct contact with the urban poor in an effort to create an "interracial movement of the poor," have not achieved notable success. Sporadic efforts to build sustained interest in problems of university reform have also failed. The anti-Vietnam war agitation and the anti-draft campaign of the SDS have been more successful mainly because of a growing but unorganized dissatisfaction with the administration's Vietnam policy rather than as a result of effective SDS planning and organization. Moreover, this concentration on the war has been reduced, and the SDS has increased its emphasis on domestic issues again. The organization has moved from issue to issue, attempting to gauge the winds of social concern on the campus.

Because of its open-ended ideological stance and its refusal to make political value judgments, SDS has become an arena for many politically interested student groups affiliated with old left political parties. They find that they can use the SDS to recruit from, and have tried, without notable success, to guide SDS policy. Although no political sect has been able to gain control of the organization, it is possible that such an event could occur in the future. SDS remains, however, the most effective "new left" student organization in the United States.

The student civil rights movement has had a more widespread effect both on the campus and in society than has SDS or any other politically radical student group. The southern Negro students who began the sit-in movement in 1960 launched a movement which is still being felt in both the North and the South. The Student Non-Violent Coordinating Committee (SNCC) developed from the struggles of the southern students, and soon became one of the most militant forces in the civil rights movement. SNCC, like SDS, has no ideological base. It is committed to equal rights for Negroes in all areas of life, and uses non-violence as a tactical necessity in its struggle. SNCC's statement in opposition to the Vietnam war came as a surprise to many in the civil rights movement, although it is quite in keeping with the organization's position as the most radical of the civil rights groups.

The prospects for the campus civil rights movement are not so optimistic as they were in the first half of the 1960's. SNCC's northern student support has clearly diminished as a result of its advocacy of "black power." White students now find themselves rejected by the movement itself. Less activity is taking place in the South as well. SNCC's well-publicized financial crisis is an indication of a serious decline in support. Civil rights will clearly remain one of the major foci of the student movement for the foreseeable future, but the widespread support for the southern movement seems to have lessened somewhat on the northern campuses.

Perhaps one of the reasons for this decline in interest in the southern movement has been the growth of northern-based civil rights activity, particularly the various social service projects in Negro slum areas of northern cities referred to earlier. Although less militant and certainly less well known than the more dramatic forms of civil rights activity, they probably involve many more students.

Considerable attention has been paid to the more extreme groups which have been part of the student left. It is quite clear that these groups have received much more publicity than they deserve in terms of their influence on the campus. The combined membership of groups like the now dissolved (Maoist) May 2 Movement, the Trotskyist Young Socialist Alliance, the pro-Communist Du Bois Clubs, and several other splinter groups is probably under 3,000, and their influence is confined mostly to large cities. These groups have tried to cooperate with both the anti-Vietnam war and the civil rights movements. They have been influential in some areas, notably in the National Coordinating Committee to End the War in Vietnam. Yet, they have been unable to "take over" any of the larger student organizations, even the rather amorphous SDS, and they have not grown substantially themselves.

The mass media are attracted to these groups possibly because of their offbeat social behavior and "way out" ideas. These left sectarian student groups spend much of their time fighting factional battles with each other and have tried to infuse their factionalism into the mainstream of the student movement, although without much success.

The State of Student Opinion

The judgments expressed earlier concerning the general lack of support for left-wing and activist causes among the student population have generally been borne out by a number of public opinion surveys. There are, for example, four national student polls dealing with attitudes toward the Vietnamese war. The most comprehensive one, completed for *Playboy* in November 1965, suggests that the majority of American students were strongly pro-war and even backed escalation at that time.

TABLE 1.

Attitudes of a National Sample of College Students on the Vietnamese War

1. Does the United States have an obligation to provide military assistance to Vietnam?
   82 per cent Yes   15 per cent No   3 per cent No Opinion

2. If we are unable to effect a negotiated settlement before the end of 1965, should we:
   A. Pull out of Vietnam completely?   6 per cent
   B. Continue to send aid in dollars only?   3 per cent
   C. Confine our military action to South Vietnam only?   35 per cent
   D. Push the war into North Vietnam?   56 per cent

3. With which of the following statements do you strongly agree, agree, disagree, or strongly disagree?
   The Administration's current policy is correct in dealing with Vietnam situation.
   18 per cent Strongly Agree   57 per cent Agree
   18 per cent Disagree   7 per cent Strongly Disagree

   Use of non-toxic tear gas is justifiable as a means of disabling the Viet Cong without endangering the lives of civilians.
   48 per cent Strongly Agree   40 per cent Agree
   9 per cent Disagree   3 per cent Strongly Disagree

   We should avoid bombing military installations and supply depots in populous areas of North Vietnam, such as Hanoi.
   15 per cent Strongly Agree   18 per cent Agree
   40 per cent Disagree   27 per cent Strongly Disagree

4. Do you feel Americans have an obligation to accept military service even if they disagree with government policies?
   90 per cent Yes   10 per cent No

Source: *Playboy Student Poll* news release, November 1965.

Interestingly enough, faculty opinion sampled by *Playboy* was less bellicose, but a majority of faculty also supported the U.S. military involvement in Vietnam. Since we have no information concerning the representivity of the *Playboy* sample, the findings are, of course, open to doubt.

The size of the pro-war majority, however, clearly indicates that the large number of student petitions presented to Administration officials express-ing support for the war, and the *ad hoc* groups which have been formed on many campuses to back the war would seem to be more representative of the main trends in student thinking than the more newsworthy anti-war protests. This conclusion is bolstered by the results of three other na-tional surveys. One conducted in February 1965 by the Louis Harris or-ganization reported that 24 per cent of the students with opinions favored negotiations and American withdrawal from Vietnam. A second, completed by Samuel Lubell in the spring of 1966 indicated that "two-thirds of the students interviewed continue to back our Vietnam policy—which is about the same proportion of support one finds in the country as a whole." The most recently completed available national survey of student attitudes, com-pleted by the Gallup Poll in May and June 1966, indicated that 47 per cent of college youth endorsed the way "Johnson is handling the situation in Viet-iam," while 23 per cent disapproved because they thought the U.S. should be more aggressive and another 16 per cent opposed the President's policies for being "indecisive" or "inconsistent." A breakdown of the reasons given for criticizing the President into "dove" and "hawk" categories suggests that about 20 per cent of this sample were anti-war, a figure not very different from that reported by Gallup for the population as a whole. A more special-ized survey by *Moderator* magazine in November 1965 found that 83 per cent of a national sample of 500 campus leaders "support the Johnson admin-istration's position on Vietnam."[67] Most strikingly, the results of a survey taken at the University of Wisconsin, home of the National Coordinating Committee to End the War in Vietnam, scene of many militant anti-war ac-tivities, and traditionally the campus with the most continuous history of student radicalism, point out the large discrepancy between the visible activi-ties of an active "new left" minority and the majority of the student popu-lation. Over three-quarters of the undergraduates interviewed and 72 per cent of the entire student body favored U.S. participation in the war. Only 16 per cent expressed definite opposition.[68]

Similar confidence in the policies of dominant American domestic in-stitutions, particularly those linked to the economic and professional elites, has also been expressed by a national sample of university students. The majority voiced a "great deal" of confidence in the medical profession, banks and financial institutions, higher education, and big corporations. Students were much less favorable to the arts, the United Nations, the civil rights movement, religion, and the labor movement. The results are presented in Table 2.

TABLE 2.

How Students View the World around Them; Responses to the Question, "How Much Confidence Do You Have in These Institutions?"

Institution	Great Deal (per cent)	Only Some (per cent)	Hardly Any (per cent)	Not Sure (per cent)
Scientific community	76	20	2	2
Medical profession	73	22	5	—
Banks and financial institutions	66	29	3	2
U.S. Supreme Court	65	28	6	1
Higher education	64	32	4	—
Big corporations	52	40	7	1
Executive branch of Federal government	49	42	9	—
The arts	46	43	5	6
Psychiatric field	44	44	7	5
Congress	39	52	8	1
The military	38	43	17	2
The United Nations	35	49	14	2
Organized religion	34	46	18	2
Civil-rights movement	33	47	19	1
The Democratic party	22	63	10	5
The press	20	57	21	2
Advertising	16	38	44	2
Organized labor	13	55	29	3
Television	13	46	39	2
The Republican party	12	53	29	6

Source: "Campus '65," *Newsweek* (March 22, 1965), p. 45, from The Harris Survey.

Perhaps more significant than the positive replies in indicating how little alienation from American institutions exists among American students is the very small percentage who showed "hardly any confidence" in the dominant economic organizations. Lubell also found as of Spring 1966 that 60 per cent of students interviewed praised the role of business, while only 15 per cent were critical. He concluded his analysis by commenting that in "their political thinking, far from being 'alienated,' the students remain basically like the rest of the country. . . ."

Most surprising of all the recent research on American student attitudes and behavior are the findings of Dr. Joseph Katz of Stanford University, who reports that a comprehensive continuous long-term study of samples of the Berkeley and Stanford student bodies indicates that a considerable majority at each school is passive and conformist:

> When we asked these students what they expected to be doing ten years from now, they often replied with a description of a suburban existence that they considered rather routine. . . . Our questionnaire and interview data confirm that most students have a strongly "privatist" orientation. They rank highest their own individual careers and future family life. Involvement in international, national or civic affairs, and in service to other people are ranked astonishingly low and there is little change from the freshman to the senior year.[69]

The conclusions reached by Katz in his Berkeley-Stanford study coincide with those derived from an examination of surveys in different parts of the country. Kenneth Keniston also reports that "a vast majority of American students remains privatistic."[70] There are various reasons for this emphasis on private individual goals, but not the least of which is the enormous increase in pressure to attain good grades which increasingly has been placed on American students, in high school, college, and graduate school. The combination of the demands to upgrade the level of American education which followed as a reaction to the Russian lead in space science (the post-Sputnik craze) and the effects of greater numbers pressing for entrance to good universities and graduate schools than there are places, even for excellent students, has changed the quality of education. Students are now pressed by their parents and teachers as no other generation in American history has ever been pushed. To relax while in school may lead to disaster. In seeking to explain the seriousness, the inability to relax, which has been attributed to many students, the philosopher Charles Frankel points out: "The students have been on a treadmill for a long, long time. There are the pressures of college boards, pressures of parents, pressures of the competition for grades."[71] These concerns are consciously reflected in the responses given by students to opinion pollsters as indicated in Table 3.

In a real sense, American students have been placed in a situation comparable to that long faced by Japanese teen-agers. In Japan, there is enormous pressure to work hard to prepare for the intensely competitive examinations for college entrance. A variety of novels and studies have pointed to the way in which this pressure upsets Japanese youngsters. And two of the consequences which are reputed to flow from this pressure are the high suicide rate among teen-agers and the often rather militant and ultra-radical political activities of Japanese college students.[72] Studies of

TABLE 3.

Main Pressures Felt by Today's Freshmen

Pressures	Total Freshmen (per cent)
Pressure to get better grades	58
How to get along socially	24
Fear of flunking out	11
Grades not fair	11
Worries about future success	10
Dating problems	8
Faculty, administration problem	8
Fear of war	7
Money worries	7
Living up to parents' expectations	6
Assessing self-worth	3
Too many dull, required courses	3
Why went to this college	3
Worried about life at home	2
How to be independent when dependent	2

Source: *Washington Post* (March 18, 1965), p. D-1, from The Harris Survey.
Note: Percentages add to more than 100 per cent because most freshmen report more than one main pressure.

Japanese student politics indicate that much of the well-publicized activism is the work of freshmen and sophomores who are able to relax upon entering the university since Japanese universities give only infrequent examinations and traditionally grade easily.

Those who are admitted do not have to work hard. Political activity drops off as they approach graduation and face a new set of competitive examinations to qualify for good posts in industry or government. One may point to similar reactions in the United States. The suicide rate among young people of high school and college age has risen rapidly while that of older age cohorts has been declining. A comparison of rates in 1950–1952 with those a decade later reveals a total increase of 4 per cent among all white American males. The suicide rate, however, jumped *48 per cent* among the 15–19 age category, and 26 per cent among those in the 20–24 years' old group. It actually *fell* for men 55 years and older.[73] (It is interesting to note that precise suicide-rate statistics exist for Berkeley and Harvard. The differences are in the same direction as the variations in drop-outs mentioned earlier: the Berkeley rate per 100,000 students for the years 1952 to 1961 was 17.44, considerably above the national and state rates for persons in the college age bracket; the equivalent rate for Harvard during the years 1958 to 1965 was 9.5, about the same as the national average.)[74]

Other relevant data pointing to increased stress among young people in school have been various reports which indicate a striking increase in resorting to psychiatrists among adolescents and college students. Such increases may reflect the increased availability of psychiatric services, but, as Richard and Katherine Gordon suggest, this possibility may be controlled by studying the "incidence of an illness that is not under a person's conscious control—a disorder that is psychosomatic, influenced by emotions, but still organic, a true physical ailment. Such an illness is peptic ulcers, ulcer of the stomach or duodenum."[75] They report that a study of the records of three hospitals in New Jersey between 1953–1955 and 1959–1962 reveals an increase of 58 per cent among those under 17 and of 63 per cent among those in the 18–24 age bracket.[76] To find out whether the increase in reported psychiatric problems was related to educational stress, the Gordons studied the record of 174 private psychiatric outpatients in the 13–24 age group in New Jersey between 1953 and 1961. They found that "the stresses of getting an education were the *primary* reasons for seeking psychiatric help" in 34 per cent of the cases in 1953–1957, in 56 per cent in 1958–1959, and in 74 per cent in 1960–1961.[77]

Studies of student politics suggest that while a higher proportion of more advanced and graduate students have liberal and radical attitudes than do those in lower division classes, the freshmen and sophomores are more likely to show higher rates of participation in demonstrations. Thus a study of a Washington peace demonstration indicates that "30 per cent were college freshmen, 15 per cent were sophomores, 15 per cent juniors, and 11 per cent were seniors. Only 6 per cent identified themselves as graduate students in a university. . . . The mean age of the demonstrators was 18½, with *45 per cent of the sample being either 18 or 19 years of age.* Twenty per cent were 17 and under." Similar findings were reported in a study of a militant Washington, D. C., student civil rights group.[78] At Berkeley, also, freshmen and sophomores were the most over-represented classes among those arrested in Sproul Hall, while graduate students, the most ideologically liberal group in the school, were by far the most under-represented in the sit-in. Over one-third of the student body is graduate, but only 19 per cent of those arrested fell in this category.[79]

These findings concerning the greater propensity of freshmen to engage in political activism may tie in with the findings of psychological research that "the freshman year is a particularly stressful one. . . . [F]or entering freshmen the sudden impact of academic requirements, homesickness, new living arrangements and peers constitute especially unsettling conditions."[80] Participation in group activity in a conflict situation may give the insecure and lonely freshman that sense of identity and involvement which he lost when leaving home and high school.

We would suggest that the willingness to break loose against authority afforded by activism, the growth in the use of drugs, and the increase in drop-outs by able students, as well as the emphasis on privatism and self-orientation reported by Katz and Keniston, are to some considerable degree a reaction to the competitive stresses placed on today's students. They are under extreme coercion, and it is not surprising that some, from extremely privileged backgrounds, strike out against the system, that they see the university as an agency of authority which fosters the "rat race," that they welcome an opportunity to secede, to get off the treadmill. But though a small minority take the activist or secessionist solutions, the great majority accept their role and conform, though they may want to do other things. As The Harris Survey comments: "the pressures to get into college and then perform well are so great that this generation does not feel many larger challenges in the world."[81]

The evidence presented here that the vast majority of American students are privatistic, careerist, and moderate in their politics does not mean that the university is a conservative environment. Some schools are, of course, but the majority of universities do seem to have a liberalizing effect on a large number of their students with regard to their attitudes to civil rights, religion, and domestic politics.[82]

But though the campus seems to be a liberalizing place for some students, it is characterized generally by the values and attitudes of the educated middle classes. Students, on the average, are somewhat more liberal than their parents. Their attitudes on issues such as civil rights, welfare state legislation, government economic planning, or the propensity to vote Democratic are more liberal than the mainstream of the middle class, particularly since 1960. Recent events in American student political life have shown that it is possible to remove students from their liberal but generally apathetic tendencies during a crisis. When the chips are down, as they were in Berkeley, a large proportion of the students supported the militants of the Free Speech Movement, even though the overwhelming majority did not normally take part in politics and have not remained active in the student movement. Similarly, such students will back a movement for civil rights in the campus community.

When one considers American students on the scale of conventional radicalism, those who attend the universities in the United States must be considered a fairly conservative and passive community. The tiny handful who make up the attention-getting "new left" apart, one must agree with the conclusion of Joseph Katz concerning the vast majority that *the primary need still is to wake up students, not to constrain them.*[83]

Despite the fact that the proportion of students in the United States who are alienated from the values of the mainstream of society and who are active in politics is very small, this minority has been able to achieve notable successes. The fact that a small proportion of the student body at Berkeley could arouse the sympathy of large numbers of students and that groups like the SDS can have so widespread an influence on the campus (even if their influence is much less than what the mass media would have us believe) is very significant. The reasons for this phenomenon are not difficult to discern. The very political vacuum on the campus makes it easier for a minority to be heard and for it to exercise an influence far beyond its numbers. A study by Glaucio Soares dealing with students in many countries indicates that even where student political activity is highly institutionalized, the numbers of those actively involved are relatively small. The ideologically committed students (of either right or left, although predominantly the left) are able to dominate university politics because of their higher degree of political commitment and level of activity.[84] A survey of the attitudes of Japanese students toward the militant Zengakuren-led demonstrations against the U.S.-Japan security treaty in 1960 showed that 60 per cent of the students thought that the activities of the Zengakuren were "too radical" while only 10 per cent felt that they were proper.[85] The Zengakuren, however, was able to control effectively the student movement and to lead it for an extended period in extremely militant political activity. President Eisenhower canceled his visit to Japan, and the Kishi government ultimately fell largely because of the activity of this militant student minority. When the heat of the political crisis was ended, however, many of the students who had been involved in the movement returned to their classes and did not continue to take part in the student movement.

The majority of moderate students everywhere are not only generally less concerned with politics, expressing interest in social or cultural activity and in their own careers, but when they do have political interests, their commitment tends to be weaker than that of the radicals. Thus, moderates will act less decisively on issues, and will be less concerned with politics in any case.[86]

The ability of American student activists to mobilize a visible base of demonstrators on large campuses from a national student population of close to six million should not be confused with the revolt of the students as a stratum. It is probably true that, in absolute numbers, more students are involved in protest activity than at any time since World War II (although it should be recalled that the pre-war student movement was numerically larger than the present movement, and that in terms of the proportion of involved students to the total student population, it was vastly more significant).[87] On the other hand, there seems to be little doubt that only a small fraction of the total student population is so engaged and that the number of students who consider themselves politically aware is also small. This small fraction has the passive support of most students when it is pressing for civil rights or academic freedom. But its support dwindles when it demonstrates against American foreign policy or for a specific ideological program.

The American Student Movement and the Developing Areas: Some Comparative Comments

The recent attention given both to student activities in the United States and to student unrest in many of the developing areas makes some comparative discussion both relevant and feasible. These comments are necessarily incomplete and are only intended to underline some of the more obvious factors which we have observed.

American student politics, like American politics generally, tends to be rather pragmatic and non-ideological. No directly left-wing party-related student organization in the United States has ever achieved a mass following. The only groups which have made a strong impact on the student population have been those concerned with a specific issue, such as civil rights, or more broadly based social action groups, such as Students for a Democratic Society at present, or the American Student Union during the 1930's. Political ideologies still have an important attraction, particularly to students in many of the developing nations, and are often the base of substantial student movements. The fact that student groups are able to fall back on ideology—usually some form of Marxism—makes it easier for such groups to survive periods of political quiescence. American student organizations, because of their pragmatic approach, have had a more difficult task surviving when struggles are not at a high pitch.

A general characteristic of student political activity is the rapidly changing focus of attention of the student activists, and the mercurial quality of student organizations. American students are not alone in losing interest in a specific issue or organization. In many countries, there has been a rather regular pattern of student political action, which rises and falls with changes in the political and educational situation in the society. Even militant mass student movements, such as the Zengakuren in Japan, are plagued by periods of student apathy. It is significant that the strongly Marxist Zengakuren has often shifted its tactics and stressed such issues as better student living conditions or reduced tram fares for students instead of militant struggle against the government.

The problems of continuity of organization and leadership which bother the American movement are duplicated in most nations which have an active student movement. In a number of the new nations, the active student movements which participated in various anti-colonialist revolutions practically disappeared following independence. These student movements functioned effectively in an atmosphere of struggle, but seemingly could not adjust to periods of political calm. Student leaders, often idealists committed to goals of rapid modernization, found it difficult to function under seemingly slow-moving regimes, and either quit politics in despair or turned to extreme radical opposition. The parallel between such behavior in developing areas and the growing alienation from adults and the liberal "power structure" which can be seen in much of the American student movement today seems striking.

The relative weakness of the American student movement as compared to those abroad undoubtedly reflects institutional differences. The variation between the system of examinations in the United States and those in other countries may, for example, have an important impact on student political developments. In the United States, students are examined regularly and must be fairly well prepared if they are to continue in the university. In many of the developing nations and parts of Europe, however, examinations take place at yearly intervals (or even less often), thus allowing considerable leeway for outside student activities. Student movements in India and Latin America have strongly resisted efforts to upgrade standards through regular stringent examinations. They have also insisted that students who fail should have the right to repeat tests, that no one be dropped for bad grades. It is interesting to note that some of the student political activists in the United States do indeed drop out of college in order to participate more fully in the movement. The full program of extra-curricular activities not related to politics which is offered in most American universities also decreases student political participation. In many of the developing areas, politics is one of the few areas open to student participation, since there is little or no provision of facilities for non-political extra-curricular activities.

There are some important differences in the larger social systems which affect the nature of the student movements in the United States and those in many of the developing nations. The image of the college student, for example, differs greatly from country to country. In many of the developing areas, the student is one of the key modernizing elements in the society, is part of a small educated elite, and is treated, if not as a member of the ruling class, at least with considerable respect. In these countries, the individual student may have a feeling of importance and of potential or actual power in his society. Student manifestos are often taken seriously by government officials, and the student organizations expect to be given a serious hearing by the government. It would be inconceivable that the President of the United States would hold protracted discussions with the leaders of the National Student Association in order to persuade them to support the government's plans for social development. Yet, this is exactly what happened in the Ivory Coast last year, and while the students eventually agreed with the President because of the threat of an end to scholarship aid, everyone recognized the importance of the students.

Student populations in many of the developing countries tend to be small, and relatively homogeneous. Often there is only one major university, which is located in the nation's capital, thus making the mobilization of student protest relatively easy. Students often come from relatively similar social class backgrounds, and many will have received their secondary educations in a small number of prestigious schools, thus building up the cohesion of the student community. The situation in the United States, with the college population approaching six million and with more than 2,000 institutions of widely disparate kinds, is not at all analogous to those in the developing areas. The fate of an individual American student is relatively unimportant, and even the largest student organization, such as the SDS, means very little given the size of the educational establishment. The size of the system also makes it difficult to organize coordinated activity.

The fairly wide range of class backgrounds, educational interests, and motives of American students makes them a very difficult group to stimulate to social action. Moreover, the vocational emphasis of American higher education is much greater than in universities in most developing areas, which have patterned their educational systems after British or French elitist models.

In the developing countries, there is an intrinsic conflict between the university and the society, thereby creating a fertile ground for student political awareness and participation. The university, as one of the primary modernizing elements in largely traditional societies, necessarily finds itself opposed to other elements in its society, and must often fight to protect its values and orientation.[88] Students are often involved in these conflicts and are key protectors of the modern orientation of the university. During the Nkrumah regime in Ghana, much of the student opposition to the government was based on the commitment of the university and of the student population to the modern values of academic freedom and to an institutionalization of an independent judiciary, a competent bureaucracy, etc. In much of Latin America, the student movements have attacked the traditional oligarchic elements in the society for resisting economic and social modernization. In the developed nations, on the other hand, no such conflict exists. The university is a carrier of the traditions of the society, as well as a training agency for necessary technical skills. It is a participant in a continuing modernizing development, rather than in the vanguard of such development. University students are not called upon to protect the values of their institutions against societal encroachments. In most cases, they are merely asked to gain the qualifications necessary for a useful role in a technological society. Thus, the place of the university in the developing and the advanced societies differs substantially, and these contrasts have an important role in shaping student political involvement.

These contrasts between the modernizing role of the university and the traditional values of pre-industrial societies may also be elaborated, as was done to some extent earlier in Chapter 1 in the culture cleavage between generations, which exists in many of these societies. Eisenstadt and Parsons have stressed the extent to which youth movements are a product of such tensions.[89] They point to the discrepancy between the values inherent in the family, i.e., those of the parents, and those which are required by a modern economic structure. The better-educated youth tend to adopt the values of the latter, universalism, achievement, equalitarianism, and the like. Attitude studies in various recently emerging nations have pointed to the sharp differences between the educated and the uneducated on a variety of issues. The educational variable seems to be more important than factors of socioeconomic status. Since age and level of education are highly correlated in less-developed nations, politically relevant value differences often involve generational tension. Such differences between university youth and the older generation are, according to Parsons, minimized in contemporary American society. He argues that the American middle class, itself relatively well educated, basically accepts the values of a modern economy. Hence, increased education will not pit youth against parents. And flowing from the logic of the analyses of Eisenstadt and Parsons is the assumption that youth movements will be much less significant in developed as compared with underdeveloped society. And as we have seen, insofar as American students have been concerned with eliminating the last major aspect of traditionalist pre-modern values, the ascriptive pattern in race relations, they have the moral support of their parents. A brief comparative look at the situation of the university and educated youth in the emerging and industrially developed societies suggests, therefore, that student activism cannot take on major proportions in the latter.

Many developing areas have highly articulated traditions of student participation in, and sometimes leadership of, political events. In Latin America, students have participated in political affairs for generations and are expected to do so. They have well-defined powers in the governing of universities. In many Asian and African countries, students were a leading force in the struggles for independence, and former student leaders often achieved political power in the post-independence governments. Since independence, the student role in many of these countries has diminished substantially although governments must still take account of the student movement. Recent events in South Korea, Turkey, Japan, Indonesia, South Vietnam, and other countries graphically emphasize the importance of the students.

The United States is a sharp contrast to this picture of semi-legitimated student political activity.[90] American students have never been particularly active politically, and they are not generally expected to participate actively in their society. Student organizations have not been important in any aspect of American life, except for the civil rights struggle. A substantial majority of the student population has never been involved in political activity. The new student left is essentially going against the major trends in American academic life. Despite recent widespread publicity, student political activity is still regarded in negative terms by a majority of the students, as well as by many educators and the general public.

It can be seen that there are both differences and similarities between the American student movement and student political activities in the developing areas. This brief discussion has served mainly to point to a few of the more obvious factors. Ironically, students in many of the developing nations recently have begun to look to the relatively small American student movement for inspiration. The success of the civil rights movement, the Berkeley revolt, and other events have been well publicized in many nations. There has been close communication between the American student "new left" and its counterparts in other nations.

Conclusion

It is clear that the student movement in the United States has played a significant role in the past few years in the civil rights struggle in the South, in focusing attention on problems of higher education through the Berkeley revolt, and in beginning the national foreign policy debate on Vietnam. Yet, the student movement has not succeeded in mobilizing a really significant segment of the student population, or in substantially influencing either its educational environment or the broader society. Some of the causes for this weakness have been presented in the contrast between the developing areas and the United States. Basically, in the United States, with its relatively stable social system and a fairly long tradition of political tranquility, radical social movements of any kind have had difficulty in establishing themselves. Many of the developing nations, however, face major social problems and are trying desperately to transform their societies, to modernize, and to industrialize. There is often real ambivalence about roles in rapidly changing societies. Major segments of the society may be impatient at the rate of change, or feel they are suffering from its consequences. In such an atmosphere, radical social movements have a greater opportunity to expand.

While the American student movement is small, and in the long run may be almost insignificant in terms of its direct impact on society, there is always the possibility that it may be a precursor to a larger left-wing movement in the United States. Students have often played a "vanguard" role in different societies and an increase in student activism has sometimes heralded social change. It is possible that the new student left of the mid 1960's may imply some changes in American society. On the other hand, it is much more likely that it is one of many unsuccessful attempts in the United States to create a radical movement in an essentially infertile environment.

Notes

1. This chapter should be read as complementary and slightly overlapping with S. M. Lipset, "Student Opposition in the United States," *Government and Opposition*, I (April 1966), 351–374. The earlier article goes into much more detail on a number of topics which are treated scantily here, while the current one elaborates on themes which are dealt with peripherally in the previously published paper. Some of these issues are also discussed in Philip G. Altbach, "The Future of the American Student Movement," *Liberal Education*, LII (October 1966), 313–324.

2. It is impossible to list all of the various material which has appeared recently concerning student political activity. Some of the books which have recently been published include: American Council on Education, *The Student in Higher Education* (Washington: American Council on Education, 1965); Richard E. Peterson, *The Scope of Organized Student Protest in 1964–1965* (Princeton: Educational Testing Service, 1966); Graham B. Blaine, Jr., *Youth and the Hazards of Affluence* (New York: Harper and Row, 1966); Jack Newfield, *A Prophetic Minority* (New York: New American Library, 1966); O. A. Knorr and W. V. Minter, eds., *Order and Freedom on the Campus* (Boulder: Western Interstate Commission for Higher Education, 1965); Seymour Martin Lipset and Sheldon S. Wolin, eds., *The Berkeley Student Revolt: Facts and Interpretations* (Garden City, N. Y.: Doubleday, 1965); Hal Draper, *Berkeley: The New Student Revolt* (New York: Grove Press, 1965); Michael Miller and Susan Gilmore, eds., *Revolution at Berkeley* (New York: Dell Publishing Co., 1965); Mitchell Cohen and Dennis Hale, eds., *The New Student Left* (Boston: Beacon Press, 1966); Kenneth Keniston, *The Uncommitted: Alienated Youth in American Society* (New York: Harcourt Brace and World, 1965). Philip Jacob's *Changing Values in College* (New York: Harper and Row, 1957) is a pioneering study in this area, and Rose Goldsen, Morris Rosenberg, Robin Williams, Jr., and Edward Suchman, *What College Students Think* (Princeton: Van Nostrand, 1960) also provides valuable insights into student attitudes. Nevitt Sanford, ed., *The American College* (New York: John Wiley, 1962) is probably the most valuable overview of American higher education published to date. There are also a great number of articles and dissertations which have appeared concerning students and politics in the United States. A particularly useful one is Barry Metzger, *The Young Radicals: Student Protest in the Nineteen-Sixties* (Senior Thesis: Princeton University, 1966).

3. See the articles cited in Chapter 1.

4. Michael Munk, "New Left: Background of the Young Radicals," *National Guardian*, September 18, 1965, p. 3.

5. Peterson, *op. cit.*, p. 33. Similar results from comparable spring 1964 data

are reported in E. G. Williamson and John L. Cowan, *The American Student's Freedom of Expression* (Minneapolis: University of Minnesota Press, 1966).

6. "Campus '65," *Newsweek*, March 22, 1965, p. 54.

7. Peterson, *op. cit.*, p. 34.

8. Glen Lyonns, "The Police Car Demonstration: A Survey of Participants," in Lipset and Wolin, eds., *op. cit.*, p. 522.

9. Kenneth Little, "Academic Protest in the United States," *The Listener*, LXXIV (August 12, 1965), 220–221, 249.

10. Michael Aiken, N. J. Demerath III, and Gerald Marwell, "Conscience and Confrontation: Some Preliminary Findings on Summer Civil Rights Volunteers" (mimeographed, University of Wisconsin, 1966), p. 12.

11. Lawrence F. Schiff, "The Obedient Rebels: A Study of College Conversions to Conservatism," *Journal of Social Issues*, XX (October 1964), 91.

12. A survey done by the Opinion Research Corporation indicates that 77 per cent of the student conservatives at Eastern colleges feel that their campuses are dominated by liberals (figures for the South and West were lower in this regard). This survey also indicates that conservative students feel that the academic community is dominated by liberals, and there is often a good deal of reaction against professors and the colleges for their liberalism. Opinion Research Corporation, *Conservatism on the College Campus* (Princeton: Opinion Research Corporation, 1962), p. A-1; for data on social origins see p. 23.

13. Peterson, *op. cit.*, p. 24. Similar findings are reported in a study of Negro college students, the higher quality of the southern Negro colleges, the larger the proportion participating in civil rights activity. See John Orbell, "Protest Participation among Negro College Students" (mimeographed, Ohio State University, 1966), p. 11.

14. Martin Meyerson, the Acting Chancellor at Berkeley during the spring 1965 semester, noted in a speech to the faculty that in his twenty years at three major private universities, he had never detected anything approaching the degree of hostility and criticism of the university by the faculty as existed at Berkeley prior to the FSM protests. He commented that when the Berkeley faculty said "we" they did not mean their university.

15. Martin Trow, "Notes on Undergraduate Teaching at Large State Universities" (mimeographed, Stanford: Center for Advanced Study in the Behavioral Sciences, 1960), p. 23. For an excellent analysis of the tensions which affect faculty and students in state universities, see also Frank Pinner, "The Crisis of the State Universities: Analysis and Remedies," in Sanford, ed., *op. cit.*, pp. 940–971.

16. The heterogeneity of large public universities has been graphically documented by Martin Trow. Among the 5,000 freshmen who enter Berkeley each year, one-quarter could not name the Secretary of State and half had never read a book of poetry for pleasure. By contrast, 90 per cent of the freshmen entering three selective liberal arts colleges could name the Secre-

tary of State, and three-quarters had read poetry for pleasure. Half the freshmen at the university owned more than fifteen books, while 70–80 per cent did at the three colleges. The results of the Scholastic Aptitude Tests (SAT) tend to corroborate these findings. At Harvard, MIT, Stanford, and Cal Tech "between 70 and 90 per cent of their entering Freshmen had SAT Verbal scores of over 600. At Berkeley the comparable figure was 30 per cent." At the private universities, no more than 21 per cent had scores lower than 500, while at Berkeley one-third scored below 500—this despite the fact that Berkeley is one of the most selective state universities. "In 1960 Berkeley admitted . . . 420 students with SAT Verbal scores of over 650, and almost a thousand with SAT scores of over 600, more at that level than enter MIT and Amherst combined." Berkeley also admitted 1,500 students with scores below 500—more than triple the number with scores that low who were admitted to Kutztown State College in Pennsylvania, *ibid.,* pp. 16–19.

17. Martin Meyerson, "The Ethos of the American College Student: Beyond the Protests," in Robert Morison, ed., *The Contemporary University: U.S.A.* (Boston: Houghton Mifflin, 1966), p. 274. For a similar point see Trow, *op. cit.,* p. 15.

18. *Ibid.,* pp. 12–13.

19. Thus Berkeley has over 400 graduate students in physics, around 200 in sociology and 350 in political science. Harvard admits around 10 to 15 graduates in sociology per year; Yale takes in fewer than 25 in political science.

20. Preliminary Report of the Wisconsin Student Attitude Survey (Madison: University of Wisconsin Survey Research Center, 1966, mimeographed), p. 2. We are indebted to Professor Harry Sharp for these data.

21. Select Committee on Education, *Education at Berkeley* (Berkeley: Academic Senate, University of California, 1966), p. 12.

22. A report indicating the varying degrees of success of graduate students in different departments of sociology attests to the sharp variations at the Big Three of the Ivy League and the State Universities in educational achievement. In the academic year 1964–1965, Berkeley had more graduate students than any other department in its field, 193, yet reported only 45 completed Ph.D.'s in the preceding nine years. Harvard, on the other hand, has 73 graduate students, but had turned out 86 Ph.D.'s in the same period of time. Similar relative differences exist between Michigan and Wisconsin, on the one hand, and Princeton and Yale on the other. *Guide to Graduate Departments of Sociology, 1965* (Washington, D.C.: American Sociological Association, 1965), pp. 12, 25, 36, 52, 65, 70.

23. For data showing some of the differences in academic and vocational orientations between good state and private schools, see Jacob, *op. cit.,* p. 113.

24. Martin Trow, "Some Lessons from Berkeley," in Lawrence Dennis and Joseph Kaufman, eds., *The College and the Student* (Washington, D.C.: American Council on Education, 1966), p. 128. The typology of different student cultures is Trow's.

25. Hanan Selvin and Warren Hagstrom, "Determinants for Support for Civil

Liberties," in Lipset and Wolin, eds., *op. cit.*, p. 514; Lyonns, *op. cit.*, pp. 521, 523; John Corry, "Drugs a Growing Campus Problem," *The New York Times*, CXM, March 21, 1966, p. 27; "Excerpts from Report of Select Committee on Education," *The Daily Californian*, CXC, March 18, 1966, p. 12; and Richard Goldstein, *Drugs on Campus* (New York: Walker and Co., 1966).

26. Kenneth Keniston, "The Faces in the Lecture Room," in Morison, ed., *op. cit.*, p. 321; see also Joseph Katz and Nevitt Sanford, "Causes of the Student Revolution," *Saturday Review*, December 18, 1965, pp. 66, 76.

27. Richard G. Braungart, "SDS and YAF: Backgrounds of Student Political Activists" (Pennsylvania State University, Department of Sociology, 1966, mimeographed), p. 9.

28. Richard Flacks, "The Liberated Generation: An Exploration of the Roots of Student Protest," *The Journal of Social Issues*, 1967.

29. Aiken et al., *op. cit.*, p. 5.

30. Keniston, *op. cit.*, p. 338. A study of the backgrounds of a sample of demonstrators in a student demonstration in Washington, D. C., which attracted students from around the country reported that almost half "felt their parents to be in support of the demonstration," while less than a quarter reported parental opposition. Frederic Solomon and Jacob R. Fishman, "Youth and Peace: A Psychosocial Study of Student Peace Demonstrators in Washington, D. C.," *The Journal of Social Issues*, XX (October 1964), 61.

31. Samuel Lubell, "The People Speak" (news releases reporting on a study of American college students), April 28, 1966, pp. 1–2. Data from the survey of those who surrounded the police car in Berkeley for over 30 hours are highly suggestive of the link between parental politics and those of student demonstrators. Exactly half of the 618 demonstrators who filled in an FSM endorsed quesionnaire indicated that they had been in previous demonstrations. When those with previous demonstration experience were compared with "first-time demonstrators," it turned out that 53 per cent of the experienced ones reported their politics as democratic or revolutionary socialist, as contrasted with 20 per cent among the initiates. Among the experienced demonstrators, 42 per cent reported "one or more parents actively involved in politics during the period 1930–1950," as contrasted with 21 per cent among those involved for the first time. Lyonns, *op. cit.*, p. 524. See also Philip A. Luce, *The New Left* (New York: David McKay Co., 1966), pp. 187–188.

32. Braungart, *op. cit.*, p. 24.

33. William Watts and David Whittaker, "Free Speech Advocates at Berkeley," *Journal of Applied Behavioral Science*, II (1966), p. 53.

34. Flacks, *op. cit.*

35. Jeanne H. Block, Norma Haan, and M. Brewster Smith, "Activism and Apathy in Contemporary Adolescents," in James F. Adams, ed., *Contributions to the Understanding of Adolescence* (Boston: Allyn and Bacon, in press); Flacks, *op. cit.*

36. *Ibid.*

37. Block, Haan, and Smith, *op. cit.*; for a review of the literature and discussion of the psychological effects of the family backgrounds of activists see also Kenneth Keniston, "The Sources of Student Dissent," *The Journal of Social Issues*, 1967.

38. Braungart, *op. cit.*, p. 8.

39. *Ibid.*, p. 16.

40. Flacks, *op. cit.*

41. Charles M. Stanton, "The Committed Student—A New and Rare Breed" (paper presented to the 21st National Conference on Higher Education, Chicago, March 15, 1966), p. 2; see also Orbell, *op. cit.*, p. 12, for comparable data on Negro students.

42. Braungart, *op. cit.*, pp. 23–24.

43. Schiff, *op. cit.*

44. Opinion Research Corporation, *op. cit.*

45. Braungart, *op. cit.*, p. 7.

46. Flacks, *op. cit.* Similar findings are reported in a comparison of members of a left activist group, Students for Peace, and a right one, the YAF, at Pennsylvania State University. The former came from much more well-to-do backgrounds than did the conservatives. See David L. Westby and Richard G. Braungart, "Class and Politics in the Family Background of Student Political Activists," *American Sociological Review*, XXXI (1966), 690–692.

47. Select Committee on Education, *op. cit.*, p. 14.

48. Lyonns, *op. cit.*, p. 521.

49. Paul Heist, "Intellect and Commitment: The Faces of Discontent" (mimeographed Berkeley: Center for the Study of Higher Education, 1966), pp. 18–19.

50. Lyonns, *op. cit.*, p. 521; Solomon and Fishman, *op. cit.*, p. 58. A study of a sample of those who sat in Sproul Hall in December 1964 indicates that 43 per cent of those reporting a paternal religious affiliation indicated Jewish background as compared to 25 per cent among a cross-section of Berkeley students. See Watts and Whittaker, *op. cit.*, p. 54.

51. Braungart, *op. cit.*, p. 26.

52. Flacks, *op. cit.*

53. Solomon and Fishman, *op. cit.*, p. 57. A study comparing participants in the FSM with the Berkeley student population reported that the social sciences gave the greatest support to the demonstrations with the humanities and fine arts running second. Watts and Whittaker, *op. cit.*, p. 51. For a pre-FSM survey of Berkeley students which shows the same correlations with general attitudes see Selvin and Hagstrom, *op. cit.*, p. 512.

54. See S. M. Lipset, *Political Man* (Garden City: Doubleday, 1960), pp. 310–343, for data and discussion of the nature and sources of differences between the politics of intellectuals and other groups, and variations within the intellectual and academic community.

55. Morris Rosenberg, *Occupations and Values* (Glencoe: The Free Press, 1957), pp. 81–83.

56. Select Committee on Education, *op. cit.*, p. 18; see also Selvin and Hagstrom,

op. cit., p. 513. Lubell, *op. cit.* (April 29, 1966), p. 3. Similar patterns have been associated with drug-users and drop-outs on university campuses. "The drug takers are majoring in the humanities or social sciences. . . . There are fewer consistent users in the sciences or in the professional schools. . . . They are vaguely leftist, disenchanted with American policies in Viet Nam, agitated because there are Negro ghettoes and bored with conventional politics." Corry, *op. cit.*, pp. 1, 27.

A report on drop-outs at Berkeley reports that they are to be found disproportionately among "those who choose to study humanities and social sciences, . . . and those who reject important aspects of American society." "Excerpts from Report of Select Committee on Education," *op. cit.*, p. 12.

57. Metzger, *op. cit.*, pp. 81–82.
58. "A Report on the Delegate Questionnaire. The Congress as a College" (Washington, D.C.: U.S. National Student Association, 1966, multilith), *passim.*
59. Opinion Research Corporation, *op. cit.*, p. 21.
60. Braungart, *op. cit.*, pp. 7–8.
61. Christian Bay, "Political and Apolitical Students: Facts in Search of Theory," *Journal of Social Issues*, 1967, contains the most comprehensive effort to draw together various studies, the most pertinent of which are based on Berkeley data, which indicate a link between intellectual attainments and liberal-left political attitudes and actions. However, it may be noted that the one Berkeley study which compared grade points from actual university records, rather than from the reports of respondents, indicated "no differences in grade point averages between the cross-section [sample of the entire student population] and the FSM in either the undergraduate or the graduate categories. . . . [I]n terms of grade point average . . . they [the FSM activists] are quite typical of the Berkeley campus population." Watts and Whittaker, *op. cit.*, p. 52.
62. Flacks, *op. cit.*
63. Richard G. Braungart, "Social Stratification and Political Attitudes: A Study of P.S.U. Student Reaction towards United States Policy in Vietnam" (Department of Sociology, Pennsylvania State University, 1966, mimeographed), p. 14.
64. David Matza, "Position and Behavior Patterns of Youth," in Robert E. L. Faris, ed., *Handbook of Modern Sociology* (Chicago: Rand McNally, 1964), p. 210; see also Lewis S. Feuer, "The Student Left in the USA," *Survey*, No. 62 (January 1967), pp. 90–103.
65. David Riesman, "The College Student in an Age of Organization," *Chicago Review*, XII (Autumn 1958), 61.
66. Peter Bart, "Students of Left Set Up Colleges," *New York Times* (December 12, 1965), p. 72.
67. *Newsweek*, "Campus '65," *op. cit.*, p. 53; Lubell, *op. cit.* The *Moderator* survey is reported in Metzger, *op. cit.*, p. 76.
68. Preliminary Report of the Wisconsin Student Attitude Survey, *op. cit.*, p. 3.
69. Joseph Katz, "Social Expectations and Influences," in Dennis and Kaufman, eds., *op. cit.*, p. 139.

70. Keniston, *op. cit.;* see also Jacob, *op. cit.,* pp. 24–29.

71. *Newsweek,* "Campus '65," *op. cit.,* p. 60.

72. Philip G. Altbach, "Japanese Students and Japanese Politics," *Comparative Education Review,* VII (October 1963), 182.

73. "Rise in Frequency of Suicide," *Statistical Bulletin, Metropolitan Insurance Company,* XLV (July 1964), 8–10; see also Louis Dublin, *Suicide* (New York: Roland Press, 1963), p. 212.

74. Dana L. Farnsworth, *Psychiatry, Education and the Young Adult* (Springfield, Ill.: Charles C Thomas, 1966), pp. 86–88.

75. Richard E. Gordon and Katherine K. Gordon, *The Blight on the Ivy* (Englewood Cliffs: Prentice-Hall, 1963), pp. 9–10.

76. *Ibid.,* p. 10.

77. *Ibid.,* p. 12.

78. Solomon and Fishman, *op. cit.,* p. 57 (italics in original). The same two researchers also studied civil rights activists. See "Perspectives on the Student Sit-in Movement," *American Journal of Orthopsychiatry,* XXXIII (1963), 873–874.

79. Watts and Whittaker, *op. cit.,* p. 49. For somewhat similar data on the police-car demonstrations see Lyonns, *op. cit.,* p. 521.

80. Joseph Katz, "Stress and Development during College Years" (paper presented at a meeting of the American Orthopsychiatric Association, San Francisco, April 15, 1966), pp. 2, 5.

81. The Harris Survey, "College—for Job or Education?" *The Washington Post* (March 18, 1965), p. D.–1.

82. This matter has been more generally discussed in several other chapters in this book, especially in those by Lipset, Altbach, and Bakke.

83. Katz, "Social Expectations and Influences," *op. cit.,* p. 139 (italics in original); on student conservatism generally see Goldsen, Rosenberg, Williams, and Suchman, *op. cit.,* pp. 97–124; Alex S. Edelstein, "Since Bennington: Evidence of Change in Student Political Behavior," *Public Opinion Quarterly,* XXVI (1962), 564–577.

84. See Glaucio A. D. Soares, Chapter 5, this book.

85. Nobushige Ukai, "Whither Students of Today," *Contemporary Japan,* XXV (1960), 702–703.

86. Glaucio A. D. Soares, *op. cit.,* and Metta Spencer, Chapter 14, this book.

87. During the late 1930's, the American Student Union (ASU), the most important general left-liberal group, claimed a membership of 20,000 out of a student population of about one and a half million. SDS today, reports 7,000 members in a student population of near to six million. Peace strikes called by the ASU were reported to have involved over 200,000 students, a larger absolute figure than any peace or anti-war national demonstrations have secured in recent times.

88. For a comprehensive discussion of the values inherent in the concept and role of the university see Michio Nagai, *The Problem of Indoctrination: As Viewed from Sociological and Philosophical Bases* (Columbus: Department of Sociol-

ogy, Ohio State University, Ph.D. thesis, multilith, 1952), pp. 36–39 and *passim*. This general theme is also discussed in S. M. Lipset, "Values, Education, and Entrepreneurship," S. M. Lipset and Aldo Solari, eds., *Elites in Latin America* (New York: Oxford University Press, 1967), pp. 41–43.

89. S. N. Eisenstadt, *From Generation to Generation* (Glencoe: The Free Press, 1956), pp. 171–176; Talcott Parsons, "Youth in the Context of American Society," in Erik H. Erikson, ed., *Youth: Change and Challenge* (New York: Basic Books, 1963), pp. 93–119.

90. For an excellent analysis of the sources of apoliticization among American students see Kenneth Keniston, "American Students and the 'Political Revival,'" *The American Scholar*, XXXII (Winter 1962–1963), 40–64.

Student Freedom and the Republic of Scholars:

Berlin and Berkeley

PAUL SEABURY

———————— **8** ————————

"East is East and West is West." But those who appreciate symmetry in politics and education will marvel at the newest refutation. In Berkeley and Berlin—i.e., at geographic poles of modern higher education—severe crises occurred during the past two academic years. Parallels between them are astonishing. The origins of these crises at the University of California and the Free University of Berlin are much the same; the respective patterns of escalation also surprisingly alike. Administrative prohibitions on political expression in each case were followed by student defiance and demands for virtually unlimited free speech and for unrestrained political engagement. Further restraints were followed by street demonstrations, teach-ins, and student protest strikes. Student groups finally in each case came to demand vastly increased rights for themselves in the self-government of the university. In each case also, inept or insensitive administrative reaction to successive stages of the crisis lent credibility to student agitators' charges that the structure of the university was authoritarian and reactionary. In neither instance was the faculty immune to the disturbances which followed. Professors in Berkeley and Berlin became sharply divided in diagnosing the causes and the real nature of the crisis, and in prescribing the means by which it should be overcome and the implications it should have for the future of the "republic of scholars." What ideal or practical balance should exist between research (*Forschung*) and teaching (*Bildung*) within the university? How great a policy role should students have in its government? Should the University be an unrestricted market place for ideas —especially political ones? Do constitutional guarantees of free speech and assembly have special applicability within a university in view of its public status, or do its unique functions require that these guarantees be modified in the name of academic freedom? Should the University—as some politicized students demand—act as critic of the existing social order outside? Should, as others say, its scholarly enterprises seek to objectively mirror the outside world in microcosm? Or—as traditionalists reply, should it remain a sheltered community of scholars and students *(Lehrenden und Lernden)*, protected from outside pressures in their quest for scientific "truth"?

The gravity of each situation—the German and the American—has placed each institution in jeopardy. Student politicization in each case has meant the intrusion of extremist views. Many faculty members, irrespective of their individual political views, came to regard the existing climate to be inconducive to their research and teaching. The internal crises have been closely watched from the outside by citizens of California and Berlin who have come to be annoyed at what they regard as the abuse of their tax money by irresponsible agitators. They have been even more closely watched by extremists of both left and right who are eager to gain ideological profit and further visibility from the intense politicization of university life and from the chance especially to exploit assembly halls once closed to them. Responsible politicians and educators are now fearful that the unrest may crumble the walls which traditionally have served in some degree to protect the university from the immediate claims and demands of Society—whose attitude toward the university in both Europe and America has been fickle, to say the least.

These crises in German and American higher education come precisely at a time when the relationship between University and Society is being thoughtfully re-examined, and when—especially in Germany—university reform is felt by many to be sorely needed. Are these disturbances symptomatic of growing pains in higher education? Or are they precursors of a new form of Western ideological politics, and the University only incidentally the unlucky arena in which they are first manifest? Ironically, both Berkeley and Berlin immediately before these troubles were generally regarded as among the most liberal and progressive academic institutions in America and Germany—despite their many other imperfections. The "Berlin Model" of academic freedom—especially its autonomy from outside political control—in recent years has been held up in sharp, and favorable, contrast to older and much more traditional universities in West Germany and, of course, to the totalitarian schools of the East. So also in Berkeley.

Only three years ago President Clark Kerr was cited by the American Association of University Professors for Berkeley's distinguished record under his leadership, in advancing academic freedom for faculty and students alike. Radical political groups had more members at Berkeley than at any other American campus before September 1964.

Berkeley and Berlin before the crises had become academic magnets for libertarian transfer students from other parts of their countries for whom the atmosphere of traditional universities has been regarded as too chafing and restrictive. The three most prominent FSM leaders at Berkeley, Mario Savio, Steve Weissman (the head of the graduate student group), and Bettina Aptheker, had transferred to Berkeley during the year before the crisis.

For all of these reasons, the importance of these events is not just whether they have mortally wounded two of the Western world's outstanding universities. They bring into question certain fundamental issues of modern university life. What is the nature and meaning of academic freedom?

I.

A Rip van Winkle returning to Berlin in 1965 would have marveled at the changes which both the Wall and the German *Wirtschaftswunder* have wrought—isolation from East Germany and from refugees has served even to hasten its integration into the general prosperity of the West. The unique quality of Berlin remains—a prosperous and democratic island in the authoritarian sea of the DDR; but its showcase function now is meaningless, except for Western tourists. The Wall serves its function well. Eastern refugees no longer come. Ulbricht's zone might be a thousand miles away; the symbolic resonance between the deadened puritanism of Ulbricht's part of the city and the brilliant vitality of West Berlin is no longer audible.

The Free University also has changed. In the early 1950's, after it had been founded by student and faculty émigrés from the Humboldt University in East Berlin, with American economic aid, its flavor had been poor, humble, and proud; its faculty and students were chiefly either from Berlin itself or from Eastern Germany; Stalinist oppression through the 1950's encouraged a steady flow of eminent scholars and students from the East which was choked only when the Wall was built in 1962. Today, the University looks like many new American universities. A vast construction program financed by the Berlin Senate has filled once vacant fields and open spaces of Dahlem with elegant modern libraries, classrooms, offices, and student residence halls. Like many new American state colleges—which it physically resembles—the Free University owes its new architectural gaudiness to Berlin taxpayers. Its annual DM 100,000,000 budget of the University comes through the Berlin government. In ten years the student body at the university has almost doubled. But the total number of East German students has absolutely declined by 75 per cent. New students and faculty members come to it chiefly from the prosperous West. (In certain respects Berkeley also owes a great deal to the tensions and prosperity of the Cold War and, more than most Western universities, to the tragedies and vicissitudes of recent history than do most other great universities. Vast American defense expenditures during World War II and the Cold War channeled American "brainpower" westward to California. In 1939 Berkeley was a lush Pacific outpost of American higher education; today, it ranks at the top of American universities in the number of Nobel prizewinners, and certainly among the top five in most scientific fields. The average quality of its total student enrollment of 27,500 may not be so spectacular as that of Harvard and Swarthmore, but hidden in it, as one Berkeley professor has put it, there are at least several "concealed" Swarthmore student bodies and probably at least one Harvard. The vast majority of faculty in its chief disciplines are *émigrés* from Europe and Eastern America.)

II.

As in any tragedy the events of the Berlin crisis moved from good intentions to disaster. Early in 1965, anticipating the impending twentieth anniversary of the collapse of Hitler's Germany, Professor Sontheimer of the Philosophy Faculty—officially responsible to the Academic Senate for problems of political education—invited Karl Jaspers to address a special university convocation on May 8. (One might wonder what reasons Germans today should have to celebrate such an anniversary; as one Berlin professor, himself a refugee during the Nazi period, put it, it was hardly worth commemorating at all. "For us it was an end, and not a beginning.") What Jaspers—known well for his sensitive views about German "collective guilt" —might have said on this controversial occasion we will never know. In correspondence with the professor, he declined the invitation on genuine grounds of ill health. But by this time the unlucky professor had been officially rebuked by an outraged Rektor for *Amtsanmassung* (excessive arrogation of authority). Very possibly, if Jaspers had accepted the invitation, it would have been withdrawn. Rumors of this event leaked to the students and to the left-wing leadership of the Free University student government.

They went a step further, inviting a highly controversial, yet far less significant speaker, Erich Kuby, to speak on the same occasion. The Rektor refused permission; Kuby, six years before, had in a speech in Berlin publicly insulted the University as being a relic of the Cold War. Using Hegelian dialectics obscurely, he then had asserted that since it had originated in 1949 as an "antithesis" to the "unfree" East Berlin Humboldt University it was trapped in unfreedom by being enmeshed in politics—a condition he regarded as incompatible with the "scientific and pedagogic tasks of a university." Since subsequently Kuby had been *persona non grata* to the official University, his invitation this time could easily be regarded as a deliberate challenge to university authority. Denied the right to speak at the University by Rektor and Senate both, Kuby nevertheless appeared at a protest meeting held the same day at the *Technische Hochschule* in Berlin. Student leaders then were able to charge the Rektor with political regimentation and with reactionary tendencies, stating that because of such authoritarian behavior he could not carry out his duties as "chief administrative officer" (*Hausherr*). Further, since Kuby had been denied permission to speak, the Rektor had violated constitutional rights of free speech.

From this point, the Kuby case led to the Krippendorff case. A week after capitulation day, a young American-trained political scientist, Ekkehardt Krippendorff, wrote an open letter to a Berlin newspaper, the *Spandauer Volksblatt*, openly attacking the Rektor and calling for public demonstrations, for financial contributions to students in their struggle for constitutional rights; he charged that the Rektor himself had denied Jaspers the right to speak at the University—a false statement which he later publicly retracted. But for this he was too late. Krippendorff, a non-tenured *Assistent* (a rank approximately comparable to that of Instructor in American universities) was dismissed; his contract was not renewed, on grounds that he had irresponsibly libeled the Rektor ("conduct unbecoming an assistant").

Between early May and late July, when this troubled semester at Berlin came to its exhausted end, there were street demonstrations, student strikes, demands by students that the Rektor resign, protests in the student *Konvent* (its representative assembly) over this matter, over Vietnam and the Dominican adventures of President Johnson, and, finally, demands by student leaders for reorganization of the university's internal structure which would give them equal representation, on the troika model, together with two faculty and non-tenured university staff, in the making of University policy. As a German newspaper, *Die Welt*, commented on July 28:

The chief question now concerns the right of unlimited political engagement by student organizations within the University; it ultimately concerns the problem of the politicization of the University.

The right of any one, at any time and any otherwise free place within the university, to speak about any subject in any way: this aspect of the struggle bears the most striking superficial resemblance to the Berkeley situation. A far more fundamental issue, however, was the students' challenge to the university's constitutional structure. Was not the behavior of the Rektor— so even a Professor of the Otto Suhr Institute charged—and of the Senate in acquiescing to it—an evidence once more of the authoritarian servility of Germans to their *Obrigkeitsstaat?*

Not that the Rektor himself had displayed political acumen in these or in several other public matters during the past year. The year before, greeting Robert Kennedy at a university convocation, he had dramatically observed in English: "It is as though the ghost [*geist*] of President Kennedy were with us!" In welcoming the Italian President Saragat, a distinguished anti-Fascist, on a second occasion, he committed a second *faux-pas* in praising Italy's great contributions to modern political thought, and especially those of Croce and Gentile (the latter, next to Mussolini, the intellectual father of Fascist thought). In the Krippendorff matter, while acting legally, he had done so without bothering to consult either the Direktor of the Institute to which the *Assistent* was attached, nor the Professor under whom he worked. The shoals of university politics are treacherous, especially when the amateur pilot—annually elected by his passengers—is a professor of entomological diseases and not a trained sailor.

In all of this, the Berlin "Model" of German university organization has been brought into question. How "free" is the Free University? Among German universities today, students and faculty in Berlin enjoy greater freedom from governmental interference than those of any other German university. Students, through representatives of their own choice, are accorded a voice in university policy-making the likes of which is simply unknown in any other university outside of Latin America. In all other German universities, it is the *Land* government—i.e., the State—which has ultimate authority over the internal administration of German universities. The Free University, through its Senate and its elected Rektor, is master of its own house; the latter, not the minister for science and education, is *Hausherr*. This in turn means that all administrative decisions ultimately are made by him or in his name. Students, elected by the student parliament *(Konvent)*, sit as full-fledged representatives in the Academic Senate. Elected student members participate with equal rights in each Faculty of the University and in its Institutes. The temper of faculty and student body alike, in West Berlin, is far more "liberal" in the Anglo-Saxon sense than those of other German universities. Berlin, for instance, is the only remaining German university which still prohibits the nationalist and traditionalist *Burschenschaften* (dueling fraternities) from engaging in official University life; the *Burschenschaften* flourish everywhere else. Like some American universities, there has been no ban as such on Communist speakers—unpopular as they have been in the past at the Free University. Professors from the East Berlin Humboldt University have publicly debated with Free University professors on such subjects as Marxism and Christianity. Kuby was denied the right to speak because of his earlier insulting remarks about the University—not because he was a Communist, which he is not.

The election of a new "liberal" Rektor for the 1965–1966 academic year seemed to portend a more amicable phase of faculty-student relations in Berlin. But this new regime had barely begun when the Academic Senate (dominated by conservative faculty) ruled that no university facilities henceforth should be used for any political activities whatsoever. This was a far more generalized and harsh deprivation of privilege than the Berkeley Chancellor's ill-considered denial (the year previous) of a small strip of campus land to students for political fund-raising, recruitment, and propagandizing. After several months of renewed student agitation, this Senate resolution was rescinded. A more liberal yet vague ruling now holds: political meetings are permitted provided they do not interfere with normal academic activities. But this satisfies no one, conservative or liberal, and its vagueness is a source of inevitable future acrimony. The matter is by no means closed.

For these and other reasons—the growing prestige of the University in German higher education, for one—more and more West German students in recent years have migrated to Berlin for their studies, thus to escape the more restrictive atmosphere of more traditional universities. As Table 1 shows, since the mid-1950's they have taken the place of East German *émigré* students, whose access to the University is now shut off by the Wall, and whose grim experiences with real political "un-freedom" moved them to play such an important role in the founding of the University and in setting its original tone.

TABLE 1.

Student Enrollment at the Free University

	1956–1957	1964–1965
West Berlin	50.8%	49.3%
West Germany	15.6	38.9
East Zone	31.5	5.4
Other (foreign)	2.1	6.4

Krippendorff's abrupt dismissal, the refusal to permit unwelcome speakers to the University, and other such actions may indeed strike many American university students in much the same way as they did the students in Berkeley who participated in the protest strikes.

If German universities are less tolerant of political dissent than American ones, it is due in part to the fact that German scholars know from recent historical experience what politicization has meant for their university in the past. One earnest handbill, written and distributed by American exchange students, denouncing the Rektor's prohibition of Kuby's speech, had this to say: "Shall the University be turned into an academic hot-house in which intellectual vegetables are grown?" Citing a Jeffersonian adage about the boundless freedom of the human spirit, they continued: "We use Jefferson's words not because we believe that America respects freedom—Johnson in recent weeks has grievously rejected it. But in America there have always been people who have held true to the ideal of freedom—without seeing the least personal advantage in it." "Do we want the University to become a mental hot-house for intellectual vegetables?" "A university should not shut its gates even to the Devil himself—otherwise it will lapse into sterile complacency." There followed the idealistic statement: "We don't just claim to be right—we claim even more: we have political reason on our side." There is more than a touch of naïveté in all this. The gates of German Universities were open to the Devil in the 1930's and like the Man Who Came to Dinner, he did not leave soon or of his own volition. It is among the older generations of scholars in the University—the refugees, the émigrés and the victims of Nazi and Soviet totalitarianism—that nostrils are sensitive to brimstone which some young German scholars do not smell. Today they control the Academic Senate, and—unlike their Berkeley colleagues in December 1964—almost unanimously rejected the claims of students and supported the Rektor's decision and his authority to make it. Many of the elected members of the Academic Senate doubtless share the views of one professor, that the "radicalization of an inflamed, so-called public opinion robs us of the tranquility which is an essential condition for research and teaching." Many of them also share the troubled views of the most respected of the former Rektors of the University, Professor Hirsch, who wrote months before the student disturbances took place:

> Students must ask themselves which image [of the university] they wish to impose on themselves: that of a student "trade union" . . . with an unavoidable tendency towards opposition against a University exclusively represented by its teaching body—or a community of teachers and scholars (*Lehrenden und Lernenden*) who according to *our* statutes possess responsibilities in common for affairs of the entire university. . . .

Yet to disgruntled student leaders like Wolfgang Lefevre, chairman of ASTA (the General Student Association), the events in Berlin—especially the Rektor's and Senate's public criticism of students' intervention in the two cases—prove that this choice is an unreal one. As Lefevre remarked in a speech before the student *Konvent* in July:

> Student representatives often have been criticized in the past (by faculty committees) for neglecting the welfare of the entire university and for caring only about their special interests. But then when they begin to show an interest in concerns of the whole university, then they are accused of exceeding their jurisdictional competence.

The Berlin drama has featured a case of actors playing the role of leftish generational protest against Johnson's Vietnam and Dominican policies, against the three German democratic parties, for peaceful accommodation with the East-zone D.D.R., and so forth.[1] But a well-organized right-wing nationalist cast stands in the wings, waiting for a swing of student mood in the opposite direction. Its constituency principally lies in the still-banned *Burschenschaften*. Its political views differ, of course, from those of its opponents who have controlled the gears of student government. But campus politicization has been as welcome to them as it is to the others. Right-wing *Konvent* representatives in January 1965 had thrown their support to the left-wing radical, Lefevre, resulting in his victory over centrist candidates as president of student government. Both extremes stand to profit from a situation where students—like German burghers in 1932—found no choice except one of two extremes.

Among Berlin students, as in American universities like Berkeley, the activists are only a small minority. At the height of the Berlin disorders only 250 students manned the barricades and actively participated in protest—a percentage approximately the same (4 per cent as opposed to 5 per cent) as that of the Berkeley "hard core" (in a university nearly twice as large), who "sat in" Sproul Hall in December. For the rest, these constitutional issues and the agitational issue of "political freedom" have been less important than the mundane objectives of getting an education and then getting a job. (Barely 48 per cent of Berlin students voted in the last student elections.)[2] But revolutions are made by minorities even in universities. The Western university has never—except in brief medieval experiments in Bologna and Vienna—claimed to be a majoritarian democracy for students and faculty together.

The "Republic of Scholars" confronts much more than the mere question of how its constitutional powers are to be divided and exercised. The Berkeley and Berlin disturbances go to the very heart of the nature of the academic enterprise itself. Differing conceptions of the university seem hopelessly intermingled in the lexicon and vocabulary both of student protest and of academic reaction to it.

In both Berlin and Berkeley, the newness, rapidity of expansion, absence of unique corporate traditions, and sharp up-grading in the quality of imported students and faculty, and a liberal atmosphere contrasting sharply with most comparably prestigious universities, have doubtless contributed to this crisis of politicization. In many faculties and departments of both universities vast numbers of students have little contact with professors, except through the intermediary of non-tenured assistants. The community of teachers and scholars which Professor Hirsch rightly regards as the traditional idea of Western universities is already radically at odds with existing reality. Berlin faculty members are overburdened with teaching and administrative jobs. The plight of many top- and middle-rank German professors is especially poignant. Their academic careers were savagely interrupted by the war; much of their precious time in the immediate postwar years was spent not in individual research but in common tasks of rebuilding the shattered universities; major research other than their *Habilitationsschrift* often has been deferred from year to year. "Angry young men"—Ekkehardt Krippendorff for one—in the new generation of scholars seem indifferent to such private woes of their superiors. German academic *Assistenten* (scholars not through with the double jeopardy of writing both a doctoral dissertation and, their qualifying masterpiece, the *Habilitationsschrift*) regard with impatience the *Sitzfleisch* of their superiors in the professorial chairs they aspire some day to occupy.[3]

Many are aggravated by what they regard as an outmoded and even "feudal" career pattern. (A young American assistant professor, the same age as an average German *Assistent*, normally acquires in his late twenties major teaching and administrative rights which the *Assistent* usually does not have until his mid-thirties.) Many of them also are impatient with what they regard as backward and traditionalist modes of scholarship—especially in the social sciences. Thus the generational conflict—seen in American universities as the revolt of the Under Thirties—is latent also in German university life. It is further complicated by growing demands from outside the University, now called by many the *Bildungsnotstand*, that it further admit and provide facilities for even larger numbers of students; that its educational programs place even greater stress on *Bildung* (teaching) than on *Forschung* (which includes both research and the training of academic apprentices for future university scholarly careers). Even in the "Berlin Model" the hand of tradition lies heavily on certain practices. At Berkeley and other progressive American institutions, demagogues such as Mario Savio have raged at the impersonality of an efficient "machine" whose IBM precision-instruments route students through a complex maze of requirements and courses; yet if German universities like Berlin are to respond to growing pressures to enlarge themselves even further, and to train more and more young scholars for "practical" careers, they also will have to relinquish many of their highly intimate and guild practices,[4] in favor of more efficient, if impersonal, administrative ones.

There is a "syndicalism" in German student radicalism which finds its counterpart in Berkeley tendencies toward anarchism.[5] Syndicalist student groups in Berlin now claim the right of equal student representation in university policy-making; at Berkeley, the demands are for minimal, if any, administrative controls of student behavior within the university and unlimited freedom of expression. In each instance there is little reason to suppose that "Society," "the Administration," or "the State" will assent for long to any formal weakening of the corporate structure of the University or to vast cessions of authority over such matters as student discipline. During 1965–1966, the new Berkeley administration has gradually been recovering powers which were yielded under pressure last year. In February 1966, three student leaders, including Bettina Aptheker, were ordered by the administration to desist from campus political activity on pain of being suspended as students. A month later, three students, including one of those enjoined from political activity in February, were dismissed by the Chancellor for repeated violations of campus regulations. A non-student activist was arrested on campus for manning a table for a political organization. It is interesting to note that the event which escalated the Berkeley protest into a mass revolt was the effort by the campus police in October 1964 to arrest a non-student for sitting behind a table. But by the spring of 1966, though the successors of the FSM could still run protest meetings with thousands present, there seemed to be little willingness on the part of large numbers of students to risk jail sentences and expulsions.

The likely resolution of constitutional issues, however, is a less important issue than the deeper one posed at Berkeley and Berlin: What is the nature of the Republic of Scholars? Who should run it, and for what purposes? The questions posed sharply now in both institutions go to the very heart of the academic enterprise itself; and regardless of whether that enterprise formally responds, in any significant sense, to demands for change and reform, its inhabitants must recognize, at least individually, the complexity of the web of missions in which the contemporary university must engage, if the equilibrium of the institution is to be restored.

It is possible to see in Berlin and Berkeley three views of the University mission each claiming to wear the mantle of academic freedom. One, the traditionalistic view, long the style of continental universities, and still prized by the Berlin faculty, sees its institution principally as a corporate body sheltered from the immediate pressures of society—indeed, protected in many ways *from* it, and able for this reason to engage, in Jefferson's words, in the free pursuit of truth in various fields of knowledge regardless of where it leads. This is the community of scholars; living for knowledge and justifying itself in its results—i.e., what it adds as increment to human knowledge. A second—and quite new—conception which has found favor in the minds of many students today is that the university should be, as it were, a society in microcosm: representing or mirroring all views, all tendencies of thought, an open place wherein even the Devil himself has the right to speak. To many now politicized students, this conception of the university is illogically linked with a third—the university as *critic* of society—as a playing field on which future political Waterloos could be won, and where regiments may be recruited and trained for more immediate battles. That these roles are by no means identical is beside the question so long as students do not see the difference between them. Added to these two general conceptions it is easy also to see a third: the university as a training school which justifies itself only so long as it performs practical tasks for society. Its instrumentalist role consists of providing skills to an endless flow of students—taxpayers' children; and he who pays the piper calls the tune. A free university is one which "serves" a democratic society.

Every free university claims to incorporate and to reconcile these differing images. Somehow a balance among them is struck. But it is doubtful that a university can survive when it pretends that these roles are harmonious, and of equal importance. Furthermore, the limitless pursuit of one of them, to the neglect of the others, can bring a modern university down in ruins. To many scholars, the idea of a university as permanent battleground of "free" political movements and ideologies is hardly more compatible with academic freedom (in its traditional sense) than that of a *gleichgeschaltet* ideological institution such as the Humboldt University in East Berlin. In Berkeley and West Berlin important scholars have made it known that they will not remain if some semblance of quiet is not regained, and some have already left. Nor will "society" which pays the bills tranquilly long endure an intense heat of university politicization without responding in some negative and possibly positive fashion to it.

In new, progressive, and quickly-renowned universities such as Berlin and Berkeley questions of this sort have come up more dramatically than in older universities. Could it perhaps be that it is precisely in such institutions, where traditions must be invented, that such issues arise in such violent form? Martin Meyerson, acting chancellor during Spring 1965 at Berkeley, in speaking to the Academic Senate observed, *inter alia*, that Berkeley, unlike other distinguished private universities at which he had taught, seemed to have little sense of community in it: "I suddenly realized one day, after being here for a year, that I never heard any of my colleagues use the expression 'we' in talking about problems common to the University." Former Rektor Hirsch of the Free University had this to say:

When the normative meaning of the concept Community within a University is not understood by the majority of those who must comprise it, then the individual —student or professor—comes to feel himself isolated and turned-inward . . . he completely fails to understand any appeals to public spiritedness; the terms "fellow student" and "colleague" are meaningless rhetoric.

As its critics like to point out, the Free University of Berlin was a child of the Cold War. Some of them today sarcastically comment that too many "cold warriors" are still in charge. Many Americans will be outraged at such views, especially those for whom Berlin and Berliners have gained special admiration and affection akin only to the Londoners of the Blitz. For them, the spirit of Berlin—its patient good humor under intense pressure—may seem to have been betrayed by these events. The Americans are still here; *Si vis monumentum circumspice:* John Kennedy's and Henry Ford's names are inscribed on two of its chief buildings. But the *Henry Ford Gebäude* was the scene of one of the most exuberant demonstrations.

Before American benefactors' tempers rise too sharply, two central features of the situation worth reflecting on are its surprising congruence with widespread phenomena in American higher education, and the fact that in Berlin as in America itself the rhetoric of extremism thus far has been voiced by libertarians in the authentic language of Western liberalism, not in that of the violent ideologies which destroyed an earlier Germany. To say this is not to take a "boys will be boys" attitude; but to see that—just as hypocrisy is the tribute which vice pays to virtue—Western liberalism today can command its due even from those who are contemptuous of its present realities and impatient with its endless difficulties.

Notes

1. When an East-zone *Volkspolizist* recently shot and killed a West Berlin pleasure boater (and seriously wounded his fiancée) who had rowed too close to the wrong shore of a border canal, the D.D.R. added another civilian to its long list of Berlin victims since the Wall was built in 1962. But Wolfgang Lefevre, the student ASTA president, dismissed it as an "unfortunate incident" and voiced the hope that it would not be exploited by those opposed to improvement of relations with the East German regime.
2. A figure which easily permits "activists" of the left and right to set the tone of student politics. The comparable Berkeley figure is closer to one-third.
3. One young *Assistent* remarked to me: "When a Professor gets his chair, that is the end of him as a scholar."
4. The tradition of academic government-by-amateurs is now being seriously examined at Berlin: should the chief university official—the *Rektor*—remain a one-year elective post, or should the American institution of a more permanent President chosen for administrative expertise be adopted?
5. The sartorial squalor which sets the dreary style of Berkeley protest would doubtless astound many Berlin "radicals," as would the verbal violence of Berkeley's demagoguery and the lengths to which rebels have been willing to go—in the name of idealism—to risk their personal careers. But then, the ritualistic style of American civil rights protest and the political successes of mass civil disobedience are not so well known in Berlin, nor are the characteristically permissive attitudes of American elders, including faculty members. As far as I know, the girl student who brought her unchained Rhesus monkey into a Berkeley Academic Senate meeting and permitted it to climb on the shoulder (and inspect the hair) of a distinguished professor of cell physiology, was subject to no academic discipline for this remarkable act. After all, as some professors might ask, who is entitled to define what "conduct unbecoming a student" *is*?

The French Student Movement

JEAN-PIERRE WORMS

9

This chapter attempts to apply an historical perspective to the analysis of the French student movement since 1900.[1] It concentrates on the history of the *Union Nationale des Étudiants de France* (UNEF). The UNEF is not the only channel for French students' political action. Indeed, it is constitutionally non-political, although this has come to mean that it is not affiliated with any political party rather than not concerned with political issues. Until recently, the UNEF was by far the most influential student organization in the French political sphere.

From 1900 to 1914: The Golden Era of Student Folklore

The rise of a national organization of French students expressing a sense of collective identity is a relatively new phenomenon in France. In 1877 the first local student organization *(Association d'Étudiants)* was founded— that is, the first organization in which "studenthood" was the only criterion for membership as opposed to the previous organizations, which recruited on the basis of religious or political affiliation. By 1900, such non-political and non-religious student associations existed in all French university towns. In 1907 these associations were federated in a single "National Union" of students which marks the birth of the *Union Nationale des Étudiants de France*. Until the end of World War I, however, the UNEF played no significant role on campus or in society.

The pre-World War I student population was a very small elite (29,000 in 1900). Students came almost exclusively from the upper bourgeoisie and prepared themselves for professional careers which were assured them.

They enjoyed almost complete financial and future professional security. The time at the university was "the good life"—the prelude to an elite position in society. Their position rendered them completely indifferent to social or political issues. They went through university as through an initiation rite. Determined to "enjoy life," they had wild drinking and singing parties, outings on the town, and generally participated in the kind of expected and benevolently tolerated student folklore described as "sowing wild oats." The student associations presided over such recreational activities. In many ways they resembled the American fraternities: high membership fees, a system of recommendation by alumni, and strong school traditions. There was very little unity in the UNEF, no feeling of general solidarity, no nationally organized action, and a great deal of energy spent in traditional local school rivalry.

1914 to 1945: The Corporate Orientation

The thirty years that separated the beginning of World War I from the end of the second signaled important changes in French higher education: the highly elitist model disappeared with its small number of upper class students secure in their status, self-indulgent, and indifferent to the world. Increasing numbers of middle class students entered the university with greater economic and professional worries. With a new style of studenthood and with different ties to society, the student organization, the UNEF, assumed new functions.

The 1914–1918 war was, of course, the first gigantic shock to traumatize the "happy-go-lucky" student body. One figure tells the whole story: two out of three students were called up. Another effect of the devastation of war was the undermining of confidence and economic well-being of the upper and middle classes. As a result, postwar students lost their carefree attitude and were strongly motivated to terminate their studies as rapidly as possible and proceed with the business of making a living.

Moreover, the universities had begun to recruit students from a wider section of the population. By 1926, there were 58,000 students in France— twice the 1900 figure. The result of significant reform in the educational system was added to this general effect of technological change: all secondary education became free in 1930. Subsequently, many children of the *petite bourgeoisie* continued their schooling up to the *baccalauréat* (terminal examination of the secondary cycle) and demanded entry to the universities. The French student population had grown to 80,000 by 1939.

However, access to universities of social classes hitherto excluded was not the only factor to affect the economic security of the student population. With the 1930's came the depression and ensuing unemployment and economic hardship. Students became absorbed in solving their material problems; their local associations and the UNEF assumed an essentially new function of pooling efforts to solve them. Grants were to be obtained from the government, subsidized housing for the increased student population and various other needs had to be taken care of: health, restaurants, sports.

The UNEF undertook to secure these benefits but the methods used to do so were influenced by its past experience. The organization had been built as a federation of fraternal or friendship societies, not as a mass movement. There was little internal democracy in the selection of leaders and the determination of policies. The national level of leadership had little power and was most reticent to use its limited power for planning mass demonstrations which might have shaken the "nepotic" structure of the UNEF. There was no national "doctrine," no sense of responsibility for future student generations or for the university system as a whole, with the result that the UNEF handled problems with piecemeal action and generally at the local level.

A few demands were coordinated at a national level such as tuition fees, grants, and social aid, but they never erupted into mass demonstrations, student strikes, or the like. Instead, the most important work was done by the local association which also acted as a charitable, mutual aid organization. Students turned to their local association for financial loans, help with housing, etc. But their most important contribution was the soliciting of help from outside with great reliance on the alumni. Thus, a number of charitable organizations, private or semi-private, were created *for* the students, like the *Cité Universitaire* in Paris, university restaurants in the provinces, and sanatoria. The local associations which had often played an important role in the instigation of such endeavors rapidly lost control. And as these charities developed they were federated on a national level either through private foundations (e.g., the Sanatoria Foundation) or through semi-public "offices" or "services" such as the *Service de Médecine Préventive*, the *Office du Tourisme Universitaire*, the *Office du Sport Universitaire*, the *Bureau Universitaire des Statistiques* (which, among other services, advised on future careers), and, most important of all, the *Centre National des Oeuvres* which dealt with the building and administration of student housing and food services.

It is obvious that politics played only a minor role in these activities. Indeed, the UNEF adhered to the most restrictive interpretation of its "non-political" constitution. Each problem was seen as practical and limited, to be faced separately from all others—without political ramifications. To do otherwise, to elaborate a global set of demands or strategy would have called for a different type of organization and a sense of some collective identity on the part of the students, a different conception of "studenthood."

The lack of militant action by the UNEF, its uninvolvement in political issues, and its inherent respect for the established political order can probably be explained in part by its structure and history and, in part, by the urgency of material problems students had to face—their economic difficulties and uncertainty of their future led them to strive for individual benefits without "rocking the boat." However, another factor seems relevant: the political atmosphere of the society at large.

This was not a time of political quiescence. The Left increased its power to the point of winning an electoral majority and forming a Popular Front government while the Fascist *ligues* (under the leadership of Maurras) became a real threat. The students participated in the political battles and growing ideological strife. Violent fist fights between students of the Left and Right became frequent in the Latin Quarter.

Two comments should, however, be made: these demonstrations were not specifically student political manifestations, but participation in national "adult" political movements. Secondly, the level at which the political confrontation took place was so "ideological" in terms of a clash between total theories of society that the current demands of the students pertaining to their more immediate basic needs could hardly be introduced into the debate. In other words, there was a dichotomy between the political involvement of students and their involvement in everyday preoccupations. This also explains why the UNEF was able to remain so aloof from raging political battles.

This describes the situation when World War II broke out. The UNEF continued to function as if nothing had changed. It established "normal" relations with the new Vichy government and even went as far as collaborating with its program of compulsory youth work camps in Germany (*Service du Travail Obligatoire*). The university suffered less from World War II than it had from the first. In 1940 the number of students had dropped from 80,000 to 55,000, but it soon increased again and reached a peak of 106,000 in 1943. Students then began to join the *maquis* in greater number—others were taken to German work camps.

There again the fact that the UNEF ignored the war was not indicative of the lack of French student involvement in political problems of the day but only of their organization's narrow corporate orientation. In fact, the first demonstration organized against the German occupation was a student agitation on the Champs-Elysées on November 11, 1940, which resulted in some hundred dead and many more sent to Germany. Subsequently, an increasing number of students participated in the resistance movement. However, when the war ended, it was obvious that whatever students had contributed to the fight against Hitler had been done outside their own organization. In postwar France, when the Resistance spirit was the focal point of national identity, the UNEF was discredited and could no longer be considered to represent French students.

1945 to the Present: Student "Syndicalism"

1. *The Resistance heritage: 1945–1950.* When the French universities resumed normal peace-time activities a large minority of students had been directly involved in the war. Of 123,000 students in 1946, approximately a quarter emerged from the *maquis* or from Germany. France had been greatly damaged by the war and it was conceivable that students might primarily be concerned with their studies and uninterested in anything else—a phenomenon which seems to have taken place in postwar America. However this was impossible in view of the enormous intellectual and moral influence of the "resistance spirit." Unlike America, where the war had tended to unify the country and dissolve most of the political battles in the common effort, France had suffered the war as a divided nation. The Resistance had led the fight as much against the Vichy Government as against the German occupation. The war had been a partial civil war and a highly ideological one at that. Political choice was a basic factor of the French involvement during the war, and France emerged highly politicized from the war.

Three "lessons" learned by the new generation of students in the Resistance were particularly relevant to the future of the UNEF. First, no representative organization, no group in society can stand aloof, indifferent to others and to national political issues, without "losing its soul." Second, the old political parties had failed to rise to the challenge of the times and were attributed great responsibility for the French debacle. In addition, rigid ideologies were highly suspect. Third, fundamental solidarities should not be forgotten between intellectuals and the working class in a country, and between all countries including those under colonial rule.

These were the main guide lines along which the "heirs" of the Resistance chose to organize student participation in the reconstruction of post-war France. A national organization was needed with a window on the world at large and its problems, and yet independent of political parties, truly representative of the specific interests and aspirations of students. A doctrine was also needed to reconcile these two potentially divergent aims.

In the Resistance, students had been affiliated to a variety of political, social, educational, cultural, and religious organizations. They federated into one single *Union Patriotique des Organisations Étudiantes* (UPOE). Should this organization assume all the tasks which the old UNEF had handled with the risk of endless faction fights inherent in this form of student "parliament," or should the slower process of "capturing" the UNEF and changing it from within be tried? The second course was finally adopted. In one year "Resistance" candidates for leadership of local associations affiliated to the UNEF had stood for most elections and had won against the old discredited leaders. The Easter 1946 annual convention in Grenoble ratified their majority.

A way had to be found for reconciling the old defense of students' corporate interest with the new ideology of social and political responsibility. This was done through a remarkable "charter" which first attempted to define "studenthood" in socially meaningful terms ("Students are young intellectual workers") and then elaborated on the ensuring "rights and duties." Despite the rather grandiloquent style indicative of the time it was written, this document deserves to be quoted extensively:

La Charte de Grenoble

Preamble. The representatives of French students legally assembled at a national congress in Grenoble on April 24, 1946, aware of the historic significance of the times,

When the French Union is elaborating the new declaration of the rights of man and of the citizen,

When a pacific Statute of Nations is being drawn up,

When Labor and youth are elucidating the bases for a social and economic revolution at the service of man,

Assert their willingness to participate in the unanimous effort of reconstruction.

True to the example of the best of them who died in the fight for freedom of the French people,

True to the traditional aims of French students when they were at the peak of awareness of their aims,

Recognizing the outdated character of the institutions that govern them,

Declare their decision to be in the vanguard of French youth as often in the past by freely defining the following principles as the bases for their action and demands:

Article I: The student is a young intellectual worker.

Rights and duties of the student as a young person

Article II: As a young person the student has a right to particular consideration from society from the physical, intellectual and moral standpoints.

Artilce III: As a young person, the student has a duty toward national and world youth.

Rights and duties of the student as a worker

Article IV: As a worker, the student has a right to work and live in the best possible conditions, to be independent, both personally and socially, as guaranteed by the free exercise of Union rights.

Article V: As a worker the student has a duty to acquire the highest competence possible.

Rights and duties of the student as an intellectual

Article VI: As an intellectual, the student has a right to the pursuit of truth, freedom being the first condition thereof.

Article VII: As an intellectual, the student has a duty:

—to define, spread and defend truth which comprises the duty to propagate and enrich culture and to assess the meaning of history.
—to defend freedom against all oppression which is the foremost consideration for an intellectual.

Thenceforth, the UNEF became a mass, democratic organization both in style and action with little resemblance to the prewar era.

The first national student strike was organized in 1947 for reduction of university fees and increased government grants. It was a total success. In 1948, after demonstrations and another strike, students won the right to a special health service financed by the National Health Service and administered by their own elected representatives. Student sanatoria, mental hospitals, clinics and medical care without cost still remain the most important achievement of the UNEF. In 1950, after three years of intensive campaigning among students, the National Convention, with a near unanimous vote, adopted the principle of a student "salary," which is still on the books of the UNEF, but not yet granted by the government. The reasoning behind this last claim is that the work of the student will ultimately be of benefit to the national community. They therefore have as much right to material independence and moral dignity of a salary as any other group of workers. Such a salary would be but a long-term investment for society. This demand is interesting in that it constitutes a paradox: along with other demands such as educational reform and financial aid to working class families putting children through university, it aims at democratizing the university and is, therefore, the expression of a privileged group contriving to abolish its privilege. And as such, it is a direct consequence of the new doctrine of solidarity elaborated at Grenoble in 1946.

Solidarity was, however, also to be applied on an international basis. Difficulties in this field were to bring the downfall of the Resistance generation of leaders. The International Union of Students had been founded in Prague in August 1946, following one year of preparatory work by a committee representing students from the U.S.A., U.S.S.R., Great Britain, France, Denmark, Belgium, Czechoslovakia, Yugoslavia, Poland, India, China, and Australia. However, international student unity could not resist the Cold War. After the Prague conference in 1948, Canada and the U.S.A. withdrew from the International Union, soon followed by most other Western countries, and the Communist delegations gained a clear majority. The UNEF remained a member trying, with increasing difficulty, to save its ideal of international cooperation. However, in France itself, the Communist party no longer formed part of the government and became increasingly isolated from the rest of public opinion. Any collaboration with the Communists was stigmatized as collaboration with the enemy in the Cold War atmosphere. The president of the UNEF was voted out of office upon his return from an international conference in 1950.

2. *A new "corporate" interlude: 1950–1956.* In the France of the 1950's the Cold War was only one aspect of significant changes in the political atmosphere which made a Left-oriented militant student organization obsolete. The enthusiasm with which the political leaders, born of the Resistance, had faced the reconstruction of postwar France had been short lived. First, de Gaulle had taken away most of their powers and then the old-style politicians entered the scene with the familiar political games. With the abandonment of a militant mobilization of energies, the economic hardship of the postwar years was beginning to tell, to which was added the moral and economic cost of a spreading war in Indochina. It is not surprising that most students returned to a conception of unionism which emphasized narrower corporate needs to the detriment of a greater involvement in national or international issues, taxed with being "political." As is often the case, such a rigid non-political doctrine was in many instances

a cover for conservative political values: many of the leaders of this period were later deeply involved in right-wing or even neo-Fascist groups. For five years French students and their union were mainly concerned with fighting for better material conditions, graduating quickly and obtaining jobs.

The left wing of the movement was, however, still in control of large student associations such as Lyon and Grenoble and was a sufficiently strong minority to influence the decisions of the majority. Thus, they succeeded in retaining the movement's militant mass tactics (e.g., street demonstrations and sometimes a strike when the Education budget was before Parliament) and avoiding a piecemeal approach to problems of student welfare. During this period, a reorganization of the *Oeuvres* (student housing and restaurants) was achieved which rationalized the entire structure in a single organization administered jointly by the Ministry of Education and elected student delegates—each wielding an equal number of votes. It was only in the fields of international cooperation and anti-colonialism that the "a-political" majority refused to be influenced.

Eviction from office taught the left that defense of student welfare could not be neglected with impunity and that a long educational effort at the grass roots level had to be maintained if the students were to accept greater social and political responsibility. Realizing the strength of a unified single student organization, they set about to recapture a majority in the UNEF. Working at the local association level, they campaigned on well-defined corporate platforms, organized a number of practical "services" for students, and generally won the respect of their electorate as efficient administrators and defenders of student welfare. Involvement in politics was advocated not on "ideological" grounds but for a limited number of issues presented as a direct outgrowth of such corporate interests or even as a precondition to the satisfaction of the immediate demands of the students (e.g., how can the state finance the necessary reforms of the university when such a high proportion of the national budget goes to the war effort?). By 1956, the left was again in the majority, but with a more solid platform and a more "educated" rank and file.

Three factors seem to have played a particularly important role in the return of the left:

a. *The improving economic situation.* Despite the game of political musical chairs, the Fourth Republic had done a remarkable job of restoring France to economic progress. In the same way that deteriorating economic conditions seem to have fostered a withdrawal into an attitude of narrow self-interest, a rise in material well-being and a glimmer of hope seem to afford the individual liberty for involvement in altruistic and long-term political action.

b. *The political situation.* Contrary to its success in the economic field, the Fourth Republic had failed politically to solve the gigantic challenge of the emancipation of the colonies. The election of Pierre Mendés-France in 1954 was a marked change in style as well as in content of political leadership and demonstrated the bankruptcy of previous governments. The need for "change" was felt throughout the country and the electorate returned a left majority to the 1956 National Assembly. The student left undoubtedly benefited from this general shift in public opinion.

c. *The political student organizations.* With the Communists as isolated among students as they were in the "adult" world, two organizations rose to prominence in the non-Communist left: the Socialist students and the Young Christian Students (JEC). The former enjoyed a high degree of independence from the Socialist party and accordingly took on a specifically "student orientation." The student world was their immediate field of political action. They provided a number of leaders for the UNEF. Similarly, the JEC was the militant student organization of the *Action Catholique* which emphasized complete immersion in the "milieu" for educational and social action. Thus they trained another important contingent of UNEF leaders. These two organizations worked in close collaboration to re-establish a left majority in the UNEF.

3. *From "issue syndicalism" to "revolutionary syndicalism": 1956–1960's.* From 1956 to 1961, the Algerian war was the main preoccupation of the UNEF, although action on corporate issues remained the basis for a large part of its student support. The UNEF involvement in the Algerian problem was indicative of the new educational and issue-oriented approach elaborated by the new leadership during the six years of their opposition. Rather than advocating outright independence for Algeria, an intensive educational campaign was launched. Within four years student opinion was ready to support a strong political stand in favor of Algeria's independence. These were some of the intermediate problems emphasized by the UNEF leadership: the suppression of Algerian "culture" under French colonial rule, the discrimination against Algerians in the French educational system and the special responsibility of the academic community in both matters: the methods used by the French army and the moral responsibility of the academic community; the cost of the war and its effect

on the budget of the university and, closer to home, the restrictions on student deferments. The UNEF was able to mobilize vast numbers of students and play an important political role in bringing together the more reluctant labor unions when the time came for effective public pressure on the government in favor of a negotiated settlement for Algerian independence.

However, when the Algerian war ended, so did this particular type of student approach to politics. "Decolonization" had greatly favored such a practical, issue-oriented political involvement. It was a highly political problem in the broadest sense of the term and not only a moral one: if a "meaning of history" had to be discovered, the rise to independence of previously dependent nations offered a clear example; yet it was a problem with obvious practical consequences in the everyday life of all and thus allowed for a practical educational approach and not an exclusively ideological one. When the Algerian problem disappeared, the UNEF, which had concentrated all its political energy on it, was left with a highly politicized rank and file but with no clear issue on which such political energy could be spent. Consequently, it suffered a deep re-orientation crisis as was the case with other left-wing political organizations and labor unions.

With no clear issue at hand, the involvement in politics of some students has become more abstract and theoretical. This trend has, in recent years, profoundly affected the leadership and policies of the UNEF and has, for the moment, resulted in a drastic reduction in its membership.

This new trend has been qualified as revolutionary syndicalism. Before analyzing its content, I should cite other factors which seem to have played a role in bringing it about.

The Gaullist regime. De Gaulle acceded to power in 1958 after a military coup d'état in Algeria thereby estranging most of the university community and particularly the UNEF. He never forgave their dissent. His government cracked down on the UNEF with a number of measures: a subsidy justified by the various services directly run by the students was abolished; the number of student representatives on the various boards where the UNEF had gained equal number of seats with the government was reduced; a rival student union was established and heavily financed by the UNR (the Gaullist party) thereby destroying the unified student representation which UNEF had established. Contact with Government officials became increasingly tense and devoid of meaning—a trend which was accentuated by the Gaullist doctrine: any representative organization was suspect and branded as standing between the leader and "his" people. At any rate, the delicate balance between militant action and constructive cooperation with the government in certain fields was broken.

Changes in the student political sub-stratum. The Catholic student organization (JEC) had encountered the wrath of the Catholic Church hierarchy who had imposed authoritative change in the leadership and policies of the organization. The Socialist students' conflict with the policies of the discredited Guy Mollet (head of the French Socialist party and largely responsible for the conduct of the Algerian war) had led them to withdraw from the Socialist party and lose most of their political influence on national policies. Thus, the two political "training grounds" which had proved so fertile in the emergence of the new issue syndicalism had vanished from the scene. In their place, the more aggressive Communist student organization (UEC) and the new-left organizations advocated a different approach to student unionism. They encountered wide support among students in a political situation where de Gaulle allowed little room for "constructive opposition."

Demographic changes. The birth rate which had stagnated before 1945 picked up tremendously from 1945 on. By 1961–1962, the effect was felt on the universities. The increase in the student population from 1950 to 1960 had been approximately 75,000 (25,000 in the first five years and 50,000 in the following five years as a result of the improved economic situation). A 300,000 increase has been predicted between 1960 and 1970.

Very little has been done in recent years in the way of university construction, student housing, and restaurants, and recruitment of professors to prepare for such an explosion of the student population. The crisis calls for radical "revolutionary" measures—not moderate reforms. Consequently, it is not difficult to understand that many students turn to what they term "revolutionary syndicalism."

The new revolutionary student ideology seems to have the following characteristics:

Suspicion of traditional "representative" democracy, in their own organization as well as in government and emphasis on "participatory democracy."
A search for a new ideology which emphasizes concepts such as student and intellectual "alienation."
As to the university, a special emphasis on grass roots participatory educational processes as a way to democratization in contrast to the previous approach which advocated structural reforms.

This new trend offers obvious similarities to the ideals of some American students. This chapter has not explained how such convergence came about.

However, knowledge of the historical development behind the evolution of the French student movement might afford some insight for understanding divergent student movements. This may be useful in future comparative studies.[2]

Notes

1. It should be noted that this chapter is not the result of a systematic study of the French student movement. I have made no first hand analysis of quantitative data; I have made no survey, nor any substantial analysis of historical material. Moreover, student political activity is not my field of research. My only qualifications for writing this chapter are on the one hand personal experience of leadership in the UNEF as a student at the Sorbonne and, on the other, a personal interest in the research on student movements presently undertaken by S. M. Lipset at Berkeley and Harvard.
2. The following is a short bibliography of sources:

    1900–1956

    Michel de la Fournière et François Borella. *Le syndicalisme étudiant* (Paris: Éditions du Seuil, 1957).

    Special issue of *Esprit*, "Les étudiants," 20 ème année (April 1952).

    1956–1961

    Pierre Gaudez. *Les étudiants* (Paris: Éditions Julliard, 1961).

    1962–1965

    Pierre Bourdieu and Jean-Claude Passeron. *Les héritiers* (Paris: Éditions de Minuit, 1965).

    Articles in *Les Temps Modernes:* Marc Kravetz, "Naissance d'un syndicalisme étudiant," No. 213 (February 1964); Jean-Pierre Milbergue, "La signification politique des rapports pédagogiques dans l'Université française," No. 227 (April 1965); Antoine Griset and Marc Kravets, "De l'Algérie à la réforme Fouchet: Critique du syndicalisme étudiant (I)," No. 227 (April 1965); and Antoine Griset and Marc Kravets, "De l'Algérie à la réforme Fouchet: Critique de syndicalisme étudiant (fin)," No. 228 (May 1965).

Students and Politics in

Latin America

———————————— **PART IV** ————————————

Academic Freedom and Higher Education in Latin America

ORLANDO ALBÓRNOZ

— 10 —

The issue of academic freedom has received substantial attention in the United States in recent years. There seems to be a fairly general agreement among scholars, with substantial public concurrence, that academic freedom is a necessary part of higher education. Academic freedom also has as important a role in the developing nations although it has been a good deal less secure in these nations than in many of the industrially advanced countries.

It can be argued that the quality of university life is even more important in the developing areas than in the advanced nations because of its crucial role in modernization and in technical training. Because academic freedom is a key element in determining the tone of academic life and is generally agreed to be an important component of scholarly research, it is a vital issue in any consideration of higher education and the progress of democracy in the developing nations.

Latin America offers a particularly interesting example of the relationship of academic freedom to the emergence of an adequate system of higher education because of its combination of economic and social traditionalism and a strong background of Western higher education. In this chapter, I want to consider some aspects of academic freedom in this area as they affect the prospects for modernization in the Latin American nations. The ideas discussed here are largely a set of observations which hopefully will be elaborated by some of the empirical research concerning education at all levels which is now under way in Latin America.[1]

Initially it should be stated that it is impossible to have complete academic freedom without freedom for the rest of society. As Polanyi has argued, "Academic freedom is never an isolated phenomenon. It can only exist in a free society; for the principles underlying it are the same on which the most essential liberties of society as a whole are founded."[2] Meaningful academic freedom, therefore, has been a rare phenomenon in Latin America, since freedom in this part of the world continues to be a hazardous enterprise. Dictatorship has been a recurrent part of its political life; and whenever a dictator has been in power, academic freedom has been severely limited.

Despite the undoubted relationship between academic freedom and the broader political situation in a nation, it is nevertheless also true that the universities in Latin America, as in other countries, have often retained a considerable degree of freedom even in the face of authoritarian regimes. The fact that the universities are sometimes the last stronghold of political discussion under dictatorial regimes increases their importance. Thus, while the university must in the last analysis keep in step with trends in the broader society, it has shown a good deal of independence.

Before entering into a discussion of the different aspects of academic freedom in Latin America, I should note that similar problems arise in North American society. In the United States academic freedom has frequently been an issue. Periods of drastic social change, the different crises in American society, particularly situations in which the country has been at war, or periods of economic tension have led to conflicts over the meaning of academic freedom.

In the past half century the principles of academic freedom have frequently been threatened, particularly when linked to the issue of communism. Many in high places have taken the position, expressed by a president of the University of Washington, that "a member of the Communist party should not be permitted to teach in an American college because he is not a free man."

During the nineteenth century, the doctrine of evolution as contained in the work of Darwin and Spencer provided a topic for controversy. Many issues were fought concerning the rights of evolutionists. There is, however, a radical difference between the issues. During the debates about evolution, the academic freedom fights revolved around individual cases, with *individuals* defending their right to teach a point of view which was different from the prevalent beliefs of the time. Today *organizations*, such as the American Association of University Professors, the American Federation of Teachers, or the American Civil Liberties Union, lead the fight, identifying each case as part of an effort to establish or preserve general principles. Concern for academic freedom has become an institutionalized part of the intellectual life of American society. Organizations are available to defend the rights of particular individuals.

In Latin America, the situation remains more in the preorganization stage. Cases are still fought on an individual basis. Intellectuals offer a united front only in cases of "national emergency" such as in Brazil today. In every country there is an organization of university professors, but as in the case of other Latin American professional bodies, it is concerned primarily with financial problems, and not with academic standards or freedom.

Although Latin America contains the oldest universities in the Americas, it is unfortunately true that few institutions of higher education in these nations are currently important centers of significant scholarship. Most of these universities have been concerned largely with the diffusion of knowledge imported from Europe or the United States. They are "second-hand" institutions, teaching, but not creating, knowledge. In this situation of intellectual dependence, it is impossible to raise the question of freedom of knowledge, of academic freedom in the true sense. Questions about freedom to innovate begin to arise only when genuine independent research exists, when intellectual activity results in divergent points of view.

To see in detail the current problems of academic freedom in Latin America I propose to discuss the different ingredients of the situation—the universities, the students, the professors, and the intellectuals.

The universities are, generally speaking, primary instruments in the process of social change, since they train the future elites of the country in scientific, humanistic and professional areas. To accomplish this task, universities are obliged to try to further the universalistic objective of finding truth, as S. M. Lipset has pointed out in his much-quoted chapter on "University Students and Politics in Underdeveloped Countries."[3]

The need for academic freedom requires that the university give institutional backing to professors against the particularistic tendencies which in every country seek to prevent innovation and change. The struggle for academic freedom in Latin America may be seen as an aspect of the struggle between those who are concerned with universalistic values, with the need for modernization and social change, and those who try to prevent such changes, who want to preserve the traditional establishment.

Such issues take on varying aspects in public and Catholic universities.

There are many variations between the two. The main difference concerning academic freedom is that the latter tend to have internal consensus about basic values and ways of finding truth, which the former lack. In the Catholic universities, truth is generally established by principle, without any possibility of discussion. Truth in this case has a dogmatic basis. In the state universities, the situation is quite different. Hence, the political issue of academic freedom in Latin America, almost by definition, is a problem of the state universities. Few of the problems discussed in this chapter in connection with professors, students, and other intellectuals have arisen in the Catholic universities. Notice should also be taken of the growing number of non-Catholic private universities on the continent. Most of these, however, are largely professional institutions, devoted primarily to preparing technicians. They are quite important, however, since it will probably be in institutions of this type in which the most important independent and free research will be done in the future.

Catholic and state universities may also be distinguished by the fact that the former tend to support traditional values, while the state universities often foster criticism of the established order. In this sense, the latter are instruments of change. The scholarly weaknesses of the state universities, which have been partly a consequence of political instability and intrauniversity political conflict, have created support for the private secular universities and research institutes. Those interested in a fruitful intellectual life increasingly find it advantageous to participate in the private institutions as a way of escaping the political tensions involved in working in a state university. These give the scholar and teacher more academic freedom, precisely because they are less involved in politics and religion. Many concerned with freeing Latin American scholars from non-academic pressures, whether those of the politicians, the church, or the student groups, have furthered the growth of secular private universities, and of independent non-profit academic research institutions. These may eventually provide the needed "demonstration effect" in the area of academic freedom for both state and Catholic universities.

Limitations on academic freedom in the public universities are to a considerable degree related to the role of students in politics. The politically active students in the universities in much of Latin America can and often do intimidate their professors. The political parties look on the *campus* as a major arena for political activities. The continued strength of political activities within the universities is, in turn, related to two elements: co-government (students' participation in the administration of the university) and the inviolability of the campus inherent in the concept of autonomy.

It is important to note that these two, the most important of the Córdoba reforms—co-government and the inviolability of the campus—have had an adverse effect on the progress of academic freedom in that they have greatly increased the politicization of the Latin American state university. Political parties, as well as politically motivated student groups, have been encouraged to use the university campus both as a recruiting ground and as a headquarters for demonstrations and activities. This increased politicization has resulted in the university becoming one of the main centers of political opposition and extremist agitation in many Latin American nations and has made many governments reluctant to permit so powerful a source of potential dissent to remain free of governmental control.

Compared to students in North America and most of Europe, those of Latin America maintain a constant and very active political life, although it should be noted that the active are relatively few, to use in an inverse way the title of the chapter on this subject by Glaucio Soares.[4] Student political activity, of course, has many positive aspects. It helps to train many of the future political leaders, contributes to the political socialization of others who will be part of the non-political elite, and provides a forum for various opinions on controversial social issues.

In some countries the sole effective criticism of the reactionary oligarchies or of the military cliques comes from the students who are the only ones who are willing to speak up. On the negative side, however, it remains true that the political activity of students has been a primary threat to academic freedom in those Latin American countries which are politically democratic. It has resulted in a situation somewhat similar to that in India, where the widespread student indiscipline has helped to demoralize the teaching staff and has impaired the dignity and effectiveness of Indian universities.

To turn to a discussion of autonomy, this concept, which has institutionalized the existence of one society inside another, encourages the members of the *campus* to sustain sharply different norms of behavior than the general community. No matter what happens within university precincts it remains an autonomous jurisdiction, which neither the national nor local police can enter without conforming to very difficult legally established procedures. Inside the campus, students live quite differently from the way of life in the community where the university is located.

These privileges inherent in autonomy are used quite consciously by the radical political parties, which can protest against the government, distribute propaganda, collect money, and engage in other oppositional activities without worrying about the police. As in tsarist Russia, non-student political leaders can find a place on campus to hide themselves from the authorities in special situations. Autonomy has also helped produce the phenomenon of the "part-time" political activist. Some of the same students who are very eager to protest against society inside the campus often behave differently outside it. They will join demonstrations inside the campus which they would not support in the larger society where they will be exposed to the dangers of repressive police action.

If autonomy contributes to the politicization of the campus, the institution of co-government increases the chances that student political activity will endanger academic freedom. *Cogobierno* means that the students share directly in the government of the university, that they have a voice in the different bodies that have power inside the university, especially at the level of the *Consejos de Facultad* (Faculty Council), where university decisions are made. It has given them substantial power on matters of academic policy and personnel. This student power has often been used for political purposes; their involvement in academic decision-making has often resulted in considerable corruption and a high degree of factionalism. Corruption means misuse. In the case of students, corruption derives directly from the power that university students have to participate in the government of the university. There are many examples of such corruption, enough to suggest the existence of a pattern in the universities of the continent. In one case (I am not in a position to name the university in question) the student members of a special body which awarded scholarships did so only to those students who agreed to "kick back" part of the scholarship stipend to the student political leaders, whether for personal or political use one will never know. In another case, a researcher appointed five assistants, but in fact hired only two. The salaries for the other three went to students who served on the university committee which had given funds to this researcher.

Even more important are the occurrences in which professors have been nominated for *catedras* after they agreed to give back part of their salaries to student leaders. As *The Economist* has pointed out in a recent discussion of Peruvian universities, the

power granted to students has led to a system of bribery, both with money and with high marks, by faculty members. "I am now correcting exam papers," said one Cuzo professor, "and at least half of these poor bastards deserve to fail. They don't know anything and they don't come to class. But if I failed them they would fire me. Believe me, I take a great risk in flunking 10 per cent of my students, which few other professors would dare to do.[5]

These provide vivid examples of the perils to development of competent scholarship and academic freedom which, involving students directly in the process of choosing faculty, have created for various Latin American universities.

Many Latin American professors will privately acknowledge having to say and publish things that they do not believe, including favorable citations to leftist authorities, in order to win or retain the support of the student activists. To publicly approve of North American scholarship opens one to the charges of being a lackey of Yankee power, an agent of cultural imperialism. And to be viewed in this light may affect one's chances to attain or keep a position, or more commonly to retain the good will of the academic community, particularly of the students.

Of course, if we consider the lack of scholarly competence and particularly the lack of objectivity of many Latin American professors, it may be argued that the faculties inhibit efforts to sustain academic freedom by their inadequacy as scholars and teachers. In much of Latin America competent faculties simply do not yet exist. Being a professor is often an honorific post which men seek not for the sake of the small honorarium, but to enhance their general social prestige and opportunities in the professions or in politics. Most faculties do not devote themselves to full-time activity at the university. The part-time professor who earns most of his income in a totally non-academic occupation is still the standard. Some would like to become full-time academics, but too many, particularly in the social sciences, prefer to keep the professoriate as an honorific position, which enables them to advance themselves in professional or political life.

It should also be noted that the distinction between teaching and indoctrination which, as Max Weber noted, must always be in the consciousness of university professors, does not exist in much of Latin America. Teaching *is* indoctrination in many cases. Most professors, particularly in social sciences, feel obliged to take a strong stand on many unverifiable aspects of knowledge. Thus the continued presence of incompetent scholars and highly subjective teachers constitutes one of the principal impediments for the emergence of academic freedom in Latin America.

The inadequacies of many Latin American universities and faculties would seem to sustain the arguments of the student activists in the University Reform Movement who insist that student involvement in university government is necessary to improve the university, to press the faculty and administration to improve in their scholarly and teaching functions. Unfortunately, however, in spite of their ideology of modernization, the organized student groups contribute to these failings by objecting to efforts to increase the standards of work required to remain in school. Student activists have resisted efforts to raise standards using the argument that higher examination standards would discriminate against students from economically impoverished backgrounds who often must work full time to attend university.

While this argument has some validity, the best way to deal with the problem would clearly be through fellowships and bursaries. Easy examinations which may be taken at the examinee's discretion as often as he desires simply undermine the efficacy of the Latin American universities as educational institutions. And students who seek an easy path for themselves cannot complain in good conscience about similar behavior by the faculty.

Finally, let us turn to an examination of the role of the intellectuals in Latin America as it affects academic freedom. The imprecise and ambiguous character of the term intellectual has been frequently discussed in the United States. The concept is even more confused in Latin America, where it has some negative connotations, in part because of the old relation between *doctor* (intellectual) and *general* (dictator). Doctors and military men belong to the intellectual community in the sense that both have a "capacity for detachment from immediate experience, a moving beyond the pragmatic task of the moment, a commitment to comprehensive values transcending professional or occupational involvement."[6]

Intellectuals in Latin America conform to Shils's definition, which argues that in underdeveloped countries intellectuals are all persons with an advanced modern education and the intellectual concerns and skills ordinarily associated with it.[7] In Latin America, intellectuals do not have an engaged attitude to the university, that is, they do not feel themselves part of the extended university community, as is true in other parts of the world. Rather they are more likely to identify with their social class, political party, religious affiliation, or other membership group.

This lack of identification with the university means that non-academic intellectuals do not see freedom inside the academy as something that they should fight for. They worry about political freedom, but not about academic freedom. Academic freedom is not institutionalized inside the universities, and non-academic intellectuals are rarely concerned about the lack of academic freedom. Like other contending socio-political forces they want the university to *support* them, not to be "free."

Another factor affecting the content of university activities in Latin America is the parochialism of intellectual life. There is a considerable cultural lag between Latin American intellectuals and those of the rest of the world. As noted earlier, they are culturally dependent on the developed countries. In Latin American capital cities this dependence is reflected in the fairly adequate knowledge of what is going on in Paris or in New York, complemented by an equal ignorance of intellectual life in neighboring Latin American countries. Latin American intellectuals have little interest or respect for the work of their compeers in other parts of the world.

In Latin America one must look to the university as the only institutionalized agency of intellectual life. There, as elsewhere, as Coser points out, "the university remains today and is likely to remain in the future the major locale for intellect."[8] On the other hand, Coser's statement about the United States that "although the university is theoretically the ideal environment for the intellectual, its institutionalized practices too often operate in such a way that the intellectual vocation within the academy is fraught with perils,"[9] is much more valid for Latin America than for the United States.

The restrictive aspects of academic life cannot be dealt with in any further detail here, but it should be noted that social science research in particular is very inhibited, that objective research in sensitive areas such as politics, religion, and sex is impossible in many countries. But as we have seen, the culprits are not solely the supporters of the political, social, and religious establishments; they also include leftist politicized intellectuals and student political activists.

In conclusion I would reiterate that discussion of the relationship of academic freedom, higher education and the process of modernization in Latin American society lacks any substantial empirical underpinning. Research on the effects of co-government, autonomy, and other factors on academic freedom is just beginning. It is, however, evident that though the university in Latin America must undergo substantial reforms, the principles of Reform which emerged in Córdoba almost fifty years ago are no longer as progressive as they seemed then. The concept of university autonomy has become an illusion, a medieval concept applied to a modern or, more accurately, modernizing society. The same thing is true for the idea of university co-government.

These ideas, of course, have a remarkably democratic sound, the notion that students hand-in-hand with their professors should try to make the best possible use of the university without external interference can hardly be disputed. In practice, however, they have not led to the improvement of the academy. It cannot be repeated too often that the politically active students are not interested in improving education through establishing academic freedom, but rather in finding political allies.

Academic freedom in Latin America is still not institutionalized. The idea of searching for truth regardless of where it may lead has been an ideal far removed from the facts of university life in Latin America. Academic freedom must still be fought for on an individual basis. The time must come when the intellectual community in Latin America will decide to unite throughout the continent in support of academic freedom. But this struggle must await the emergence of the social conditions which sustain democratic freedoms, the acceptance of the value of opposition beliefs in the polity generally. This, unfortunately, has not happened in most of Latin America as yet.

Notes

1. Some research on academic freedom in Latin America has been done. See particularly Rudolph Atcon, "The Latin American University," *Die Deutsche Universitätszeitung*, XVII (February 1962); Luigi Einaudi, "University Autonomy and Academic Freedom in Latin America," *Law and Contemporary Problems*, XXVIII (Summer 1963), 636–646; John P. Harrison, "The Confrontatation with the Political University," *Annals of the American Academy of Political and Social Sciences*, CCCXXXIV (March 1961).
2. Michael Polanyi, *The Foundations of Academic Freedom* (London: Society for Freedom in Science, 1947).
3. Chapter 1, this book.
4. Chapter 5, this book.
5. Special Correspondent, "Peruvian Students," *The* [London] *Economist*, January 29, 1966, p. 405.
6. Lewis Coser, *Men of Ideas* (New York: The Free Press, 1965), preface.
7. Edward Shils, "The Intellectuals in Political Development," in John Kautsky, ed., *Political Change in Underdeveloped Countries* (New York: John Wiley and Sons, 1962).
8. Coser, *op. cit.*, p. 291.
9. *Ibid.*

A Comparison of the University Reform
Movements in Argentina and Colombia

KENNETH N. WALKER

11

Student politics in Latin America is looked upon by many observers as something endemic to Latin American culture, personality, institutions, or all three. While it is probably true that much of the general character and frequency of student collective action can be accounted for by specific characteristics of Latin America, including relatively unstable or despotic governments in many of these societies, we now know that student political rebellion in the Western hemisphere is not restricted to the lands south of the United States, especially after the Berkeley revolt. But the political role of students is, by and large, of more political significance in Latin than in North America, given the direct opposition by student movements to national governments on frequent occasions.

There are a number of characteristics which differentiate Latin American from North American universities and colleges, which may account for the disparity in the frequency and intensity of student politics between the two continents. Salient among these characteristics are the lack of a full-time faculty and the presence of student participation in university government in most Latin American universities. The University Reform movement has often been pointed to as a significant force in bringing about student participation in university government, and as a factor in maintaining student political involvement at a high level. There are relatively few studies in Spanish dealing with the origins, development, and consequences of the University Reform movement, and almost none in English. It is generally known, however, that the movement began in Argentina and spread to other Latin American nations, with varying consequences for student politics and universities in the societies in which it took hold. A comparative analysis of the origins and effects of the Reform movement in Argentina and another society in which the movement developed under quite different conditions, Colombia, should contribute to a deeper understanding of the present character of student politics in Latin America, especially in these two countries. This chapter will provide a brief historical account of those aspects of the origins of higher education in Latin America which are relevant to a discussion of more recent student political movements, and will assess the development of the University Reform movement in relationship to the character of student politics in the two societies.

The historical antecedents of Latin American universities derive from the structure of Spanish universities of the fifteenth and sixteenth centuries, the period in which the first Latin American universities were established. The participation of students in university government was instituted in these first universities, including the election of rectors and of "catedráticos," or holders of university chairs. The proportion of student representation was reduced, however, from that of the University of Salamanca, the Spanish university on which Latin American universities were modeled,[1] but the autonomous status of the university was retained.

Although there were often complaints of viceregal interference in the choice of rectors, or in the recommendation of candidates for degrees, the University was one of the few corporations in America that retained any degree of autonomy.[2]

Writers on the Latin American university and the university reform movement suggest that the tradition of student participation in university government during colonial times is an important precedent for the claims made by the university reform movement in the twentieth century. However, it should be noted that at the University of San Marcos in Peru, students did not participate in the election of rector. Students were under the direct disciplinary control of the rector, who had the authority to mete out severe punishment for acts committed by students within or outside the university environs. The students' most important decision-making role appears to have been that of voting for contestants to university chairs.[3] This latter privilege was eventually withdrawn, due to the tendency of professors to ". . . succumb to the temptation to popularize and cater to the student's plebeian tastes. . . ."[4] Thus the precedent for student participation in university government is perhaps more appropriately referred to the University of Bologna, where students originally had the sole power to employ and dismiss professors.

The university was established and maintained primarily for the education of select members of the elite, and was slow to respond to intellectual and scientific currents from Europe and North America, to broaden its educational content to provide a wider and more practical content to meet the needs of new professions, or to conduct research directed to the economic and social problems of Latin American societies.[5]

Development of the University Reform Movement in Argentina

Argentina provides the setting for the first and most significant effort at university reform in Latin America. While the origin of the University Reform is generally given as 1918, the date of the famous Córdoba Manifesto, its antecedents were some years earlier. As early as 1871, law students at the University of Buenos Aires mounted a university reform movement which had some effect on the structure of that university, and students of law and medicine at Buenos Aires were active in a reform movement from 1903 to 1906. In 1908 the University Federation of Buenos Aires was founded, and in the same year the first Congress of American Students was held, where the principle of student representation in university directive councils was proclaimed "by acclamation."

The First International Congress of American Students accepts as an aspiration, which should be put into practice as soon as possible, the representation of students in the directive councils of university education, by means of delegates, named directly by them and renewed as frequently as possible.[6]

This principle was proclaimed subsequently in the second and third Congresses of this body, in 1910 and 1912, and in 1916 the University Federation of Buenos Aires sought unsuccessfully to obtain student representation in the superior council of the university.[7]

In 1918, at the University of Córdoba, what appears to have been the first large-scale attack by a Latin American student body against the university system took place. A student strike was declared, the university was closed by the Superior Council of the University, and the Radical party government of President Hipólito Irigoyen intervened, resulting in the institutionalization of several university reform demands as university law. The principal reforms enacted were the following: attendance at university to be free and conditional only on successful completion of secondary school studies; students, professors, and graduates to be represented on the governing councils of the university and of the faculty; the rector and deans of faculties to be ex officio members of the superior council of the university, and to be elected, the deans by majority vote of faculty coun-cils, and the rector by the university assembly, composed of equal represen-tation of students, faculty, and graduates; and professors to be free to teach and students free to attend classes, without compulsion or restriction. Addi-tional reforms were also enacted, including provision of university exten-sion courses for the public, regulations concerning examinations, and the periodicity of the "cátedra" or chair, by which professors are subject to appointment or reappointment every six years, by election within the fac-ulty directive councils, decided by a two-thirds vote of delegates.[8] These reforms were not enacted all at once, nor did they remain in force continu-ally in Argentine universities from their inception, since there have been several counterreforms, in 1923, 1929–1930, 1943, and 1946, involving in some cases military occupation of the universities and the enactment of presidential decrees abrogating university statutes which embodied univer-sity reform principles.[9]

The causes and consequences of the University Reform movement as these bear on a comparative analysis of the student political context in Co-lombia and Argentina are of major concern, since the relative success or failure of the movement has determined the character and shaped the con-text of contemporary student politics. It appears that the major impetus for the movement was a reaction against the archaic and oligarchic structure of the university, characterized by nepotism, an emphasis on formalism in lectures and an absence of practical training, and the domination of the university by a self-perpetuating governing council with little concern for the interests of students or lower status professors or for the cultural needs of the nation, and with little or no support of original research, develop-ment of new fields of study or new methods of teaching.[10] The following passage from the "Córdoba Manifesto" of 1918 presents a perhaps exag-gerated image of the old university, but expresses its ideological definition by reformist students.

Up to now the universities have been the secular refuge of mediocrities, have pro-vided a salary for the ignorant and a safe hospital for invalids, and what is worse, have provided a place where all forms of tyranny and insensitivity could be taught. The universities have thus come to be faithful reflections of a decadent society, offering a sad spectacle of immobile senility. Before these closed and silent houses, wisdom passes silently or enters distorted and grotesque into the service of bureaucracy.[11]

Such conditions were probably widespread in Latin American universi-ties, despite considerable cultural diversity among Latin American nations.

A typical indictment of Latin American universities up to recent times emphasizes the discrepancy between the needs brought about by major social change, and the inadequate response of the universities, which continue to prepare professionals for only a limited number of fields, and to emphasize a metaphysical, speculative approach to knowledge, rather than an experimental, pragmatic one concerned with social realities.[12]

Considering the apparently widespread decadence of the university in nineteenth-century Latin America, one may ask why the reform movement developed first and with such intensity in Argentina rather than elsewhere. An adequate answer to this question would require a comparative analysis of this situation in all of the Latin American nations during the latter part of the nineteenth and the early twentieth century. A partial answer, however, may be provided by a close look at the development of the movement in Argentina, from the perspective of the theory of collective behavior of Neil Smelser.[13] The advantage of this theoretical approach is that it provides categories for analysis in terms of the major components of social action, permitting the specification of the presence or absence of conditions which appear to be crucial for the character and outcome of collective behavioral phenomena. These conditions are defined in sufficiently abstract terms to permit the analysis of different social movements in varying social contexts and avoids the difficulties for comparative analysis inherent in the natural-history approach to collective behavior. The theory provides a set of determinants which, Smelser asserts, must be present for collective behavior to occur and specifies the consequences of variations in the character of these determinants for the type of collective behavior which ensues. Two types of social movements are defined, among other types of collective behavior. These are the "norm-oriented" and the "value-oriented" movements. The first is defined as ". . . an attempt to restore, protect, modify, or create norms in the name of a generalized belief,"[14] the second as ". . . a collective attempt to restore, protect, modify, or create values in the name of a generalized belief."[15] While the University Reform movement had some overtones of a value-oriented movement, in its nationalist emphasis on moral and social regeneration, its major focus was on alteration of the norms governing institutions of higher education in Argentina, and later throughout Latin America. Thus the determinants of collective behavior in the form which results in a norm-oriented movement will be applied to an analysis of the inception of the Argentine university reform movement, and to account for the less successful character of this movement in Colombia.

According to Smelser, the determinants of collective behavior are (1) structural conduciveness, (2) structural strain, (3) growth and spread of a generalized belief, (4) precipitating factors, (5) mobilization of participants for action, and (6) the operation of social control. All of these are necessary for the development of some form of collective behavior, the first five as positive and the latter as a negative, or counter-determinant. Social control serves to prevent collective behavior, or to channel it once it has begun."[16]

1. *Structural conduciveness.* "The most general condition of conduciveness concerns the possibility for demanding modifications of norms *without simultaneously appearing to demand a more fundamental modification of values.*"[17] The University Reform movement limited its demands to modifications in university structures in the name of the need to democratize and modernize them, and in the interests of the nation as a whole. While the values appealed to as a basis for legitimating the demand for institutional reforms were general ones, they were held to be consistent with national values and interests, while the universities were held to be in the grip of old and outmoded values.[18]

a. "In general, the discontented must have *some* degree of access to some method of affecting the normative order."[19] The Reform movement, as it turned out, had direct access to and a hospitable reception from the newly elected Radical president, Hipólito Irigoyen, who not only intervened in Córdoba University, but in other universities, and institutionalized many of the demands of the movement by presidential decree. Here it should be pointed out that while universities were nominally autonomous, the national government promulgated the basic organic laws of each university. As Luigi Einaudi points out, in practice the question of autonomy has centered on the means of selection of the rector, and when the university itself chooses the rector, it is considered autonomous.[20] Students sought to be included in the process of electing the rector, but in this sense they were not seeking university autonomy, since governing councils of the universities already chose their own rectors.

The marked success of the movement in Argentina must then be attributed to an important degree to a sympathetic government. The Radical party had developed from a movement of middle class elements directed against the Conservative oligarchy in the late nineteenth century, which became institutionalized in the Unión Cívica Radical party, with the goal of the secret ballot and the enfranchisement of all adult males.[21] A liberal wing of the Conservative party developed which also espoused these goals, and in 1912 it succeeded in passing the Sáenz Peña law, granting universal and secret male suffrage. Irigoyen was elected in 1916 with a majority of the popular vote, but a majority of only one in the electoral college, due in part to opposition from within his own party.[22] Thus it may be argued that, without the access to a sympathetic president, the movement may have become a value-oriented one with revolutionary goals, or may have reverted to "hostile outbursts," defined as "action mobilized on the basis of a generalized belief assigning responsibility for an undesirable state of affairs to some agent."[23] Its success as a norm-oriented movement permitted its institutionalization and its symbolic value as a model for similar movements elsewhere in Latin America.

b. "Any discussion of structural conduciveness must refer also to the lack of alternative channels for expressing dissatisfaction."[24] During the early stages of the 1918 movement and later there were acts of violence and force, including seizure of various universities on occasion, and resulting in the imprisonment of students. These manifestations may be considered an aspect of the uncertainty of the effectiveness of appeals to the president, since initial reforms did not immediately grant student participation in university government, perhaps the principal change in norms sought by the movement, and thus recourse to other forms of protest were sought. The effectiveness of social control by the government and the willingness of the government to intercede and eventually to institute the demanded reforms limited the use of violence by the student movement.

c. "Like all collective outbursts, a norm-oriented movement requires a certain ability to communicate if beliefs are to be disseminated and action to be mobilized.[25] University students are especially well situated in this respect, as a collectivity with a high degree of access of members to one another, due to their joint presence at university centers. As the Córdoba Manifesto and others like it attest, Argentine university students were in full command of an impelling rhetoric to dramatize and justify demands and actions, especially to fellow students in other university centers, and served as calls to action by students in other universities to mount similar demands and actions.

2. *Structural strain.* This term is used as a general referent for words like "mal-integration," "disorganization," "conflict," "anomie," and others in the literature on collective behavior referring to some kind of trouble people experience in their environment, which results in one or another form of collective behavior.[26] Strain is discussed in terms of what Smelser

terms the four "components of action—facilities, organization of motivation, norms and values." The most relevant components for locating strain in the environment of Argentine university students appear to be norms and values.

a. "Any disharmony between normative standards and actual social conditions can provide the basis for a movement whose objective it is to modify the norms. This is particularly true when either norms or social conditions undergo rapid change in a relatively short time."[27] The period during which the university reform developed, from about 1890 to 1918, was a period of rapid social change in Argentina, with the influx of large numbers of European immigrants, rapid urbanization, industrialization, and political conflict between the middle classes, represented by the Radical party, and the oligarchic Conservative ruling party.[28] Clearly the norms governing universities were inappropriate to these conditions, which brought pressures for modernization and democratization in all spheres of Argentine life.

b. "The rise of new values frequently creates bases for defining certain social conditions as 'evils'—social conditions which previously had passed less noticed."[29] The years preceding and during the reform witnessed the influence in political and social life of new values and ideologies. These included radicalism, socialism, anarchism, communism, especially through the influence of the Russian revolution, and the influence of World War I.[30] Carlos Cossio also attributes an important change in Argentine intellectual life to the 1916 visit of the Spanish philosopher Ortega y Gasset, in which he introduced neo-Kantian philosophy[31] to an Argentine audience. The influence of these values and historical events is evident in the populist democratic, anti-clerical, anti-imperialist, nationalist, and pacifist sentiments of the movement, although present in a diffuse and sometimes incoherent form.[32] The cumulation of these "modern" values and ideas provided ample ideological armament for judging and condemning the "old university."

3. *Generalized beliefs and the role of precipitating factors.*

For a norm-oriented movement, the generalized belief includes a diagnosis of the forces and agents that are making for a failure of normative regulation. It also involves some sort of program—passing a law, creating a regulatory agency, scrapping an antiquated custom, etc. Norm-oriented movements are committed to the belief that adoption of this program will control, damage, or punish the responsible agent, and thus erase the source of strain. The combination of all these components results in a "cause" in the name of which the aggrieved mobilize and agitate for normative change.[33]

The Córdoba Manifesto, cited above, provides all of these elements of a generalized belief, including diagnosis, remedy, and an element not mentioned but presumably an important one for gaining broad support, that of legitimation of the grounds for proposing the diagnosis and reforms. This latter element was put forth as an assertion of the right of inherently virtuous and as yet uncorrupted youth to play its part in university government unselfishly and wisely.

Youth lives in an ambience of heroism. It is disinterested and pure. It has not yet had time to become corrupt. It can never be mistaken in choosing its own teachers. Flattery and bribery would obtain no advantage with youth. (Córdoba Manifesto.)[34]

The remedies in the forms of proposed university laws were set forth in considerable detail, in messages to the Minister of Education.[35] It must be assumed, of course, that the generalized belief expressed in the Córdoba Manifesto and subsequent declarations were the result of a cumulative development, beginning at least with the first International Student Congress in Montevideo, and proceeding through a succession of conflicts at the University of Buenos Aires during the intervening years.[36]

a. "Precipitating factors focus the belief on a particular person, event or situation."[37] The major precipitating event which gave the movement its initial national and international impetus appears to have been the expulsion by indignant students of the members of the University Assembly of Córdoba University, from the meeting called for the installation of the rector opposed by the students. This was followed by a student strike and the closing of the university by its Superior Council. The events which preceded the action of the students are the following. The University of Córdoba was one of the most backward in the country, opposing intellectual currents which challenged the dogmas of the Church. Although the University was secular and established by the national government, it remained in the control of a small group opposed to all reform. Tulio Halperin characterizes this group as follows:

... the University was in the hands of a group bound together by all sorts of ties, not only ideological or religious ones, and was disposed to avoid every change which menaced the solidity of their domination. This situation was linked to the existence of a more or less secret society—the *Corda fratres*—like that of the mysterious *"Congregation"* of the French Restoration, to which was imputed the goal of assuring the triumph of ideas which promoted the prosperity of those who sustained them.[38]

Student opposition to the hegemony of this group had taken the form of a series of public lectures challenging Catholic dogma, in 1916, and diagnosing the ills of the university. These lectures aroused considerable public interest and strong opposition from the clergy. They were followed in 1917 by a series titled the "popular university," with courses on public hygiene, civic virtue, penal law and political economy.[39] Student opposition gained support from the national government, which intervened in the University in April 1918, following a student strike and the closing of the University in March. The University statutes were modified and new elections for deans and members of the University Assembly were held, in which all those candidates with student support won. But in the election for rector, a candidate of the *Corda fratres* won, and the students reacted as described above, apparently because they felt betrayed by those they had supported for election.[40]

The experience by the students of defeat in the midst of what had appeared to be an assured victory led to the dramatic occupation of the assembly hall and to the impassioned Manifesto, which together gave a symbolic significance to the movement which it had lacked previously. This may be considered an example of the "power of limited setbacks to invigorate a movement."[41] The outcome of the election for rector had the advantage for the movement of giving concrete evidence of the corrupt character which students had imputed to the faculty and served to legitimate their direct action, contrasting their moral superiority to that of the faculty and rector.

The acts of violence, for which we were wholly responsible, were done in behalf of pure ideas. We stopped an anachronistic uprising, and we did so in order to raise a new spirit in these ruins. Those acts also represented the measure of our indignation in the presence of moral destitution and cunning deceit, which pretended to infiltrate itself under the guise of legality. (Córdoba Manifesto.)[42]

4. *Mobilization of the movement for action.* "Characteristic of the mobilization of the norm-oriented movement is the complexity and time involved in organizing and implementing its program."[43] Smelser outlines three phases of mobilization characteristic of norm-oriented movements, "the incipient phase, the phase of enthusiastic mobilization, and the period of institutionalization and organization."[44] The incipient phase would appear to be that of the period prior to 1918, perhaps beginning as early as 1871, with the formation of the "thirteenth of December" movement by law

students at the University of Buenos Aires. Reform-oriented movements or activities appear to have been sporadic in the years preceding the second decade of the twentieth century, and confined to individual faculties. The period 1903–1906 was one of student protest and strikes at Buenos Aires, culminating in reforms which made the "academias," the term applied then to the faculties, a more integral and less autonomous part of the university, and provided for greater participation of professors in university government.[45]

The period 1918 to the early twenties represents the "phase of enthusiastic mobilization," since during this period occurred the organization of the Argentine University Federation, the Córdoba revolt, the first National Congress of Students (of Argentina), government intervention at Córdoba and the reform of the statutes governing Córdoba and Buenos Aires Universities, providing for the participation of students in university government. Beginning in 1919 and continuing into the twenties, the reform movement spread to other Latin American countries, with varying success in the institution of reforms. In Argentina the movement became institutionalized with the formation of university governments involving the representation of students, and other reforms. The period from the 1920's up to the present may be considered the period of institutionalization and organization. There were several attempts at counter-reform during this period, the most notable during Perón's rule, but these were vicissitudes of the universities as a whole, not merely of the movement. Once the principle of direct student participation was assured, the movement became a party, winning all elections at the University of Buenos Aires up to 1961, and providing an organizational base for liberals and leftists. As Smelser states, ". . . a successful movement usually begins to focus on other, related reforms, or becomes a guardian of the normative changes it has won. . . ."[46] Clearly the university reform movement conforms to the latter alternative. Each time the basic principles of university reform were abrogated by the government, the adherents of reform struggled to reinstate them. Following Perón's overthrow in 1955, students seized the universities and carried out an orderly "counterpurge" of Perónist professors, re-establishing student involvement in university government before it was officially reinstated by the national government.[47]

5. *Social control.* This determinant is primarily that of the response of society to a movement, primarily through its political or other agencies of social control. The character of this response determines whether the movement maintains its character or becomes another type of movement.

a. "Differentiation of political from other aspects of social control makes for greater toleration of norm-oriented movements."[48] The reform movement appealed directly to the relevant political authority, that of the president, through his minister of education. There was no ambiguity concerning the locus of relevant authority, since the national government made the law concerning the institutions of higher education and was empowered to intervene in disputes of sufficiently serious proportions.

b. "The success that a given agitation has in the political arena influences a movement's course of development."[49] The dependence of the movement's success on the fact that a newly elected Radical president had just entered office on a platform of widening democracy has been pointed out above. Although Irigoyen's government had wide popular support and could be characterized initially as democratic and modern, there were strong personalist tendencies in his rule, and, though universal manhood suffrage prevailed, he was careful to ensure nomination of his own supporters as candidates for office. Regarding the Radicals' orientation to the university reform movement, the Argentine historian José Luis Romero says the following:

Although the Radical government, because of its militant opposition to the oligarchy, supported the university reform movement, and consented to modify the statutes regulating the institutions of higher education, the party was nonetheless remote from the true spirit impelling the young students who sensed the revolutionary restlessness of the day.[50]

Thus it was not necessarily common ideals and principles but rather a common enemy which provided government support for the university reform movement.

Without the generally favorable response of Irigoyen, the movement might have become diverted into "hostile outbursts," or expanded into a value-oriented, revolutionary movement. In fact the movement's tactics often included what may be considered "hostile outbursts," but most characteristic was the seizure of universities, presumably to dramatize the lack of legitimacy accorded by students to university government, and as a means to ensure intervention by a sympathetic government.

The Colombian Student Movement
for University Reform

Colombia, like nearly all other Latin American countries, was influenced by the Argentine student movement, and took as a model many of its proposals and much of its diffuse ideology. This emulation was not successful in bringing about major reforms through direct action, however, and the reform law which was eventually promulgated, in 1935, was not a direct consequence of student pressure, as in Argentina, and reveals only a moderate influence of the movement. Although the historical evidence for student political action in this period is inadequate, it would appear that the movement was not broadly supported by students, and also lacked the crucial advantage of the Argentine movement in 1918, that of a sympathetic government. To place the analysis in a comparative perspective, and to seek to explain its lack of success as compared to that of the movement in Argentina, the analysis will be organized in terms of the determinants of collective behavior, as in the preceding discussion.

1. *Structural conduciveness.* As noted above, the possibility for demanding modification of norms without also appearing to demand a more fundamental modification of values is the most general condition of conduciveness. To assess this possibility requires a brief discussion of the origins and situation of the student movement in Colombia. It appears to have begun, at least officially, in the early 1920's. The first national student congress took place in 1923, although documents are available only for the second congress in 1924. While the documents from this meeting and the writings of Germán Arciniegas, apparently the major spokesman of the movement, concentrate on critiques and proposals for reform similar to those put forth by the Argentine movement, several of the most active participants appear to have been involved in more radical political activity oriented to the society at large. This suggests that the movement at this stage may have been compromised by tendencies toward a value-oriented movement. The period of the 1920's was one of considerable social change and political conflict. Colombia was much less developed economically and socially than Argentina, as reflected by the greater predominance of agriculture in the economy and the primarily rural character of the populace, and was less influenced by European events and ideologies through the mass media and trade with Europe, than was Argentina. World War I and its aftermath nevertheless brought about change through the impact of new international markets, the influx of foreign capital, and, as in Argentina, the influence of revolutionary socialist doctrine.[51] With increasing urbanization and industrialization, unions were organized and labor-management conflict increased in the cities, while Indian and peasant uprisings occurred in rural areas. During this period socialist and Communist parties were formed, largely by young intellectuals. Fluharty describes the role of the young intellectuals as follows:

This potent brew of social ferment was ably stirred by a new generation of young intellectuals. Rejecting the old ideas regarding equality, these young men, many of whom were destined to become national political leaders, were irresistibly drawn into the social fray. Gabriel Turbay, Luis Tejada, Hernández Rodríguez, and Moises Prieto organized the Communist Party. Intrigued chiefly by the doctrine of the class struggle, they actually knew little about Marx, and cared less. Others, Dios Romero and Mario Cano among them, sponsored labor syndicalism, and men like Germán Arciniegas, Armando Solano, and Juan Lozano plunged happily into the strong current of socialism running through the nation.[52]

Several of those mentioned above, including Arciniegas, Turbay, and Prieto also signed declarations presented at the second Colombian student congress in 1924.[53] The young intellectuals' involvement in Marxist study groups contradicts Fluharty's statement that they knew or cared little for Marx. This group included Turbay and Prieto, among others.[54] The implication of these involvements in radical political and intellectual movements suggests that the University Reform movement may have been invigorated by radical fervor, on the one hand, while alienating potential student members, on the other hand, for the same reason. While the Argentine reform movement was radical in its demands for university reform, and while it was influenced by socialist ideology and theory and by the example of the Russian revolution as a model for the seizure of power, it nonetheless limited itself to reforms which were possible within a government dominated by the party then in power. In contrast, Conservatives dominated Colombian elections, primarily through fraud and coercion, from 1886 to 1930, when a Liberal party candidate won.[55] Thus the advent of radical left politics occurred in a period with no apparent political outlet except revolution or agitation.

a. *Access to methods for affecting the normative order.* An example of the limited access to such methods available to the reform movement at that time is provided in a message from students to the members of a German educational mission, invited to Colombia for the purpose of proposing educational reforms.[56] The message contains a comprehensive critique and set of proposals for university reform, modeled on those of the Argentine experience.[57]

Proposals for reform were made to Congress by the group composed of the German Technical mission and their three Colombian university professor counterparts, in 1925, including the proposal that the university " . . . should be a juridical institution governed by its own legal bodies; that is, the faculty staff, the university council, the rector, and the representatives of the student body."[58] While the students may have been influential in the drafting of this proposal, it was not enacted into law, although it constituted a precedent for subsequent reform.[59]

b. *Lack of alternative channels for expressing dissatisfaction.* Short of seizing the universities by force and seeking to impose reforms, an action which would not have met with government support, the most likely channel of reform lay in influencing the government, which, as in Argentina and everywhere in Latin America, determines the constitution of public universities. On the other hand, alternative channels did exist through involvement in various left political movements and groups, as noted above, and while these were not concerned directly with university reform, they offered a base for attacking the same oligarchy which resisted reform in the universities. The influence of such involvement, which was perhaps proportionately greater than that on student activists in Argentina in 1918, is evident in the declarations of the Third National Congress of Students in 1928. In addition to goals of university reform were several relating to broad social reform, including "equality of life chances," the "ideological liberation of women," and the legal equality of women. Another goal was defined as "national defense, demanding the effective nationalization of petroleum and the conservation of the integrity of the national patrimony. . . ."[60]

2. *Structural strain.* This factor was present especially in the form of new values which provided a basis for defining persisting social conditions as evil, and discussed above. But the incorporation of critiques of university structure and content with broader critiques of national life may have had the effect of weakening the impulse for university reform as such, and of diverting energies of student radicals into broader and more diffuse movements, lessening the norm-oriented character of the student movement becoming a value-oriented one.

3. *Generalized beliefs and the role of precipitating factors.* Generalized beliefs have been discussed in part above, in terms of the various pronouncements of student congresses and elsewhere, particularly in the writings of Germán Arciniegas, who became to an important degree the major ideologist of the movement. What might have been a precipitating event, focusing attention on the movement and gaining militant support, occurred in the context of a broader conflict. Although details are lacking in the available account, "the university," presumably students at the National University in Bogotá, led ". . . a formidable movement of popular protest against a system characterized by nepotism, incapacity to deal with pressing so-

cial and economic problems enhanced by the worldwide depression, and led by a president . . . incapable of dealing with imperialism."[61] A law student was killed in a battle with police, the date of which event has since been commemorated as a "symbol of the struggles for the transformation of the State."[62] This event occurred during a period of widespread social discontent and revolt marked by a peasant uprising in the banana zone against the United Fruit Company, put down by the army, and numerous strikes in the cities, arising from bad working conditions, low pay, and general dislocation of the economy brought on by the depression.[63] Student activity, while significant, was part of a general social movement, or perhaps was involved in a number of interrelated movements, which had in common a desire to remove the oligarchy from power. A Colombian observer described the character of the social movements of the period as follows:

With one thesis or the other . . . that of the conserving of the Liberal Party, or that of making new parties, the new generation understood that the people were obligated to battle, together, to gain their social rights, their political and their religious rights. All the revolutionary currents of the epoch . . . Socialists, Communists, syndicalists and anarchosyndicalists . . . participated in the same doctrine.[64]

The consequences of these pressures from below led to the candidacy of Olaya Herrera on behalf of a coalition government, a solution by the oligarchies of both parties to avoid revolution and to reduce pressures for major changes in the socio-economic structure by the choice of a candidate committed to moderate reforms, with ties to both parties.[65] At least one writer credits the student movement with playing a "decisive" role in bringing about the end of Conservative rule, but he also asserts that student influence was effective for only a brief period of time.

The conclusions of observers of this period are that the young radicals did not pursue the struggle with the oligarchy and sought neither to further the social revolution nor to continue the struggle for university reform, since their real concerns were to gain entrance to the political oligarchy.

The student leaders used the Federation of Students as a trampoline to jump into the political arena, to perform on the model of the traditional parties. They turned in the direction of bourgeois politics, offering the programs of the University Reform for the purpose of renovating the old bourgeois programs.[66]

This judgment is concurred in by Fluharty, though in somewhat broader terms, referring to the young intellectuals as a whole.

The brash young men confronted the oligarchies and threw down the gauntlet. Inspired by the new ideas that came down every wind, they became the voice of Colombia's future, her nascent social conscience. For the most part, they were laughed out of the arena. The oligarchy was certain that when they had established themselves, when they had made a mark and gained a stake in the society, these young firebrands would recant. The fever would die, the innovations pall, the challenging ideas lose their validity. By and large, the oligarchy was right....[67]

He goes on to discuss the Liberal party leader Jorge Eliécer Gaitán as an exception to this generalization, as one who was committed to radical reform throughout his life, and who never compromised his principles.[68]

The preceding discussion suggests, then, that the university reform movement was transformed into an abortive value-oriented movement, and failed to realize the goals of either university reform or of the broader revolutionary movement within which it became involved. The explanation appears to lie in several directions, all related to the particular characteristics of Colombian society and its situation at that time, but generalizable in terms of the theory of collective behavior utilized here. The conditions for a value-oriented movement in Colombia during the twenties and early thirties were clearly present, including the existence of large numbers of politically alienated in the population, an inflexible political structure, and the failure of the government to provide solutions to increasing economic misery, combined with the capacity of the government to prevent or control hostile outbursts.[69] But what might have become a revolution was prevented by the capacity of the oligarchy to respond sufficiently to pressure to put forward a moderate, reformist candidate, and thus to remove the appearance of intransigence and inflexibility in the face of demands for reform.[70] The Olaya Herrara regime was not sufficiently responsive, however, to prevent intensification of protest, but the propitious occurrence of a broader war with Peru in 1931 appeared to offer an escape valve for revolutionary pressures, channeling protest into nationalist fervor and legitimating the imposition of martial law.[71]

Thus the student movement became diverted into a value-oriented movement which was diverted from its revolutionary course. We may here contrast the fortunes of the Colombian with that of the Argentine student movement. The latter developed during a period of considerably less structural strain and thus was not diverted into a value-oriented movement, but remained focused upon the explicit issues of university reform. It also had the advantage of being allied with a middle class political movement, in the form of Radicalismo, which came to power prior to the major "precipitating event" of the Reform movement, and thus was in a position to accede to the demands of the movement as a further realization of the tenets of the Radical party's expressed concern for the extension of electoral democracy.

The comments quoted above concerning the apparent readiness of Colombian student leaders to forego their radical posture, once assured a place within the traditional oligarchy, suggests a further contrast between characteristics of the middle class in the two societies. One North American observer has asserted that those who occupy middle class positions in Colombian society are largely descendants of upper class families, and maintain a predominantly upper class identification. This is assertedly due to the presumed low rate of upward mobility and to the high rate of reproduction of upper class families, with consequent downward mobility of offspring who do not inherit sufficient wealth to maintain an upper class style of life, and who enter middle class status in the professions, teaching, and business, but maintain upper class family and social contacts.[72] This thesis has been challenged by a Colombian anthropologist who asserts that there is considerable social mobility, both upward and downward. He argues that there is and has been "for a long time" a "genuine" middle class, in the sense of its having derived from lower class origins, and also that the upper class families with downwardly mobile members are those which ascended two or three generations ago, and "have not had sufficient time to form a family tradition, to feel inextricably linked to the upper class."[73] Since neither writer offers data to support his thesis, the issue is unresolved, but nearly all observers of Colombian life have commented upon the existence of an identifiable political oligarchy, based on economic power and occupying the seats of political power, both elective and appointive. The opportunity to share power with the oligarchy may be an especially compelling one in a relatively small country like Colombia, with limited access to power outside the traditional parties. Thus radical student leaders may have been more easily persuaded or encouraged to "sell out" there than in Argentina, for example, where power has been more widely dispersed during the twentieth century, at least.

A moderate university reform did come about in 1935 with the passage of the Organic Law of the National University of Colombia. With respect to the Reform movement, its most important section was that referring to university government, to be exercised by a rector, a "síndico" or treasurer, a secretary general, and a directive council. The latter was composed of nine members, including the Minister of National Education as its President, the university rector as vice-president, and seven other members, including two representatives of the national government, one representative elected by the deans of schools and faculties of the university, two elected by the professors, and two elected by the students.[74] Student representation is thus granted in the law, but is considerably less than the one-third established in Argentina and recommended by Germán Arciniegas in the law which he proposed to the Colombian House of Representatives in 1932. He proposed a Directive Council, to be composed of the president, secretary, treasurer, and controller of the university, the rectors of faculties, heads of university departments and representatives of each faculty, the latter to include two each from the professors, students, and graduates of the university for each faculty. The functions of this body would have been broad and comprehensive, including the election of rector and faculty heads, and control of all matters pertaining to the organization of the university and the formulation of the educational program of the university, including matters concerning examinations, degrees, and courses of study.[75] The enacted organic law, on the other hand, while it contains similar functions for the directive council, states that the council should "approve the plans, methods of teaching, and of research and other regulations submitted to it by the academic council," a body composed of deans and directors of faculties and schools, without the representation of students or professors.[76]

The 1935 law was nevertheless a considerable move toward reform, and it did allow for student representation. But the distinct difference between the reform instituted in Colombia compared to that in Argentina lies not only in the substantive difference in the content of the reforms, but in the fact that reform in Colombia, while perhaps reflecting the influence of the student movement in some degree, was not precipitated by direct student pressure, but was rather enacted independently by a legislature dominated by a reformist Liberal party majority, elected in 1935 following the 1934 election of Liberal Alfonso López as president. Under López important reforms were instituted benefiting labor, including the right of workers to organize and strike, a minimum wage, the eight-hour day and forty-hour week.[77] Thus university reform was a consequence of the shift to a reformist government, as was the Argentinian reform movement, but since it was not directly instigated by a militant student movement prepared to strongly protest the modification of its principles embodied in a body of "generalized beliefs," as had been the case in Argentina, it was unable to significantly affect the law, which granted students little more than token representation in university government.

The consequences of this difference would appear to be the following. In Argentina, the successful culmination of the university reform movement granted students a major decision-making role in university and faculty governing councils, institutionalized the movement, and established a political subculture in which student elections were significant for the actual conduct of university affairs. A party was formed (Reformista) to embody and defend the principles of university reform, providing the organizational base of subsequent movements for reform or for opposition to the government. The failure of the movement to become institutionalized in Colombia meant that collective student political action lacked a stable and persisting base, and rather tended to be discontinuous, responding to specific issues by the formation of temporary *ad hoc* organizations. Thus Colombian students have had considerably less direct influence on university government and policy than have their counterparts in Argentina. One would also expect that student political organizations have been less responsive to the mass of students and more easily manipulated by their leaders, since there has been a lack of the open and competitive university student party structure which has existed in Argentina. In other words, one would expect a greater tendency to oligarchy within student political organization in Colombia, along with a tendency toward organizational instability. This last point is conjectural for the period from the 'thirties to the 'fifties, but recent developments would appear to support this contention.

Consequences for Contemporary Student Politics

Perhaps the major difference between the pattern of student politics in Colombia and Argentina, which bears out the contention that the relative success or failure of the University Reform movement in the two societies has determined the course of subsequent political organization and activity, lies in the presence or absence of a relatively stable national federation of university students in the two nations. In Argentina, the continuing existence of the Federation of Argentine University Students (FUA) has provided a basis for concerted political action, among and within the universities. An example is the well-organized campaign conducted against the 1955 government decree-law, which authorized private, predominantly Catholic universities to grant degrees, formerly permitted only to state universities.[78] The student campaign was unsuccessful, and its failure perhaps contributed to the decline of leftist representation within university government and within student councils. But the development and maintenance of the Federation as an outcome of the successful University Reform struggle earlier has provided a well-established structure for political conflict, as well as norms for the conduct of such conflict. In Colombia, on the other hand, there have been several attempts to form anew a national student federation in recent years. The present National University Federation (FUN) appears to lack legitimacy among a large proportion of students, and to be dominated by leftist student leaders oriented toward Maoist or Castroist political means and goals. Its character and ideology may be due in part to the absence of a well-institutionalized and persisting organization for national student politics in the past, leading to its being easily controlled by a minority of student radicals.[79] Students in Colombia have apparently been less ready to contest such control, in part because of the ephemeral nature of student federations in the past, and the lack of significant student participation in university government.

Thus a wide spectrum of student parties competes for office in university government in Argentina, and a much narrower spectrum in Colombia. There appears to be little representation from Catholic or non-Marxist student groups with the FUN in Colombia. In Argentina, groups reflecting a non-Marxist, "humanist" ideology have had majorities in recent elections.[80] The struggle among all ideological groups has tended to take place in the arena of the Argentine University Federation, since the fruits of victory mean significant influence within university government. In Colombia, since students lack significant representation within university government, student politics tend to be turned outward toward national and international issues, and to provide a platform for student revolutionaries.

It would appear, on balance, that in the Latin American environment, where the belief that students should participate in university government is widely held and founded to some extent on the reality of university structure, that such participation may contribute to the civilizing of politics, and to the development of democratic norms of political action which carry over into non-student life.[81] The denial of participation by students in university government does not inhibit the development of student political activism in Latin America, but may rather facilitate a more ideological, utopian political orientation among student politicians who lack the experience of pragmatic involvement in university affairs, in which authority for decision-making implies a responsibility to the university community, and thus a check on the tendency toward an "ethic of ultimate ends," in Max Weber's phrase.

To conclude, it would appear that where the University Reform was successful, as in Argentina, it provided an important impetus toward needed reforms in the character and conduct of higher education, a defense of academic freedom against the claims of the state, and a politicizing experience for students in the democratic process. Where the movement was relatively unsuccessful, as in Colombia, student politics would appear to be more alienated from university and society, and less responsible in its choice of means. The different fate of the movement in these two societies was due to quite different conditions and events, differences, however, which are part of the broad historical trends in these societies and which must be taken into account if one is to interpret the character of student politics in the two nations.

Notes

1. Gabriel del Mazo, *La reforma universitaria y la universidad latino-americana* (Resistencia: Universidad Nacional del Nordeste, 1957), pp. 77–78; Roberto Mac-Lean y Estenos, *La crisis universitaria en Hispano-América* (Mexico, D. F.: Universidad Nacional, 1956), pp. 89–92.
2. Clarence H. Haring, *The Spanish Empire in America* (New York: Oxford University Press, 1947), p. 230.
3. David Rubio, ed., *La Universidad de San Marcos de Lima durante la colonización española* (Madrid: Imprenta Juan Bravo, 1933), Vol. 3, pp. 47–56, 151–154, *passim;* John Tate Lanning, *Academic Culture in the Spanish Colonies* (London: Oxford University Press, 1940), pp. 44–56.
4. Lanning, *op. cit.,* p. 56.
5. For the state of science and medicine in the colonial period, see Lanning, *op. cit.,* pp. 93–111; Haring, *op. cit.,* pp. 238–242.
6. As quoted by Gabriel del Mazo, *Estudiantes y gobierno universitario* (Buenos Aires: Libreria "El Ateneo" Editorial, 1956), p. 25.
7. Del Mazo, *op. cit.,* p. 27.
8. Del Mazo, *Estudiantes y gobierno . . . , op. cit.,* pp. 29–73; Carlos Cossio, *La reforma universitaria* (Buenos Aires: Espasa-Calpe, S. A., 1927), pp. 119–173.
9. Del Mazo, *Estudiantes y gobierno . . ., op. cit.* pp. 74–96.
10. See Carlos Cossio, *op. cit.,* pp. 39–86, for a characterization of the "old University."
11. "The Argentine Youth of Córdoba to the Free Men of South America," in Federación Universitaria de Buenos Aires, *La reforma universitaria, 1918-1958* (Buenos Aires: 1959), p. 23.

12. Mac-Lean y Estenos, *op. cit.*, pp. 13–17.
13. Neil J. Smelser, *Theory of Collective Behavior* (New York: The Free Press of Glencoe, 1963).
14. *Ibid.*, p. 270.
15. *Ibid.*, p. 313.
16. *Ibid.*, pp. 15–18.
17. *Ibid.*, p. 278. (Italics in original.)
18. See Del Mazo, ed., *La reforma universitaria* (La Plata: Centro Estudiantes de Ingeniería, 1941), Vol. I, pp. 1–114, for documents concerning the movement in its initial, 1918 phase.
19. Smelser, *op. cit.*, p. 282.
20. Luigi Einaudi, "University Autonomy and Academic Freedom in Latin America," *Law and Contemporary Problems*, XXVIII (1963), 640.
21. James R. Scobie, *Argentina: A City and a Nation* (New York: Oxford University Press, 1964), pp. 200–201.
22. *Ibid.*, p. 203.
23. Smelser, *op. cit.*, p. 9, 284.
24. *Ibid.*, p. 285.
25. *Ibid.*, p. 286.
26. *Ibid.*, pp. 47–48.
27. *Ibid.*, p. 288.
28. See Scobie, *op. cit.*, pp. 189–214, 275–277.
29. Smelser, *op. cit.*, p. 289.
30. See Sergio Bagú, "Como se gestó la reforma universitaria," in Federación Universitaria de Buenos Aires, *op. cit.*, pp. 28–33; Cossio, *op. cit.*, pp. 102–104; Del Mazo, *La reforma universitaria . . . , op. cit.*, pp. 10–12; Einaudi, *op. cit.*, p. 638.
31. Cossio, *op. cit.*, pp. 104–107.
32. Tulio Halperin Donghi, *Historia de la Universidad de Buenos Aires* (Buenos Aires: Editorial Universitaria de Buenos Aires, 1962), p. 132.
33. Smelser, *op. cit.*, p. 292.
34. Federación Universitaria de Buenos Aires, *op. cit.*, pp. 24–25.
35. Del Mazo, ed., *op. cit.*, pp. 9–28.
36. Halperin, *op. cit.*, pp. 106–129. Moderate success was achieved at Buenos Aires in the inclusion of all faculty members in the electoral body for faculty and university governing councils.
37. Smelser, *op. cit.*, p. 294.
38. Halperin, *op. cit.*, p. 129.
39. Del Mazo, ed., *op. cit.*, pp. 465–467.
40. See Halperin Donghi, *op. cit.*, pp. 130–131; Del Mazo, *Estudiantes y gobierno . . . , op. cit.*, pp. 34–35; Federación Universitaria de Buenos Aires, *op. cit.*, p. 9.
41. Smelser, *op. cit.*, p. 294.
42. Federación Universitaria de Buenos Aires, *op. cit.*, p. 25.

43. Smelser, *op. cit.*, p. 296.
44. *Ibid.*, p. 298.
45. Halperin, *op. cit.*, pp. 78–122; Del Mazo, *Estudiantes y gobierno . . ., op. cit.*, pp. 22–28.
46. Smelser, *op. cit.*, p. 306.
47. See Nancy Delmas, "The Revolution in Argentina's Universities," *The Reporter* (January 12, 1956), pp. 26–30.
48. Smelser, *op. cit.*, p. 306.
49. *Loc. cit.*
50. José Luis Romero, *A History of Argentine Political Thought* (Stanford: Stanford University Press, 1963), p. 223.
51. Vernon Lee Fluharty, *Dance of the Millions: Military Rule and the Social Revolution in Colombia, 1930–1956* (Pittsburgh: University of Pittsburgh Press, 1957), pp. 28–29.
52. *Ibid.*, p. 29.
53. Del Mazo, ed., *op. cit.*, pp. 104–106.
54. Diego Montaña Cuellar, *Colombia: País formal y país real* (Buenos Aires: Editorial Platina, 1963), p. 131.
55. Jesús María Henao and Gerardo Arrubla, *History of Colombia*, trans. and ed. by J. Fred Rippy (Chapel Hill: The University of North Carolina Press, 1938), pp. 54–541.
56. See Germán Arciniegas et al., "Mensaje de la juventud a los miembros de la misión pedagógica," in Del Mazo, ed., *op. cit.*, Vol. II, pp. 100–104.
57. See Arciniegas, "Carta a los antiguos alumnos del gimnasio moderno," in *ibid.*, pp. 110–111.
58. Orlando Fals Borda, "Basis for a Sociological Interpretation of Education in Colombia," in A. Curtis Wilgus, ed., *The Caribbean: Contemporary Colombia* (Gainesville: University of Florida Press, 1962), p. 208.
59. *Loc. cit.*
60. Quoted in Montaña Cuellar, *op. cit.*, p. 136.
61. *Ibid.*, p. 137.
62. *Loc. cit.*
63. Fluharty, *op. cit.*, pp. 36–41.
64. Antonio García, *Gaitán y el problema de la Revolución Colombiana* (Bogotá: Cooperativa de Artes Gráficas, 1955), p. 257; as quoted in Fluharty, *op. cit.*, p. 40.
65. *Ibid.*, p. 42.
66. Montaña Cueller, *op. cit.*, pp. 137–138.
67. Fluharty, *op. cit.*, p. 29.
68. Fluharty, *ibid.*, p. 30.
69. See Smelser, *op. cit.*, pp. 313–381, for a discussion of the determinants of value-oriented movements.
70. *Ibid.*, pp. 330–332.
71. Fluharty, *op. cit.*, p. 45.

72. T. Lynn Smith, "Observations on the Middle Classes in Colombia," in Theo R. Crevenna, ed., *Materiales para el estudio de la clase media en la América Latina* (Washington, D. C.: Unión Panamericana, 1951), Vol. VI, pp. 1–14.

73. Gerardo Reichel-Dolmatoff, "Notas sobre la clase media en Colombia, II" in *Notes e informaciones en ciéncias sociales*, III (1952), No. 13, p. 4.

74. Colombia, Ministerio de Educación Nacional, *Compilación de disposiciones sobre régimen de universidades, 1888–1952* (Bogotá: Imprenta Nacional, 1953), p. 122.

75. Germán Arciniegas, *La universidad colombiana* (Bogotá: Imprenta Nacional, 1932), pp. 166–170.

76. Colombia, Ministerio de Educación Nacional, *op. cit.*, pp. 123–125. Perhaps the most significant difference between the law proposed by Arciniegas and that later enacted by Congress is the inclusion in the latter of government representatives on the directive council to the extent of three out of nine members, including the Minister of Education as president of the council. This would appear to considerably reduce university autonomy, placing it more directly under control of the government. This insertion of government representation within the directive council was contained in a law proposed in 1935 by a member of congress, and which presumably influenced the drafting of the enacted law. He criticized Arciniegas' proposal of a Directive Council for the large number of student and former student representatives which it proposed, which would lack "seriousness and permanence," but he did not attempt to justify the inclusion of government representation. Carlos García Prada, *La Universidad Nacional de Colombia y su organización*, (Bogotá: Imprenta Nacional, 1935), p. 10.

77. Fluharty, *op. cit.*, p. 53.

78. See "La Universidad de Buenos Aires y la libertad de enseñanza, *Revista de la Universidad de Buenos Aires*, Quinta Época, III (1958), 506–522.

79. This characterization of FUN is based on a reading of Colombian newspaper accounts, and various Colombian student political publications, including *Federación Universitaria Nacional* (October 1964), the official organ of the Federation.

80. See Mario Peralta and Ramón Gutiérrez, "Análisis comparativo de la trayectoría de los movimientos estudiantiles, Trabajo No. 1—Universidad de Buenos Aires," *CREA Boletín* (1963), 5–9.

81. See Kenneth N. Walker, "Political Socialization in Latin American Universities" (paper presented at the International Seminar on the Formation of Elites in Latin America, University of Montevideo, June 6–11, 1965).

University Experience and Political Unrest

of Students in Buenos Aires

DAVID NASATIR

---— **12** ---—

It is known that higher education has numerous effects on the lives of those who partake of it: expanding their knowledge, modifying their tastes, preparing them for occupations, introducing their mates. Its role in developing and shaping their political beliefs is not known, although in recent years this has been a topic of increasing theoretical and empirical interest.[1] In his work, *Political Man*, S. M. Lipset claims:

Education presumably broadens man's outlook, enables him to understand the needs for norms of tolerance, restrains him from adhering to extremist doctrines and increases his capacity to make rational electoral decisions.[2]

Yet in her book, *What College Students Think*, Rose K. Goldsen gives evidence for increasing conservatism throughout the college years.[3] In contrast to the above, Philip E. Jacob, after an extensive review of the available evidence, has concluded that higher education probably has little or no effect on attitudes and values.[4] And Peter I. Rose has suggested that it is quite possible that each of the above conclusions may be true—under certain conditions.[5] This chapter is an attempt to illuminate some of those conditions.

Rose Goldsen has stated,

... If young people are exposed for four years to institutional norms and values in the very milieu in which they are explicit and authoritative, they will become socialized to the predominant values of that milieu and will come to acknowledge their legitimacy.[6]

Thus, to the extent that the norms of the university differ from those of the society at large, systematic differences should be observable among the values and norms of students and non-students. These differences should be observable, as well, among the students themselves to the extent that the milieu in which they play out their roles as students differs.

A simple test of the impact of university life can be devised, then, by comparing the responses of students and non-students to questions indicative of deeper normative orientations. To the extent that there are systematic differences in the contexts of their everyday lives, we may expect differences in their responses to such questions. Similarly, to the extent that there are important differences within the larger student context, there should also be differences in the responses of students from these subcontexts.

University students throughout the world have a political significance out of proportion to their numbers. They constitute the future elite of their societies and, frequently, have an image of that future at variance with their daily experiences. This is especially true, perhaps, in developing nations where students have more opportunity to come in contact with new ideas and products as well as greater skills in articulating feelings of deprivation and demands for change. One area in which the impact of university life should be most evident, therefore, is that of political interest. For whatever else it might be, bringing about large-scale change, like the preservation of the status quo, is an eminently political task. It may be expected, therefore, that an interest in politics will be more widespread among students than among other youthful members of the population.

But elite potential and cosmopolitanism are not the monopoly of students alone. The children of elite families are exposed to factors at home which might well produce similar contacts and skills. And it is, of course, precisely these children who are also most likely to be students. Therefore, before attributing a special "politicizing" impact to the university, it is necessary to examine the manner in which political interest is manifested by youth in general and to determine whether such interest is especially associated with highly politicized subcultures among students.

In order to illustrate more clearly the role played by the university in developing an interest in politics, a study of some 1,600 Argentine youth was undertaken. Argentina presents many interesting contrasts to the United States which facilitate such a study. It is relatively easy to locate groups of young, middle-class Argentines who do not attend institutions of higher education as well as children of manual laborers who do.[7] Comparisons of a kind not possible in the United States (where it is quite difficult to locate youth from middle class families who have not been associated with some institution of higher education at one time or another) can thus be made in an effort to distinguish the effects of higher education from those of social class and family background.

In order to simplify the analysis somewhat, the following discussion will be based only upon the responses from 630 students of the University of Buenos Aires and 489 non-university youth from the metropolitan area that constitutes greater Buenos Aires. Random samples of approximately equal size were drawn from the lists of eligible voters in each of the ten faculties (professional schools) which constitute the university.[8] In order to be included in the lists it is necessary to be formally registered as a student in the particular school and to have finished at least one course during the electoral period prior to the one in which the list is to be employed.

Non-university youth were selected according to a quota sampling technique. Interviewers were sent throughout the greater metropolitan area of Buenos Aires with instructions to obtain interviews from subjects between eighteen and twenty-five years of age, who had never had any contact with any university (including those who had started but not finished even the first course). Examination of the University census provided an estimate of the age, sex, and social class distribution of the students and these parameters were used in constructing the remaining quotas for the non-university youth.

That some differences in political interest do exist between groups of university students and non-university youth comes as no surprise. Table 1 shows rather clearly what might have been expected all along; students respond more often than non-students in that they sometimes or even fre-

TABLE 1.

More Students Frequently Interested in Politics Than Non-Students: Answers to the Question "Do You Ever Get as Excited about Something That Happens in Politics as about Something That Happens in Personal Life?"

	Frequently	*Sometimes*	*Never*	*No Answer*	*Total*
University Students*	38%	48%	13%	—	(630)†
Non-University Youth*	26%	41%	32%	—	(489)

* University of Buenos Aires and non-university youth from Buenos Aires.

† Number in parentheses indicates size of sample from which percentages were computed.

quently get as excited about something that happens in politics as about something that happens in their personal life. While only 13 per cent of the students say that they never develop such an interest, a complete lack of interest is characteristic of 32 per cent of the non-students. In fact, non-students more often respond that they *never* get excited about politics than that they *frequently* do. Students, in contrast, claim frequent interest almost three times as often as they claim complete lack of interest.[9]

These differences are not simply differences in subjective orientations but are also reflected in the behavior of the two groups. Tables 2 and 3 reveal the same type of relation between university attendance and talking about politics with friends as was observed in Table 1. In Table 2, 45 per cent of the students claim that they frequently talk politics with

TABLE 2.

More Students Frequently Talk Politics Than Non-Students: Answers to the Question "Do You Often Talk Politics with Your Friends?"

	Frequently	Sometimes	Rarely	Never	No Answer	Total
University Students	45%	38%	12%	4%	—	(630)
Non-University Youth	26%	34%	19%	22%	—	(489)

their friends in contrast to 26 per cent of the non-students claiming such activity. Where only 4 per cent of the students say that they never talk politics with their friends, 22 per cent of the non-students may be considered relatively apolitical.[10]

A final indicator of political interest can be obtained from analysis of the role played by the students and the non-students in political discussions. Table 3 shows that almost one-fifth more (69 per cent) of the students claim that they intervene in political discussions rather than listen in comparison with the 50 per cent of non-university youth making such a claim.

TABLE 3.

More Students Usually Talk in Political Discussions Than Non-Students: Answers to the Question "In These Conversations Do You Usually Intervene or Listen?"

	Intervene	Listen	No Answer	Total
University Students	69%	29%	19%	(630)
Non-University Youth	50%	38%	11%	(489)

No matter what indicators are used, students are clearly more interested in politics. The question is, of course, why do such differences exist? Are they due to differences in family background? Differences in the values of youth who select the university rather than the market place? Or are they, in fact, due to the impact that the university experience has upon those that participate in it?

That some part of the differences between students and non-students may be attributed to differences in family background is to be expected. Just what that difference is, however, is not clear. Many studies in the United States have demonstrated the political apathy of working class families, but there is a reasonable doubt that this same pattern might hold in a society only recently emerged from a totalitarian regime characterized by its emphasis upon creating political consciousness in the working classes. Table 4 shows that, in some degree, the expectation that children of manual workers would manifest interest in political matters with less frequency

TABLE 4.

Father's Occupation Is Positively Related to Interest in Politics

Father's Occupation	Interest in Politics			
	Frequently	*Sometimes*	*Never*	*Total*
Unspecialized Workers up to Foreman	30%	40%	30%	(258)
Technicians and Managers	30%	52%	17%	(208)
Professionals and Owners of Businesses	35%	45%	20%	(653)

than children from middle-class and professional homes is verified. Where 70 per cent of the workers' children claim that they get excited about politics sometimes or even frequently, 82 per cent of the children of technicians and managers and 80 per cent of the children of professionals and owners of businesses express such an interest. What is important here is not the existence of such a relation between father's occupation and child's level of political interest, but that the differences between students and non-students persist.

Table 5 shows that in each category of father's occupation there is still a consistent tendency for students to express excitement about political events more often than non-students. This difference is brought about in a rather interesting way. Rather than a consistent increase in political in-

TABLE 5.

**More Students Frequently Interested in Politics Than Non-Students
Even When Controlling for Father's Occupation**

Father's Occupation	Education	Interest in Politics			Total
		Frequently	Sometimes	Never	
Unspecialized	University	42%	43%	16%	(113)
up to Foreman	Non-University	24%	40%	45%	(145)
Technicians and	University	34%	53%	11%	(123)
Managers	Non-University	24%	51%	26%	(85)
Professional and	University	39%	48%	13%	(393)
Business Owners	Non-University	29%	41%	30%	(260)

terest for both groups as higher statuses of father's occupation are examined (as marginal frequencies presented in Table 4 might suggest), a differential sensitivity to political interest can be observed. That is, a marked influence of father's occupational status can be seen in the case of the political interest of the non-students, but diverse family backgrounds appear to have only slight influence upon the level of political interest of the university students. The students express a generally high level of political interest regardless of the occupation of their fathers, but such interest is more likely to be found among the non-students who are not from the homes of unspecialized workers and foremen, although even youth from middle class homes, if they are not affiliated with the university, are less likely to get as excited about politics as do university students.

Although father's occupation is a well-established indicator of family life style, there are always some problems associated with accurate characterization of occupational titles into analytical categories. It is surprising, therefore, that when the more clearly defined variable of father's education is substituted as an indicator of family values, the above relation changes fundamentally. Table 6 shows that the relation we have come to expect between students and non-students continues to hold true for children of fathers with only a primary school education. Where 83 per cent of the students claim that they frequently or sometimes get excited about political matters, only 60 per cent of non-students make such a claim. Although the percentage of students excited about politics remains relatively stable regardless of the educational level of the student's father, a sharp increase in political interest is associated with increasing level of father's education for non-students. The effect is so pronounced that among the children of university educated fathers, the original relation between the

TABLE 6.

**Father's Education Accounts for Much of the Variation
between Students and Non-Students**

Father's Education	Education	Interest in Politics			
		Frequently	Sometimes	Never	Total
Primary	University	37%	46%	15%	(336)
	Non-University	21%	39%	40%	(225)
Secondary	University	38%	50%	11%	(204)
	Non-University	26%	46%	27%	(147)
University	University	39%	49%	12%	(181)
	Non-University	42%	46%	12%	(85)

interest in politics of students and the lack of interest associated with non-students has essentially disappeared; both groups express their interest with almost equal probability.

Thus it is reasonable to conclude that a considerable part of the differences observable between the population of students and that of non-students, with respect to political interest at least, is due to factors antecedent to the university experience. The differences in political interest are associated with the level of education and the type of occupation engaged in by the youth's father.

But the similarity of students and non-students from educated families in fact says little about the politicizing process of the university experience. We still do not know if the university imparts an interest in political events that is separate from such an interest which may normally develop in young adults as they take on the full responsibilities of citizenship. It is necessary to focus upon dynamic factors to probe the adequacy of dynamic formulations.

It is reasonable to assume that some change will be manifested on the part of students and non-students as well simply due to their changing age roles in the society. However, an examination of Table 7 reveals very slight relations, not regular, and not nearly of the magnitude that one might expect to be associated with a fundamental social process.

There are, however, many kinds of students. If, as other research would lead us to believe,[11] some part of the university's impact is transmitted through informal primary associations, such effects should be more pronounced for those students in some way more "integrated" into university life.

But what is university life? The university is not a homogeneous entity.

TABLE 7.

Age Is Not Strongly Related to Political Interest either for Students or Non-Students

Age	University Students Interest in Politics					Non-University Youth Interest in Politics			
	Fre-quently	Some-times	Never	N.A.	Total	Fre-quently	Some-times	Never	Total
17 or less	—	—	—	—	(1)	—	—	—	(1)
18–19	43%	41%	14%	2%	(44)	28%	34%	37%	(220)
20–21	38%	51%	11%	1%	(180)	22%	50%	27%	(127)
22–23	36%	48%	11%	—	(157)	21%	47%	32%	(77)
24–25	37%	55%	8%	—	(105)	33%	40%	27%	(63)
26–27	43%	43%	14%	—	(56)	—	—	—	(1)
28–29	28%	51%	20%	—	(35)				
30–35	49%	31%	20%	—	(45)				
36 or more	14%	56%	28%	—	(7)				

It is entirely possible that the differences among the various faculties are greater than the similarities, at least with respect to the process of politic socialization. A look at Table 8, where the degree of political interest has been tabulated for the students of each faculty, reveals the truth of this supposition. Although the variation among faculties in the proportion of students responding that they never become very interested in political matters is considerable, the variation in the proportion claiming that they frequently develop such an interest is even greater. A first glance might

TABLE 8.

Political Interest Varies from Faculty to Faculty

Faculty	Interest in Politics				
	Frequently	Sometimes	Never	No Answer	Total
Law	55%	35%	10%	0%	(63)
Economics	45%	41%	12%	2%	(65)
Architecture	44%	44%	12%	0%	(64)
Exact Sciences	41%	37%	22%	0%	(68)
Agronomy & Veterinary	40%	37%	13%	0%	(68)
Medicine	38%	40%	22%	0%	(65)
Pharmacy	28%	52%	19%	1%	(68)
Philosophy & Letters	26%	65%	9%	0%	(67)
Engineering	21%	62%	17%	0%	(63)
Dentistry	17%	59%	24%	0%	(41)

lead to the conclusion that such variations are due entirely to the subject matter of the various faculties. The law school presents the highest proportion of politically interested students (55 per cent claiming that they frequently become interested in political matters) while dentistry presents the lowest (17 per cent making such a claim). Some suspicion is immediately cast upon this hypothesis, however, when the relatively high position of architecture is noted (44 per cent of the responses claim a frequent interest in political matters) and contrasted with the relatively low position of philosophy and letters (where only 26 per cent claim a frequent interest).

An alternative hypothesis which might be entertained at this point derives from the variable time demands made by each faculty rather than the content of its courses. Table 9 shows that there is, indeed, some relation be-

TABLE 9.

Time Spent in the Faculty Is Related to Political Interest

	Interest in Politics				
Time in Faculty	Frequently	Sometimes	Never	No Answer	Total
Less than 5 hours/day	43%	44%	14%	—	(441)
Five hours/day or more	27%	57%	16%	1%	(180)

tween the amount of time spent in the faculty each day and the degree of interest manifested in politics. Where 43 per cent of the students in the faculty, spending less than five hours per day, claim a frequent interest, 27 per cent of the students, spending more than five hours per day, express such an interest. The decrease in interest is associated with an increase in contact with the university; but a drop in interest is contrary to expectations based on a theory that the university experience, in and of itself, has a politicizing effect. It is entirely possible, of course, that this effect is due to an unequal distribution of contexts with respect to political interest. It may be that a special process of adult socialization does take place here, but that the majority of the daily activities of the students most involved in university life are carried out in contexts with relatively low political interest.

The data presented in Table 10 provide a test of the above hypothesis. A rough classification has been made of the various careers that exist in the

TABLE 10.

Political Interest Is Not Awakened by a Highly Politicized Context

Context	Time in Context	Interest in Politics				
		Frequently	Sometimes	Never	No Answer	Total
Low Level of Interest	Less than 5 hours/day	28%	54%	16%	—	(158)
	5 hours/day or more	22%	62%	15%	—	(110)
High Level of Interest	Less than 5 hours/day	51%	40%	10%	—	(294)
	5 hours/day or more	34%	52%	16%	—	(70)

ten faculties of the University of Buenos Aires. Those departments with a percentage of students expressing frequent political interest above the mean level of such interest for all students were classified as high level of interest contexts. Similarly, in those departments where the percentage of students expressing frequent interest was below the mean level for all students the classification was that of a low interest context. In addition, students were classified by the average number of hours per day that they reported spending in their faculty.

The most suggestive aspect of Table 10 derives precisely from the above division. Although the observed decrease in interest might have been expected in contexts characterized by their low level of political interest (i.e., students more involved in the context would be more like the contextual characteristic in their political interest), the hypothesis of contextual influence is weakened somewhat by the decrease in political interest associated with involvement even in high interest contexts. Where 51 per cent of the students in the high interest contexts less than five hours per day claim a frequent interest in political matters, 34 per cent of those in the faculty more than five hours per day make such a claim.

The data presented up to this point cast some doubt upon hypotheses of adult socialization in the university situation; at least in regard to the development of political interest. All of the tests employed, however, have ignored the most essential aspect in any process—change over time. Table 11 presents a final test of the socialization hypothesis by comparing stu-

TABLE 11.

**Political Interest Does Not Develop over Time Even with
Insertion in Highly Politicized Contexts**

Amount of Interest	Year	Part-Time Students				Full-Time Students			
		Fre-quently	Some-times	Never	Total	Fre-quently	Some-times	Never	Total
Low	1	50%	20%	30%	(10)	—	—	—	(03)
	2	34%	46%	18%	(35)	30%	50%	10%	(10)
	3	20%	58%	20%	(30)	18%	66%	16%	(38)
	4	35%	56%	09%	(34)	28%	52%	21%	(29)
	5 & 6	25%	75%	00%	(12)	—	—	—	(04)
High	1	42%	58%	00%	(24)	—	—	—	(03)
	2	44%	49%	07%	(55)	31%	46%	23%	(13)
	3	56%	37%	06%	(80)	35%	50%	15%	(20)
	4	52%	35%	15%	(55)	54%	36%	09%	(11)
	5 & 6	50%	30%	18%	(65)	28%	56%	17%	(18)
	Thesis	53%	47%	00%	(15)	—	—	—	(05)

dents at various levels within their careers, in high interest and low interest contexts while taking into account the amount of time these students spend, on the average, in those contexts.

An examination of these data fails to reveal a pattern of steadily increasing political interest over the years, even for those students spending proportionately larger amounts of time in high interest contexts. A marked curvilinearity is to be observed instead. A steady increase in the proportion interested over the first four years is followed by a marked dropping off among the most advanced students.

A slightly different pattern may be seen for the students spending less than five hours per day in the same type of high interest context. Interest becomes more widespread sooner, and fails to drop off with approaching termination of the university career.

In contrast to the "full-time" students, the "part-time" students develop their interests while integrated into the larger social context. The interests thus developed are, presumably, consonant with their other activities. Full-time students at the last stages of their academic careers, on the other hand, are faced with a special problem of impending status transition. Data are not yet available to test the supposition that political interest is once again widely manifest among such students upon their successful transition to the status of full-time, non-student professionals.

In summary, a slight increase may be observed in the proportion of students in high interest contexts who are frequently interested in politics when progressively more advanced students are considered. This is true both for "part-time" and "full-time" students although more pronounced among the former. If first and second year students are compared to all others, the proportion claiming a frequent interest in politics rises from 31 per cent to 35 per cent among the full time students and from 43 per cent to 51 per cent among their part-time colleagues.

Examination of the responses for students in low interest contexts reveals the opposite effect: political interest becomes less widespread as students progress through the university. Thirty-seven per cent of the students in the first two years of study in low interest contexts claim a frequent interest in politics. The level for more advanced students, however, drops to 24 per cent. A similar phenomenon is observable among the full-time students in the low interest contexts; i.e., the frequent expression of political interest drops from 31 per cent to 21 per cent.

The socializing impact of the university may be observed most clearly in Table 12. As we have seen, the initial degree of interest varies between students and non-students and among the students themselves; there are also differences between more advanced students and the newcomers as there are among older and younger non-students. But the magnitude and direction of the changes appear quite systematic.

In general, full-time students express a high degree of political interest less frequently than do the part-time students. But all students become, in time, more like the context in which their studies are carried out. Since, as Glaucio Soares has pointed out,[12] it is the small proportion of activists that creates an image of the university as a political hotbed, it is worthwhile noting that political interest can also decay in the university; it is, in part, a question of the nature of the student environment. It is even possible, as shown in Table 12, for political interest among older students to be less common than would have been expected had they not entered the university.

In conclusion, attention is drawn to the heterogeneous character of the large university, not only in the United States, as Rose points out,[13] but in Buenos Aires as well. Consequently, in order to examine the impact of the university experience, some finer breakdowns are necessary. In the analysis of political interest presented here, we have seen that when this is done, the university experience may be observed to have multiple and even op-

TABLE 12.

Changes in Political Interest

	Percentage Expressing Frequent Interest in Politics	
	Young*	Old
Non-students	28	24
	(221)†	(268)
Students		
Low interest contexts‡		
Part time§	37	24
	(45)	(76)
Full time	31	21
	(13)	(71)
High interest contexts		
Part time	43	51
	(79)	(215)
Full time	31	35
	(16)	(54)

* "Young" is less than twenty or not yet a third-year student. "Old" is twenty or over or third-year student or more advanced.

† Numbers in parentheses are bases of percentages.

‡ Low interest contexts have a mean score on the political interest factor less than 0.00 High interest contexts have a mean score equal to or greater than 0.00 (The mean of the factor score is 0.0; the standard deviation is 1.0.)

§ Part-time students are on campus less than four hours per day. Full-time students are on campus four or more hours per day.

posite effects. Thus, it has been shown how changes do take place in the political interests of students. In the apolitical atmosphere which prevails in some parts of the university, political interest tends to become less common among older students; in more politicized settings interest spreads. As in many other areas, an understanding of the context in which students spend their time and develop their conceptions of the world is vital to an understanding of the impact of university education.[14]

Notes

1. See, for example, Nevitt Sanford, ed., *The American College: A Psychological and Social Interpretation of the Higher Learning* (New York: Wiley, 1962); see also Alex S. Edelstein, "Since Bennington: Evidence of Change in Student Political Behavior," *Public Opinion Quarterly*, XXVI (Winter 1962), 564–577.

2. Seymour M. Lipset, *Political Man* (Garden City: Doubleday, 1960), p. 56.

3. Rose K. Goldsen et al., *What College Students Think* (Princeton, N.J.: Van Nostrand, 1960), p. 123.

4. Philip E. Jacob, *Changing Values in College: An Exploratory Study of the Impact of College Teaching* (New York: Harper & Brothers, 1957).

5. Peter I. Rose, "The Myth of Unanimity: Student Opinions on Critical Issues," *Sociology of Education*, XXXVII (Winter 1963), 129–149.

6. Goldsen, *op. cit.*, p. 198.

7. According to a study by Otis Dudley Duncan and Robert W. Hodge, "Education and Occupational Mobility: A Regression Analysis," *American Journal of Sociology*, LXVIII (May 1963), 644, "The data are consistent with the supposition that education was becoming a more important determinant of occupational status, in terms of both its net influence apart from level of origin and its role as a variable intervening between origin and destination."

   In contrast to the situation in the United States, see Sugiyama Iutaka, "Mobilidade Social e Opurtunidades Educacionais em Buenos Aires e Montevideu, uma analise comparativa (I)", *America Latina*, VI: "Formal education in these cities does not appear to be as important a route to higher social status as might on other grounds have been expected" (p. 39). See also Tabela 11A, p. 36, "Buenos Aires, Nivel Educacional do Entrevistado em Relaçao ao Nivel Educational do Pai, e au sea status Relativo."

8. It is important to note that differences in the enrollment among the various schools are very great, and, since the samples taken were of about equal size from each faculty, it is not proper to generalize to the entire student population of the University of Buenos Aires without giving proper weight to these differences. This has not been done here and the reader is warned accordingly.

9. This is consistent with data presented by S. M. Lipset, *op. cit.*, regarding political apathy.

10. It should be noted that this is a very relative apathy. At the *most* politicized of the eleven North American campuses reported on in Goldsen's book, 54 per cent of the students said "no" to the question, "Do you ever get as worked up about something that happens in politics as something that happens in personal life?" (*op. cit.*, appendix 13, p. 218).

11. See, for example, "A Contextual Analysis of Academic Failure," by D. Nasatir, in *The School Review*, LXXI (April 1963).

12. Chapter 5, this book.

13. P. I. Rose, *op. cit.*

14. Acknowledgment is gratefully given for support obtained from the Comparative National Development Project of the Institute of International Studies, University of California, Berkeley, directed by Seymour M. Lipset; and from the Committee on Research of the Los Angeles Division of the Academic Senate of the University of California.

The Professional and Political Attitudes

of Chilean University Students[1]

MYRON GLAZER

13

The need in developing societies for highly trained professionals is well documented by economists, sociologists, and other social scientists. Recent writings on a number of developing countries emphasize the importance of expanding the educational recruitment base, building new professional groups, improving the quality of teaching, and staffing rural positions. The writers generally assert, furthermore, that professional commitment is of prime importance in developing areas, for the assumption is made that this commitment will result in motivation to spur economic and social development, and the consequences of this commitment, then, will be positive in meeting and solving the most pressing problems facing these countries.[2]

It has been stated, moreover, that student involvement in other activities, especially political ones, can only draw student energies away from their trainee role and undermine their professional identification. Such criticism has often been leveled, especially against students in Latin American countries.[3]

It was to investigate the validity of such broad assumptions that I conducted a research project in one developing country, Chile.[4] This chapter will be directed toward an analysis of the extent and nature of professional commitment among Chilean university students, the positive and negative effects of political involvement on such commitment, and its consequences for the process of modernization.

Several criteria were considered before selecting Chile as the country in which to conduct the empirical research. Chile has long been in the process of economic development, beset by many problems, and torn by controversy concerning alternative solutions. Many of its schools, nevertheless, enjoy the reputation of training very competent professionals, whose work has been highly esteemed in their own nation, as well as in international organizations and foreign countries.

Chilean university students, furthermore, have traditionally been socially concerned and politically active as spokesmen for the most under-privileged in the society, although the extent of their involvement has fluctuated during different periods in Chilean history. Prior sociological research has shown that university students were an especially active and effective political force during the 1920's and 1930's.[5] In more recent years, university students seemed to be moving toward a greater preoccupation with local university issues and toward lesser involvement in national affairs. The year prior to the presidential election of September 1964 seemed to provide an excellent opportunity in which to observe and study student activities and attitudes during a period of greatly heightened national tension, in which candidates of conservative, center-left, and extreme left positions vied for the nation's highest elective office.

Data Collection Procedure

To gather data several approaches were utilized. Contemporary Chilean newspaper and journal articles, as well as scholarly and government sources, were used to secure a picture of the official and popular thinking on educational problems in general, and the student role in particular. Persons well acquainted with Chilean education, including social scientists, university professors, professional practitioners, and current university students were relied on as informants. Finally, a lengthy interview schedule, completed and tested during the first few months after my arrival in Chile in September 1963, was utilized to obtain the attitudes of a representative sample of university students.

The twenty-four page interview schedule included several major sections: family and educational background, professional training experiences and attitudes, political background and experiences, and political attitudes. The professional part of the schedule was strongly influenced by the approaches utilized in recent studies of United States graduate education.[6] The political questions were constructed almost entirely on the basis of my observations of Chilean national life and of the intense political struggles which characterized the country in late 1963–1964. The schedule was pre-tested and was discussed at great length with Chileans from different professions and of all political persuasions to ensure that our queries focused on those matters held to be most relevant by local observers.

The actual interviews were conducted with students in four schools of the University of Chile in Santiago, the largest and most important university in the country. The schools from which the sample was drawn are training students in fields which are essential for national development and include medicine, engineering, secondary school teaching, and physics.[7] My aim was to interview approximately 100 students in each of the schools,[8] and thirty-five names were drawn at random from those enrolled in each of the first, middle, and final years of their course of study.[9] However, the pressure of time and the great difficulty in locating some of the students forced us to accept a minimum of 30 in each of the years selected.[10]

Degree of Professional Commitment

Among those questions bearing on professional attitudes, there were several which attempted to elicit (1) the means which students would employ to achieve professional success, (2) the types of job characteristics most important to them, and (3) their desire to implement their professional knowledge.

The Means. In determining the means which students regarded as necessary for the attainment of their goals, we focused on several aspects: how the students define the realities of advancement in Chilean professional life, what they believe this situation ought to be, and finally, how students would choose for themselves in a conflict situation.

We first listed six characteristics on an ascription-achievement continuum ranging from social position of family to professional ability. The students were asked to rate, in order of importance, the three characteristics which, in their opinion, were currently most important in obtaining a desirable position in their professions.

Their responses indicate that students are very much aware of the great contemporary significance of such features as family background, personal contacts, and political affiliations in influencing career opportunities. Although there are important variations by school, a very substantial number of the total group rate these as more potent than achievement-oriented criteria of professional ability, grades, and recommendations of one's professors (Table 1).

After the students indicated which factors they felt were actually important in obtaining a good position, they were asked what they thought

TABLE 1.

Actual Factors Necessary to Obtain a Good Position by School

School	All Achievement	Primarily Achievement	Primarily Ascriptive	All Ascriptive	Doesn't Know	Total
Engineering	5	37	45	7		94
	(5)*	(39)	(48)	(7)		(100)
History	6	25	36	27		94
	(6)	(27)	(38)	(29)		(100)
Physics	13	12	3		2	30
	(43)	(40)	(10)		(7)	(100)
Medicine	19	48	29	1	2	99
	(19)	(48)	(29)	(1)	(2)	(99)

*Numbers in parentheses indicate percentage. Percentages may not add up to 100 due to rounding.

such factors ought to be (Table 2). Their responses readily demonstrate that there is a marked difference between the students' conception of what is and of what should be. In every school the vast majority of the students have stated that the achievement-oriented characteristics should be the determining, or at least predominating, factors in influencing students' future career opportunities. The students, then, strongly reject the ascriptive factors so characteristic of a traditional society, in favor of universalistic norms of evaluation.

The respondents were subsequently asked how they would choose in the following situation in order to test more fully their attitudes in this area:

TABLE 2.

Factors That Should Be Necessary to Obtain a Good Position by School

School	All Achievement	Primarily Achievement	Primarily Ascriptive	All Ascriptive	R	T
Engineering	51	34	9	—	—	94
	(54)	(36)	(10)	—		(100)
History	57	32	5	—	—	94
	(60)	(34)	(5)	—		(99)
Physics	26	3	1	—	—	30
	(87)	(10)	(3)	—		(100)
Medicine	78	18	2	—	1	99
	(79)	(18)	(2)	—	(1)	(100)

Two professors have asked you to serve as an assistant and you can only accept one of these positions.

Professor "A" is very highly thought of as an expert in his field and you are certain that you will be able to learn a great deal from him. However, he has very few contacts which would be of help to you in getting a job after graduation.

Professor "B" is also a competent professional. Even though you do not have as high regard for his ability, you know that he has many contacts that will be of great help to you when you begin to look for a job.

Which position would you choose?

The overwhelming majority of the students in every school and every year respond that they would like to work with Professor "A" (Table 3). Thus, when asked to project themselves into a future conflict situation, their responses again are consistently away from the customary paths of interaction in the society and indicative of a high degree of professional commitment.

TABLE 3.

Which Professor Would You Work with by School?

School	Definitely "A"	Probably "A"	Definitely "B"	Probably "B"	Other	T
Engineering	45	31	3	15	—	94
	(48)	(33)	(3)	(16)		(100)
History	64	20	4	6	—	94
	(68)	(21)	(4)	(6)		(99)
Physics	21	6	—	2	1	30
	(70)	(20)		(7)	(3)	(100)
Medicine	58	33	—	8	—	(99)
	(59)	(33)		(8)		(100)

"*Symbolic*" vs. "*Instrumental*" Orientations. Students were also asked to select the two characteristics of a future job most important to them. The factors listed ranged from good income and high prestige to the opportunity to serve the community (Table 4). The responses in all the schools focus most heavily on the opportunity for "professional growth" (56-77 per cent). Strong emphasis is also given to the importance of service to the community, especially by student doctors (63 per cent) and teachers (49 per cent). Furthermore, little significance is given by the students to income or prestige, with the exception of the engineers who place strong emphasis on the former (38 per cent).

TABLE 4.

Two Most Important Characteristics of a Job by School

School	Political Liberty	Social Prestige	Income	Gain Professional Recognition	Perfect Skills	Help People	Other	R	T
Engineering	35	16	36	10	53	38	—	—	94 (2)
	(37)	(17)	(38)	(11)	(56)	(40)			200
History	30	5	20	14	73	46	—	—	94 (2)
	(32)	(5)	(21)	(15)	(77)	(49)			199
Physics	13	3	7	2	21	11	3	—	30 (2)
	(43)	(10)	(23)	(7)	(70)	(37)	(10)		200
Medicine	26	10	11	11	73	62	4	1	99 (2)
	(26)	(10)	(11)	(11)	(74)	(63)	(4)	(1)	200

To test more specifically the range of attitudes to the "symbolic" vs. "instrumental" orientation to task performances, we asked the students to choose between the following positions:

You have just graduated and have been offered two jobs.

Job "A" is a very distinguished position, especially for a person of your age. However, there will be very little opportunity to apply the most modern methods you have learned in your education.

Job "B" is a job of much less prestige, but you will have the opportunity to use directly your professional knowledge and the opportunity to improve your skills.

Which would you choose?

Although some engineers (19 per cent) and teachers (13 per cent) show a preference for the more "symbolic" position, the overwhelming majority of the students select the more "instrumental" path[11] (Table 5).

To specify consistency of response and possible explanatory variables influencing degree of professionalism, we have constructed a scale combining the three last questions utilized above.[12] The results emphasize the heavy concentration of students in the high professional category (Table 6). In attempting to specify who are the students who are high, mid, or low on the scale of professional commitment, we found that background variables of sex, socio-economic status, religion, and secondary school do not offer any explanation. In all schools professional attitudes seem to be most correlated with the important variable of degree of political involvement.

TABLE 5.

Accept Job Which Has More Prestige or Allows Use of Training by School

School	Prestige		Training		R	T
	Definitely	Probably	Definitely	Probably		
Engineering	5	13	39	37	—	94
	(5)	(14)	(41)	(39)		(99)
History	5	8	61	19	1	94
	(5)	(8)	(65)	(20)	(1)	(99)
Physics	1	1	20	7	1	30
	(3)	(3)	(67)	(23)	(3)	(99)
Medicine	3	2	71	21	1	99
	(3)	(2)	(72)	(21)	(1)	(99)

TABLE 6.

Position on Professional Scale by School

School	High Professional	Mid Professional	Low Professional	T
Engineering	31	21	42	94
	(33)*	(22)	(45)	(100)
History	54	22	18	94
	(57)	(24)	(19)	(100)
Physics	20	3	7	30
	(67)	(10)	(23)	(100)
Medicine	62	21	16	99
	(63)	(21)	(16)	(100)

* Numbers in parentheses indicate percentage.

Degree of Political Involvement

In the training of young professionals experiences in the informal structure of the university have an importance beyond the formal socialization that each student undergoes. Some students join or sympathize with political groups which may be affiliated with national parties and whose activities are often directed toward influencing both national and university events. Others, less involved, attend lectures and speeches and participate in the ubiquitous political discussions which characterize university life in many developing societies. In periods of political crisis this latter group rallies to the call of the political activists and provides the mass base for strikes, demonstrations, and other manifestations of student discontent. A third group of students is alienated from any form of political activity and rejects the importance of such participation. Emphasizing non-membership and freedom from all "deals" or compromise, some see themselves as independent critics of the social order while others, uninformed or disinterested, have no political position that can be measured.

To place the students politically, categories were devised, dividing them into three groups. In the first, or "activist" segment, are those who stated that they were leaders, members, or sympathizers completely in accord with a particular university political group. In the second, or "weak political" category, are those students who sympathize with one group but who have strong reservations either about it or about the usefulness of any type of political involvement. Also in this category are those who did not state that they sympathize with any group, but who voiced a distinct preference for one of the national parties and who voted for its affiliate in the university election. Members of the final category include those students who claim no political affiliation, who define themselves as having no interest in politics, and who show no consistent voting pattern.

The Relationship between Professional Commitment and Political Involvement

Table 7 indicates the high correlation between degree of professionalism and degree of political involvement. Thus, 64 per cent of the activists are to be found in the high professional category and only 13 per cent are in the low professional group. In contrast, while 41 per cent of the non-politically active students are also highly professional, fully 33 per cent are in the low professional category.

These results challenge the widely asserted view that political activism is a direct impediment to professional modernization.[13] The implication of

TABLE 7.
Position on Professional Scale by Position on Political-Critical Scale

	High Professional	Mid Professional	Low Professional	T
Activist	56	20	12	88
	(64)	(22)	(13)	(99)
Weak	79	27	45	151
	(52)	(18)	(30)	(100)
None	32	20	26	78
	(41)	(26)	(33)	(100)

this position is that were Latin American university students less politically active, they would almost inevitably devote their energies to professional concerns, which, in turn, would accelerate development of their countries. The Chilean evidence strongly questions the existence of the polarization. Rather, political and social ideology seem to give strong impetus to the rejection of the remnants of traditional society and increase the desire for change and modernization. Among these students, there is often a direct marriage between their political and professional goals.

Important areas of role conflict do, nevertheless, exist. One frequent source of such tension involves strikes within the university. How do students who are both highly political *and* highly professional resolve the conflict over the strike situation? Are they more or less likely to support the strike, even when it means interference with the intake of important professional knowledge?[14]

Table 8 clearly shows that among all professional categories, the political activists are most "definitely" in favor of the strike and least numerous in the "no" category. It is especially notable that among the high pro-

TABLE 8.

Would You Vote to Strike by Position on Political-Critical Scale and Position on Professional Scale

Professional	Political-Critical	Definitely Yes	Probably Yes	No	R	T
High	Activist	38	11	6	1	56
		(68)	(20)	(11)	(2)	(101)
	Weak	24	36	18	1	79
		(30)	(46)	(23)	(1)	(100)
	None	10	12	10		32
		(31)	(38)	(31)		(100)
Mid	Activist	10	7	3		20
		(50)	(35)	(15)		(100)
	Weak	8	15	4		27
		(30)	(56)	(15)		(101)
	None	5	10	4	1	20
		(25)	(50)	(20)	(5)	(100)
Low	Activist	5	5	2		12
		(42)	(42)	(17)		(101)
	Weak	13	15	16	1	45
		(29)	(33)	(36)	(2)	(100)
	None	6	13	7		26
		(23)	(50)	(27)		(100)

fessionals, the percentage of "definite" responses among the activists (68 per cent) is more than double the combined percentage of students in the other two groupings (30 per cent and 31 per cent). Degree of political activism, therefore, appears to be a vital intervening variable influencing students' attitudes in favor of the relative significance of the strike.

The strike is a key mechanism used by Latin American students attempting to influence university and national policy. Their concerns were crystallized in, and given direct impetus by, the University Reform Movement of 1918. Beginning in Argentina, it spread to all Latin American countries with varying degrees of intensity. In Chile, historical circumstances limited the effectiveness of the Reform Movement. Nevertheless, Chilean students are very much influenced by the Reformist tradition, and the strike can be best understood as their most effective weapon, both facilitating and inhibiting legitimate improvement of the university.

Though our earlier findings have indicated that the two student roles tend to be complementary, the response to the question of a strike demonstrates that there are important areas of potential role conflict. This often extends beyond the strike issue and can have consequences for the student's concept of the primary purpose of his entire university education, especially in times of heightened national political tensions. To test students' attitudes further, the following problem was posed.

"A" says that the most important factor for the development of Chile is to have well-trained and prepared people. Therefore, the major responsibility of the student is to devote the majority of his time to learning the materials in his field and only a minimum of time to other activities.

"B" says that Chile needs basic social changes before it can bring about any other changes effectively. He believes that the student has a responsibility to devote a good part of his time to political activities, even if this reduces somewhat the amount of time he can spend on his studies.

With whom do you agree?

Our results strongly support our previous findings. Chilean students, generally, see the intake of technical knowledge as the primary rationale of university study.

Yet differences, again, arise among those with varying degrees of political involvement (Table 9). Although a majority of activists in all schools (56 per cent) choose the central importance of professional concerns, this group is still less committed to the professional choice than the weak political (67 per cent) or non-political (79 per cent) groups. Conversely, the

TABLE 9.

**Technical Competence ("A") vs. Basic Social Changes ("B")
by Position on Political-Critical Scale**

	Competence		Changes				
Political-Critical	Definitely "A"	More "A" than "B"	Definitely "B"	More "B" than "A"	Neither	Other	T
Active	20	29	12	21	2	4	88
	(23)	(33)	(14)	(24)	(2)	(5)	(101)
Weak	50	52	10	30	6	3	151
	(33)	(34)	(7)	(20)	(4)	(3)	(101)
None	32	30	2	7	2	5	78
	(41)	(38)	(3)	(9)	(3)	(6)	(100)

activists are most convinced of the need for basic social change (38 per cent).

These responses confirm our previous findings in regard to the strike. Although we found a high correlation between high professional commitment and political activism, and while both orientations are geared toward the central importance of modernization of the social system, conflict does at times arise over the most effective means for the attainment of social and economic change and how students may best affect this change.

Implications for Economic Development

The burden of the discussion in this section will be upon an exploration of the following questions:

1. Which students are willing to engage in pioneering activities with the urban poor and in rural areas?
2. Which students are willing to accept positions which will increase the stature and teaching level in the university?
3. Are students susceptible to foreign employment?

The medical student. There is an active concern in Chile with extending professional services to the urban slum dweller and to the rural poor. One attempt to develop such services occurred during our stay. This was a major summer program involving 82 fourth, fifth, and sixth year students from the School of Medicine. The site was Chiloe, one of the most primitive and rural provinces. The thirty day trip was sponsored jointly by the School of Medicine and the National Health Service, in order to give the students "an integrated vision of the medical reality that they would have to face upon the completion of their studies."[15]

In this environment students experienced a completely different set of circumstances from those in the medical school. In addition to the vaccination program carried out, students were exposed to one of the major causes of mortality, infant diarrhoea. The neophyte physicians introduced basic concepts about the necessity of washing hands with soap and water, gave lessons on what to do in areas where soap was not available, and generally supplied very fundamental information.

In servicing these consumers, medical students encountered a whole new set of problems. In addition to the stark medical needs, they learned that providing service often involves the ability to justify treatment and educate prospective patients about their needs. Students had discussions with community leaders, public meetings, and showings of films to indicate the importance of vaccinations, which are, of course, taken for granted in the more metropolitan and developed areas of the country.[16] This kind of experience points up some of the concerns of the medical students. One of our keenest informants said:

In hospital training we are given careful instruction on how to speak to patients, to instruct them on medicinal, psychological and diet remedies. We might well tell them to take their blender and make a banana and milk combination, etc. What good does this type of instruction do for people who never heard of a blender and have neither bananas nor milk?

As a result of their involvement with the realities of contemporary Chilean society, many other medical students also indicated to us that their training does not sufficiently emphasize or prepare them to face and solve their country's major medical problems. Excessive emphasis on specialization has the contrary impact. Thus amidst new exposure and changing concepts of what a medical education is all about, the whole training program has been called into serious question. For example, a medical school delegate to the FECH, the student federation, has summarized the results of three conferences involving medical students. The underlying theme of his statement is the necessity for an integrated and dynamic approach to medical education. What is needed, he argues, is a thorough realization of what Chile is, a rejection of the wisdom of the past, and of over-zealous borrowing from the practices of the medical professions in highly developed countries.[17]

This significant stream of criticism and social consciousness among the students is by no means the total picture. Most resist positions in small towns with primitive medical facilities or with marginal consumers in the large cities. Youthful idealism is not sufficient in a social structure in which the highest rewards still lie in specialization, work in large Santiago hospitals, and a private practice geared to middle and upper class urban dwellers. Thus, a great tension exists between the current road to high prestige and professional success, and what is idealistically recognized as an important social problem, but thus far given only sporadic attention. In essence the combination of high specialization and the current distribution rewards produces a situation in which the excellence of medical training does not result in the alleviation of basic national health problems.

The history students. Student decisions as to future professional tasks, institutional positions, and locations are central not only to personal, but also to national development. To gain further insight, we asked the history (teaching) students about a variety of future employment situations. The student-teachers place the highest positive evaluation on public secondary school positions in a middle class urban area. The next most desirable position is in the university, although it is well known that such jobs are very difficult to obtain.

Although there are no secondary schools in the "callampa" slums, these prospective teachers were asked how they would evaluate such a position were it available to them. There is no greater contrast in Chilean society than that between the callampa and the solid middle class neighborhood. As in most centers of rapid population growth, there are extraordinary differences between those who are well-to-do and relatively secure and the newcomers who arrive from the countryside without wealth, education, or personal contacts and who live on the edge of the community in tumbledown dwellings made from scraps of wood, cardboard, and other readily available material.

In view of the contrasts it is very impressive that a large number of students consider working in such depressed areas (56 per cent). Variation in decision making is somewhat clarified when the students are divided by their degree of professionalism and political activism (Table 10). Not only is it the activists in every professional group who are most willing to work in a callampa, but it is also the activists within the high-professional group (78 per cent) who are most affirmative and those in the low professional category (50 per cent) who are least so. It is also important to stress that the other students in the high-professional group are more willing to ac-

TABLE 10.

History Students' Willingness to Work in a Public School in a Callampa by Position on Political-Critical Scale and Position on Professional Scale

Professional	Political-Critical	Yes	No	R	T
High	Active	21 (78)	6 (22)		27 (100)
	Weak	12 (63)	6 (32)	1 (5)	19 (100)
	None	5 (63)	3 (38)		8 (101)
Mid	Active	7 (70)	3 (30)		10 (100)
	Weak	3 (38)	5 (63)		8 (101)
	None	2 (50)	2 (50)		4 (100)
Low	Active	3 (50)	3 (50)		6 (100)
	Weak	2 (33)	4 (67)		6 (100)
	None	1 (17)	5 (83)		6 (100)

cept such employment (63 per cent) than are students in almost any category. High professionalism, therefore, is a key characteristic among those willing to pioneer in new and difficult types of urban employment and becomes even more potent when combined with high political involvement.

When our focus shifts to attitudes toward working in the countryside, we find that degree of political activity becomes an inhibiting variable. Now it is the most active who are among the least willing to accept rural employment among all the professional categories. High professionalism is therefore neutralized by high political involvement (Table 11). The most politically active students are most willing to accept difficult employment if it permits them to remain close to the hub of national events, but least willing to accept it when it entails living in rural areas.

The engineering students. The engineering students, who more often emphasize their interest in prestige and financial rewards than do their peers in the other schools, are also less unwilling to accept rural positions. For them, these activities do not involve great sacrifice. Financial rewards

TABLE 11.

History Students' Willingness to Work in a Public School in a Rural Area by Position on Political-Critical Scale and Position on Professional Scale

Professional	Political-Critical	Yes	No	R	T
High	Active	14 (52)	13 (48)		27 (100)
	Weak	13 (68)	5 (26)	1 (5)	19 (99)
	None	6 (75)	2 (25)		8 (100)
Mid	Active	4 (40)	6 (60)		10 (100)
	Weak	6 (75)	2 (25)		8 (100)
	None	2 (50)	2 (50)		4 (100)
Low	Active	3 (50)	3 (50)		6 (100)
	Weak	3 (50)	3 (50)		6 (100)
	None	2 (33)	4 (67)		6 (100)

upon graduation are more abundant outside the large cities, as are challenging opportunities for professional growth. The ambitious engineering graduate need have less fear of rural "exile" than his teaching or medical school peers. Many engineers see this type of employment as an initiation into highly desired entrepreneurial or administrative positions in the major cities, which they hope to obtain at the peak of their careers. In this sense there is less conflict between the engineering students' goal of professional advancement and the needs of national development.

This entrepreneurial and managerial orientation is highly indicative of, and may be highly functional in, the transitional stage of industrialization. Engineers believe that their skills enable them to move into a great variety of positions, instead of merely preparing them for highly specialized work.[18] Though this is also true, to some extent, of industrialized nations, the overwhelming emphasis on entrepreneurial and managerial goals is much more characteristic of a society which has not yet reached the point where specially trained administrators capture high-level business and government positions. This entrepreneurial and management-oriented spirit can be functional in a society where large sectors of the country are still vastly untapped by business enterprise or controlled by backward and monopolistic firms.

There are also very serious dysfunctional aspects of this attitude, which have been described by Fischer in his discussion of Asian professionals. The goal of administrative employment has not resulted in efficient bureaucracy but often has culminated in waste of much valuable talent.

For example, engineers, chemists, and economists prefer to be administrators while leaving complex technical tasks to individuals who have had little specialized training. Surveys made of activities of elites in Thailand, Burma, Indonesia, and India indicate that in some fields as many as 60% of those trained are not using their skills or the specialized knowledge which university training has given them.[19]

Another significant difference between engineering and all other students is the pronounced lack of enthusiasm for university positions by the former. Pay and prestige differentials, of greater importance to engineering than other students, distinguish industrial and government from university opportunities and place the university in a poorly competitive position. We did, however, have very extensive contacts with one planning center in the University of Chile. This group is staffed by highly competent young engineers, who emphasize the central role of economic factors in influencing the attainment of technical goals. The great significance of this group lies in its ability to recruit some of the most able graduating students. Although the impact has not yet been sufficient to affect general student evaluation on university positions, some change is under way. The cycle of the best engineers going only to better paying industrial and government positions, reinforcing the low prestige of full-time university positions and undermining the quality of teaching, is slowly being challenged.

The science students. In contrast to the responses of the engineers are those of the physics students. For them, a university position is the only one consistently rated very highly. No other institution commands a comparable degree of loyalty and even the prestigious international organizations are only mildly attractive. In Chile, however, the situation for scientists is extremely difficult. The profession is not old and established like teaching, but it nevertheless suffers from low prestige and salaries. It is unformed and disadvantaged in the competition for good students, jobs, and appreciation of its contribution. While there is superficial recognition of the need for training people in the basic sciences, there is at the same time a strong feeling in powerful quarters that Chile cannot yet afford to support scientists working, for example, in experimental or theoretical physics. When the time comes that the country is ready to use such skills, it is argued, it will be able to acquire the necessary researchers.

Dedijer's discussion on the difficulties facing science in certain types of developing countries is pertinent here. Where there is little effort to modify industrial products because of near-monopolistic practices, innovative contributions are little solicited.[20] Research is then almost always "pure," "simply because its results are never demanded or used by their native agriculture or industry."

Thus, on the one hand, Chilean newspaper articles discuss in laudatory terms the creation of an Institute of Science to give degrees in physics, mathematics, biology, and chemistry to fill a large gap in manpower needs.[21] At the same time, the floundering Institute has its budget cut annually, is forbidden to buy equipment needed for a recently formed research group, is limited to no more than fifteen students per year and is in every way discouraged by university authorities, who show little concern that the entire Institute may be still-born.[22]

The contrast which clearly emerges between newspaper publicity and reality is reflective of many educational issues. From reading the papers and following the forums, commissions, and planning sessions held, one gets the distinct impression of tremendous public concern and action. A closer look at the situation reveals that enthusiasm on a surface level far exceeds the willingness to accept and carry out the structural changes necessary to achieve the stated goals. Powerful people in the university can then deplore the poor training of mathematics and science in the secondary schools, which results in large part from inadequate training of high school teachers. Yet, they simultaneously refuse to accept fully that in order to improve teacher training, Chile must attract scientists to the university who are well educated and deeply involved in their specialties. Chileans who have gone to the United States and England to obtain Ph.D.'s in mathematics, physical science, or biology find it difficult to remain in their country to train future professionals when they are denied the support necessary to work in their fields of specialization. Ironically, under these conditions the best trained and most professionally committed young scientists may be precisely those who are most driven to foreign employment.

Foreign employment. Many of the science students define foreign employment as an opportunity for gaining greater professional competence.

For others, it is a guarantee of professional positions, no matter what the situation is in their own country. Indeed, this tendency to look favorably upon employment in other countries is widespread among the other students as well (Table 12). In this situation, the variables of political involvement and professional commitment offer no explanation, nor did any of the others we tested.

TABLE 12.

Do You Want to Work in a Foreign Country after Graduation by School

School	Yes	No	Undecided	T
Engineering	47	27	20	94
	(50)	(29)	(21)	(100)
History	55	20	19	94
	(58)	(21)	(20)	(99)
Physics	19	6	5	30
	(63)	(20)	(17)	(100)
Medicine	38	32	29	99
	(38)	(32)	(29)	(99)

There is considerable public concern about the exodus of high talent manpower, and criticism is severe of those who succumb to the temptation of foreign employment. Many proposals have been put forth to counteract the trend.[23] Some students, nevertheless, consider opportunities for personal and professional advancement more important than a commitment to the solution of national problems. For them, the alternatives are simple. For others, who are more dedicated to national development, the decision is replete with conflict. It is a dilemma which young professionals face with increasing frequency. Dedijer sums up this situation very clearly and his discussion appears applicable in Chile even for those young professionals who have not studied abroad.

The reluctance of the highly trained young scientist from an underdeveloped country to return to his own country upon completion of his training is not simply attributable to deficient patriotism or enslavement to the money bags and fleshpots of the advanced countries. In many cases it is motivated, at least in part, and in some cases it is entirely motivated by the knowledge that it is difficult to do good research in their own countries. Not only is equipment and financial provision incomparably poorer than it is in the advanced countries, but scientific administration is usually far more bureaucratic and antipathetic to the needs of scientists for freedom from petty controls.[24]

Conclusion

The evidence collected from our study of students at the University of Chile in Santiago shows a high degree of professional commitment among student doctors, engineers, physicists, and history teachers. This should not, however, compel an automatic assumption that such commitment has only positive implications for Chilean economic and social development. For those students who are very committed to high quality professional performance, the attractions of working conditions in the advanced countries or in international organizations are very frequently irresistible. This is particularly true in science where jobs in Chile are scarce, where facilities for advanced research are limited, and where few opportunities exist for post-graduate specialization. Similarly, in medicine students are well trained, are ambitious to specialize, and are often under-motivated to deal with the primitive health problems which beset much of rural Chile.

It becomes quite evident, then, that qualitative professional training is in itself not sufficient for solving the manpower shortages from which Chile is suffering. As is the case with many Latin American countries, the greatest problems exist in building new professional groups and motivating members of the traditional professions to work with low income groups in urban and rural areas, where professional services are desperately needed, but are virtually nonexistent. In such situations a special kind of professional identification is demanded. Professionals are needed who are not only technically competent, but also aware of their country's problems and motivated to assist in their solution.

We maintain, furthermore, that political involvement can, at times, serve to support directly the type of professional commitment most geared to solve the society's most urgent problems. The Chilean evidence indicates, for example, that there is a marked difference in students' willingness to pioneer by practicing their professions in remote geographical areas and with those urban groups who have hitherto been excluded from the market for professional services. Attempts to explain the divergent student orientations by the use of such variables as sex, socio-economic background, and religion were unsuccessful. Our results indicate that the most potent variable is the degree of political involvement exhibited by the student. In contemporary Chile this type of involvement most often consists of an identification with the reformist or revolutionary national political parties. Our evidence strongly leads to the conclusion that political ideologies which are supportive of social change, which emphasize the importance of modifying or drastically altering the social order, which reject the current distribution of rewards, which deny the innate inferiority of the economically underprivileged, which advocate the broadening of the society's opportunity structures, and which emphasize the responsibility of youth to engage in this process as part of their student role can be highly functional in directing youthful energies into those channels most needed by the society.

On the other hand, our investigation also indicates that in certain situations political involvement does conflict with the trainee role and can have negative results. Under certain conditions political activity and affiliation can inhibit the propensity to pioneer professional services where there is a conflict between the needs of the political and professional roles. Moreover, in other instances it can directly interfere with the intake of professional knowledge by drawing off too much of the students' time and energy into political activities.

We believe that although these results are limited by time and space factors, they give further evidence to the complexity of the student role. There is an urgent need for further research before broad and often questionable generalizations are made about the degree of student professional commitment, its possible contribution to national development, and its relationship to political activism.

Notes

1. I am indebted to the Inter-University Study of Labor Problems in Economic Development and the Industrial Relations Section of Princeton University for providing the time and facilities for the preparation of this chapter. Professor Frederick H. Harbison has been an enthusiastic advocate of the Chilean project from its inception, and I am pleased to acknowledge his essential support. Wilbert E. Moore and Melvin M. Tumin have been my most important teachers, and I am ever aware of how significant they have been to me. Mr. Terry Lichtash and Penina M. Glazer contributed, as always, editorial assistance and moral encouragement. The Henry L. and Grace Doherty Foundation and the Center for International Studies of Princeton University supported my fifteen months of travel and research in Latin America.

2. The writings of the members of the Inter-University Study of Labor Problems in Economic Development have especially emphasized the need for high-level manpower. See, for example, Frederick Harbison and Charles A. Myers, *Education, Manpower, and Economic Growth* (New York: McGraw-Hill Book Company, 1964).

3. See R. P. Atcon, "The Latin American University," *Die Deutsche Universitäts*

Zeitung, February 1962, pp. 7–49; J. P. Harrison, "The Role of the Intellectual in Fomenting Change: The University," *Explosive Forces in Latin America,* J. J. Tepaske and S. N. Fisher, eds. (Columbus: Ohio State University Press, 1964).

4. See M. Glazer, "The Professional and Political Attitudes of Chilean University Students" (unpublished Ph.D. thesis, Princeton University, 1965).

5. See Frank Bonilla, "Students in Politics: Three Generations of Political Action in a Latin-American University" (unpublished Ph.D. thesis, Harvard University, 1959).

6. The questionnaire of James A. Davis and his colleagues was especially important. Also see R. K. Merton, G. G. Reader, P. L. Kendall, *The Student Physician* (Cambridge, Mass.: Harvard University Press, 1957); H. S. Becker and J. Carper, "The Elements of Identification with an Occupation," *American Sociological Review,* XXIII (February 1958), 50–56; I. H. Simpson, "Patterns of Socialization into Professions: The Case of Student Nurses" (paper presented at the meetings of the American Sociological Association, August 1960). The questionnaire appears in M. Glazer, *op. cit.,* Appendix II.

7. The goal was to choose schools in traditional fields (medicine, engineering, and teaching) and in a new one (physics). Another basis of selection was to compare schools of high prestige (medicine, engineering) and those of lower prestige (teaching, physics) in the general society. A third aim was to include schools that are oriented toward working with people and thus with social issues (medicine, teaching) and ones that are oriented toward technical and scientific achievements (engineering and physics). A final goal was to select schools that were reputed to be very politicized and left wing (teaching, medicine), a school that was somewhat more conservative (engineering), and one that was apolitical (physics). The plan to interview in a fifth school, which is training students for a new career in public administration, had to be abandoned when first my wife and then I were bedridden for five weeks each with hepatitis.

8. This number, of course, represented a different percentage of the total student body because of the variation in enrollment in the different schools. Thus, in Engineering, with almost 1,500 students, our sample represented about 6 per cent of the students. In Medicine, which had 1,225 students, it represented about 8 per cent. History had approximately 250 students and the number interviewed there was somewhat less than 40 per cent. In Physics 75 per cent were sampled. The high dropout rate in History resulted in a total population of less than thirty-five students in certain years. To ensure an adequate sample, the decision was made to combine the second and third years for the midpoint, and the fourth and fifth years for the final point. In Engineering and Medicine the problem of sufficient numbers did not arise. However, the six year curriculum in both cases led to the decision to combine the final two years in order to reduce the gap between the mid and final points. This, we felt, would have been too great had we simply sampled from the first, third and sixth years.

9. This was true in all cases, except the final years in Medicine. There, the stu-

dents are divided and assigned to different teaching hospitals throughout the city, and our random sample was drawn from only one hospital. From conversations with informants we could not determine any differences among the students assigned to the different hospitals.

10. In general, excellent cooperation in both Engineering and Medicine resulted in our completing over 90 per cent of our stratified random sample in those schools. Far greater difficulty arose in the School of History. Not only was it an extremely challenging task to track down respective respondents because many did not regularly attend class, but also lists of students, up-to-date and easy to acquire in the other schools, did not accurately reflect actual enrollment in History. The greatest modification of the sampling design occurred in the School of Physics. Since total enrollment consisted of only forty students, we had planned to interview them all. Serious political difficulty, however, necessitated an end to our work after thirty students had been interviewed. It was my impression, however, derived from informal discussions with students and professors at the school, that there were not outstanding differences among the ten students whom we had not interviewed. This observation was confirmed when we reported our initial findings to our informants in the school. For a full discussion of the problems encountered, see my article, "Field Work in a Hostile Environment: A Chapter in the Sociology of Social Research," *Comparative Education Review*, X (1966), No. 2, pp. 367–376.

11. E. Wight Bakke believes that the student "image" in Mexico and Colombia is still "confused." Students have not yet "digested" the two major components of a professional as a person who has prestige and contacts or as a person who is concerned with the implementation of knowledge. There is a very strong movement toward identification with the latter, however. "Students on the March: The Cases of Mexico and Colombia," *Sociology of Education*, XXXVII (Spring 1964), 214–215.

12. A simple point scale allocated 4 points to those who "definitely" chose the more instrumental job, 2 points to those who "probably" would make this decision, and 0 points to those who "definitely" or "probably" would choose the job offering great social prestige. Similarly, students were awarded 2 points for any one or 4 points for choosing any two of the following: opportunity to increase professional knowledge, to gain professional recognition, or to work directly with people to improve their life situations. Zero points were given in each case where students chose social prestige, income or political freedom as primary job characteristics. In the final question students "definitely" deciding to work with the more competent professor were given 4 points, those "probably" working with him were allocated 2 points, and those who did not want to work with him 0 points. On the basis of this scoring procedure 12 points were the maximum which any student could secure. Those with this total and their peers who achieved 10 points were rated as "high" professionals. Students with 8 points were placed in the "mid" professional category and those with 6 or less in the "low" category.

13. See R. P. Atcon, *op. cit.*; and J. P. Harrison, *op. cit.*

14. The question posed to the students was: There is a probability of a student strike in your faculty for what you consider to be a justifiable reason. You are an officer on the Centro de Alumnos and can have an important voice in the decision to strike or not. At the same time you are involved in several interesting and important courses in which you are receiving valuable professional training. You would vote: a. definitely to strike; b. probably to strike; c. probably not to strike; d. definitely not to strike.

15. *El Mercurio*, January 18, 1964.

16. Similar changes also seem to be occurring in other Latin American countries. E. Wight Bakke reports that in Mexico and Colombia, the concept of the university "as a servant of the people" has been growing. "In both countries the medical students spend a substantial portion of their final year carrying medical service to a particular village which lacks such service." There have been attempts, supported by the medical students, to include other students in this type of program. *Op. cit.*, pp. 213–214.

17. J. Raffo, "Problemas de la enseñanza," *Cuadernos médico-Sociales*, IV (December 1963), especially p. 38.

18. Engineering students frequently point to the fact that the president of Chile from 1958–1964 was an engineer by training and that his entire first cabinet was made up of engineers.

19. J. Fischer, "The University Student in South and Southeast Asia," *Minerva*, II (Autumn 1963), 52.

20. S. Dedijer, "Underdeveloped Science in Underdeveloped Countries," *Minerva*, II (Autumn 1963), 79.

21. Within a period of only a few months in late 1963 and early 1964, a rash of articles appeared heralding the importance of basic research. These also spoke approvingly of the University's initiating study in scientific investigation and a physics course for secondary school teachers. For example, see *El Mercurio*, October 29, 1963, November 30, 1963, and January 21, 1964.

22. These observations derive from lengthy conversations with members of the Institute's staff; these scientists are an impressive group from the standpoint of education background, commitment to their work, and desire to remain in their country. Confirmation of their statements came from enlightening discussions with persons knowledgeable of the thinking of officials in the highest university councils.

23. *El Mercurio*, October 14, 1963; October 18, 1963; May 23, 1964. Emigration of trained professionals also plagues highly industrialized societies. See *Time*, February 21, 1964, p. 46.

24. S. Dedijer, *op. cit.*, p. 68.

Indian Students: Attitudes
and Activities

—————————— Part V ——————————

Professional, Scientific, and Intellectual Students in India

METTA SPENCER

14

Studies of the political orientations of students in the universities of several different countries have shown a rather consistent pattern of political allegiance, participation and information when one compares students in different majors or faculties. In general the leftist students (who are often more politically active and better informed than are the conservative students) are found in the humanities and social sciences. The evidence has been summarized by Seymour Martin Lipset, who comments on the Indian universities that commerce is the major studied by the most conservative partisans, while students of "sociology, economics and anthropology" incline more toward the left. Science students are in between.[1] Evidence from the National University of Colombia shows the faculties of Law and Economics leading "education, psychology and sociology," who in turn lead the natural sciences in radicalism.[2] One minor departure from the pattern of highly active social sciences was reported in a study of three faculties in the University of Buenos Aires, where Silvert and Bonilla show that students in the exact sciences and even medicine are more *active* in politics than the economics students, in that they more often participated in street rallies or party meetings. However, the most *radical* faculty in Buenos Aires is letters and philosophy, which includes social science departments.[3] In Mexico, also, the economics faculty of the National University is by far the most leftist, with law second. The responses of commerce, engineering, and medical students are much more conservative.[4]

Data from universities in Teheran, Pakistan and the United States show greater leftism among humanities and social science students than among scientists and professionals. In Teheran, literature and law students lead the others in leftism with 56 per cent and 60 per cent leftist responses respectively, as contrasted with engineering, which included only 23 per cent leftists.[5] A similar relationship was discovered in the 1952 survey of eleven U.S. universities, in which humanities students led the others in leftism (even though in those McCarthy-era days their "leftism" was a timid variety); engineers, business administration, education and agriculture students were more conservative.[6] Further, the Pakistan survey of four universities in 1963 showed humanities and social science students leading in leftism, with science in the middle and the professions least leftist.[7] Likewise, in his study of Puerto Rican students' identity, Soares controlled for father's education and found substantial differences in leftism remaining when he compared intellectual, science and professional students. Intellectuals were most and professionals least leftist.[8] In most cases the radical partisans are also the most active and informed students.[9] This is true in the case of the Indian students. The various majors generally show similar variations for leftism, participation and information.

Several fields of study share similar "intellectual or cognitive styles of performance," and we shall group the students from the Indian sample into three different categories according to nature of the appropriate cognitive performance. We shall designate commerce, law, military, and other professional students as "professional," students in the humanities and so-

TABLE 1.

Major and Leftism, Participation, Information, in India. BSSR, 1952.
Per Cent of Students in Different Fields of Study Who Are Leftist,
Who Participate in Politics, and Who Are Well Informed about Politics

Fields of Study	Leftist	Participate	Informed
Commerce (104)	24	51	42
Science (461)	31	39	49
English (59)	48	51	44
Other languages (24)	59	55	34
Political science (94)	44	75	65
Sociology, economics, anthro. (193)	48	57	55
Law (136)	45	55	55
History (55)	55	58	60
Other professions (276)	28	40	44
Philosophy, psychology, education (236)	29	49	40

cial sciences will be considered as "intellectuals," while the remaining students are all "science" students.[10]

Because in India the leftist students tend to be the best informed and most politically dedicated of all students, we shall be interested in examining this constellation of "politicized leftism" as the dependent variable to be explained. Hence, we shall employ a very comprehensive measure of politicization constructed from many items relating to party and international bloc allegiance, interest in participation in politics, information about politics, as well as extreme attitudes of discontent with the political responsiveness of public officials. The scale reflects not mere leftism, but active, protest-oriented, highly informed political involvement. Even grouped in this gross fashion, some minor differences appear. Professionals are 21 per cent, scientists 22 per cent and intellectuals 28 per cent politicized leftists. This is typical of the pattern found in the other countries—the "intellectual" cognitive style, as exemplified by social science and humanities students, is associated with radical activism, with science and professional students following in that order.

To what can this pattern of variation be attributed? At least three modes of explanation occur in speculative discussions but have rarely, if ever, been subjected to systematic examination. The first mode is the explanation in terms of the different pre-existing *personality* traits of students who enter different fields of study, the second is the explanation in terms of differing *characteristics of the roles* for which the academic disciplines prepare students, and the third is in terms of *differential recruitment* from different social classes, regions, or backgrounds into the professional, scientific, and humanistic or social scientific fields of study.

Personality, Politics, and Field of Study

The first explanatory mode points primarily to personality variables—emotional predispositions, cognitive styles, basic values, and the like, which presumably antedate and "fit" both the field of study and the political style which the person selects. Assuredly, there are important differences between the personalities of students in the different academic disciplines, and these differences do exist before the field of study is selected. Unfortunately, no specific link has been demonstrated between the traits characteristic of the different fields and particular political orientations. Any satisfactory argument in the first mode should demonstrate that the constellation of traits or attitudes characterizing students in particular departments, when controlled, explains away the association between political viewpoint and academic field.

The difficulty here lies in discerning the relevant personality characteristics which precede and guide the decision as to occupational choice and politics. Morris Rosenberg, after reporting that Ginzberg's search for personality determinants of occupational choice was fruitless, nevertheless points to several significant attitudinal sets which occur differentially among students preparing for different occupations. Faith in people, for example, is greater among American students who plan to enter "people-oriented" occupations, who tend to "move toward" people, while it is lower among business students, who mistrust people, "move against" people, seek extrinsic rewards for their work but who have high administrative skill. A strong self-expressive orientation is found among students of the arts and sciences, who "move away" from people.[11] The attitude of faith in people appears to be a significant aspect of personality, relevant both for occupation and for democratic values.

Goldschmid has also demonstrated that personality differences existing at the time students enter the university can be used to predict choice between humanistic or scientific pursuits. He finds science students more interested in matters of practical, immediate application; he finds them prudent, conventional, with strict control of impulse, a restricted range of interests, introverted, logical, valuing form and structure, impersonal, with critical habits of thinking. Humanities students, on the other hand, value personal independence, freedom from rules and constraints; they are self-centered, expressive, anxiety-prone. They have wide interests, are responsive to social and political affairs, seek social contacts, like innovation and ambiguity, and think in an intuitive cognitive mode.[12] This view of their social responsiveness conflicts with Rosenberg's assertion that humanists "move away" from people, but Rosenberg is comparing them to social-service occupations, while Goldschmid includes social-service persons in the humanities and compares them with scientists.

Bereiter and Freedman say of American students that social scientists are generally the most liberal, followed by humanists and natural scientists, while engineering and agriculture students are consistently the least liberal. Liberalism is usually correlated with intelligence, but engineers regularly are most intelligent and least liberal. Applied fields are conservative.[13] Whether the explanation be "intelligence" or the different personality characteristics that are found among students, it is possible that pre-existing attitudes explain partisanship.

Roles, Politics, and Field of Study

The second mode of explanation is also plausible—that is the interpretation by reference to differences in the roles for which the academic departments prepare students. The importance of "anticipatory socialization" phenomena has been demonstrated in Rosenberg's study of U. S. students. He found, for example, that students shifted their values over time to fit those typical of the occupation to which they were committed.[14] There are important differences in the types of careers and behaviors appropriate to scientists, intellectuals and professionals. Not only are different opportunities for reward open to graduates of those fields, but there are different expectations as to the boundaries of legitimate concern, the spheres of competence proper for people in different fields.[15] The different opportunities and exceptions as to *future* professional roles may account for some of the variation in, say, preferences for politics relating to the redistribution of income and opportunity. Seymour Martin Lipset has noted,

Students engaged in the courses of study which entail something like apprenticeship for a definite profession, e.g. engineering, medicine and preparation for secondary school teaching, where employment prospects are fair, are likely to be less rebellious than students in courses of study without determinate destinations and in which the pattern of instruction does not require personal contact between teachers and students. The most insecure of all are those without specific aims or prospects, who will have to compete for ... inconsequential posts.[16]

It is reasonable to assume that persons preparing for the less privileged professions will be more likely to entertain ideas of political reform and that the different political styles between major fields of study proceed from the awareness of the differential opportunities attached to the respective roles.

A second aspect of the mode of explanation stressing role differences refers not so much to differences in privilege attached to academic roles as to differences in "proper scope of competence" attributed to such roles. We see in many areas an increasing "professionalization" of fields of study which had previously been public domain. Just as in Goldschmid's study humanities students engaged in a wide variety of interests, the "intellectuals" who emerge from a humanistic education have a very wide latitude of intellectual territory; the "functional specificity" of the intellectual's role is considerably less than that of the scientist and even less than that of the professional. The limits of relevance and of specialized expertise are quite hazy in the case of the intellectual so that engagement in political or social controversy may be seen as an integral aspect of the role. Apart from the concern with aesthetic matters, the great task of the intellectual is social criticism, the defining of new social issues. Some intellectuals do remain "detached," as Rosenberg commented, while those who enter highly "people-oriented jobs" draw upon their faith in people as a primary resource for their work. The archetypical intellectual, however, is concerned with human values of the widest variety, considering other people from a subjective point of view (rather than instrumentally or objectively, as Rosenberg's businessman does) while still retaining a critical posture, looking for significant problems. The dual function of social empathy and social criticism makes it probable that the intellectual will press hard for social changes and challenge politically conservative institutions. By contrast, the professional focuses on small discrete areas.[17]

Differential Recruitment, Politics, and Field of Study

The third mode of explanation of the differences in political performance of students in different departments alludes to the differential recruitment patterns of the sexes, age levels, regions and social classes into those departments. The students in different majors do, often enough, differ in social origins. It is a bit of poetic license to designate the social science and humanities students in India as "intellectual," for in fact they are rather frequently students who were not successful in obtaining places in professional or scientific departments because of low intellectual qualifications. The intellectuals are, on the whole, older than professional students and *much* older than the elite science students. Intellectuals come more often from rural regions, are more often married, non-Hindu, female, impoverished, and more often live in private lodgings than do professional and science students. Not all these differences are correlated with leftist activism, however, and therefore cannot be invoked as explaining the relationship with fields of study. In fact, the women students are slightly more conservative than the men, and religion and marital status are not particularly related to political involvement. Nevertheless, the different concentrations of students from situations relevant to politics may, indeed, account for some of the differences between majors.

Testing the Explanations

Although no definite or methodologically ideal treatment of these matters is possible with the materials afforded by the Indian survey of university students, it is nevertheless possible to make an approach toward ascertaining the value of the first and third modes of explanation. We cannot assess here the significance of explanations based on anticipatory socialization for special roles, but we can in a sense add weight to it by the method of eliminating alternative explanations. We must establish the degree to which students in different disciplines are engaged in radical left-wing politics and thereupon determine whether these differences may be explained away by the predisposing social circumstances or by certain personality orientations which also predispose one toward radical political involvement. *To the extent that controlling personality or the demographic background differences reduces the differential degree of politicized leftism between the intellectuals, scientists, and professionals, we shall conclude that the first or third mode of explanation, respectively, is adequate.* We have no measure allowing us to control role differences to see whether the second mode of explanation would account for the differences between the politics of different majors.

Our analysis employs data collected by the American University and Lucknow University in 1952, through the Bureau of Social Science Research. Respondents were 2,044 students of eleven Indian universities and the questionnaire design was based on that used by Cornell researchers in the study of eleven U. S. universities.[18] Besides items bearing upon social origins and current life situations, there were questions about political preferences, level of information and very general attitudes, such as those Rosenberg used to measure "faith in people." The attitudinal items were treated to factor analyses and the factors which emerged were examined for the correlations with the politicization scale.[19] Those dimensions which seemed to represent general personality orientations and which were correlated to any appreciable degree with politicization were grouped together to form a multi-dimensional "psychological predisposition" variable, which, if held constant, might be expected to reduce the association between major field of study and politicization, if indeed (as asserted by the first mode of explanation) those psychological attributes are the primary source of that association. Such a composite variable is only useful for this special purpose; it is wholly meaningless as a measure of any theoretical construct except "those attitudes which are correlated with leftist activism," which is hardly a trait of great theoretical clarity.

To obtain a similar composite variable for controlling demographic variables of the third explanatory mode, we selected several "background" variables known to correlate with leftism. Controlling that composite variable might be expected to reduce the association between major and po-

liticization if (as asserted in the third explanatory mode) differential recruitment from different social circumstances accounts for the apparent
association between field of study and politics.

On the other hand, if neither the psychological nor the predisposing social circumstances reduce the association, the second mode of explanation
(anticipatory socialization) gains a certain weight, although the first and
third modes are not ruled out in any conclusive sense, inasmuch as other
personality or social variables not entering our measures may be of decisive
importance. The multi-dimensional variables used here were not derived
from theoretical considerations.

Of the two varimax and oblimax factor analyses, one treated items relevant to modernism and the other items particularly relevant to authoritarianism. Eight factors appeared in each analysis, and for present purposes
we are interested only in using the relevant factor scores as variables to
construct a composite psychological predisposition index, which, if controlled, tests in a very general way the first mode of explaining the association between major and leftist activism.

From the traditionalism analysis we utilized the factor scores from five
factors and from the authoritarianism analysis we used three. The dimensions entering the personality composite index were these eight: (1) A factor which we call "traditionalism" which accounted for .13 of the total
varimax communality, and which had highest loadings (.52) on disapproval of common social relations with different communal groups and disapproval of free association for men and women. (2) "Trust," a factor very
similar to Rosenberg's "faith in people," accounting for .11 of the total
communality, had highest loadings (.75) on agreement that people can be
trusted and that they help others. (3) "Will power," a factor accounting
for .11 of the total communality, was composed mostly of the agreement
(loading .99) that will power is the most important quality for success. (4)
"Non-fatalism," which we titled a factor which accounted for .10 of the
communality, and which had its highest loading (—.98) on the view that
fate is the cause of most things that happen to one. (5) "Non-religiosity,"
a factor accounting for .10 of the communality, had its highest loadings
(.68) on the expression of no need for religious faith. (6) A factor which
we called "limited respect for authority," accounting for .09 of the communality, represented (.99) the belief that respect for superiors was not
the most important quality for success. From the authoritarianism factor
analysis, (7) "Emotional well-being," a factor accounting for .14 of the

communality, was composed largely of items relating to infrequency of upset stomach, nervousness, and the like. (Loadings were about .53 for these items.) (8) "Authoritarian militancy," a factor accounting for .14 of the total communality, had highest loading (.44) on the agreement that insult to national honor must always be punished, even if it leads to war, and on the belief that children should be taught to obey and should be treated more strictly. In no case were the factors which had high loadings on one factor also important components of another factor, although that is not important for the present anyway.

Factors 1 through 4 and factor 7 were negatively correlated with politicization, while factors 5, 6, and 8 were positively correlated. The other factors were not put into the variable, because of low correlation with politicization and because they accounted for too small a proportion of the communality.

We found, then, that politicized leftist-oriented Indian students have modern values on caste, family, and communal relations, are mistrustful of the good will and helpfulness of most other persons, skeptical that "will power" has much efficacy in bringing about success, fatalistic (not in the traditional sense of "fate" but in the conviction that "social and economic" conditions beyond one's own control" cause more things than one's own efforts do).[20] They are less often religious and do not regard "respect for superiors" as important for success. They report more symptoms of psychological distress and more authoritarian values in matters of child discipline and military retaliation than do less ideologically committed students. The profile outlined by these factors is a rather angular silhouette!

The composite demographic variable was constructed from five items. The graduate students were more politicized than undergraduates, the students from rural areas more so than those who lived in cities, those who lived in hostels or private lodging more so than those who lived with parents or other relatives, and those attending Calcutta, Travancore, Osmania, or Bombay Universities more so than students attending universities in other regions. On the basis of these facts we were able to control the composite "social predisposition" of the students.[21]

When the relationship between major and politicized leftism was examined, controlling first the psychological composite variable and then the demographic social-background variable, we found that *neither of the composite variables reduced the association.* Further, although there was some disproportion in the number of "psychologically predisposed" students in the humanities and social sciences, there was no evidence of differential recruitment from consistently predisposed social circumstances into the different academic fields.

We must conclude that the variables introduced as "plausible specimens" of the third explanatory mode (differential social recruitment) are not ade-

TABLE 2.

Percentage of Politicized Leftism among Academic Fields, Controlling Pre-disposing Social Background (Percentage of Politicized Leftists)

Low Predisposition for Leftism in Social Background			High Predisposition for Leftism in Social Background		
Professional	Intellectual	Scientific	Professional	Intellectual	Scientific
(174)*	(209)	(154)	(214)	(255)	(181)
21%	26%	23%	22%	31%	25%

* Numbers in parentheses indicate size of sample from which percentages were computed.

TABLE 3.

Politicized Leftism among Academic Fields, Controlling Psychological Predisposition

Low Psychological Predisposition for Leftism			High Psychological Predisposition for Leftism		
Professional	Intellectual	Scientific	Professional	Intellectual	Scientific
(365)*	(378)	(330)	(85)	(134)	(70)
16%	23%	20%	34%	47%	36%

* Numbers in parentheses indicate size of sample from which percentages were computed.

quate to account for the variation in politicization between the different academic branches. A similar inference must follow from inspection of Table 3, the table which was constructed to test the first explanatory mode, the "personality" approach. Hence, at least those personal values and traits which are available in the present questionnaire and which are related to political style do not account for the association in question.

When the distinguishing psychological (or general attitudinal) characteristics are held constant the major continues to differentiate the politically engaged leftists from the non-politicized, although the attitudinal factors themselves make more difference than the major ones. Nevertheless, among those whose psychological "bent" is fitted for radical activism, the field of study has a stronger influence on actual political involvement than it does among the student sample as a whole. The direction of association among the fields of study remains the same—intellectuals are consistently most politicized and professionals least. The psychological differences between intellectuals are considerably more decisive for their political involvement than for professional and science students. That is, the traditional, religious, non-authoritarian, trusting, deferential, emotionally secure humanities students who believe in the causal efficacy of will power and one's own efforts are far less politicized than are the other intellectual students. One could argue that the intellectual is situationally free to engage in politics if he is temperamentally so inclined, while the students of professional and scientific subjects are inhibited by the limitations of the roles, regardless of whether or not their psychological characteristics would make political activity appealing.

Personality dimensions do seem to have important connections with political style, but the fields of study also have an independent effect which is not explained away by pre-existing psychological or social differences—at least not by those which we have introduced here. The social background composite variable does prove telling in Table 4 in specifying the connections between the psychological and the political.

The kind of social situation the student is in has a different effect depending upon his ideological or psychological "set"—so much so that the student whose psyche is non-political according to our concocted personal-

TABLE 4.

Politicized Leftism among Academic Fields, Controlling Psychological and Social Predispositions (Percentage of Politicized Leftists)

Low Social Predisposition for Leftism					
Low Psychological Predisposition			High Psychological Predisposition		
Professional	Intellectual	Scientific	Professional	Intellectual	Scientific
(131)*	(123)	(115)	(25)	(40)	(21)
18%	26%	23%	24%	33%	33%
High Social Predisposition for Leftism					
Low Psychological Predisposition			High Psychological Predisposition		
Professional	Intellectual	Scientific	Professional	Intellectual	Scientific
(152)	(143)	(129)	(40)	(66)	(36)
15%	22%	19%	42%	52%	39%

* Numbers in parentheses indicate size of sample from which percentages were computed.

ity scale, is negatively (albeit insignificantly) responsive toward the social effects which predispose normally toward leftist activism. To put the matter in a way which is more congenial to sociologists, the psychological orientation which a student develops is decisive in the development of political style, and especially so for students whose situation in the social structure would normally favor this activism. Just as we saw that the intellectual student was "free" to engage in politics if he found the idea temperamentally appealing, while science and professional students lacked the open option, we also see a similar effect in the case of the students whose "social background" is conducive to radical activism; for them much more depends upon their personal orientations. For other students, the social background sets limits on what personal inclinations can do, or at least the tables lend themselves to this speculation. Actually, only by introducing all these variables simultaneously do we reveal the magnitude of the differences which each of the variables makes. The effect of social background is greater here than before because it is specific for those with high psychological predisposition.

Within each group the intellectual students remain the most politicized of all and in all except one group the professionals are the least politicized. The social and psychological dimensions have an effect on leftist political activity, but academic discipline has its own independent effect and is not explained away by these variables. One can still speculate about why this is so: possibly the divergent role expectations are significant. Of course, we have not exhausted all possible psychological and social background factors which could conceivably explain the association away. The field is still open for explanations of the first and third modes.

Conclusion

Politicized leftism was found to be high among students whose personality orientations and values were modern, mistrustful (or lacking "faith in people"), who regarded "will power" and one's own efforts as causally ineffective, who were non-religious, and who considered respect for superiors inconsequential for success, who were emotionally unstable and authoritarian with regard to child discipline and military aggression. Such active leftists often came from rural areas and lived as impoverished graduate students in hostels or private lodgings at Calcutta, Travancore, Osmania, or Bombay universities. Nevertheless, holding all these facts constant, the kind of academic major in which they were involved made a substantial difference in the political style which they adopted. Students in the social sciences and humanities were more politicized and more leftist than were science students, who in turn were more so than the students preparing for professions. Especially among those whose social circumstances were normally conducive to politicized leftism, everything turned upon their personality orientations; demographic facts were by no means single-handed determinants.

Personality characteristics, social background and academic major were significant independently for the development of political behavior among Indian students. The influence of the major did not stem from differential recruitment of psychologically or demographically predisposed students. Quite possibly, anticipatory socialization for different levels of social status and different types of cognitive endeavor accounts for the differences which intellectual, scientific, and professional students showed in acquiescing or protesting against their political condition.[22]

Notes

1. Seymour Martin Lipset, Chapter 1, this book. This note presents information from several different countries. Indian data are from Bureau of Social Science Research, *Political Attitudes of Indian Students* (Washington: The American University, 1955), p. 47.
2. Kenneth N. Walker, "Determinants of Castro Support among Latin American University Students," *Berkeley Journal of Sociology*, 1964, p. 47.
3. Kalman Silvert and Frank Bonilla, *Education and the Social Meaning of Development; A Preliminary Statement* (N.Y.: American Universities Field Staff, 1961), pp. 127–128, as cited in Lipset, *op. cit.*
4. *A Study of Opinions of University Students in Mexico* (Mexico City: Industrial Research Associates, 1964), pp. 16–19, 20–43, as cited in Lipset, *op. cit.*
5. The Teheran Survey was conducted by EMNID, a German Research Organization in 1963. N 300. Leftism here was measured by admiration for U.S.S.R. and dislike of private ownership.
6. Data from Harvard, Wayne, UCLA, Fisk, Wesleyan, Cornell, Michigan, Texas, Dartmouth, Yale, North Carolina were collected by Goldsen et al., researchers at Cornell.
7. EMNID also conducted this survey in Pakistan, sampling from Karachi, Lahore, Peshawar, and Dacca Universities, 1963.
8. G. A. D. Soares, "The Politics of Intellectuals," in S. M. Lipset and Aldo Solari, eds., *Elites and Development in Latin America* (New York: Oxford University Press, 1967).
9. See especially, G. A. D. Soares, Chapter 5, this book. Soares argues that radicalism of either the right or the left is associated with heightened political

involvement and that both the radicalism and partisan activism stem from the student's relatively well-integrated self-image as both citizen and student.

10. A happier procedure would be to group according to the respondent's self-identification as professional, intellectual, or scientist rather than according to the assessment of the researcher about the nature of the majors. Soares found considerable diversity in self-identification among students of the same fields of study. Social scientists, in particular, have the option of identifying as scientists, professionals or as intellectuals. Unfortunately, subjective classification is not available for Indian students.

11. Morris Rosenberg, *Occupations and Values* (Glencoe: The Free Press, 1957), pp. 34–48.

12. Marcel Lucien Goldschmid, "The Prediction of College Major in the Sciences and Humanities by Means of Personality Tests" (unpublished Ph.D. dissertation, Department of Psychology, University of California, Berkeley, 1965). Goldschmid's procedures were precise; he tested his subjects by psychological inventories and established the position of the major by a panel of judges ordering the fields on humanistic-scientific continua. Correlations between personality and major proved significant.

13. Carl Bereiter and Mervin B. Freedman, "Fields of Study and the People in Them," in Nevitt Sanford, ed., *The American College* (New York: Wiley, 1964), p. 568. The greater "conservatism" of the applied fields can hardly be attributed wholly to the lower socio-economic status of such students, for in many aspects of political policy, lower classes are not conservative.

14. Rosenberg, *op. cit.*, p. 83.

15. The privileged and satisfied standing of professionals is discussed in S. M. Lipset and M. Schwartz, "The Politics of Professionals," in H. M. Vollmer and D. L. Mills, eds., *Professionalization* (Englewood Cliffs: Prentice-Hall, 1966), pp. 299–309. This is especially relevant in India, where the professional students have higher aspirations relative to their parent's income than intellectuals or scientists.

16. Lipset, *op. cit.* Political rebelliousness in the non-communist countries is usually synonymous with "leftism." We cannot demonstrate whether those academic groups which would be leftist here tend to be rightist or "Capitalistic" in the communist nations, as would be expected if political deviance stems from *any* protest against the status quo, whatever the status quo may be for the student.

17. G. A. D. Soares, "The Politics of Intellectuals," *op. cit.*

18. The Cornell research is reported in Rose Goldsen et al., *They Went to College* (Princeton: Van Nostrand, 1960), and in Rosenberg, *op. cit.* The Indian data were collected at Aligarh, Agra, Benares, Bombay, Calcutta, Delhi, Lucknow, Madras, Nagpur, Osmania, and Travancore (now Kerala) Universities. Stratification was made according to as many of the following variables as possible: academic class, major field, division of the university, and sex. Within each stratum sampling was random; each university was asked to obtain a given number of questionnaires proportional to its size. Normally,

questionnaires were administered to the students in groups. *Political Attitudes of Indian Students.*

19. The factor analyses were carried out by G. A. D. Soares with the research assistance of Marguerite McIntyre. I am pleased to have the opportunity to use factor scores in the present research. One methodological difficulty should be made explicit; we treat the attitudinal factors as personality or psychological traits, presuming their antecedent status. While other researchers have demonstrated that the effects would take place *whichever* came first (Rosenberg notes this, p. 22), we cannot do so here. One could, I suppose, interpret these attitudes as role-expectations instead of personality traits, as I have done.

20. In other factor analyses fatalism has been an attribute of the traditional rather than the modern orientation. It should be apparent from the Indian responses, however, that materialistic determinism is, for the moderns, just as compelling a philosophy as the traditional fatalism.

21. Because of interaction among the components, the composite social-background variable did not discriminate as well between politicized and non-politicized students as did the psychological composite variable. In fact, each of the individual components of this variable correlates as highly as does the variable.

22. I wish to thank the Institute of International Studies, University of California, Berkeley, for supporting my research.

Indiscipline and Student Leadership

in an Indian University

JOSEPH DIBONA

15

In India no subject has been of more compelling public concern than in-discipline among college and university students. Riots, mass protests, and violence are but the poignant index of the gulf separating emerging elites from incorporation into the social and political order of their nation. The assessment of what causes such disturbances varies greatly. With rare ex-ceptions, evaluations do not deal with specific cases, concrete in time and place, but attempt to relate the phenomenon to a general understanding of Indian society, history and culture.[1] This chapter attempts to contribute further to our understanding of student indiscipline through an analysis of student action and leadership on a single, north-Indian campus. Field re-search[2] for this study was conducted during 1963 and 1964 at the University of Allahabad, the locale of a number of student disturbances.

The Problem

At the time of Indian independence, there was an unquestioned acceptance of the dramatic link between universities and modernization, and substan-tial financial outlays were allocated to higher education in each of the Five-Year Plans.[3] Of the sum reserved for education, in the Third Plan 20 per cent was designated for higher education despite the disproportionately small number of students involved. In 1965–1966 primary through sec-ondary enrollments (ages 6-17) totaled 64 million while all university en-rollment was slightly over one million.

Despite high expectations and generous financial provision in terms of the limited resources of the country, there has been widespread dissatisfaction with the outcome—a succession of strikes, massive demonstrations to intimidate heads of institutions, pitched battles, disrupted examinations, and physical attacks on respected professors and administrators.[4]

Economic Explanations

Explanations of student indiscipline in India may be roughly organized under the three categories: economic, psycho-social and political. The economic explanations, inspired perhaps by McCully's thesis, maintain that the universities and the needs of the economy, when incongruent, develop stresses of which indiscipline is but a symptom.[5] Since the inception of the Indian university system in mid-nineteenth century and especially today, the instrumental, vocational view of education has been the accepted one.[6] What is rapidly changing, however, is the ratio of students to inadequate opportunities. The total college enrollment increased in four years (1950–1954) from 396,000 to 651,000. The result has been overcrowding, increasing failures as poorly equipped students flock to the colleges, and unemployment among the graduates.[7]

Of Majumdar's sample of Lucknow degree holders, 14 per cent were unemployed five years after graduation. Rao found between 60 per cent and 70 per cent of Delhi's poorest graduates (those with only "pass" degrees) employed eight years after graduation as minor clerks, a job designed to accommodate high school graduates. However, student expectations are based on the performance of past graduates, who invariably were able to go much further with the same academic qualification. This relentless devaluation of degrees mirrors the sluggish Indian economy and contributes to the student's frustration. The weakness of the hypothesis linking slow development to indiscipline, however, lies in the difficulty of demonstrating the relevance of unemployment to campus politics.

Psycho-Social Explanation

By far the more popular explanation of student indiscipline dwells on the social and psychological distance between the student and the teacher, as contrasted with the remote past when the *guru* personally guided the novice toward the realization of some shared transcendental reality. The teacher's loss of authority and prestige was found by the UGC Committee on Student Indiscipline as a crucial factor in the current situation.[8] During the rapid expansion of education many unqualified teachers entered the profession, and their presence has had a demoralizing effect on the student body. Recommended reforms invariably suggest that numbers be reduced, the student-teacher ratio be bettered and teachers encouraged, through monetary and other means, to spend more time with the students. Despite the best efforts for over a decade, the most apt description of the Indian campus remained, in the words of Chancal Sarkar, "Where the Demoralized teach the Disgruntled."[9]

Not only has the classic relationship between teacher and student been lost, but the whole hierarchical structure of Indian society, which formerly stressed caste seniority and the joint family as immutable values, has begun to erode.[10] Today the age of marriage is increasing in India and the campus is full of mature but unmarried boys and girls whose curiosity about each other is shocking to many adults. The testing of authority comes as a welcome relief from the rote memorization required for passing examinations, as Edward Shils has eloquently explained:

A mind which cannot attach itself to intellectual objects, a libido which is prevented from attaching itself to sexual objects, a spirit which resents the burden of familial discipline and resists incorporation into modern impersonal adult institutions—what direction can it take except rebellion, blind causeless rebellion?[11]

Political Explanations

Perhaps the most appealing explanation of student unrest lies in its relationship to the larger political movements that have transformed India from colonialism to democracy. As early as 1905 students burned Lord Curzon in effigy and boycotted college examinations as a protest against the partition of Bengal.[12] Later, Gandhi himself toured northern India convincing students that their educational institutions were somehow anti-national. In 1936 the All-India Student Federation was formed with the help of such leaders as Mohammad Ali Jinnah and Pandit Nehru, whose program called for the replacement of English by the vernacular languages, fee reduction and student representation on the governing bodies of universities.[13] By the time of the Quit-India Movement of the 1940's, students all over the country were active in promoting the ends of the Congress through demonstrations and protest marches and strikes against their schools. S. M. Lipset and others suggest that the early agitational tradition of students in developing countries has persisted into the present.[14]

A second aspect of the role of politics and indiscipline are such matters as teacher factions, the intrusion of local politicians into university affairs and the support of student leaders by organized national parties. In a country where literacy is still minimal, a wide gulf separates the university student from the mass of the rural peasantry. He is spiritually and intellectually very close to the locus of power and, if ambitious, may aspire to a political career. Since recruitment to important party positions is ill developed, one of the few channels of advancement comes through activities on campus. One vice-chancellor criticized the "... craving for power in student organizations of those who seek to obtain concessions of all types or interfere in matters which do not pertain to their sphere . . ."[15] and called for the abolition of the student Unions which have become notorious as centers of agitation.[16] A survey of Poona University student opinion found the majority of the students holding that political parties were responsible for student indiscipline.[17]

Students may deliberately foment struggles in order to gain recognition by established leaders, but genuine ideological struggles also develop on campus. Immediately after independence, leftist parties were most powerful on the Indian campus. Sondhi has said that the Communist party was the only one that had an attractive program for youth.[18] This has begun to change recently and a rightist swing has now become evident in some parts of India.[19] Congress, although organizationally inactive on the student front, remains the dominant political party in India as a whole. As opposition parties gain adherents on campus, this source of conflict can easily increase.

Due to the factional nature of state and local politics in India, the universities have often become battlegrounds in caste or regional alignments. Many elections for campus office will have implications for the larger political struggle going on in the state legislature. The campus then becomes a microcosm of the special caste or other interest divisions that are vying for control of the state government. In most states the Governor (as Chancellor of the university) acts according to the advice of the state government. In order to put pressure on the government or intimidate a particular faction, the student groups are a powerful weapon in the arsenal of political intrigue.

Ostensibly the Lucknow student agitation in 1959 was to protest the moral turpitude of a Dean who was expected to be advanced to Vice-Chancellor. The student leaders freely admitted that they had been advised by a powerful ex-Minister seeking revenge against the Dean who had been one of his opponents. At Aligarh University, historically the center of Muslim nationalism in India, there was a communal faction seeking to maintain the particularistic quality of the university. The student Union elections there were fought in 1961 on outright religious lines, and riots resulted in 10 dead and 43 wounded.

The most publicized instance of collusion between political faction and student group has been Banaras Hindu University, where the Report of the 1957 Enquiry Committee found the university to be a "hot bed of intrigue, nepotism, corruption and even crime," and named the dominant "Eastern Uttar Pradesh" teacher-politicians as the real menace to campus peace.[20] Before the recommendations of the committee could be promulgated, the students attacked the home of the Vice-Chancellor and also a local newspaper which was not sufficiently sympathetic to their demands. Based on this incident, Weiner wrote:

The agitation at Banaras Hindu University suggests that close faculty-student relations do not ensure a disciplined and orderly university when factional conflicts divide the faculty or separate the faculty from the university authorities.[21]

Students, when aware of their unwitting role behind the façade of conventional student-demand rhetoric, often become demoralized and lose faith in all ideals.[22] One solution that has been advanced calls for the elimination of all elections on campus.[23]

History of the Institution

It is evident from the above discussion that little agreement exists concerning either the nature or cause of student indiscipline. Hypotheses must necessarily be built up from a firm knowledge of local conditions both in India and elsewhere. As a means of testing this general orientation, the present study of indiscipline at a single north-Indian university is undertaken.

Probably the Northern sections of India have had more student disturbances than others. And of the North probably the most populous state of India, U.P. with 73 million persons, has had the most. It is, of course, difficult to say which university has had the most "indiscipline" but, if informal opinion were assessed, Allahabad would not be far from the top. Over the years it has acquired happier associations as well. It has a reputation for "autonomy," has often fiercely resisted governmental interference in its internal affairs, and has produced some of India's greatest intellects.

When Allahabad was established in 1887, it did no teaching but instead set syllabi, affiliated colleges in an area of thousands of square miles, examined students and granted degrees. The institution was primarily an examining body, did no teaching and required no buildings. The Vice-Chancellor ran the entire establishment out of a small office with one assistant. The governing body of the new university included some Indians, but its affairs were dominated by Englishmen, the English language, and subjects inspired by Oxford and Cambridge precedent.

The first students came from the urban middle classes and quickly gave Allahabad a reputation for success in the all important Indian Civil Service examination. As an elite institution, it attracted the most highly motivated persons in the population and ensured a kind of socialization best suited to life in a dependent colony. There was the strong vocational bias, but there was also the internalization of new values such as impersonal justice, merit as opposed to caste, and a recognition of the rights of the individual. The carriers of these concepts, in turn, created a new generation of minds which today shape the forward thrust of Indian development.

After World War I, the Sadler Universities Commission formulated reforms for all Indian universities. At a time when more and more Indian participation in government was anticipated, it was clear that the college system was inadequate for the close supervision and moral indoctrination of students. For this reason Sadler recommended the formation of universities which not only examined but taught, and in which there were students and teachers living in close association. Allahabad gave up its affiliated colleges to the newly formed Agra University, acquired a campus, and built hostels for the students. Native control began, but with continued elitism. "Everyone," said the new Vice-Chancellor, G. N. Jha,

claimed it almost as a right that the first place in every examination should be won by an Allahabad student and everyone who passed out from here felt sure that he should be either a judge of the High Court or a leader of the Bar or, at least, the Vice-Chancellor of the university.[24]

The Indian Civil Service, "the steel frame of Empire," was directly recruited most frequently from Allahabad, and the generalist demands of that vocation formed the ethos of the pre-independence institution.[25] Science, commerce, technology, empirical and entrepreneureal values were ignored during that period. A sympathy and rapport with the English developed here to its highest degree, and it is no surprise to learn that A. N. Jha, the Vice-Chancellor who ruled until independence, was no friend of the nationalists and their agitational politics. Allahabad was a place where liberals, who believed in moving gradually to freedom through constitutional means, could feel at home—a place of tree-shaded hostels and cricket and tennis lawns.

As the number of students increased, the support from the government and the quality of the school began to decline during the depression of the 1930's. The tutorial gave way to the crowded lecture hall. No new hostels were built, and the mass of new students became commuters with little interest or loyalty to the old traditions of the university. The system of finance also changed from a system of block grants which ensured a modicum of autonomy to a yearly scrutiny of each and every budget item by the Education Minister. More important, as many new teachers entered, a Kayasth[26] faction arose to challenge the Brahmin hegemony, and each election, for even minor posts, became a battle royal between these two groups.

Large numbers of students were now coming from poorer homes where they had not learned English well, and for the first time a pro-Hindi agitation developed during the 1930's.[27] The creation of new universities in Lucknow, Aligarh, Nagpur, Agra, and Banaras meant that students had no need to travel to Allahabad for their education, and the recruitment pattern tended to draw more from the economically depressed rural region of Eastern Uttar Pradesh.[28]

The first Kayasth Vice-Chancellor who took office in 1946 was supported by both factions. But the subsequent elections, dominated by local teachers, became so acrimonious that they threatened the stability of the school. Changes in the method of selecting the Vice-Chancellor were introduced which gave more power to the state and central government at the expense of the university's autonomy. The university has tried, and it still continues to do well in the national competitive examinations although the universities of Delhi, Madras, and Punjab are now supplying more recruits to the prestigious Indian Civil Service than Allahabad. English remains the prestige language on campus although Hindi is better understood by the students. Most of the undergraduate classes are now in Hindi, and examinations are increasingly written in the *devanagri* script. The older intellectuals seem least able to accommodate to the masses of rural youth inundating the classrooms.

Varieties of Indiscipline

Indiscipline may be a useful device for studying more pervasive change in Indian society since universities more acutely reflect changing social pressures than other institutions. In India, political structures have been greatly transformed since the colonial era, while the family, especially in the villages, has been altered but slightly. The universities have changed both greatly and not at all. Structurally, they are the same institutions they were in the nineteenth century, but the social composition is entirely different.

To define indiscipline, many instances of indiscipline at the University of Allahabad were examined and organized into the following five categories: (1) Breaches of minor university rules (instances of this might be walking on the grass or shouting in corridors); (2) Student efforts to promote their interest as students (this would include fee reductions, changes in examinations and provision of water coolers); (3) Conflicts with townspeople usually over some real or imagined disregard of student status; (4) Instances when national politics have inspired students to action (this was true at the time of the freedom struggle as well as when the Chinese invaded India); (5) Student action as an extension of teacher or political factional conflicts on campus.

Breaches of minor university rules. In the nineteenth century the teachers from Oxford and Cambridge who came out to the East for colonial service took their socializing tasks seriously. The devotion and service of these early pedagogues inspired abject adulation and conformity in some students, but touched others not at all. Mr. Gordon, an early mathematics teacher, for example, was considered an "utter failure." He could not manage the class and was teased by catcalls. During the annual Lawn Party, students would descend like a tide on the sweets as the teachers tried vainly to maintain order. Professor Jennings, as Principal in 1913, strictly fined students who were found walking on the lawns.[29]

Similar incidents are defined as "indiscipline" today at Allahabad. The difference is that now such minor infractions are seldom punished, for it is difficult to make charges stick. The university must follow the rule of law in punishing a student. Witnesses must be presented, the accused must be given a chance to defend himself, and, in serious cases, the Executive Council itself must act. After all that, the student may still appeal to the High Court which has the original jurisdiction in such cases. Disciplining students can also be a dangerous prospect, especially if the Proctor chooses to make an example of a powerful student leader with the ability to mobilize others. In such an environment, the Proctor's office is effectively neutralized. There is no authority foolhardy enough to antagonize students by enforcing minor regulations.

Student efforts to promote their own interests. The degree is the *sine qua non* of academic achievement in India. For the poor, anything which may inhibit the acquisition of that coveted prize is certain to arouse anxiety, but the legal structure of the universities and the attitudes of teachers and politicians conspire to exclude students from concern with examinations, fees, syllabi, and courses—the facets of academic life most important for their success. The students are now willing to bring the force of their numbers to bear on such questions. As the Dean of one Law Faculty remarked, "I would not dare to limit admissions, it would mean endangering my life."

As early as 1898, there was an uproar over a paper set in the B.A. examination because it contained questions which were beyond the reduced course prescribed for the examination. The resultant agitation successfully brought a more lenient marking of the papers.

By now the problem is a perennial one and contributes to the awesome tenseness that descends on the campus during examination time. So long as the questions are within the bounds of the expected, there is no trouble. The difficulty arises, however, when teachers prepare questions which are no longer part of the syllabus. This can happen when questions are drawn (as is too often the case) from notes and old examinations without recourse to the most recent changes. Unfortunately for the student, paper setters are chosen on the basis of seniority, the most senior having first choice of the most lucrative jobs. These men may not actually be teaching the courses they are writing questions for and indeed just the reverse is thought to ensure greater impartiality. The whole enterprise is surrounded with incredible secrecy, and when the "mistake" occurs, there is no one to whom the students can appeal. At best they can walk out of the examination and at worst turn in a senseless fury and riot blindly against the whole educational system.

Conflicts with townspeople. In the early years of Indian universities, education prepared students for a preferred station in life. Despite the fact that the degree means less today than it did in the past, the students still regard themselves as emerging elites and demand all the deference and ceremony formerly reserved for a much smaller and more select body. Others in society who interact with students are not likely to fulfill such expectations. University clerks, for example, are considered by students the most difficult people in the world to deal with. With outsiders such as shopkeepers, police, and ordinary tradesmen, however, the students are more successful in asserting their higher status. Police may not, for example, enter the university campus even to arrest criminals—this is hallowed ground.

The Mansarover Affair of 1959 illustrates how a "prestige" issue can, through the intervention of highly politicized students, become escalated into a major student crisis. It began when a policeman arrested a student who had cycled through his stop signal. The policeman was forced to apologize, but the campus had been aroused by what they concluded was a blatant disregard of student rights. A fight between a student and a theater manager occurred shortly after which might never have amounted to anything were it not that a senior Communist student, already a nine-year veteran of Allahabad campus politics, entered the fray. The student Union elections were imminent, and each of the candidates for the office of president organized demonstrations in front of the District Magistrate and then the cinema. Rocks were thrown, insults exchanged, and in the melee with police, three persons were shot and forty-three arrested.

Indiscipline and national politics. While the involvement of students in politics during the 1930's and 1940's is often taken as the prototype of present-day actions, in Allahabad these were of minor consequence.[30] During the 1920's the non-cooperation movement was debated by the Union in a perfectly "proper" way, and although one instructor was dismissed, no notice was taken of Gandhi's call to abandon the schools.

By the time of the Quit-India Movement in 1942, students were finally drawn into the freedom struggle in sizable numbers, but after 1947 a change was necessary. Both Nehru and J. P. Narayan asked students to forego political activities. Instead, work and study were to be the key words of the new era. Although the Youth Congress ostensibly disbanded, student Union elections continued to be fought on political lines as late as 1959 when party labels ceased to be used, at least overtly.

Since independence, two student disturbances have been attributed to involvement in party or international politics. One occurred in 1952 when Mrs. Eleanor Roosevelt visited the university. A threat of violence developed and forced cancellation of her projected talk before the student Union. The whole incident was vaguely anti-American and anti-Congress party. As a personal insult to the Prime Minister it underlined the nationalist leader's loss of student respect.

The second incident took place after the Chinese invasion of India in 1961. The student Union wished to organize a solidarity demonstration against the foe. The Vice-Chancellor, a loyal Congress supporter, knew it would develop into an attempt to discredit V. K. Krishna Menon, then Defense Minister, and by implication the Prime Minister. Communists would also be attacked as a national threat. He refused to sanction the demonstration (which took place anyway) and again the university was in the grip of "indiscipline."

Agitations involving larger factional interests on campus. This variety of indiscipline represents a new development in the changing character of Indian higher education. This phenomenon is the most complex form of indiscipline because it must be understood in relation to a wide range of cultural and social practices which are not the same in all universities. At Aligarh University the conservative Muslim wing of the faculty is pitted against the liberal central-government supported wing. At Banaras the "Eastern U. P. group" previously referred to, while no longer dominant, remains a force in that place. At Allahabad, as we shall see, the Brahmin-Kayastha split has expressed a continuing rivalry for some time. In addition, there are aspects of administrative arrangements which are not present in all universities. Aligarh and Banaras are centrally supported, receiving the bulk of their revenues from Delhi, while Allahabad is a state institution relying on the good will of the Chief Minister and Education Minister of U. P. In Allahabad the conflict between the autocratic Vice-Chancellor, A. Jha, and the Nehru family, whose home stands within sight of the campus gates, cannot be discounted.

In 1953 a bitter struggle developed for control of the Vice-Chancellor-ship when the Brahmins tried to wrest control from the dominant Kayasth faction on campus. The court, dominated by university teachers, was responsible for choosing the highest administrative officer. The election neatly dichotomized the entire campus—forcing every teacher to align himself with one faction or the other. By the final count there was only a one vote margin in the Kayasthas' favor and that because one sick man was hauled in on a stretcher. A dynamic new Governor announced his intention of curing chronic student indiscipline by making membership in the Union voluntary and by eliminating Communist influence. Immediate opposition developed amongst a section of teachers as well as a large number of students at Allahabad. A student-teacher factional coalition made up of the Brahmin teachers who had lost the election, and the Communist-led student Union opposed the Chancellor's actions. Opposed to this group was the Kayasth faction controlling the University administration, the Government apparatus and a handful of students.

In March the Union president was expelled for calling an unauthorized strike, but with a new president the students again refused to attend class and the university was ordered closed for three weeks. When the hunger strikers began to rally more sympathy, it was clear that the government's policy could be successfully resisted. The chief student demands were met; the Union was to remain compulsory and the university agreed to collect the Union fees. The teachers alone could never have embarrassed the administration and the government—on the Indian campus students make the difference. When the calamity was debated in the state legislature, the Education Minister agreed it was the teachers who had instigated the students to go on strike and he added—without justification—that they had been threatened with failure in the exams if they did not cooperate.[31]

During 1954 each side harassed the other. The Convocation had to be postponed for fear of riots because the Chancellor threatened to address the meeting. The new date was set the following year so close to examination time that it was hoped students would have their minds elsewhere and it would be safe. Despite extreme precautions the students blocked the passage of the Governor and started a fist fight in the midst of the solemn procession.

It was strongly hinted that until control was firmly in local (Brahmin faction) hands, there could be no peace. A compromise was tried when a new Vice-Chancellor, neither Brahmin nor Kayasth, was chosen in 1957. Immediately some teachers sought to invalidate the choice by a legal maneuver and by the use of students. Some of the students most active in the Mansarover demonstration were informally blacklisted and could not enter the university when they applied. One of the students went on a hunger strike and rapidly gained support. High level committees could not control the now organized students, who descended on the house of the Vice-Chancellor on November 26 and threatened his life. The next day there was a complete strike of the campus. On November 28 the Executive Council met secretly to work out a solution. But they were discovered by a howling mob of students who surrounded the home where they met, broke the furniture and held the entire Executive Council prisoner until they had officially acceded to the demands of the student leaders. Only after the papers were duly handed over to the students were the officials permitted to go.

There were no major eruptions at Allahabad until the 1963 riots which again began with minor issues. One concerned reinstatement of an expelled ex-Union president, another demanded that some boys not be turned out of their hostel and a third sought (and was granted) a reduction in the fine for not attending parades. The student leaders and especially the Union president became the undisputed voice of all the students, who were soon convinced that the authorities were callous despots.

The faculty was still divided along the old caste-faction lines which now had strong pro- and anti-government sentiments. The Kayasth supporters endorsed the government's efforts to impose more stringent restrictions on the hiring of teachers. The anti-government forces were made up largely of the old Brahmin faction plus Congress dissidents in the state legislature. The Allahabad Teachers Association went to Lucknow in 1964 and met with both the Education Minister and the chief of the Congress opposition, who was considerate of their demands. On September 27 the gates of the university were inexplicably locked and the Vice-Chancellor fearing violence closed the school *sine die*. Some 10,000 students from university, school and college descended on the home of the Vice-Chancellor, where student leaders threatened to kill him and his family unless student demands were met. The police used fire hoses, tear gas and finally a *lathi* charge to quell the disturbance and arrest thirty of the leaders.

Leadership

In any student agitation today the most significant single individual is the Union president. He is the only elected person in the university who is *ex officio* spokesman for the entire student body. It is not that he acquires certain qualities as a result of his election but rather he is chosen because he has demonstrated ability. In the past, when the office was more like that of chairman in a debating society, this was not so. Today the student leader is the head of a large, easily aroused and possibly dangerous body. Because of this, the Union president exerts an influence in university affairs second to none. In addition to representing the student body, he may solicit complaints and on their basis formulate issues which he will proceed to negotiate with the Vice-Chancellor or government official. If necessary, he can call a strike and effectively close the university. With none of the formality of student participation in administration which characterizes some of the South American universities, the Indian student has achieved a similar importance in Allahabad. Theoretically, the president's policies must be ratified by the general meeting *(aam sabha)* of students, but in fact this is often a device for gaining additional support for a line already agreed upon. Because of his singular importance it may be helpful to look more closely at this new student role in the university.

Political. When the Union was established in 1923, it was a cultural and debating society, representing but a small segment of the student body. After 1937 the formation of a separate union for Muslim students further weakened the Union's potential force. Urban middle-class men, already fluent in English, sought office for the experience of parliamentary procedure, useful for a legislative or administrative career. Not all the leaders prior to independence were enthusiastic supporters of university policy. The Union was suspended from 1926–1927 and again between 1942 and 1945 during the Quit-India movement.

After 1947, the political competition amongst parties was reflected in the elections of the student Union. The militant right-wing R.S.S. (*Rashtriya Seva Sangh*) fought openly against the Communists. Power shifted from one camp to the other with the ill-organized Youth Congress running a poor third. In 1947, the R.S.S. candidate won, and in 1950 Asif Ansari, a Communist, was elected. The Communist party was again successful in 1952, 1954, and 1957. After the Chinese invasion, the Communists ceased to be a political force and in 1961 the elections were fought for the first time without party labels. Most recently the Socialist party of Ram Manohar Lohia has been successful. Both in 1963 and 1964 his supporters have held power in Allahabad. What is striking, however, is that regardless of which political party has its adherents in control of the Union, student indiscipline continues. During the 1954 Convocation Riots the Communists were in power; in 1959 when the Executive Council was surrounded and coerced into capitulation, the R.S.S. was strong and in 1963 it was the Socialists. In the disciplinary action taken after the Mansarover incident and the 1963 riots, students of all political persuasion were incriminated.

What is the purpose of political affiliations at all, if the use of power on campus appears irrelevant to the ideology maintained? It is a matter of considerable prestige. To capture the office of president at Allahabad gives the incumbent party leader recognition throughout India. Any time violence is threatened, the party leader will have to be consulted by the authorities and this, in turn, may facilitate political horse trading at a higher level. Another important exercise of influence comes at election time when the student leaders are drawn into the countryside to help elect particular candidates. As one ex-president said in 1964, "We are defeated now but wait 'til the elections come, then we are strong." During the by-election for Nehru's seat at Phulpur in 1964, all parties used students in the campaign, but the Socialist candidate had the additional advantage of the strength of the Union at his disposal. It is sometimes felt that student political involvement may lead to elected office. This has been true of Congress leaders in the past, but it seems of little importance for Allahabad. No past president of the Union has achieved even local recognition in any political party. Less important is the influence that a president can exert on the minds of the students by inviting political speakers of his own persuasion to address the general meetings. For, whatever their motives, parties do have a limited importance on campus. They are often accused of financing student elections, but that is difficult to determine. When Lohia addressed the students in 1963, just prior to the big riots, he did exhort them to stop attending classes that were held in English and to so disrupt the lessons that teachers would have to leave and not return until all the English books were translated into Hindi.

If ideology is of limited use in explaining student agitation, what motivates political action? Politics on campus represents the power of personal affiliations between individuals and groups. Teachers, senior politicians, ex-Union presidents or others who have served and suffered for the student cause command great respect and have considerable influence in student affairs. When a student demonstration becomes imminent, the Union president will surround himself with a number of senior individuals of proven ability, including ex-leaders no longer students. The leadership is often able to enlist the active support of students in remote parts of the state and may have close associates even among national politicians. Because of their elite status, students have entree into the highest administrative ranks. Moments before the arrests of 1963, the Union president, according to plan, slipped away to arouse the students of Lucknow, Kanpur, and Banaras. Another absconding student took refuge in the Delhi home of a cabinet minister, and a third was sheltered by a high police official in the state who was related to him. Not to appreciate the network of personal and political connections of India's top student elite is to fail to comprehend the complex nature of student indiscipline today.

Because of its importance, the office of president is always hotly contested. Money is lavishly spent on tea, loudspeakers, scented papers, and small impromptu bands. Each candidate's supporters canvass the students in hostel, town or classroom. The qualities most important for success are seniority and a demonstrated ability to fight for student rights, and it is likely that a candidate will have at least a B.A. and preferable an M.A. as well. The successful Communist candidate in 1950 had a ten-year record as a student agitator with numerous jail sentences to his credit and the successful candidate in 1959 was a leading *provocateur* in the Mansarover incident. On several occasions prospective candidates have sought to enhance their image by going on hunger strikes. They have not always won office, but it is a recognized channel for developing availability.

Social and personal. Because most student leaders are senior men in the university community, they are also older than the average student. While they must be able to identify with the great mass of poor students, they are not themselves deprived; often, in fact, they are scions of wealthy families. Prior to Independence, the student leader was, like the body of students, more middle class, but today he reflects the rural origin of the majority of students. Likewise, before Independence, the student leaders were persons of some academic achievement. Today this is no longer the case. The Union presidents do not come from the small percentage of "Toppers" who get the First Division marks. They are not the athletes and are too young to have been Freedom Fighters. If one could find a single quality that they all possess it would be verbal ability. Veritable torrents of words flow easily from their lips on even the most inconsequential occasions. As superior orators they can move a disinterested and largely apathetic crowd into a cohesive group of dedicated supporters who will implicitly follow directions. This charismatic quality which converts mobs into movements is what makes the student leader both feared and admired by university and governmental authority.

This is possible because the political and administrative leaders today are close to the students both in origin and orientation. Since the proliferation of institutions of higher education it is unusual for students to come to Allahabad from distant places. Over 90 per cent of the students come from the rural areas of Eastern U.P. Many Union presidents were essentially of the land, but like all educated men cannot return there because opportunities only exist in the city. To come from such a background is to understand the difficult problems of adjustment facing the average shy and poor freshman student. It is to know how much help is required to find a place to live, a restaurant to eat at, a classroom, a teacher, a book in the library. The university provides none of these services. Before the hostility of clerk and university authority, the student has no one to turn to but the Union leader. In the Union building he finds the few newspapers that can be read, the only seat, hard though it be where he can rest and smoke, a place to buy a cup of tea, a cool drink of water, and if he is lucky, sympathy.

Cultural. The importance of caste is decreasing all over India and any student leader is quick to condemn the institution as retarding India's progress in the modern world. It is true, however, that the largest single caste represented at the university remains, as it is in most Indian universities, Brahmin. It is also true that most of the leaders have come from that caste with Thakurs[32] second. Fifteen of the twenty-five Union presidents since independence have been Brahmins, seven Thakurs and only one Muslim.

But whatever his caste the Allahabad student leader believes in many of the traditional Hindu values. In a way this new point of view represents a departure from the pre-independence British orientation that characterized his predecessors. When the object of higher education was an administrative job with the British bureaucracy, it was natural to share the Englishman's love of Shakespeare, his faith in progress, and belief in the parliamentary forms of justice. Today one is more likely to hear a Union speaker extoll Tulsi Das, the author of the local Ramayana, as the "greatest poet that ever lived." The important festivals for the students tend increasingly to be the Hindu festivals of *Shiv Ratri* or *Holi* and all political harangues allude to the importance of duty, piety, and respect for elders. Of the thirty-odd leaders arrested and held five months in jail for the 1963 riots, none of them objected to their parents' choosing their spouse. At home in the village, although it is otherwise on the campus, they observe all the caste ceremony and ritual attached to food and bathing.

In the university the expression of popular nationalism tends to be more secular in its appeal. Outside the Union is the statue of a hero who was shot by the British in 1942 as he attempted to raise the Congress flag. Inside are the portraits of other eminent Indians (Chandra Sekhar Azad and Bhagat Singh) complete with revolvers and bandoliers. These men, along with the religious, are the "true" teachers of India, the orator proclaims.

But it is in language that the clearest evidence of the new rural assertion on campus is evident. The average student who is weak in English must seek classes in Hindi but the books are not yet in that language and he must compete with a segment of the urban middle classes who are well trained in that language. Although above average in English ability, some student leaders will prefer to use Hindi even when addressing foreigners. English is still used (although decreasingly) in the graduate classes where it remains the language of learning, but Hindi is now the language of student action, and campaign speeches are delivered in a blend of Hindi and English. This is a departure from the past when the university socialized young Indians to be like Englishmen and the language was scrupulously correct.

Student motivation. What is it that makes the student leader act the way he does? The leader has, above all, an overwhelming sense of moral indignation not generally shared by his fellow students. There are, by contrast, a small number of boys from rural areas without any feeling of resentment or hostility present in the mass of students. They come from their farms full of hope, and honor their teachers with obsequious devotion, and after they graduate and return to the village they are not discontented with the lack of occupational opportunities but bask in the peasants' adulation of their learning. Although many of them continue at the university for ten, twelve, or more years and their goodness and virtue are acknowledged by other students, they would never be chosen as leaders.

Additionally, there are still a minority of middle class students at Allahabad: sons of professors, officials, rich businessmen, and absentee landlords, who speak English well, wear Western clothes, and enjoy Western entertainments such as dancing, driving, tennis, and Ping-pong. They are impatient with the new rustics on campus and tend to sneer at their too frequent demonstrations. The old student leaders were drawn from this class, but today the mass of students feel they are careerists who would use the Union for their own ends. A third segment of the student population are the urban poor—sons of small shopkeepers, clerks, teachers, and the like. They are poor, miserable, and have little hope of success in life. Their background and experience is urban and their aspirations firmly fixed on wealth or governmental positions. The rural boys see them as unreliable leaders who cannot be counted upon to uphold the students' interests above their own.

The most successful student leaders who have an agrarian background are keenly at odds with the entire nature of Indian higher education. These rural alienated youth have no sympathy for or understanding of the elaborate administrative forms which are designed to protect the individual, award merit and ensure justice for all. For the farmer newly arrived on campus, rules are but burdensome machinations to prevent him from achieving his goal of a degree. Examinations, merit, impartiality, and law cannot but work to his detriment. Not knowing the language, not having "connections" apart from the Union, without hope of success, he is alienated from the politics of the faculty, the dead weight of the curriculum, the official rhetoric of obedience and restraint. He hopes for someone who can cut through the decay and enable him to relate to what he knows is important. The poverty of the villages, the fierce grip of privilege, and the lack of conviction in adults—these are the things that touch his heart.

Conclusion

In a way these strong feelings are not new. During the freedom struggle they were clearly formulated as part of the platform of *Swaraj*. Now that independence is two decades old they are being rediscovered. Adult Indians, hearing the old slogans anew, are slightly embarrassed. But if these feelings represent dissatisfaction with the status quo, they do not represent revolution. They justify the outbreaks of violence but are too vague to serve as platform for consistent action. In many ways, the new student strength is conservative: cow worship, vegetarianism, respect for parents, and caste are important. This school may represent a new popular nationalism which threatens the Nehru image of India as a secular, democratic and liberal society.

The issue of indiscipline is not simple. Theories of economic deprivation or of psychological alienation lack applicability. The data presented here are drawn entirely from a single north-Indian university but India is not encapsulated in the narrow confines of one university. It will be necessary to study other institutions for even a preliminary understanding of this problem to grow.

Notes

1. See "Student Indiscipline—The Case Study of an Institution," *Educational Studies and Investigations,* I (Delhi; Ministry of Education, 1962); *Randhir Singh Enquiry Report 1956,* I & II (Allahabad: University of Allahabad, 1956); *Reports of the Banaras Hindu University Enquiry Committee* (Delhi: Ministry of Education, 1958); Margaret Cormack, *She Who Rides a Peacock* (New York: Praeger, 1961), see especially "Why Student Indiscipline" for accounts of disturbances at Annamalai and Lucknow Universities in 1959. For a fictionalized account of a Calcutta hunger strike see K. Bhaskara Rao, *Candle against the Wind* (Bangalore: Samyukta Karnatak Press, 1963).

   On the other hand, empirical socio-economic surveys include: American University, *Political Attitudes of Indian Students* (Washington: Bureau of Social Science Research, 1954); American University, *The Indian Student* (Washington: Bureau of Social Science Research, 1954); Calcutta University, *Hundred Years of the University of Calcutta* (Calcutta: University of Calcutta, 1957), contains a synopsis of a 1954 survey of undergraduate living conditions; Shanti S. Gupta, *Report of the Socio-Economic Survey of College Students of Aligarh* (Aligarh: D.S. College, 1957); M. S. Khan, *Report of the Socio-Economic Survey of University and College Students of Aligarh* (Aligarh: Aligarh Muslim University, 1957); Poona University, *A Socio-Economic Sample Survey of College Students in Poona City 1955–56* (Poona: Poona University, 1960); V. K. R. V. Rao, *University Education and Employment: A Case Study of Delhi Graduates* (Bombay: Asia Publishing House, 1961); V. M. Sirsikar, *Social and Political Attitudes of Post-Graduate Students of the University of Poona 1960–61* (Poona: University of Poona, 1963); *Survey of Living Conditions of University Students* (Delhi: Ministry of Education, 1961).

2. The field research in India was supported by an International Development Fellowship from the East-West Center, Honolulu, Hawaii.

3. The statistical data are drawn from *University Development in India, A Statistical Report* (Delhi: University Grants Commission, 1962), Chapter 11, "Third Five Year Plan."

4. See Humayun Kabir, *Student Indiscipline* (Delhi: Ministry of Education, 1955), p. 1.

5. Bruce T. McCully, *English Education and the Origins of Indian Nationalism* (New York: Columbia University Press, 1940). His thesis briefly is that the graduates of colonial universities, "unable to rise above the status of petty clerk, formed a kind of rootless educated proletariat whose dissatisfaction with their lot" led to that grossest form of indiscipline, the nationalist movement.

6. Malathi Rao, "Institutional Failure," *Seminar*, XLIV (1963), 21–24; V. S. Matur, "Examination and Indiscipline," *Education Quarterly*, VII (1955), No. 28, pp. 348–349; N. V. Tirtha, "Rural Expectations Concerning Education in India," *Teacher Education*, IV (1960), 40–47; A. A. Khatri, "Social-cultural Factors in Guidance of College Students," *Journal of Vocational and Educational Guidance*, VIII (1961), No. 1, pp. 30–36.

7. *University Development in India: A Statistical Report, op. cit.,* p. 56; B. Da Cruz, "Student Discipline," *Progress of Education*, XXXIII (1959), No. 8, pp. 278–280; G. S. Bhargava, "Student Unrest in India," *Eastern World*, XV (1961), No. 2, pp. 14–15; A. K. Kamat and A. G. Deshmukh, *Wastage in College Education* (Poona: Gokhale Institute of Politics and Economics, 1963). For studies of unemployment, see D. N. Majumdar, *Unemployment among the University Educated, A Pilot Inquiry in India* (Cambridge: M.I.T.: Center for International Studies, 1957); V. K. R. V. Rao, *op. cit.*

8. *Report on the Problem of Student Indiscipline in Indian Universities* (New Delhi: University Grants Commission, 1960), p. 6.

9. This is the title of the lead essay in his book, C. Sarkar, *The Unquiet Campus, Indian Universities Today* (New Delhi: A *Statesman* survey, 1960). See also K. G. Saiyidain and M. S. Kotiswaran, "Indian Union Social and Economic Position of Teachers," *Yearbook of Education*, 1953, pp. 473–483; P. Parija, "Steps to Ensure Full-time Occupation Needed," *Amrita Bazar Patrika* (Sep-

tember 16, 1956); *Report on the Problems of Teachers in the University* of *Bombay* (Bombay: University of Bombay Teachers Association, 1954); *Papers Read at the Second Conference of the College Teachers of the Poona University Area* (Poona: Poona University Teachers Association, 1955); *Proceedings of the Vice-Chancellors' Conference 1960* (Delhi: Ministry of Education, 1961). See especially Appendix IV, Report of the Committee on Student Indiscipline, p. 131.

10. S. H. Patwardhan, "Society and Students' Indiscipline," *Progress of Education*, XXXIII (1959), Nos. 10–11, pp. 336–341; A. K. Saran, "Teachers and Society," *Seminar* (March 1960); M. Cormack, *op. cit.*

11. Edward Shils, "Indian Students," *Encounter* (September 1961), No. 96, p. 20.

12. Myron Weiner, *The Politics of Scarcity* (Chicago: The University of Chicago Press, 1962). See especially Chapter VII, "Students."

13. M. Muni Reddy, *The Student Movement in India* (Lucknow: K. S. R. Acharya, 1947), pp. 143–144.

14. Seymour Martin Lipset, Chapter 1, this book. Shyamnandan Sahay, "Character Roles of Students as a Step against Indiscipline," *Amrita Bazar Patrika* (September 23, 1956); Joseph Fischer, "The University Student in South and South-East Asia," *Minerva*, II (1963), No. 1.

15. *My Idea of a University* (Delhi: Ministry of Education and Scientific Research, 1957), p. 2.

16. G. C. Chatterjee, "Drastic Remedy," *Tribune*, January 22, 1960, p. 4.

17. V. M. Sirsikar, *op. cit.*, p. 35. See also J. Krishnamurthy, "The Place of Politics," *Seminar* (March 1960), No. 44, pp. 25–27, and a report of 50 principals' opinions regarding politics on campus in "Student Indiscipline and Remedies," *Amrita Bazar Patrika*, June 11, 1960.

18. G. D. Sondhi, *A Plan for Youth Welfare* (Delhi: Ministry of Education Publication No. 223, 1956).

19. Philip G. Altbach, "Rightist Swing among Indian Students: The Vidyarthi Parishad and the Indian Student Movement," *Peace News* (February 5, 1965), No. 1493. See also *Organizer*, February 17, 1958, for a report on the *Rajasthan Vidyarthi Parishad.*

20. *Report of the Banaras Hindu University Enquiry Committee* (Delhi: Ministry of Education, 1958).

21. Weiner, *op. cit.*, p. 175.

22. J. Ray, "The Evils from Which Our Education Is Suffering," *Progress of Education*, XXXV (November 1960), 112–116.

23. Humayun Kabir, *op. cit.*, pp. 8–9.

24. *Convocation Speech* (Allahabad: University of Allahabad Minutes, 1922).

25. A study conducted in 1960 of the 200 members of the I. C. S. in India. Sixteen per cent were from Allahabad, only exceeded by Madras with 21.8 per cent. However, it is recalled that Madras is a much larger affiliating university and the strength of this tradition is clear. See R. K. Trivedi and D. N. Rao, "Higher Civil Service in India: A Sample Survey," *Journal of the National Academy of Administration*, VI (July 1961), 5 ff.

26. A caste of scribes who kept records for the former Muslim rulers. This caste has the highest corporate literacy rate in India. In 1921 there were .4 million Kayasths in U.P. with 30,000 literate in English. Brahmins, with 4.4 million in U.P., had the same number literate in English.

27. Numbers of students increased from 1,279 in 1926 to 6,830 in 1956 while the ratio of students to teachers doubled from 14 to 28. *Progress of Allahabad University* (Allahabad: Allahabad University, 1958), p. 21. During the period 1939–1956 hostel accommodations rose from 1,000–2,000, but those living elsewhere increased from 1,000–5,000.

28. Based on a 20 per cent sample survey of entering students in 1964, over 50 per cent came from Allahabad district, and about 90 per cent from Eastern U.P.

29. An account of early collegiate life in Allahabad is contained in A. Jha's *A History of the Muir Central College 1872–1922* (Allahabad: Allahabad University, 1938).

30. In statistics collected by the Indian National Congress, convictions of persons arrested for taking part in *satyagraha* between 1930–1934 were most frequent in Bengal, Bihar, Punjab, Andhra and Bombay City in that order with the smallest number in Uttar Pradesh. Jagdish S. Sharma, *India's Struggle for Freedom* (Delhi: S. Chand Company, 1960), pp. 78–79.

31. *Northern Indian Patrika* (December 18, 1954).

32. A landowning caste of U.P. An approximate count is possible through analysis of the names of the leaders of the Allahabad Student Union.

Index

academic freedom, 31–32, 148–195; and admission to practice, 150, 156–158, 160–161; American universities and, 183–188, 284; and anti-monopoly teaching, 183, 184; Berlin model of, 168, 254, 258, 263; conflicts concerning, 151–155; and evolution theory, 183, 284–285; infringements of, 150, 156; and Keynesian economics, 183–184, 187; in Latin America, 283–292; and loyalty oath, 183–185, in principal types of modern university, 155–189

academic systems, *see individual countries*

actions groups, student activism and, 58, 68–70

Adams, Henry Carter, 184

Afghanistan, disturbances in, 114

Africa, academic system, 162–163, 166, 179–180; intellectual elite, 6; nationalism of, 4; scientific writing, 4; student disturbances, 6, 107; student movements and organizations, 91; students and politics, 19–20, 74, 75, 91, 241, 243; university teaching, 4

Agger, Robert, 127

Agra University, 377, 378

Alabama, student protest against racial integration in, 97

Albórnoz, Orlando, 229, 283–292

Alexander, Robert, 23

Alexander I, 171

Alexander II, 171

Algeria, student movements in, 199

Algerian war, 24, 276–278

Aligarh University, 375, 378, 383

Allahabad, University of, 372, 376–390

All-India Students' Federation, 89, 374

Alliance for Progress, 128

Altbach, Philip G., 74–93, 103, 199–252

American Association of University Professors, 184–185, 188, 255, 284–285

American Civil Liberties Union, 284–285

American Council on Education, 213

American Federation of Teachers, 284–285

Americans for Democratic Action (ADA), 204, 225–226

American Student Union, 239

anarchism, 263, 300

Anglo-Saxon community of nations, 98–99

Ansari, Asif, 385

Aptheker, Bettina, 255, 263

Arciniegas, Germán, 305–307, 311

Argentina, Conservative party, 298–300; Córdoba Manifesto, 295, 296, 299, 301, 302; Federation of Argentine University Students (FUA), 312; Radical party, 298, 300, 304, 309–310; Sàenz Peña law, 298–299; student strikes, 119, 295, 301; students and politics, 33, 129–130, 134–138, 300, 303, 309–314; university-recruitment pattern, 30; University Reform movement, 23, 287, 291, 295–304, 309, 314; *see also* Buenos Aires, University of; Latin America

Argentine University Federation, 313

Army-Navy football games, 108

Asia, academic system, 162–163, 166; expansion of university student popuntion, 18; intellectual elite, 6; nationalism of, 4; scientific writing, 4; student demonstrations, 22; student insecurity, 18; student and politics, 74, 243; university teaching, 4; *see also individual countries*

Asquith Commission, 104

Association Générale des Étudiants de l'Université de Montréal (AGEUM), 99, 100

Association of Vietnamese Revolutionary Young Comrades, 13

Austria, academic system in, 162, 166

Averroism, 153

M.